THE
PERSONAL SESSIONS
Book 1 of
The Deleted Seth Material
Sessions
11/15/65–12/6/71

THE EARLY SESSIONS

The Early Sessions consist of the first 510 sessions dictated by Seth through Jane Roberts. There are 9 books in *The Early Sessions* series.

THE PERSONAL SESSIONS

The Personal Sessions, often referred to as "the deleted sessions," are Seth sessions that Jane Roberts and Rob Butts considered to be of a highly personal nature and were therefore kept in separate notebooks from the main body of the Seth material. *The Personal Sessions* are expected to be published in 6 to 9 volumes.

"The great value I see now in the many deleted or private sessions is that they have the potential to help others, just as they helped Jane and me over the years. I feel that it's very important to have these sessions added to Jane's fine creative body of work for all to see." –Rob Butts

THE SETH AUDIO COLLECTION

Rare recordings of Seth speaking through Jane Roberts are available on audiocassette and CD. For a complete description of The Seth Audio Collection, request our free catalogue.. (Further information is supplied at the back of this book.)

For information on expected publication dates and how to order, write to New Awareness Network at the following address and request the latest catalogue. Also, please visit us on the Internet at www.sethcenter.com

New Awareness Network Inc.
P.O. BOX 192
Manhasset, N.Y. 11030

www.sethcenter.com

THE PERSONAL SESSIONS
Book 1 of
The Deleted Seth Material
Sessions
11/15/65–12/6/71

© 2003 by Robert Butts

Published by New Awareness Network Inc.

New Awareness Network Inc.
P.O. Box 192
Manhasset, New York 11030

Opinions and statements on health and medical matters expressed in this book are those of the author and are not necessarily those of, or endorsed by, the publisher. Those opinions and statements should not be taken as a substitute for consultation with a duly licensed physician.

Cover Design: Michael Goode
Photography: Cover photos by Rich Conz and Robert F. Butts, Sr.
Editorial: Rick Stack
Typography: Raymond Todd, Michael Goode

All rights reserved. This book may not be reproduced in whole or in part, without written permission from the publisher, except by a reviewer who may quote brief passages in a review; nor may any part of this book be reproduced, stored in a retrieval system, or transmitted in any form or by any means electronic, mechanical, photocopying, recording, or other, without written permission from the publisher.

ISBN 978-0-9711198-4-0
Printed in U.S.A. on acid-free paper

I dedicate The Personal Sessions
to my wife, Jane Roberts,
who lived her 55 years
with the greatest creativity
and the most valiant courage.
-Rob

A NOTE ON THE COVER DESIGN PHOTOGRAPHS

June 2003. A note about the photographs Michael Goode used in his striking cover design for The Personal Sessions *series.*

The central colored photograph of Jane and the lower right and left-hand shots of her and myself were taken by my father, Robert F. Butts, Sr., in Sayre, PA a year or so after our marriage in December 1954. The upper right one of Jane in trance for Seth was taken (among many others) by Rich Conz, a photographer for the Emira, NY *Star-Gazette, while he witnessed Session 508 on Nvember 20, 1969. (See Volume 9 of* The Early Sessions.*)*

I don't know who photographed the young Jane Shown on the upper left, but she saved that picture all of those years for me to inherit upon her death in September 1984, when she was 55.

My inventive and versatile father had always taken photographs, and in his later years turned professional, photographing many weddings and other events in the Sayre area (and also Jane's and my wedding at the home of my younger brother Loren and his wife Betts in Tunkhannock, PA). To help my father, my mother Estelle trained herself to hand-color his black and white photographs, for color film was not available then—and so she colored Jane's portrait. Now I wonder: do my long-deceased parents, and Rich and the unknown photographer of the young Jane, all know that their creativity will grace the covers of a series of books that I so lovingly dedicate to them, as well as to Jane and each reader? I believe that they do, each in his or her own way.

—Rob

INTRODUCTION
BY ROB BUTTS

September 20, 2002. How strange, I found myself thinking as I prepared to write this introduction, that 37 years would pass before I'd start publishing this series of personal sessions and excerpts that had been dictated by my wife, Jane Roberts, for Seth, the "energy personality essence" she spoke for while in a trance state.

In reviewing them, I'm very pleased to discover that these sessions are as fresh, as creative and perceptive, as they ever were. Talk about the elasticity of "time," as Seth often did! How much do we consciously know, or think we know, about that ultimately mysterious quality within which we construct our universe, our planet, the most minute portion of each one of us, mental or physical, during each moment of our lives? That ineluctable universe within which we swim so beautifully day and night, one that, according to Seth, we also create—and all at once, no less! As Seth told us in Session 20, on January 23, 1964: "Time and space, dear friends, are both camouflage patterns, therefore the fact that the inner senses can conquer time and space is not, after all, so surprising. To the mind with its subconscious, and to the inner senses, there is no time or space...." If only we could really grasp consciously those innate qualities that we value so highly, yet take for granted! I think that my writing this introduction, then, is basically timeless behavior.

I also think that in her unique private and public ways Jane explored time as well, as evocatively, as anyone ever has. An immodest statement, I submit, but I'm proud to have shared in her creativity, and I offer *The Personal Sessions* series as a testament to what she sought to accomplish in all of her writings—and did indeed accomplish, in my opinion.

Obviously, this introduction will be incomplete. It will also be rather unorthodox—more like a series of conscious and unconscious reminiscences and free associations, moving back and forth in time as I approach sets of ideas from various angles while seeking to learn more about my wife even now, 18 years after her death. Jane's death may have been physical, yet she still lives, still offers insights, still makes me reach to understand and grow as I mourn her passing. She died at the age of 55. What more could she have accomplished in our camouflage reality had she chosen to live physically for, say, even another decade? Wonderfully penetrating things, I'm sure—and I believe that she is indeed doing so, "where she is now."

Do I think it a "coincidence," then, that I received the page proofs, or galleys, to check for Volume 1 of *The Personal Sessions* from publisher Rick Stack on September 5, 2002, when Jane died on the same day 18 years ago?

No, I think that seemingly innocuous little happening is one more sign of how this reality we're all creating together works in its often mysterious, and often ignored, fashion.

Some will disagree with my felt premise and this is their right, of course. But after working with Jane and the many complicated and interwoven facets of the Seth material that she produced for more than 20 years, I no longer believe in "chance" or "coincidence." I humbly submit that somehow, somewhere, there are connections, intuitions, whispers and shouts and facts that proclaim our greater reality's depth and being, its independence of our ordinary conscious ideas of space and time. More and more, but especially since Jane's death on September 5, 1984, I have tried to be open to those fascinating and unending interrelationships we create individually and en masse and so live with.

Thus, I opened up several years ago to ask Rick to publish the nine volumes of *The Early Sessions* through his New Awareness Network, Inc. And now, I open up even more to his publication of *The Personal Sessions* series. As this group of sessions slowly accumulated, often as "deleted" or unpublished portions of "regular" sessions, Jane and I took it for granted that since they were personal they would stay that way. Every session is obviously personal, since Jane delivered them all, but now I'm encouraging the overall intimacy of these personal sessions to seek their own intimate freedom—and of course I know that doing this will not only help others, but me too.

Yet every so often in this series I'll be including sessions that are also of more outgoing subject matter—more like the sessions in Jane's published Seth books. Later volumes of *The Personal Sessions* will also include a whole book that Jane delivered for me on the great 17th-Century Dutch artist Rembrandt Harmensz van Rijn. This book has never been published. It's not a Seth book, but one of the three "world view" books from highly creative people in the arts that Jane tuned into on her own as gifts for me. The other two are *The World View of Paul Cézanne* (1977), and *The Afterdeath Journal of an American Philosopher: The World View of William James* (1978). When we get to the Rembrandt material in this series I'll offer my interpretation of Jane's very interesting world-view material.

I add that none of those books stress reincarnation, or any claims that Jane or I (or both of us) had or have psychic relationships with any one of that celebrated trio. My wife simply knew how interested I was in those very creative individuals. I still am. I know I'm in good company with the many who have been and who are nourished by their works. One personal example: for many

INTRODUCTION

years I carried a beat-up old paperback edition of James's *The Varieties of Religious Experience* beside me on the front seat of my old Ford Taurus. Without conceit, I also feel that the works, the ideas, of those three are in their own ways reminiscent of the Seth material. (I don't believe it would ever have occurred to Jane to make a statement like that!)

My goal, then, has come to be the publishing of all of Jane's work, or at least as much of it as I can, including not only the Seth material but her poetry and fiction and notes and journals—to finally be able to offer it as a great whole for study in what we call the "future." For if all of a person's lifework isn't known, how can its true worth in all of its human complexity ultimately be known? Sometimes I think I'm a slow learner: It took me a while to realize, for example, that the responses to the Seth material by mail and in person—and now electronically—are actually myriad extensions of that work, showing in all of their varieties the questions and answers it's raised and the beneficial effects it's had on the many who have communicated since Jane held her first real session on December 2, 1963—and on those who still do. The mail in any form is great! Seldom does a day go by that I don't answer letters. I'm glad to do it, even when I fall far behind.

The kindnesses of others became especially helpful in all of those years that we went through the phases of Jane's physical "symptoms," as we called them—from our growing emotional questions and torment about them to success and relief and then through torment again and again. All of that, we gradually learned, proved to be one of the major challenges we had created and participated in, mixed in as it was with our other successes and failures.

Jane's symptoms consisted of a pervasive loss of flexibility—hardly noticeable at first, quite innocuous—that slowly over the years became more and more physically debilitating. Eventually she became unable to walk.

But first: One day in late November 1963, Jane sat at her writing table in the living room while I left to paint in my studio at the back of the apartment. We often followed this routine when we didn't have to be out of the house. My wife liked to tune into a radio station that featured classical music while she worked; she kept its volume low enough so that it didn't bother me. After some time on that particular day I realized that all was quiet—too quiet—out there in the living room. When I went out to see what Jane was up to I was greeted with her breakthrough accomplishment—one that, to put it mildly, was to lead to very unexpected challenges and growths in our lives: Jane held up a sheaf of typewriter paper upon which she had scribbled in large handwriting an essay that had come to her as fast as she could write it down: *The Physical Universe as Idea Construction*. She didn't know where the work had come from, how she had produced it. She'd felt as though she was out of her body some of the time, out on the first floor's porch roof looking in at herself. "What does it mean?" she asked as we discussed it. She was exhilarated, intrigued, cautious, wondering about its ideas—that basically each one of us creates our own reality in the most intimate terms, for example.

She was of course very familiar with the spontaneous role her creative self enacted when she was writing, especially in her poetry. But this? We were to learn that the conscious yet intuitive pace of her realizations was carefully meted out by her psyche: just so much at a time. For the first few days after I finally got it through my head what Jane was really saying in her essay I couldn't accept the idea that each one of us literally, really, creates our own reality. Conventional thinking simply couldn't, wouldn't accept that, I said, although I didn't regard myself as a conventional thinker. But her breakthrough had set the agenda for our lifetimes-to-come: idea construction, all right!

Very soon after that initial revelation, Jane and I began the actual sessions when we sat with a Ouija board on December 2, 1963. See Volume 1 of *The Early Sessions*. Hardly a "coincidence," that psychic and psychological progression, from an easy-to-use popular device to something much more personal and encompassing like idea construction. Yet the board had played its part. One can even say that Jane's basic intuitive knowledge of idea construction led us to use the board in the first place.

We'd borrowed the board from our landlord, James Spaziani, who hadn't had any success using it with his family. He was to later just give us the board. Jimmy (long deceased) was a kind and outgoing landlord and restaurateur who lived with his wife and three children on the second floor of the old converted horse barn and carriage house in back of the apartment house he owned at 458 West Water Street, where Jane and I lived. He also owned a well-known dine-and-dance establishment in Elmira, Lib's Supper Club, which my wife and I frequented before the onset of her symptoms. Jimmy was the chief cook at Lib's. Busy as he was, he always welcomed us when we stepped into his kitchen to say hello.

Jane had read about the Ouija board and expressed casual interest in it, but hadn't tried to obtain one; nor was there a local supplier. What conscious and unconscious communications, we were to wonder, had led her to mention the board to Jimmy? What kind of a "coincidence" was that, anyhow? Out of all of the apartments for rent in Elmira, why had Jane chosen that one? She had found the apartment. She came to Elmira with me after I'd begun working for the greeting-card company, Artistic, to look for a place for us so we could move from Sayre and save the time and expense of commuting 30 miles a day, five days a week. She found the empty apartment 5 at 458 on her first day of looking. When I picked her up after leaving work she directed me to the apartment, and that was that. Jimmy had lost interest in psychic phenomena long ago.

In fact, he had to dig the board out of his cluttered attic to give to us. Yet he had initially investigated the topic, and after *Idea Construction* his gift sent us on our way in no uncertain terms. We didn't even have to order a board!

Would we have done just that on our own? How else might the sessions have begun—would Jane's *Idea Construction* have led us into them at all as we came to know them? How far back into camouflage time should one try to trace such connections?

At the board, my wife clumsily reached a personality named Frank Watts, an American schoolteacher who told us he'd died in 1931. He gave us very brief, halting and sometimes disconnected answers during our first three board sessions. Yet in that third session Frank Watts told us that Jane had "Too much aggression." That she had been a "Medium." in a previous life, that her present "Timidity has roots of rage." from "Previous hates unresolved." that she "Must conquer now." When I asked Frank Watts about those unresolved hates, he replied "No information direct permitted."

It's easy to note in retrospect that such remarks were clues, clear indications or projections of at least possible troubles that we needed to explore in depth, but the whole affair with the board was so new to us that in our inexperience we felt no urgency to at least try to do so. We had no experience to go upon.

Would Seth have cooperated in such a venture? It didn't occur to Jane and me to even ask. We moved beyond Frank Watts's "Timidity has roots of rage." Seth announced his presence in the next, fourth, session: "I prefer not to be called Frank Watts. That personality was rather collarless (as spelled out on the board)." Also: "I was Frank Watts to learn humility." So with our obvious consent and the great variety of his very intelligent and fluent discourses, Seth became the discarnate entity who spoke through Jane for the next 20 years and eight months. That "energy personality essence" did his best, always honestly, I'm sure, to help my wife, both as far as he was able to but also, as I came to believe, as far as he was allowed to. Not only because of Jane's intense early fears in this lifetime, I felt, but also because of past lives, as Frank Watts had indicated. How unusual, I thought as I recorded the sessions in my homemade shorthand, that the conflicts displayed between the two main portions of her immensely creative personality were so open, even while she had the potential to help so many others. And did. Jane was living her challenges just like each one of us does, and her efforts were inextricably bound up with the world even as, I was sure, we were creating our human versions of the earth and its own reality. This taught us that even with Jane's talents there was more, always more, to create and to learn from. How exciting and frustrating at the same time! In all modesty, there seemed to be much that we could do, feel, want, offer to others. Our mail alone began to speak written volumes, almost always approvingly, that we had never anticipated. How could we have known that would happen? As with other details of our experiences to come, many were still unknown to us on conscious levels—we'd have been incredibly wise to have known it all in advance! Like each one of us, Jane as a physical creature still had to travel her literal paths to experience and knowledge.

During her journey (and mine) I helped her publish 19 volumes of the Seth material, fiction, and poetry, and since her death in 1984 I've added 12 more so far, including this first volume of *The Personal Sessions*. I'm sure that Jane knows what I'm doing, and identifies with the poignancy I feel as I begin this latest publishing venture. That very poignancy enriches the value of this long-range endeavor for me as, I trust, it will for others.

I'm married now to a very beautiful, intelligent and much younger lady who in her own unique ways offers me invaluable love, assistance, and reinforcement. I often feel that Laurel Lee Davies, a native of Iowa who came to me from California on August 23, 1985, 11 months after Jane's death, helped transform me. No coincidence, that! After we had corresponded for a while I called Laurel on February 2, 1985. We met at the hill house in Elmira on August 25 of that year. From the very beginning our relationship seemed perfectly natural, as though we had always known each other. (We feel reincarnational relationships but have yet to explore them.) Laurel helped revitalize me; our years together have been full and creative and productive—and yes, at times controversial. But always she has helped me, just as, I trust, I have helped her. I'm still amazed by the challenges two human beings can create and resolve for themselves within the inconceivable beauty and mystery of All That Is. Each one of us springs into creativity while All That Is gives us the supreme privilege of doing so—and thus, I feel, constantly surprises itself.

The camouflage days pass with blessed speed as Laurel and I savor them in all of their complexities. Our journey together continues with new insights, new challenges, new understandings. We were married on December 31, 1999. Thank you, Laurel. I love you.

I've noted that many of the sessions in this personal series will not be complete, but deleted excerpts from published sessions. Often over the years Jane and I tried to balance the subject matter of the sessions as Seth sought to help us in whatever way. This approach included what I thought Jane allowed him to say.

That overall format developed, then, out of the needs and abilities of and permissions of the three of us—two physical, one nonphysical. As the sessions piled up and books were published that balancing between public and private material came to seem quite natural; it actually became another portion of Jane's abilities that was as creative in its way as any other aspect of the sessions: if the personal sessions were available, why not take them? Often they helped greatly, as the record will show in my attempt to publish all of the Seth material. Jane, then, grew in more ways than one at once.

This seems obvious in retrospect. Her multitudinous abilities also showed in the ESP classes she held from 1966 through 1975, with a few informal meetings after that. When I finish these volumes of personal sessions I'll be publishing with Rick Stack's New Awareness Network the transcripts of many of those always hilarious, incredibly active, crowded and loud meetings: full of Seth sessions, member dialogues and repartees and questions that erupted in those weekly classes that Jane held in our apartment's small living room. I didn't attend most of them. Usually on class night, Tuesday, I was secluded in my studio at the back of our second-floor apartment, typing from my notes the session Jane had held for the two of us the night before; then I'd be caught up for the Wednesday-night session to come.

Often, I could hear a powerful Seth through two closed doors. And so, we learned more than once in warm weather, could neighbors and passersby on West Water Street when our windows were open. But those occasions were relatively minor: consider the situation *inside* the house! Long ago, the three floors of the old house, a typical turn-of-the-last-century "mansion" on the main street three blocks west of Elmira's business district, had been converted into eight apartments. All were continuously occupied during the 15 years Jane and I (and Seth for the last 11 of those years) lived there. Turnover was low, and we knew most of the other tenants, although no more than one or two of them at any time had an inkling of what we were up to with first the sessions and then the addition of the ESP classes. Even now I still correspond with two of those "ex-tenants"—loyal friends indeed!

I'm also still embarrassed to contemplate the merciless racket Jane, Seth, and their students made after class began in 1966. The floors and ceilings of the old house were not soundproof. And in retrospect I'm apologetic and grateful that during our whole tenure there not one tenant ever complained to our landlord, Jimmy Spaziani, about the noise we subjected that captive audience to once a week for those nine class years.

Nor am I trying to justify class behavior by noting that Jane and I and our guests were much better behaved during the Friday-night gatherings in our apartment. A fine group of young friends with both similar and quite different interests than ours slowly developed, each one, each couple, dropping in at the end of the workweek to relax and talk. All knew of Jane's abilities, of course, her growing career with its attendant publicity, but that was only a minor subject amid wide-ranging discussions. Once in a while Seth would come through—though usually only by invitation—but that wasn't the norm by any means. There were too many other things to discuss! Sue Watkins, a dear friend who was to write several books about Jane's work with the Seth material, lived just down the street for a while before moving to the country. (Sue's latest, *Speaking of Jane Roberts*, is crowded with much frank and loving information about Jane and me that I have no room to go into here.) Peggy Gallagher and her husband Bill worked for the Elmira Star-Gazette; as a reporter Peg wrote several well-received articles about Jane and the Seth material. The Gallaghers were the best friends anyone could have, but we loved everyone. Especially as we came to realize that our having such friends made up for interactions with others that Jane and I had largely missed out on in our own earlier relationships. Valuable!

On Saturday nights just the two of us often went dancing in the local joints while Jane was still able to—and I still like rock-and-roll.

Given our situation, I took care of my wife as best I could. As the years passed our lives became more and more restricted physically. It became increasingly difficult for Jane to walk in public. When we went food shopping, for example, she would sit in the car in the parking lot, perhaps reading, while I pushed the grocery cart up and down the aisles. We gradually gave up on vacations, in the usual sense of traveling. Strangely, the traveling aspect of the symptoms bothered us the least: we were too immersed in our daily lives with either full-time or part-time jobs (in the beginning), but always with writing, painting, the Seth material, ESP class, seeing friends, and so forth. Jane did conduct several quite successful long-distance experiments with the Gallaghers when they vacationed in the Caribbean Islands. We made dated notes and times of her impressions so she could check them when our friends returned. Interpreting the impressions was sometimes quite difficult. Jane did have direct hits listed, but for other impressions Peg and Bill couldn't agree on the accuracy and/or timing of certain activities. And sometimes they said the impressions were just wrong.

Reading these private sessions, one can legitimately ask: "Well, if Jane Roberts was so smart and Seth was so great with all of that personal stuff, why did she come down with the symptoms to begin with? Why couldn't he cure her, or at least help her?" My answer right here is that those questions were and still are answered to the best of the abilities of Jane, Seth, and myself in these private sessions, even while I keep in mind Frank Watts's references to Jane's "Timidity has roots of rage." from "Previous hates unresolved." These sessions will detail in many ways and times why my beloved wife, even with all of her creative dedication to her chosen path, ended up with what finally came to be her intractable physical impairments. Part of the answer, as I've already noted, is that because of her strong fears from early childhood on, Jane did not *allow* Seth to tell us all he could have. Not that she was consciously aware of why she refused, and not that the elimination of that barrier alone would have magically wiped away the challenges the two of us were creating. But again and again I felt, I knew, that reincarnational factors were involved, concerning not only Jane, Seth, and me, but a number of other "past" personalities and influences from any of the three of us, and in various camouflage time frames. And what about that influence from the "future," since Seth maintained that all is now? I didn't berate Jane to open up more psychically. I saw her struggles (and had plenty of my own). I sensed walls, barriers, and complications there. Some of them arose from the very uniqueness of her position. After all, here she was, speaking in trance for a personality who told us he'd last lived on Earth in Denmark 300 years ago—even if there is no such thing as time!

Seth, very briefly and with his underlining in Session 54 on May 18, 1964: "I could not tell you in the beginning in so many words that Ruburt (Jane) is myself, because you would have leaped to the conclusion that I was Ruburt's subconscious mind, and this is not so. When you understand the construction of entities, then you will understand how this can be so. Ruburt is <u>not</u> myself <u>now</u>, in his present life; he is nevertheless an extension and materialization of the <u>Seth</u> that <u>I was at one time</u>. Nothing remains unchanging, personalities and entities least of all…I realize this is somewhat difficult, but…Ruburt is <u>now</u> the result of the Seth that I once was, for <u>I</u> have changed since then."

The session is crammed with fascinating material. See Volume 2 of *The Early Sessions* series of nine volumes, published by New Awareness Network, Inc.

Yet I also knew that there was more that Seth could have said; that if Jane had allowed herself to cooperate—but hardly surrender—more completely, the creative Seth portion of her psyche could have helped her more. Much more. Yet I can also honestly state that neither one of us ever felt any sense of blame, toward ourselves or others.

Instead, I think Seth knew that even though he was—and I'm sure still is—in certain senses a portion of Jane's psyche, brilliant counterpart that he was and is, he too had in his own way and for his own reasons desires to contend with Jane's chosen background this time, with her frightened and restricted upbringing and with his obvious advantage of a much more detailed overall knowledge of the life experiences—past, present, and future—involving the three of us. Yet Jane and I didn't ask him to predict for us in national or global terms. Nor for that matter did it occur to us, uninformed though we probably were, to ask about predictions or even "just" the probabilities concerning our own physical lives, let alone our physical deaths. Not that we would have received any answers! All Seth ever told us was that we were in our last physical incarnations. Why didn't we push him for more specific answers? He'd have certainly said something, since he was never at a loss for words!

Yet Jane and I began to truly understand that the challenges, potentials, and probabilities in our lives could easily outstrip our ordinary daily capacities to grasp them. We began to feel that the probable realities alone that we could create and explore, for example, were "probably" endless in ordinary terms. Now, all of these years later, I'm sure of it.

In 1931 in Saratoga Springs, New York, Jane's father, Delmer Roberts (or Del) chose to exercise the probability that he would leave his wife Marie and their daughter Jane, who was not yet three years old. Marie's mother, Mary Finn, called Minnie, lived with the family and often served as Jane's nanny. Jane was a second child following her mother's earlier miscarriage. Already Marie was showing signs of arthritis. Jane and I came to believe that it was hardly accidental that her mother quickly became bedridden—for life—following the departure of her husband. Minnie Finn was killed by a hit-and-run speeding motorist one icy winter day on her way to the corner store to buy the young girl some shredded wheat for supper—a tragedy that Marie never stopped blaming her daughter for. The two went on welfare. A series of housekeepers, of varying abilities and temperaments and staying powers, were provided for them over the early years. The young Jane spent almost two years in a Catholic orphanage for women while her mother was hospitalized. Some of the housekeepers had been—and some still were—prostitutes, Jane told me. They took care of Marie's physical needs—tasks that in her later teens Jane would often take care of herself. With welfare's help Marie set up a telephone answering service for local doctors that she ran from her bed. The two women's Catholicism became even stricter: it was often bolstered by the head of the local church coming to Sunday dinner at the old two-family house at 92 Middle Avenue, in one of the lower-income sections of Saratoga Springs.

It wasn't too long however before Jane, already writing rudimentary poetry, began to have creative conflicts with the doctrinaire priests. She told me how eventually one of the older priests burned certain "forbidden" books of hers in the backyard incinerator, including one she particularly admired: Edward

Gibbon's *Decline and Fall of the Roman Empire*. There were other conflicts also, that Jane didn't reveal to her mother: certain persistent hints and requests as she began to mature, Jane told me more than once, for favors from a young priest that she intuitively rejected. She left the church when she was 19, despite Marie's bitter objections.

A strong saving grace in all of the personal and household turmoil she lived in, Jane told me often, was her relationship with her maternal grandfather, Joseph Burdo, her "Little Daddy," as she called him because of his diminutive size. Even as a youngster she had been well aware that she felt psychically connected to him. Joseph Burdo had become estranged from his wife, Minnie Finn, long ago. He was a man of few words, yet he nurtured in his granddaughter a love of nature that she was to cherish for the rest of her life. In Appendix 1, Volume 1 of *The "Unknown" Reality*, published in 1977, I partially quote Seth as saying that Joseph Burdo was "Part of a very strong entity. However, extremely inarticulate in his last life, due to an inability to synthesize gains in past lives... That is, in his feeling of unity with All That Is, he excluded other human beings...." He lived alone in rented rooms and worked at various jobs in town; he was a doorman, a watchman. He drank and gambled at the local casinos and played the horses at Saratoga Springs' famous racetrack. He took Jane on walks in the nearby woods. "When he spoke of the wind," Seth remarked, "she felt like the wind, as any child will unselfconsciously identify with the elements." He died in 1949 at 68, when Jane was 20 years old.

A year later Jane made the naive mistake of seeking comfort in a marriage to a new friend, Walter Zeh, who was having his own difficult life with just one parent. By then both were attending Skidmore College in Saratoga Springs. Jane was on a liberal arts scholarship awarded to her because of her gifts and work in writing; her husband, a World War II veteran, qualified under a government program and majored in philosophy. Skidmore suspended Jane's scholarship at the end of her third year because she'd attended an all-night party with three professors and three other students; along with discussions of philosophy there had been drinking and smoking, but very modestly on her part. Her marriage was in the process of breaking up when we met early in 1954. I made no judgments about that relationship. Walt and I got along well.

A note about how the "past, present and future" evolved and combined in an unexpected way within Seth's concept of simultaneous time. Jane divorced Walter Zeh in 1954, and published *Seth Speaks* in 1972 and *Personal Reality* in 1974. She died in 1984. During all of that time we had no communication with Walt, as might be expected, although we often talked about him and wished him well. Yet a year or so after Jane's death Walt wrote to me, and we began a most interesting correspondence although we were never to meet. Walt gave me background information about Jane's history, and his own, and the welcome news that he had married again and fathered several children. For many years he worked for the New York State government in Albany. His passion was railroading, and after his retirement he and his wife traveled extensively by rail.

Walt passed along his discovery of the Seth material to his family. Our correspondence eventually faltered, then ceased. Finally, I received news of his death from one of his sons. He too had become interested in Jane's work, and had many questions. I replied, but heard no more from the Zeh family. I think about them often.

And how did Jane and I meet? I too am a World War II veteran; after three years of service in the Air Force Transport Command I was discharged in 1942. I spent several years freelancing as a commercial artist in the Sayre, Pennsylvania area while living with my parents, Robert Sr. and Estelle (my father called her Stell). They were, I could see, getting older. I felt protective toward them; both of my younger brothers had left home, and one had married. I preferred the small-town life, but had about exhausted my professional options after doing medical illustrations for the local but well-known Robert Packer Hospital (some drawings won prizes in traveling exhibitions), working briefly in radio, painting signs, and so forth. Then I went back to doing comic-book art by mail for various New York City publishers. Finally I decided to return to the city indefinitely to go into advertising illustration, a field that paid much better. I told myself that I had to get back into the world out there.

I packed my suitcase and art materials the day before I was to leave Sayre. At suppertime that night I received a telephone call from Ed Robbins, an old friend I'd gone to art school with in Brooklyn, New York before World War II. The results flowing from that call, which was so of-the-moment, were to change my life forever—and Jane's too! Ed offered me a job as an artist in his upstate hometown of Schuylerville, some 11 miles east of Saratoga Springs and on the Hudson River. He was writing and drawing the Mike Hammer daily and Sunday comic strips for his friend, Mickey Spillane, and was having trouble meeting those remorseless weekly deadlines for the syndicate that distributed the feature to newspapers coast to coast. Ed knew I'd done comic-book work: would I be interested in helping him get his strips to the syndicate on time? The pay would be good. I could live with him and his wife Ella and their children until I found a place for myself if our arrangement worked out.

Well, the pay wouldn't be as good as I could earn in New York City, I explained to my parents, but my living expenses would be much lower. Besides, I'd be close enough to visit them often, so what could I lose? I could always go

INTRODUCTION xiii

to the city. What I didn't understand until later was that Ed's seemingly innocent call had set into motion a series of events that one by one would magically fall into place and create a much larger, much longer and more penetrating overall experience. I wasn't used to consciously thinking in such terms.

Ed told me that his car was in a garage for repairs. Tomorrow he was to take the bus from Schuylerville to mail his weekly set of strips to the syndicate via the faster service provided by the post office in Saratoga Springs. If I drove upstate, he suggested, I could meet him late in the day at the post office, and then we could go out to his place. Evening was approaching at the end of my 200-mile trip when we met. Now Ed had a new idea after we'd become reacquainted. I paraphrase all of his dialogue even though my memory is good: "Bob, there's a couple you've got to meet—her name's Jane Zeh and her husband is Walt. She writes poetry, did a column for *The Saratogian*. I think she's got real ability. They have an apartment here in town, and her mother lives on Middle Avenue. I'd like to see the place where she grew up—it's not far out of our way out of town…" Ed added that a few days later, on Saturday night, the Zehs were to join a gathering of friends at his and Ella's home in Schuylerville.

Ed guided me through a poorer section of Saratoga Springs to Middle Avenue. It was almost dark. The narrow "Avenue" had a sidewalk only on his side of the car. On my side was an abandoned red-brick grade school behind a wire fence.

Ed wanted to find number 92, the old double house that Jane had described to him as being her childhood home. We had crawled halfway along the avenue, between its dim corner streetlights, when my car's headlights brushed over a shadowy feminine figure walking in our direction. Indeed, I was driving past the lady when Ed, looking back, exclaimed: "Hey, wait, Bob—that's her! That's Jane right there now. Pull over—" He was lowering his side window even as he spoke. Yes, it was Jane Zeh, expressing surprise in a clear musical voice at such a "chance" meeting as she came even with the car. I could see only part of her silhouette as Ed introduced us and told her I'd be working for him. Jane didn't have a license to drive. She said that if she happened to be in Schuylerville during the day she'd stop in at Ed's studio in town and say hello. (She did, but several weeks later.) Right then, she told us she was on her way to see her bedridden mother, Marie, as she often did at that time of night. She pointed out number 92, a few doors ahead of us. I said something innocuous to the effect that I looked forward to meeting her and her husband next Saturday night.

And so the first time I met my wife-to-be I heard her but didn't really see her….

When he spoke through Jane for the first time in Session 4 on December

February 2, 1954: I was so struck by Jane's beauty that I asked her to pose for me soon after we met in Saratoga Springs, New York. She wasn't to begin creating the Seth material per se until December 6, 1963.

8, 1964, Seth not only gave us his own entity name—Seth, of course—but those for Jane and me: Ruburt and Joseph. He was quite amused that Jane didn't particularly like the name Ruburt. "Strange to the strange," he told us. See Volume 1 of *The Early Sessions*. Yet Ruburt and Seth met on certain common grounds that were to be developed in depth over the years. Indeed, each one of us had particular qualities of life—memories, emotions, events—to explore "this time around." I'm sure that Jane and Seth, those two parts of our triumvirate, are relatively involved in their afterdeath challenges, each from her and his nonphysical viewpoint. Just as I'm doing in this earthly environment that I'm helping to create—preparatory, possibly, to joining them "later" in our ordinary terms of time. That, I'm sure, is a privilege I'll have full freedom to carry out, if I choose to.

I never saw my wife blame Seth because she had her symptoms, nor did I ever refuse to help her hold the sessions until she got rid of them. Almost unconsciously, it seemed, the three of us were committed to creative growth in spite of all obstacles, whatever their cause or nature, or the amount of camouflage time involved.

Nor again, in presenting these private sessions and Jane's and my travails, am I looking for sympathy. Instead, I'm passionately interested in presenting our work with Seth so as to contribute in whatever ways possible to our understanding of this reality we're all creating together. And, dear readers, the participation of each one of you in those efforts help make that possible. I thank you, one and all.

I also feel that now, years later in earthly time, Jane and Seth are free of each other yet more closely knit than ever before. And me? Yes, I chose to be creatively involved (as I still am, obviously) for my own intuitive reasons—not only as an intensely interested observer and recorder, but as an artist too. Much of my art is rooted in the Seth material, in ways I couldn't have anticipated before Jane and I began our work together. Seth once said that without my steadying influence Jane may never have developed the sessions as we know them. That may be true, but I'm also sure that she would have expressed her innate creativity in other surely literary ways—and maybe in psychic ways, too! Why not? Look at her *The Physical Universe as Idea Construction*. But those more acceptable ways, like her "regular" essays but like her poetry most of all, were the ones she had worked in and with from a very early age.

They were also the forms, with the addition of fiction, that she worked within for the first nine years of our marriage on December 27, 1954. She began the sessions in December 1963.

By the age of three I was already drawing—scribbling, experimenting—

and began writing stories in grade school. Many of them were fantasies involving cowboys and Indians and detectives and world adventurers that I crudely illustrated on my yellow school pads. I still have a collection of those: strangely innocent but moving. (I was especially fascinated by horses, but have yet to ride one!) While a sophomore I wrote a novel that I typed on the same kind of yellow paper and bound into a book, I even tried—unsuccessfully—to sell it. I still have that book, also.

It was no accident, Jane and I often said, that we were so quickly attracted to each other. Not only because of our simple love for one another and our mutual interests—but even then, I came to understand, because we could intuitively sense the fine creative adventure in consciousness that was to become the Seth material. (We didn't give a thought, however, to anything like reincarnation, let alone to such connections involving us.) Even now, 18 years after Jane's death in 1984, I'm as committed to our work as ever. I have no reasons or motivations to present myself as being really cautious or asking my wife to be careful as she began to unleash the great flow of creativity that was to follow. I welcomed it after my first hesitance at accepting her themes in *Idea Construction*, and as it created its many-faceted path through our lives. On November 26, 1963, when Jane and I received those first incoherent "messages" on a borrowed Ouija board, our world views began to change, to enlarge. And more and more the Seth material became as deeply intertwined with my visual art as it did with Jane's written art.

Nor did I brush aside my deep concerns about her symptoms because of the excitement stemming from the appearance, then the steady growth and complexity, of the sessions. Instead we became involved in a long process of trying to understand my wife's impairments as they fluctuated over the years, and then finally did not leave her completely at all. Seth told us a number of times that Jane did not have arthritis, like her mother Marie did, but had instead started to develop deep self-protective defense mechanisms at an early age as a result of her chaotic and fatherless upbringing.

Even her early intuitive connections with her grandfather, "Little Daddy," helped only so much. Add to those early fears her later fears of rejection not only by the mainstream publishing world because of the "psychic" nature of her work, no matter how good it was—but also by most of the world in general because of her chosen and unique way of expressing her great creativity: the Seth material. Seth also told Jane that her mother was "an old enemy," thus implying a reincarnational relationship, but we didn't demand details at that early stage. Nor did Jane want to. Once again, I felt there were more such hidden conflicts.

Pardon me for using the phrase every so often, but as the years passed and after her two very brief stays in Elmira's St. Joseph's hospital, Jane finally came to be deeply skeptical of the value of conventional medical help. It hadn't helped when it was offered. The connections involving her mother's bedridden condition and her tempestuous temper, including her suicide attempts, both faked and real, troubles with a succession of housekeepers, the lack of a father, the almost two years she spent in a Catholic orphanage while Marie was hospitalized, the death of her beloved grandfather, the whole strained atmosphere within which the gifted and impressionable child was growing, as well as her conflicts with church dogma and personalities, had, all together, powerful effects indeed. Neighbors tried to help. One gifted Jane with a male dog—a Sheltie—from the city pound. Jane named that loving young creature Mischa, and he was to offer her great comfort for years, just as he did to me when later we met. And I learned that the symptoms were not only a possibility that was native within my wife, but were to become corrosively alive within her all of those years later. Jane took me to meet her mother in the old double house on Middle Avenue three times. The first time, Marie cursed me from her bed; the next two times she ignored me.

Within a few weeks Ed Robbins' and my labors on the Mike Hammer detective strip came to an end due to policy differences with the syndicate distributing the feature. Both of us ended up out of work. I never did get to settle down in my own place in Schuylerville! A "coincidence," of course, that my work for Ed ended at the same time Jane told him that she and Walt had amicably agreed to part. Ed talked about moving with his family to New Paltz, a small community about 110 miles south, near the Hudson River; he might find commercial work there with a friend. I thought of returning to my parents' home in Sayre, and then going on to New York City as I'd originally planned to do before receiving that life-changing call from Ed.

I had kept my very strong feelings for Jane to myself, or so I'd thought, and despaired at the idea of never seeing her again. I was the complete amateur at dealing with the personal interactions of others. I visited Walt and Jane at their apartment in Saratoga Springs and told them I'd be leaving the area. Jane discussed the decision she and Walt had made. Then, directly to me: "I'm leaving town, with or without you. So which is it going to be?" I was quite unprepared, yet knew at once what my answer would be. Even though I'd had no thought of interfering with, or taking advantage of, any complications between them. I can see Walt now, sitting by the window of their second-story apartment's small living room, nodding at Jane's words, his eyes wet. There was never a harsh word between us. Jane's dog, Mischa, slept at her feet. It was only after Jane had begun the Seth material a number of years later that we realized that

I drew Jane a few weeks before our marriage on December 27, 1954. We had always been dedicated to our arts, but little did we realize what great changes were to take place in our lives and how we were to help ourselves and others with Jane's gift of the Seth material.

she and Walt, both coming from dysfunctional families, had chosen to come together at just the right time for their own mutually creative learning purposes—and that with those purposes fulfilled, each of them was ready to move on by the time I met them. At the time, however, I wasn't ready to consciously understand such interlocking emotional relationships even though I was playing a part in one of them.

Getting a divorce in New York State was difficult in the 1950s, but easy to achieve in Florida. Jane's father, Del, traveled with his trailer from Los Angeles to meet us in Daytona Beach, Florida; we followed him to Marathon, in the Florida Keys, where we lived with him and Mischa and Del's Great Dane, Boo, in that wonderful climate while Jane put in the required few weeks of residency that Florida divorce law required. I found work painting signs, and prepared samples of advertising art to show art directors in New York City once we'd returned north. Besides writing for herself, Jane worked briefly as a cashier in a newly-opened food market; she left the job after a few days when the manager made advances to her. Her divorce was granted without being contested, the papers signed. Del paid the costs. We thanked him, said good-bye to him and Boo and headed north with Mischa in my ancient Cadillac. We hoped we had enough money to get to my parents' home in Sayre, PA. We made it with only one flat tire on the way.

Jane and I were married on December 27, 1954 at the home of my younger brother Loren and his wife Betts in Tunkhannock, PA, some 55 miles south of Sayre. Betts's father, Leonard Meeker, who was a Methodist minister, performed the ceremony. In his later years my father, Robert Sr., had trained himself to become an excellent professional photographer. As a wedding present he created an album of the ceremony that Jane and I treasured. I still do. We rented an apartment in Sayre. I painted signs, then designed clothing labels for a printing plant there, and painted and wrote on weekends.

Jane made her first sales of short stories—science-fiction fantasies. And riding her old-fashioned secondhand bicycle she also sold cutlery and household supplies door-to-door for two out-of-town manufacturers, and did well at those efforts, too! She turned down an offer to be a district manager for one of the companies. In 1960 we moved 15 miles across the Pennsylvania border to Elmira, NY, to live in Jimmy Spaziani's apartment house on West Water Street. I designed greeting cards for a nationally known company, and was to work there off and on for several years. Jane worked part-time as a secretary for Elmira's Arnot Art Museum, and wrote two unpublished novels—and one that did sell. *The Rebellers* was published in a two-novel paperback edition that she disliked intensely. Without judging the other author's work, she just didn't want to share her first book with anyone else.

She began the sessions on December 2, 1963 and published *The Seth Material* in 1970. Before that welcome event, however, we had held 510 sessions over five years and two months, mainly for ourselves as we sought to understand and let develop her most unusual abilities as she spoke for and wrote about Seth, with all that such creatively unorthodox behavior implied. We never asked others in the field to help us play "the psychic game," as we understood it from our reading. We just wanted to do our own thing. Mischa died, and I buried him in a flower bed in back of 458, as we called the house; we were left with our two cats. Those 510 sessions have now been published in nine volumes by Rick Stack of New Awareness Network, Inc. (See that last volume for my drawing of Mischa.) It took a while after the publication of *The Seth Material* for the first seemingly innocuous signs of conflict within Jane's psyche—the symptoms—to appear.

My father died in a rest home in 1971, my mother in 1973. Both were buried in the family plot in Tunkhannock. Without judgment or rancor I note that my parents never seemed to have the slightest interest in Jane's work (although they loved her dearly), while taking my own abilities for granted as they had done all of my life. It was easy to look at signs and commercial art and paintings; they only knew that Jane wrote poetry and fiction, but never asked to read any of her work any more than we offered it to them.

Professional writing was simply outside of their experience. They did understand that we had a creative relationship with the arts, and that we obviously loved each other. For whatever psychological and psychic reasons, the lack of communication on that score between the two "sides" suited both. I don't remember Jane and me showing my parents any of the Seth material, for example, and trying to explain what we were searching for within it. For all of the six years that we held the early sessions, we never mentioned them to my parents as we sought to go our own way. Nor did we discuss with them the information Seth occasionally gave us about them. For that to be possible, my parents would have had to understand what the Seth material was all about. There was no animosity about the situation, let alone conscious curiosity about what to do, on either side, although now I think there must have been at least an unconscious telepathic understanding and acceptance among the four of us.

During this time also Jane's mother, Marie, lost her home in Saratoga Springs, NY, and was placed in a state-run nursing home in nearby Middle Grove. Through the mail mother and daughter patched up their volatile relationship enough to begin exchanging letters fairly regularly. Jane never told Marie about the Seth material, or her symptoms. Marie even accepted me as her daughter's husband. The two gave each other Christmas gifts. Jane sent her mother nightwear and stationery and other small useful presents. Marie always sent her daughter sweaters that she had knitted with great difficulty because of her misshapen fingers; invariably the garments were too large. Seth suggested that Jane not wear them in any case because of the roiled emotions that had existed between the two almost from Jane's birth; gifts from the mother could still carry those feelings. Mother and daughter were to never meet again: Marie died shortly before 1975. By then it wasn't easy for Jane to travel, and we didn't make the approximately 400-mile roundtrip to attend the funeral. Later the nursing home was closed by the state. A mutual friend sent us photographs of the big old red-brick building, three stories high, shuttered and dark and deserted among the trees and in the snow.

And guess what: I finally understood as Jane's symptoms began to slowly grow that her choices were her right, and stopped my innuendos that it was perfectly all right for her to be open to outside help—so why wasn't she? Seth was way ahead of me. I don't recall that worthy ever suggesting to my wife outright that she seek medical help, let alone insisting that she do so. Was this because Jane wouldn't allow him to say that, even if he wanted to? As noted, at times I'd felt that that was the case. It's easy to proclaim that we human beings live short of our potentials in those terms—for if such potentials didn't exist, how could we sense or aspire to them? But I'm hardly being original when I insist that each life is so intensely real that it seems most difficult to truly believe that we can have it any other way—let alone have more than one! Our challenges in *this* physical/nonphysical existence reign supreme, regardless of other possible long-term influences like reincarnation or time travel, for example. Or—yes—even religion: a subject I would like to explore in depth if ever I can create the several years of camouflage time necessary to do so. So even if Seth did help, still Jane chose to live her own life within the face and force of her own very creative present personality. Seth did offer insights, excellent ones of certain very creative depths that we more than welcomed, while all the time being quite aware, I think, that the beautiful young woman through whom he spoke—who *let* him speak—had her own agenda at the same time. And even though we agreed with Seth's reincarnational material involving the three of us, and our families, still it was also intensely personal for my wife in *this* life that she go her own way.

I also believe that even as Jane dealt with certain long-range challenges, *her doing so also influenced Seth*, perhaps in ways we cannot know. I do not recall that I have him on record concerning that possibility, and regret that I didn't ask him about it, and in detail.

As I've written, Jane's two short and fruitless stays in the hospital had left her deeply skeptical about the value of conventional medical treatment in her case. She was still most reluctant to return to St. Joseph's, but when her symptoms became so severe that I could no longer care for her at 1730 she went back into the hospital in April 1983. For the last time. For one year and 9 months until her death. In all of that camouflage time I missed spending several hours a day with her in room 330 just once. The Elmira area was hit by more than a foot of snow. I couldn't get my car out of the garage; the streets weren't plowed, businesses remained closed. Radio bulletins advised all except emergency workers to stay home. I couldn't get through to my wife by telephone. Sometimes I would call her late at night to offer reassurance.

Jane was still productive during much of that last stay, however. With Seth she dictated, if slowly, *The Way Toward Health*. For herself she dictated poetry. I read to her the fan mail I brought each day, and between the two of us we kept up with answering it. She had periods of modest motion improvement, but they didn't last. Various medications helped a little (with side effects at times), but the medical establishment had no cure to offer. Jane obtained her greatest relief from the daily baths that were given her so lovingly by staff members. We became friends with a number of them; they helped us celebrate birthdays and holidays in 330. At no time did we tell anyone what we were writing about, or its sometimes nonphysical source, so to speak. Staff knew only that Jane dictated to me often, that we got a lot of mail, and that I kept copious notes. We had a few visits from local friends, but it didn't take us long to learn that many people avoided hospitals as much as possible. We could hardly object to that: after all, for whatever strong personal reasons Jane had done her best to stay out of the hospital, and I had acquiesced to her decisions. People out there in the world had their own challenges.

I do want to record that while we took great comfort in receiving the mail, we also came to receive through it an additional and totally unexpected gift—one that literally we would never have asked for even if we had thought of it. Maude Cardwell, an older Seth reader in Austin, Texas, had for several years been publishing a modest monthly journal on the Seth material that she called *Reality Change*. When I wrote her about Jane's latest hospitalization Maude, without mentioning her idea to me, suggested to her readers that donations would help Jane and me cope with our hospital bills. I would have never had the nerve to make such a statement. St. Joe's, as we called the hospital, had never dunned us for money in the past, and wasn't doing so now. Our considerable daily charges were mounting, but we had emotionally pushed their import into the background. I was able to make modest payments out of royalty income I had been saving, but this was difficult to keep up because most of that money was paid to us but twice a year. Imagine, then, our great surprise when the readers of *Reality Change* began to contribute: small checks; medium checks; the occasional larger check. I have every one of those letters and my heartfelt answers in a separate file that I plan to add as a unit to the collection of Jane's and my work in the archives of Yale University Library.

The checks kept arriving as Jane's health very slowly cotinued to deteriorate even with all of our creative activities in 330. As the months passed I became more and more consciously caught up in the signs of her approaching physical death. See the final sessions and notes in *The Way Toward Health*, which I published in 1997, 13 years after her passing. Questions? There was no end to them, and there still isn't. Like, why had I stayed way later than usual on the night of her death—so late that I fell asleep in my chair beside her bed after she had fallen asleep? Usually I left 330 before 10 PM. When at last I startled awake, Jane had died, at an estimated 2:08 AM on Wednesday, September 5, 1984. How did my dear wife react, feel, at the moment of her death? In the minute AFTER her death? How did Seth respond in those same fleeting intervals? How did the two of them greet each other, and perhaps join? Had he spoken with me after those precious first moments, could Seth have given me information that Jane, for whatever reasons, hadn't wanted us to acquire from or through him? Did Jane, did Seth, watch me make the two pen-and-ink drawings of my beautiful wife as she lay so quietly in her bed, at peace at last? (I still plan to do paintings based on that art.)

If they chose to do so together, how did Jane and Seth explore the new reality they were committed to? Could I have briefly joined that reality, and perhaps recorded a few aspects of it in my own dream reality, aside from the after-death paintings of Jane that I was to produce over the next several years? What, I could ask, did Seth really think of the portrait I'd painted of him way back in June 1968? I had envisioned him as portly, middle-aged, and bald.

A month later, in Session 168 on July 7, he did tell me that the work was an excellent likeness; Jane had liked it from the day I began working on it. And why hadn't I ever painted the two of them together? I could even insert myself into the art, since I'm the third member of the triumvirate. In short, I believe there's no end to our abilities in whatever reality we choose to create and explore.

Apart from my questions and speculations, I think it significant that Jane had waited until she had produced the first 207 sessions of the Seth material, over a period of a year and 11 months, before she really began to allow Seth to come through with outright personal material about her—as if first the two had to learn to know each other that well by bridging not only space but our historical or camouflage time. This opening volume of *The Personal Sessions* begins with an excerpt from Session 208, on November 15, 1965. During the nearly two years before that there were very sporadic mentions by Seth about Jane's challenges, usually occurring as brief interludes that we deleted from the published sessions. Of course, neither one of us ever considered the possibility that many years later these personal sessions would be published.

For example: In Session 510, on January 19, 1970 in Volume Nine of *The Early Sessions*, Seth remarked: "Now. I have been helping Ruburt. The energy that I would put into sessions has gone into some private talks to him while he slept. These have resulted in necessary insights on his part that will themselves cause the release of energy from the inner self." And my notes follow: *(For the last several days Jane has been telling me about a string of insights and revelations she has been experiencing, both asleep and awake. She feels these are very beneficial and has been putting them to immediate use. She feels she has lately realized a group of truths that she hadn't understood before, etc.)*

Trust, then, entered in in a unique way, even before Jane opted more consciously for more direct help from Seth within the limits she created. As I've noted, she avoided doctors and the hospital as much as possible until her last long stay in St. Joseph's.

For whatever reasons, she had resolved along the way to do her own thing in her own way—with two exceptions. She went to Andy Colucci, a dentist (and friend) who had his office around the corner from where we lived on West Water Street for routine cleaning (she had perfect teeth); and on rare occasions one or both of us visited Sam Levine, a doctor who had his office on the ground floor of his building next-door to 458. We'd see him for an inoculation, say, or treatment for a cold. Did Doctor Sam ever hear Seth's booming voice in the summertime, when windows were open, or the uproarious racket made by the members of Jane's ESP class on Tuesday nights? Yes he did, he told Jane, but he didn't understand what was going on—only that there were many extra cars parked in the neighborhood on Tuesday nights. And Jane wasn't about to explain: "Hi, Sam. Hey, I'm speaking in a trance state for this nonphysical entity called Seth—a guy I knew in Denmark three hundred years ago. I wonder if you can help me deal with some of my symptoms, as I call them. They might be connected with my psychic work..." Not a chance! Doctor Sam was a very kind but reserved Jewish doctor who helped many people on a daily basis. Yet I do think that even if he hadn't accepted Jane's mediumship per se, still he would have recognized it as being a portion of her psyche.

But even trying to take into account all that Jane accomplished, I know that while I proofread the galleys of *The Personal Sessions* as Rick Stack of New Awareness Network sends them to me volume by volume, I'll still come across

I converted this image of Seth from the full-color, nearly life-size portrait I painted of him in oil from my vision in 1968. I show him from the waist up as he beckons to the viewer—Rob.

material that is new to me. Each discovery, large or small, will be a new truth. This has happened often as I've worked with the Seth books over the years. Readers have written describing similar experiences. I make no pretense of keeping in mind the contents of the more than 16,500 typewritten pages of the Seth material and notes. I only know and feel, that the material will help me and others, and I do appreciate the participation of each reader.

Many have written; many still do. I like each letter, even the occasional disapproving ones, and reply as best I can. Sometimes I send copies of my drawings and paintings. I've always been gratified by the response to Jane's work, just as she was and, I know, still is. I claim little credit for her success, however. I only helped her. I'm simply pleased by, and very respectful of, the public response to the Seth material. That response is much more important and helpful to the material than my own feelings—though obviously I'm quite aware of these, and respect them too!

Jane and I were very surprised at the initial reception of *The Seth Material*, then *Seth Speaks* and *Personal Reality* (our shortened terminology for those first two Seth-dictated books.) Since we had no experience with "fan mail," for example, we had no expectations, but as the Seth titles and Jane's own books were published she came to spend many a weekend answering that most welcome mail. I helped out when I could after typing sessions, often doing commercial art at least part-time, and trying to paint. The mail rapidly became a quite humbling education in itself. The writers of those letters opened up in specific terms worlds that we'd have never known about otherwise, and, eventually, they did so not only from this country but also from abroad. Seventeen language translations as I write this. How interesting to see that each one of us was indeed creating our personal reality within the overall reality of the universe that all of us were also creating, uniting all—everything—in complicated fashions far beyond our ordinarily accepted understanding. Time travels for sure; travels not only through the psyche but through time—even if Seth did call that quality we were so used to "camouflage time!"

Periodically, after answering the mail, I add it to the archives of the Seth material at Yale University Library as an integral part, a reinforcement, say, of Jane's great body of work. It's well preserved there. I speculate that eventually someone may write a book showing the great variety of reader reactions to the Seth material. It would—and will—be a vital addition to the work my wife began, and so help perpetuate it. Producing such a loving compendium would require much study. And a continuing one, as long as more mail arrives....

I'm sure that Seth and Jane, whether or not they're together, per se, have each been more than a little amused to watch me at my labors here—but also compassionate and sharing from "where they are now." I'm pleased to believe that they have psychically joined me as I write this introduction, and that they know I have tried to be objective. I also feel that they will be with me as I enter into this account's final episode, one involving Laurel's and my most interesting meeting with a group of visitors.

*   *   *   *   *   *   *

Finally, then: I was working on this introduction late in October 2002 when Laurel and I were visited by five members of the Houston, Texas, Seth group: Winter Calvert, Theresa Smith, Jim and Debbie Serra, and Yvette Silva. I had corresponded with a few members of the group, and Jim and his wife had visited me some time ago. The five were accompanied by Richie Kendall; he's an old friend from the days of Jane's ESP class—one of the New York City boys, as Jane used to fondly refer to that group. Richie had also visited Laurel and me twice last summer with Mary Dillman from his new residence in Westport, Connecticut.

Our guests, with others who didn't make the trip to Sayre, had been visiting the collection of the Seth material in the archives of Yale University Library in New Haven, CT. The archives contain a complete copy of my original typed pages of the Seth material in its 46 three-ring binders; many editions of the Seth books and Jane's "own" books in English and in translations; her published and unpublished novels; her journals and poetry; her notes and papers, and mine; various published Seth journals; treatises and websites on the Internet (some nice, some not so nice); plus other relevant, indeed very evocative material like the reader correspondence from this country and abroad. I'm still adding to the collection. It's open to the public.

Mary Dillman, a volunteer, works with and cares for the collection at the library. She has been, and is, a great help in organizing that mass of material, coordinating and computerizing it for researchers in a number of interesting ways that Jane and I hadn't thought of doing "way back when" my wife was delivering the sessions. Ways that, indeed, wouldn't have been possible even if we'd had the camouflage time to carry them out in those long-ago days. The blinding speed and depth of association via modern technology simply hadn't existed.

Shortly before they were to leave Yale, Jim Serra had e-mailed Laurel and me from New Haven to confirm his and his friends' visit. The members also had plans for visits in upper New York State and in Maine before heading back to Texas. Laurel and I always find such infrequent meetings very evocative—

unique signs of the reach of Jane's work to a variety of individuals, each with his or her own creative and intuitional skills. This is both humbling and worthwhile, that Jane's love and inspiration has helped so many others. And still does.

We talked with our guests about many things psychic and psychological most—but not all—of the time. Theresa Smith showed Laurel and me color photographs of her very original modern art in progress, and talked about her goals. I encouraged her to keep developing. Then I showed the group some of Jane's art and my own.

Of the two of us I was supposed to be the artist in the conventional sense, yet I'd always felt that I couldn't rival Jane's amazingly simple but brilliantly colored art that was so true to her innate psychic knowledge—while seemingly ignoring it! But she didn't ignore it at all, I learned along the way, for she created and explored a spontaneous and innocent reality that freed her from all other concerns. Her art contained our origins, I felt, by strongly calling attention to her obviously creative and intuitive knowledge. She painted a tree rising out of the earth with brilliantly colored apples, for example. It was, after all, an epitome of what our reality has led us to create and enjoy. What could be better? She wasn't bound by the mundane rules of perspective, with its everyday limits that most of us never surmount or subsume: she created her deceptively childish world each time she painted. I could go on and on. Jane's work is not large-scale by any means. One of my goals is to see her art, all of it, reproduced in color in 81/2" x 11" portfolio style at a modest price. Susan Ray of Moment Point Press used three of Jane's paintings as cover art for her books; *God of Jane*, *Adventures in Consciousness*, and *Psychic Politics*.

I showed our guests the portrait of Seth that I had painted from my vision in 1968, as well as my paintings of Jane both before and after her death. Some of the latter were from visions, some simply from my memory of her and what she was trying to tell me or from what I was trying to understand. I also showed our visitors several of my portraits from my own past lives, both male and female, that Seth had mentioned long ago, or that I'd tuned into through dreams. The points I stressed to the group mainly concerned my basically unconventional interests. I do some abstract art. Beyond an occasional foray, however, I no longer have an abiding interest in simple literal portraits or still-life or landscape images per se. But then, I asked, what more literal odyssey would there be than to investigate one's own past lives, male and female? It took me a while to start thinking that way after Jane began speaking for Seth. The subject matter is endless, free of time and age and style in unique ways. And here again, I envision publishing a portfolio of my art, with the necessary text. I see Jane's and my art as reinforcing the Seth material in quite original ways.

For my own amusement, I can't resist digressing a bit here. Please forgive me.

I do admit that in recent years I've wondered more and more why artists don't deal with at least their own past-life images. Surely these would be as original as any conventional self-portrait. Surely the artist could have, would have, insights into such existences but for a number of reasons—fear of ridicule, for example—choose not to investigate them. Especially in public ways! Yet artists are supposed to be uninhibited to express their feelings and knowledge. An incredibly rich and very nearly untapped, psychic and psychological field lies open for exploration, I think, waiting, waiting. I also believe that opening up past-life fields would enrich us all. In my naiveté I can see a whole genre of art growing. My own projected portfolio of art will include at least several past-life images of me. I've already painted them (but can always add more). Recently I finished a past-life portrait from my vision of a friend Jane and I had known years ago. Jim hasn't seen it; we lost touch with him before moving to the hill house in 1975. Why did that past-life image of him come to me in 2002? I painted my image of Jim with tiny crosses in the pupils of his eyes, and with his eyes themselves brimming with tears. I wrote: "Always very religious in his lives, Jim cried with compassion for his fellow human beings." The resultant oil is one of my best.

Of course, it could be much trickier for the artist to paint a past-life portrait of the client who poses with that result in mind. Questions abound. Can the artist relax enough to let a pertinent image of the sitter come to him or her? What if the client doesn't like the results? The looks? The time frame? The race, the sex, the implied behavior? Well, to start the sitter could always tell the artist about his or her own dreams and hunches, and help the poor guy out that way. That is, while taking it for granted that the artist believed in reincarnational possibilities....

Back to conventional reality.

At the end of the first day of the group's most interesting visit. Richie and Yvette left to return to Connecticut. Jim and Debbie and Winter and Theresa left for the Holiday Inn in Elmira, New York, 15 miles across the Pennsylvania border. At the Inn in 1997 and 1999 Laurel and I had been guests at well-attended Seth conferences organized by Lynda Dahl and Stan Ulkowski. Our rich memories of those gatherings are nourished each time we drive past the Inn on our way to the hill house. We met our guests at the Inn the next morning, and the six of us drove in our three cars to a nearby country restaurant for breakfast. Then, with Laurel driving and our friends' cars following, we traveled up a steep and winding hill just outside the city to not only a fine view but to Quarry

Farm, an old-fashioned but large and elegant wooden homestead where Mark Twain had done some of his finest writing. No admittance, private property, a sign proclaimed, so we stood in the driveway just off the road to study the farm and its open and peaceful setting. Then back down into the city and to the campus of Elmira College. Jane had lectured to a class in creative writing at the college after the publication of *Seth Speaks* in 1972. There on the school's green sward stood the small many-windowed gazebo that Mark Twain had worked in during his summers at the farm; it had been relocated to the college long ago. Not surprisingly it was locked, but still easy to inspect—and also to just accept as the people of Elmira and those in the college went about their daily activities. Mark Twain had been one of Jane's favorite writers.

Next, at Jim's request we visited the apartment house at 458 West Water Street that Jane and I had lived in when we moved to Elmira from Sayre in 1960. We had stayed there until 1975, when we purchased the hill house at 1730 Pinnacle Road in West Elmira. Some years after we had moved out, the apartment house was painted a garish green, a color that was quite out of keeping with all of the other houses in the neighborhood. Now, the color is unevenly faded. The whole sprawling house looks shoddy, sagging almost, in need of general repair.

Actually, Laurel and I drive past 458 often, without paying much attention to it on our way from Sayre to the hill house. But now we were there on its grounds, focusing upon that precious symbol where Jane and I had lived for 15 years. I hadn't set foot in 458 since the day we'd moved to the hill house 27 years ago. Incredible! Already, as I pushed open the heavy front door for the six of us, I felt like an intruder, that my footsteps were stirring up the past. We tramped noisily up the narrow and turning stairs to face a fire door guarding the second floor. Past that, we were in the narrow hall that led to a similar door guarding a stairwell at the back of the building. The hall was much shorter and gloomier than I remembered it to be. The sounds of our voices were crowded; the space we stood in seemed to be so confining, with the doors at each end, that I marveled that my dear wife and I had lived in the house for all that time. Apartments 4 and 5, the ones Jane and I had rented (we could afford only Apartment 5 for the first several years) opened off each side of the hall. Apartment 4 was empty; its door was on a short chain that let me push it open a bit to peek into a now-deserted living room that Jane and I had known so well.

The door to Apartment 5 was closed. Locked? Was anyone home? I didn't try to find out as all of us stood there. Seth had first come through Jane in the living room of that apartment, in Session 4 on December 8, 1962. Thirty-nine years ago. I couldn't believe it....

I pushed open the back fire door and the six of us clumped down the open stairs that Jane and I had used so many times. I worried about being an intruder into the domain of the people who lived in those dingy apartments now. Indeed, as we left the stairs two dogs in a back apartment set up a furious barking as they scratched at what I knew were kitchen windows. A friend of ours had lived in that apartment (and I still correspond with him). I was embarrassed: the dogs' racket must have bothered everyone in the house. We saw no one, however, and the barking magically ceased as we moved around to the east side of 458 and surveyed it from a small paved parking lot. Once in that spot there had been flagstones and benches beneath an extended roof supported by four sets of wooden pillars. The tin-covered roof had born layers of old vines that had climbed up the pillars from our living-room windows on the second floor. Jane had liked to throw seed and bread crusts into the vines for the squirrels and birds to root out. The pigeons, cardinals, sparrows, blue jays and others had flown over from the Chemung River a quarter of a block away.

Early in this introduction I wrote that late in November 1963 Jane had had an out-of-body experience while writing her essay, *The Physical Universe as Idea Construction*—that she had looked in at herself from the porch roof outside our windows. That had been the porch she referred to. Long gone.

From the parking lot I pointed out to our guests the windows of Apartment 5 as they marched along the side of 458 on the second floor. Our landlord, Jimmy Spaziani, had told us that the entire apartment had been the master-bedroom complex of the wealthy merchant who had built the house for his family more than a century ago. The kitchen with its three tiny windows near the front of the house had been a closet; the three bay windows of the living room where Jane had held the sessions and her ESP class had been the main bedroom. Next comes the oversized bathroom with its stained glass window, tiled floor, and marble shower with eight nozzles. Jane and I had really enjoyed that shower! Then comes a smaller room that we had used as a bedroom, with one window in the back wall of the house. Finally, there's the last room with its windows on three sides as it juts out on iron posts from the back of the house. Originally it had been a sun parlor. The room is open underneath. It had been my studio, and I'd had to insulate the floor.

I also described to our guests the great Seckel pear tree that had grown so beautifully in the back yard, with some of its branches—and fruit— within my reach from the windows of the studio. It must have died years ago, as did its companion, the apple tree I had drawn to illustrate Jane's poem, "The You-ness of the Universe," in her book of poems, *Dialogues of the Soul and Mortal Self in Time* (1975). At the Sayre house I have the large oil painting I did of the sunlight streaming through the windows of the studio on a certain day early in August: the only day in the year that the ever-moving sun casts that particular intriguing pattern of light and shadow across the bare wooden floor.

While we were surveying the house I saw a young black man step off the front porch and stroll out to the sidewalk. He didn't turn to walk up or down the street, however, as one might expect, but casually stood there and turned to look at our group a few times as we talked and took pictures. Evidently we'd bothered at least one tenant after all, to the point of sending a sibling, say, to try to see what we might be up to, if anything. Perhaps deciding that we were no threat, our observer sauntered back into the house. I never did see anyone peeking out at us, though.

During our talking, Jim Serra asked me a key question (which I paraphrase along with my answer).

"Rob, do you think the community—Elmira—has any idea of the historical significance of this house, as far as Jane's work goes?"

It wasn't hard for me to answer, with no judgment or resentment implied. "No, I don't think anyone here in town has the faintest idea of anything like that."

Actually, outside of our own small group of friends, including ESP class members, plus the well-received articles Peg Gallagher had written for the *Elmira Star-Gazette*, Jane and I hadn't stirred ourselves to become known in Elmira, even after the Seth books had begun to sell. In our own creative ways we had been loners, (as I still am) basically; our passions had been to focus on what we could learn both for ourselves and others in the long term, and especially through publishing to reach a larger audience. This became even more so for us as Jane gradually became more restricted physically because of her symptoms.

We had always been very comfortable in the community, and grateful indeed that we had the privilege of living there on our own terms, even though in those early years we usually took in so little money that we lived pretty much from week to week, with no security. Before we moved out of 458, though, Jane's books began to appear in local and chain bookstores, and the very interesting mail from readers kept increasing, to our great pleasure.

The Butts family does have a bit of history in Elmira, though. Here are a few clues for anyone even remotely interested. In the last two decades of the 1800s my grandfather Otis and his wife raised four children on their farm in Wellsboro, PA, a farming community some 50 miles from Elmira, New York. At the age of 15 my father, Robert Sr., followed his three older siblings, Jay and Ernest and Ella, in leaving the farm. All did well, each in his and her way. Ernest left the northeast and never married. After Jay and Ella had each married they settled in Elmira. Jay and his wife had children. My father married Estelle (Stell) in Newark, NJ in 1917, and I was born two years later in Mansfield, a small community near Wellsboro.

My parents lived briefly in Elmira, and then moved to Sayre in 1923 after having traveled to California. Hardly strange, then, that I found work as an artist in Elmira, and that Jane and I moved there in 1960, five years after our marriage. I still have third-and-fourth generation relatives in Elmira, although I'm not close to them. This is as much my fault as anyone else's. Jane and I became so wrapped up in our own little worlds that we didn't try to reach out. I tell myself that I should try to do that, even now, however.

The last stop in our group's little tour was to visit the hill house. 1730 Pinnacle Road sits on a corner lot up a modest hill on the western outskirts of Elmira. Jane and I fell for it the first time we saw it. It's a one-story dark-green-painted dwelling with a big stone fireplace, and has a screened-in side porch and a one-car garage in back. The woods continuing on up the hill begin only 50 feet from the garage. The setting had—and has—privacy without being isolated from other homes not far away and it had plenty of room for our few possessions and work projects. That was a real treat to us.

Often I think of the routines Jane and I settled into upon moving into 1730 in 1975. She was 46; I was 56. Now it seems that all of those years to follow passed in a flash. Routines, yes, but also ever-changing ones that still revolved around the simple elements of the work we loved and carried out amid the unexpected freedoms of living so much closer to the environment we had always taken for granted: the writing and painting, the sessions and mail, the publishing of books, the visits of friends and fans, some even from Europe. The hill house was the first property either one of us had ever owned, yet even within that loving context Jane gradually had more and more trouble walking even while the Seth material continued to grow in reach and flexibility, to attract a wider and wider audience. We saw deer in the back yard and put feed out for them and the birds. (The deer went into hiding during the hunting seasons.)

We quickly made friends with the family across the road. Joseph and Margaret Bumbalo had three children, all living away from home. The youngest, John, who visited his parents occasionally, was attracted by the ideas in Jane's work. (Now that was a coincidence!) He had, and still has, no doubt, a most powerful and moving baritone voice. He was also restless. When we met, John had little interest in an operatic career, as far as I recall, yet had taken professional singing lessons and given auditions. When he crossed the road to visit I would encourage him to sing a bit for us a cappella. The few brief times he did so I thrilled to the power and quality of his voice; I could feel it surging within me, as could Jane. John's masculine power, while different from Jane's Seth voice at its masculine strongest, represented the only time I've personally heard a voice that could match Seth's voice at its best. Both voices could make my ears ring, conjuring up deep-seated wordless emotions that usually lay unsuspected within the psyche. Very revealing, Jane and John.

Another part of my routine at 1730, a somewhat selfish one I saw in retrospect, involved first walking and then running late at night. I'd always been active in sports, and later in dancing with Jane, but as her symptoms slowly deepened I became more and more reluctant to leave her alone except when I had full or part-time jobs. By the time we bought 1730 we could exist without my outside income for the most part as we concentrated on the Seth material. I had my chance, I told Jane: on other than session nights I was free to leave the house. I started out walking, but soon my nighttime excursions turned into running on those hilly streets in our neighborhood. Jane was reluctant to see me go out late at night, but I reassured her that she would be all right in the house and that I would be all right outside of it—and each one of us always was. My solitary treks became most enjoyable, no matter the time of year. I came to know intimately all of the dead-end streets opening off the main road, Coleman Avenue, like steps in a ladder that led up the hill to Pinnacle Road. I encountered wildlife on those streets. I told Jane that my record was six deer at one time. I stopped moving; they stopped; each side stared at the other in the porch light from a house across the street....

When Jane entered the hospital for the last 21 months of her life, I could run all I wanted to. I usually spent the morning typing the session she had delivered the afternoon before for *The Way Toward Health*, answering mail, running, and running errands. I went to her room at noon and stayed until the evening, seven days a week, every week. I still remember asking myself as I trotted along on my 65th birthday on June 20: "Should I still be doing this?" My answer was yes, for that action, free of any other personal responsibility, helped me stay connected with the outside world in my own way. Jane died later that year. John Bumbalo did me an enormous favor in the hours following Jane's death. When I came home from the hospital for the last time in a year and 9 months, John went to Jane's room 330 and very carefully gathered up all of the belongings and artifacts we had accumulated there and brought them to me in 1730: my paintings and drawings, the letters from readers that I had put up on the walls (the hospital never complained), the session notebooks for *The Way Toward Health*, our books and magazines and newspapers and clothes, the flowers and other gifts from readers and from some of the nurses—all of those things that seem to accumulate almost by themselves as one seeks to create a home wherever that may be.

John "settled down" eventually; he lives with his wife and children in Seattle, Washington. I saw him once several years later when he visited his mother. He was immensely proud to show me his very young first son. His mother Margaret retired to Florida after the death of her husband Joe. We still keep in touch. I'll always treasure her exceptional kindnesses to me during Jane's long and final hospital stay.

Laurel and I have lived in Sayre since early in 2000 while 1730 sits there unoccupied. The trees and bushes around the house are taller and more luxurious than ever. They make it harder to see the house from the street corner, almost as though they're offering protective shelter in their own ways. We hire help to maintain the lawn, while each year I vow to fix up the place. Laurel makes the 15-mile trip from Sayre much more often than I do: to look the place over, to pick up the junk mail that's still addressed to us there in spite of the notices I've sent out, and to scatter feed for the birds and animals. She knows I still feel sadness about 1730. I sometimes think I'm almost cowardly about visiting it, as though I fear my emotions could still erupt if I weren't careful. And of course they do, but I let them out without a struggle usually, in a very subdued manner. And today my feelings about visiting 458 with our guests were also fresh in my psyche.

Jane and I lived in the hill house while she had her greatest initial successes with publishing the Seth material, and before she went into the hospital for good on April 20, 1983. Of course 1730 is still a large part of my life, as it is of Laurel's, even while we use it for storage of all of the treasures it still contains: many of my paintings, files stuffed with records that are destined for the collection at Yale University Library, Laurel's books and mine, and her records and possessions—all of those intimate signs of life that now seem suspended in our creations of space/time. Laurel came to live with me there on August 23, 1985, 11 months after Jane's death. And may I add that she wasn't /enamored of my late-night running either. Now, at 83, I walk or run just about every day over the streets I knew so well as a child—only I do it in the daytime. It's a treat, a privilege, to be able to do it each day. Then I do some painting. I have evenings free to answer mail and write and proofread books like this one. While I still feel the pull of all of those secret nighttimes out of 1730....

Please forgive me for having used too many dates in this account, dear reader. It's my habit to be as specific as I can when communicating with others.

Once our three cars were parked in or near 1730's driveway, Debbie Serra helped me unload the overstuffed roadside mailbox and carry the pile to my

SUV. As we milled about the side porch and garage area and began talking about 1730, Jim politely asked if he and the other three guests could see the inside of it. Laurel just as politely declined. The cozy house that Jane and I had loved so much looked dark and forlorn. The door and window shades were drawn. The house needed painting. The porch's screen door was wired shut in a crude way that wouldn't keep anyone out.

Then a strange little challenge began to develop. There were two cars lined up in the driveway. Without intending to, Laurel and Debbie became separated from the rest of us as they stood in back of the car nearest the road, while Winter, Jim, Theresa and I were clustered near the front of the other car as it was pointed toward the house. The four of us were so busy talking that we actually missed the little drama that followed: Laurel briefly mentioned it to me right after it took place—telling me that a very large bird, a hawk or an eagle, had flown from low over the house seemingly right toward her and Debbie before zooming back up to perch high in a tree in the backyard of the house across the road. Amid the other conversations going on I didn't really appreciate what the two women had experienced until Laurel went into detail about it the next day. By then we were back in Sayre by ourselves as we sought to understand the meaning or message that was involved.

First, though, as the afternoon began to lengthen our guests left us at the end of their most delightful collective visit. Laurel and I had thoroughly enjoyed meeting them; we'd badly needed a break from our endless routines of work, even if those were mostly creative. There were handshakes and thank-yous and hugs all around. Jim and Debbie, and Theresa and Winter wanted to visit the wine country of upstate New York, and then continue their vacation in Maine before finally heading back west and home. Laurel and I were left standing alone in 1730's driveway. But not for long. She hadn't brought birdseed along as she usually does to scatter around the house, so down the hill we went to the little store at the intersection, then back up to the silent and shuttered house....

That night in Sayre, and the next day, Laurel mentioned her near encounter with the hawk or eagle several times before we finally got down to really discussing what had happened at 1730. I drew a crude map of the house and its grounds as seen from above. The front of the house, facing Pinnacle Road, cannot be seen from where all of us were standing in the driveway to the side and in back of it. On the map Laurel showed me how the bird had suddenly zoomed into view low over the house from Pinnacle Road, and then flown even lower toward the two women near the back of the second car in the driveway. Laurel exclaimed now about the bird's enormous wingspan as it had seemed to fly right at her. It had made no sound except for the rush of air through its wings. Obviously my wife hadn't been prepared for its seemingly friendly behavior.

What had puzzled us both from the time of the episode was that Jim, Winter, Theresa and I, standing only two car lengths away from the two women, hadn't become aware of the episode even if we hadn't been staring in its general direction.

Now here is Laurel's own account of our guests' visit, and what was to her—and to me—a most unusual event.

* * * * * * *

DECEMBER 20, 2002
DESCRIPTION OF THE VISITORS IN OCTOBER, 2002
BY LAUREL LEE DAVIES-BUTTS.

Meeting the Houston Seth Group was a nice event for Rob and me. Jim and Debbie had driven by to meet us earlier in the summer, and we had corresponded by e-mail discussing their visit. The Houston Seth Group went thru not one but two powerful hurricanes just a month before they visited, a week apart! So we were looking forward to our visitors for several months before they arrived, and worrying about their situation as well.

On Sunday we went out to breakfast, and then went to some of the Samuel Clemens/Mark Twain historical sites. (I am a student of mediumship, as well as a reader of and believer in the Seth material. Mark Twain and his wife [as well as Jane Roberts, Robert Butts, and Seth] called Elmira, New York, home for years, and appear to still be psychologically involved with the sites.)

Then we went to 458 West Water Street. Our visitors that weekend included a television executive, a power company builder and planner, and people working in the fields of finance, law, writing, and art.

Each individual, as has always been the case with visitors, had many talents, with a personal viewpoint, and private belief system, regarding meeting with Robert Butts, of the Seth material (and myself), and of seeing Rob and Jane's apartments and home.

The Seth material, as Jane and Rob spoke and wrote it between 1963 and 1984 has brought insights and inspiration to millions of people, including myself. I have often been interested in the vast differences in the goals and characters of the many readers who visit and correspond. The Seth material was magical to me as soon as I started reading the first book I found in a used bookstore, *Seth Speaks*, in 1979. Many other readers have felt the same way. Rob and

Jane and Seth's magic has brought new interest and purpose into the lives of many different kinds of people. The exact number of readers is unknown, but over the years many people have visited and have written to Rob and Jane.

On this October day last fall, as we stood in Jane and Rob's driveway, (now my driveway also) at Pinnacle Road, Rob and most of the group started looking around the front of the house. I stood talking at the entrance of our driveway with a writer in the group.

As we stood talking another visitor dropped by also, rather literally, as a hawk or young golden eagle flew in! He or she appeared flying out of the Southwest, soaring down over the top of our house and flew right up to Deb and me to say hello! It was incredible to me as it took place, as I have never met a flying hawk or eagle face to face before. I have for many years had specific positive symbolic-seeming events with flying creatures and this seemed to be another one. Deb felt the same way. The hawk or eagle was completely in control in his or her flight, Deb and I were at no time in danger, but he or she flew in and actually looked at us almost face to face and then showed us a full in-flight wing span a meter wide (three feet or more) as he or she turned up the angle of flight and soared back up again, just over our heads. The creature flew across the road, soaring up into the branches of a tall tree, where it stopped and perched, and looked at us. Deb and I stood looking at the bird that sat with its profile to us—like a new friend who had flown in! We continued talking and were not looking at the bird when it flew away; we did not see where it disappeared to.

The symbolic and actual addition of this visitor, who not everyone was there to meet, has been a delightful magical event that I have been thinking about ever since.

Perhaps he or she was a magical symbol of the powerful natural universe coming to visit, in the driveway of our Pinnacle Road house, along with individuals from the television industry, the power industry, the arts and financial worlds. At the same moment a large hawk or small eagle decides to drop by and say hello!

This specific real and magical event added to the fun of the weekend for me immensely but it also symbolizes the interesting power of the Seth Material, and the odd elements the work has juxtaposed in our time period. Unusual visitors of intelligence and power were the watchword of the day!

But unusual visitors have delighted Jane and Rob over all their years of work, as you read about all through the years of the Seth archives.

As Rob and I looked up hawks and eagles in our bird books I am unable to say for sure what the bird was. It appeared larger than the hawks who appear in our area and are often seen flying overhead. It seemed smaller than the golden brown eagles that soar around the mountains nearby. Perhaps it was a young eagle, or a large hawk with slightly more brown or golden feathers than our bird books show. Flying wingspan approximately straight on was about 3 and one half feet.

*   *   *   *   *   *   *

Laurel sent a copy of her letter to Debbie Serra, who in this busy season included these passages in her e-mail reply of December 30, 2002: "...I also believe there are some people and perhaps animals more sensitive to the 'old ways' and beliefs in our communicative relationships with one another. The bird that swooped near us was spectacular. He or she knew we were not a threat. I think he or she was also testing our sensitivity which is why the bird remained in the tree regarding us."

At the hill house Jane and I used to see such birds, but soaring and circling high above, perhaps with their superb vision searching for small birds and animals. We never saw one behave as Laurel described. A sign of a message from the universe, she said! I thought of trying to paint a portrait of a hawk or an eagle. I thought of its enormous beauty and energy, the creative energy that sustains us all, in whatever form we choose to create and to live by and with. Thank you, Laurel and Jane and 458 and 1730 and our guests, for reminding me of that as I bring this introduction to *The Personal Sessions* to an end—even while I feel its persistent challenge to grow into a book of its own. Maybe someday...?

Robert F. Butts
Sayre, PA
December, 2002

SESSION 208 (DELETED PORTION)
NOVEMBER 15, 1965 10:29 PM MONDAY

(Personal material from the 208th session, November 15, 1965. Not included in the regular record. Delivered at our request.

(Jane speaks very rapidly, eyes open most of the time. Voice average.)

Now. I have had several matters to discuss with you.

Our sessions in general, the matter of spontaneity and discipline, your own fears, rather natural enough, concerning any subconscious effect I might have on Ruburt.

These are rather important matters that should be discussed. The question concerning the broken dishes rather amused me personally. There are, then, the separate questions concerning your health, Joseph, and Ruburt's.

Now I realize that you obviously are mainly concerned with the annoying physical symptoms. And since we cannot cover everything I suggest that we discuss these points first.

I would <u>not</u> like the matter of the sessions in general, and the subconscious influence question, to go by the board however, and in one way or another we must find time for those matters.

I will now, ordinarily, pick up any <u>dangerous</u> warning signals concerning your health or Ruburt's, but it is still a good idea to query me now and then directly.

I would suggest perhaps a session, or part of a session, perhaps once a month, to be directed along these lines. Under most circumstances the tail end of a session such as this will do well.

Now, on your part we will use the word envy rather than jealousy. *(Jane smiled.)* There is a difference. This has to do with your friend *(J. Spaziani)*, and an excellent friend he is indeed. You are <u>itching</u> to have what he has, quite literally. This should be clearly understood, for envy is a potentially dangerous emotion.

There is a difference between <u>wanting</u> more, which is legitimate, and envying those who have more, for in such cases you harm not only yourself but those whom you envy.

A simple and weak salt solution will help clear up the physical symptoms, applied twice daily.

A serious and humble consideration of the man's problems, which are very difficult indeed, should help clear up the envy.

("Yes.")

For upon his shoulders rests the burden of what he owns, and he fears with a steady, nearly unending <u>panic</u> that he will not be able to keep this, through ill health. The panic is wild and like a storm. Basically you do not consider the terms. You do not realize that he has long ago made a bargain to give his family those things which he feels will content them, only to find them less content. For to deliver these things he must, because of his nature, deprive them of other more important considerations.

<u>You</u> would feel twice as trapped in his circumstances. He wants to share with you what he has, and in your visits, to which he and his wife look forward, in your acceptance of his hospitality and food and drink, he hopes for some justification.

There is an affinity between you. He likes to think that under different circumstances he could live as you live. The need for money literally strangles him. He wants to help <u>you</u>, rather normally, because he feels rather illogically but understandably, that in helping you he helps a part of himself. For there is an isolated characteristic in him, and a completely undeveloped talent, though not in painting.

There is little need for you to itch to have what he has. Because of your past existence as a landowner, you <u>particularly</u> are resentful of those who own land. This was one of my main reasons for suggesting strongly that you buy the specific property, a while back. Such a procedure would have satisfied a <u>strong</u> demand of your nature, but it would <u>not</u> have <u>isolated</u> you to an unhealthy degree, since it was close by.

Acres were hardly involved. Nevertheless any reasonable plot of land would have satisfied this to a <u>reasonable</u> and <u>realistic</u> degree. You cannot afford to satisfy it at this point to a large degree, and in <u>any</u> case your desire for land would have to be completely allowed to dominate all other considerations, to be completely satisfied.

Now, to make you feel better: had you bought the house, you would have been exactly as well off now as you are, no more and no less. Ruburt's book would still have been written. He would not have had to stay at the gallery but two months longer.

That is all of the land.

Now. The envy applied to your friend should be easily dissipated, since you understand it. Envy by itself however is something else again. I want to tell you how to handle this positively, for it can work <u>for</u> you.

There is nothing wrong, and much beneficial, in strongly <u>imagining</u> yourself as the possessor of property. To imagine yourself <u>enviously</u> (underline) as the owner of <u>another</u> man's property is harmful.

To suggest vividly that you will find property that you will like and can afford, will help you attain it.

I do not know how tired you are. Now or later we can discuss your hand.

("Go ahead.")

(It was about 10:53. This delivery began at 10:29, at the end of the regular 208th session. I was very pleased to obtain the above material, for it confirmed what I had learned on my own through using the pendulum this week.)

First of all, all this is connected with the question of discipline and spontaneity of sessions, for I could have spoken at any time.

("I thought you could have.")

It may <u>appear</u> that Ruburt is too easy or too willing to hold sessions. However his ego is very well in control, so well in control that on occasion when I would have spoken on these very matters I have not been allowed to do so. Of course I realize the time limitations, and others.

Do you want a break?

("A short one.")

(Break at 10:58. Jane had been dissociated as usual. Her pace had been quite fast, her eyes open and closed; she resumed in the same manner at 11:09.)

Now, as briefly as possible. The hand was connected with the envy, and also with the difficulty involving the penis. This is somewhat complicated.

The envy caused you to be angry at the hand, which was not bringing you the financial results that envy required. Therefore you punished the hand. Subconsciously your reasoning went like this: "If I were any shape of a man, the hand would bring me what I wanted." And translating this into literal terms, you changed the shape of the penis.

You did not incapacitate the penis or the hand, you see. You did not after all blame yourself that much. *(Seth amused; I laugh.)*

Ruburt, incidentally, simply because of his nature and through no design, was of benefit to you here, since he never commented on the penis in an adverse manner.

("I knew that.")

Now. The symptoms would vary at times. You also felt that in <u>order</u> to satisfy envy, you would have to change yourself from your direct course to a crooked course. Here again, the shape of the penis.

The hand faltered out of <u>two</u> reasons, for two reasons.

You faltered in your purpose subconsciously, so the hand was allowed to falter. You were not steady on your course, and the hand faltered. Yet because you are an artist above all, you also punished yourself for your envy with the faltering hand, so that the hand expressed two needs.

("Why was my hand better last week?")

Now lately the hand has improved because the envy itself was given direct expression through the itch. The itch therefore became the punishment for the envy that it expressed. This was a more direct, less involved, less frightening symptom, a localization in other words. The envy being realized subconsciously for what it was, isolated in such a manner, meant that the hand need no longer falter.

(This too I had learned through the pendulum. However I wouldn't say the itching was a less frightening symptom.)

Since we are bringing all of this into the open, the symptoms should begin to disappear quickly.

We have something else here however to say concerning the penis, which is very amusing under the circumstances, and <u>not</u> simple.

On the one hand you are pleased because Ruburt does not demand a large amount of physical goods, in usual terms. On the other hand you have the hilarious suspicion, <u>when</u> you are envious of others, that if he wanted more you would get more for him. You could blame him, and therefore have your cake and eat it too; so that the penis difficulty is also aimed in his direction, rather literally.

It is also so aimed in another manner. For when you are envious you become angry at yourself, but also angry at him, for you cannot help thinking that if he worked harder, if he did something, of what you are not certain, then he would make more money, and you could still have what envy demands. So here again the penis difficulty, for he sat home full time writing, while you work part time, and yet he has not made all that money.

One more thing here. A connection with your mother, in that you <u>feel</u> that she never considered your father a true, <u>straight</u> man because he did not do well financially.

The manipulations here should be obvious, and they result again in the shape of the penis. All of these difficulties are not organically serious. Functionally they certainly are not beneficial however, and they should now begin to better themselves. Much of this has already been worked out by your own subconscious, and with this session the situation should quickly begin to show signs of improvement.

The penis difficulty may last longer, for it is more involved, but it is in no way dangerous to you, and left alone it will disappear.

I will leave you to tell me when you need a break, or when you want the session terminated.

("Let's take a short break then."

(Break at 11:29. Jane had been well dissociated. Her delivery had been fast,

her eyes open much of the time, and she smoked steadily. Her voice sounded somewhat dry. My hand had long ago gone half numb. She resumed again in the same manner at 11:39.)

Now, I simply do not know where to begin with our friend Ruburt. First of all however, one small point. I have <u>never</u> manipulated his subconscious, in any manner, and <u>both</u> of you called me the evening of our last unscheduled session. We will devote some time to this whole matter.

(Here Seth refers to the unscheduled session held on Friday, November 5, for Ann Diebler, Paul Sinderman, and Marilyn and Don Wilbur. A few notes about it preface the 206th Session. Consciously I had not wanted to have the session, since I thought our guests not well-enough prepared.)

Now as to Ruburt's health.

One session is not enough here. For the interconnections that exist between the two of you, several sessions would give you an excellent basis for understanding yourselves in relationship to one another. I do not know where to begin.

The back problem was particularly easy for Ruburt to pick up, because of his mother and the arthritis, and because of this Father Ryan, whose back was injured. He constantly picks up and reacts to <u>your</u> moods, subconscious as well as conscious, interprets them, and translates them into physical realities, because of your psychic closeness and his strong telepathic abilities.

I am sparing no one here, incidentally, for your benefits. He is prone to criticism; that is, he is prone to being criticized. He picked up the feeling that although you wanted him home writing, you were also envious and resentful. Yet he loves you. He felt you were being stiff-necked, and identified here.

He adopted the stiff-necked symptom, which has been with him off and on. He also felt guilty however at being taken care of, for the stiff neck was also therefore a punishment. He feared he was being taken care of as his mother was; and that you must resent it symbolically, as he resented it, taking care of her, and therefore the bed difficulty.

For the bed reinforced the mother image for him. There is much more here, and we will cover what we can, and fill in when we can. The poor eyesight <u>and</u> the sinus are both, on a much limited scale, adaptations of his mother's more frightening and more successful efforts to close out portions of reality.

The sinus is made worse by heat, because at home he always wanted to open the windows and escape, and could not. You should, whenever you move again, have all rooms with more than one window if at all possible, for this also has a connection with the thyroid. The need to escape is now latent only; but windows symbolize the <u>way</u> to escape, and closed places frighten him.

This session may help, but the mechanisms are so involved that it will be a while, even with my help, before this need for spaciousness, comparatively speaking, leaves him.

I am suggesting, Joseph, nothing. However as far as <u>sleep</u> is concerned alone, he would sleep best in the back room or the front room, neither of which I believe is practical at this point. In any case this is not activated on all occasions by any means.

Now. The pressure has also several origins.

One, along with the recent irregular periods, is fairly obvious. His book is to be published, and since he is a female the book is his baby. It will not be completely born until it hits the light of day. We have then pressure pains, extended abdomen, and irregular periods. *(Seth much amused here.)*

This is not all however, and I do not spare him.

He feels that your eyes are upon him to see that he puts in a full working day, and he feels that he must because you do. Without your help he feels guilty, staying home. His nature is strongly intuitive and spontaneous. It needed discipline, and you helped here to a truly astounding degree.

Now however he feels under <u>pressure</u>, hence the pressure again in the abdomen, again connected with his work; for he feels that he must be at the typewriter five or six hours steadily, daily, or he is not keeping up his part of the bargain.

Now. He would produce as much, if not more, and of better quality, were he not so rigorous in this respect. For after a certain point of discipline is reached, he will operate well and effectively. But ideas will come to him in better fashion if he allots part of the day to spontaneous thinking. He sops ideas up in a spontaneous manner, and when it seems that he plays, even to him, he is working.

This feeling was heightened after a discussion in particular that you held in your room, and this is connected with your relationship, because he left his mother when he was <u>sick of taking care of her</u>. His loyalty, once captured as you have captured it, is unbelievably enduring, but he is never sure basically of the loyalty of someone who supports him, which is regrettable.

One the other hand, this fear works <u>for</u> him, because he works harder as a writer to pay you back. So it is not entirely negative or destructive, but partially channeled in a constructive fashion.

Your own background is important here, and he picks up your past feelings, you see. You truly have no respect for your mother, in the one instance that your father supported her, and she pushed him. There is a connection here with Ruburt's insistence on spending a part of his money on the apartment tangibly, where you could see it, and be reminded that he helped out.

At the same time it makes you slightly angry, for you feel two things. One, that it is little enough; and two, because of your own envy of others who have more, that perhaps Ruburt means that you should have bought these things, while he means nothing of the sort.

The pressure, I am sorry to say, has also some connection with our sessions, in that he feels caught betwixt and between; somewhat under pressure to hold sessions regularly, although he may not feel like particularly doing so; and under pressure not to hold sessions when he may feel particularly like doing so. This in relation to the abdomen.

He feels more pressure to hold sessions now regularly because of our doctor, and more pressure not to hold sessions when he feels the urge to, because of your own fears; that is, your fears and his fears.

This I intend to clarify. Now. Ruburt is bearing up well this evening, with my help. I can clarify further here on his health after a break, or you may end the session.

("I guess we'll end it then.")

I will then wish you my best and heartiest regards.

("I'd like to thank you very much.")

I am indeed, under usual circumstances, at your beck and call. *(Seth amused.)*

("Good night, Seth."

(End at 12:11. Jane was well dissociated. Her pace had been fast, her voice about average, her eyes open wide most of the time. She had smoked many cigarettes and her voice was somewhat dry.)

SESSION 223 (DELETED PORTION)
JANUARY 16, 1966 SUNDAY

(Omitted from the regular session copy to avoid any possible embarrassment to the Wilburs, Marilyn and Don, of Wellsburg, NY.

(Jane and I had visited the Wilburs at their trailer in Wellsburg last Friday evening, January 14, 1966, and met for the first time their 2-year old son, Scotty. When we left Jane forgot her pocketbook and Marilyn returned it Saturday morning; she had her son with her and Jane had more time to observe him. After Marilyn left Jane and I discovered that both of us had been alarmed by the child in some vague way; his actions had been quite overtly strong, we thought, involving such things as pretending to kill our cat Willy, taking swings at Jane and me, etc. We found

it hard to like him subjectively, even while dismissing these demonstrations.

(Toward the end of the session as Seth, Jane and I sat talking alone, after the departure of the Gallaghers, Seth volunteered the information that Scotty was a greedy child. He belonged to an entity that was strongly attached to physical life on our plane, Seth said; the entity having experienced many physical lives, and still refusing to leave earth as we know it.

(In addition the child knew it was not wanted, but had insisted upon being born. Knowing it was not wanted, it paid back its parents. It was destructive, and psychically older than they —Seth confirming my suspicion here. The child was to cause its parents much trouble, but they were strong enough to cope with it.

(An added note, omitted from the regular session copy:

(When I spend too much time going out, Seth told me, too many evenings in a row visiting or dancing, I get depressed because I feel it is a waste of time in spite of the psychic benefits to be derived from being with others. This feeling stems from my mother, who "must always be up and at it," Seth said, and also from my Aunt Alice, who used to be a missionary, and whom I have met but once or twice. She is now very old.

(When I act this way it affects Jane deeply, frightening her. I am now aware of this however, and Seth told me I saved the situation last Saturday evening at Mihalyk's by asking Jane to dance.)

SESSION 239 (DELETED PORTION)
MARCH 7, 1966 MONDAY

Now. I did not resume the session for obvious reasons... Ruburt is not particularly pleased with what he knows I am about to say, but I am not held by the same social rules that hold him in this particular manner, and I know Philip *(Seth's entity name for John Bradley)* perhaps better than he does.

Now. We have fear and rage on the part of the girl, for despite the children she is yet a girl, and a very nice one. However the relationship between her own parents has been destructive. The father has wanted domination, and to some extent has forced his wife into a position of dominance which she strongly resents. Because of this she lashes out at her husband. I am speaking now, you understand, of the parents of Philip's wife.

Now, the girl respects Philip because he will not be dominated. On the other hand the woman image that she understands, because of her mother, is a dominating woman image. To <u>her</u> she fails as a female if she cannot hold him in line. At the same time her personality is far different than her mother's, and less focused.

Also she loves Philip, and would not consciously want to dominate him if she could. He senses this subconscious need of hers however to hold him, and resents it vigorously. She attempts to dominate him in her own way, and on a subconscious basis, and it is indeed by appealing to him through helplessness. At the same time she does not want him to give in to her.

She tries to dominate in more feminine ways. Her mother's domination had more masculine aspects. We will have more to say concerning this, and I hope some helpful comments after our other material....

With the girl's background it is natural enough that an independent male would both frighten and fascinate her. It was this way from the beginning of their relationship.

What he does not understand is the rage that she is containing. There is considerable strength to it, and he should recognize this. She does not <u>want</u> to dominate him through feminine wiles, and yet subconsciously she feels driven to do so.

She feels <u>threatened</u> by serious conversations, Philip, for she fears the unknown. She <u>feels</u> like a child when a parent says, "Now, we must discuss this seriously." Such a discussion threatens the status quo.

The trivial conversations which you were all discussing would be helpful here, as reassurance. Your own ideas concerning various issues could be profitably inserted when you are not emotionally upset over them.

Your anger is interpreted simply as violence, and she fears it. Ideas expressed at such occasions will be strenuously fought by her. You must make an emotional bridge, for she will not understand an intellectual one. But the emotional bridge must not be of a violent nature.

This is all you have achieved so far in that regard.

She fears, for one thing, that you could run the house more efficiently than she can, and basically that you do not need her. She is not certain of her own merit, and achieves her self-approval through your auspices.

She is not a partner and you are indeed in difficulties. She can <u>become</u> a partner however, but anger will only minimize her importance in her own eyes, and therefore in yours.

One of the children is suffering to some extent psychologically because of the dilemma, and you are too much the autocrat with this child, a female.

This is merely a question of relationships, where any thought of blame is meaningless. The situation can be salvaged.

Now, give us a moment again.

Her father has been more destructive to her psychological health in some respects than her mother, for he gave her the image of males as weak.

The strong male is therefore a threat, while he also represents security. There seems to be some situation arising particularly on Wednesdays, that is important emotionally to her. I am not certain as to what this refers.

She does not realize basically, subconsciously, her importance to you. If you can make her see this you will be able to maintain that sense of independence that is important to you. If you cannot she will be driven to snatch it away.

If you cannot communicate important ideas, then you must communicate trivial ones. The big conversation, in which you attempt to communicate your ideas, only frightens her. The idea should be communicated when you are not emotionally upset, and you should not adopt the tone of a parent speaking to a child.

Now. I am rather an old man to be speaking in such terms.

However, in the main you are doing two things wrong. You are treating her primarily as a woman rather than an individual person, but you are not treating her as a desirable woman rather than an individual person.

If you treat her as a desirable woman, you will find a difference in your home atmosphere. If <u>you cannot do this</u>, then you must treat her primarily as an individual person. But if you treat her as a woman primarily, it must be as a desirable woman, or she will find no content as a woman or as an individual.

And if you treat her as a desirable woman, she will become one. You are treating her as a <u>wife</u> and mother, primarily. With this particular individual this is not adequate. She wants to be regarded as a desirable woman who happens to be your wife and a mother.

She will be much more content and pliable to reason if you can manage, regardless of your intellectual tendencies, to approach her in that light. She needs drama, within the framework of the home, and she wants this from you. It will take some effort on your part, but if she feels that you spend time with <u>her</u> simply because you want to be with her, this will go a long way in solving your difficulties.

And if you cannot do this honestly, then your difficulties are more serious than you realize. The effort will be more than worth your while, but the effort must be an honest one, or she will sense the hypocrisy.

Do you have any questions, Philip?

([John:] "No, not specifically.")

I realize that you feel as if you are in a vicious circle. In many cases however you do not ask, but have a tendency to command her. Not in words so much as in attitude. She does not feel truly desirable. You can do much to change this.

If your relationship is as important to you as I believe it is, then you will make the effort. The simple fact is that you do need her, and you have not communicated this. Obviously there are reasons for <u>her</u> behavior, and changes also that she can and should make, but I am speaking to you and not to her.

There seems to be someone, three houses away, a woman with whom your wife could make friendly and profitable contact. Either the woman is younger, or seems so.

The adjustments necessary are not all on your part, but your adjustments can initiate hers. These remarks, Joseph, do not have to go in the record.

("All right.")

Now. Several hours devoted on occasion to intimate relationships of sexual nature would be advantageous, simply because of the implied suggestion that you were not only willing but anxious to devote yourself to her. The energy that you have could be focused momentarily into a physical acknowledgment that would have strong psychic overtones for both of you. The physical relationship then would indeed open psychic channels, where understanding becomes intuitional. This would be to both of your benefits, and she would understand what you so poorly put into words.

You are concerned, and have made efforts, but you are better equipped simply because of your personality structure, to make these efforts. She is at this point like a child in the woods, but the potentialities are there for an excellent relationship.

(End at 11:59.)

SESSION 241 (DELETED PORTION)
MARCH 14, 1966 MONDAY

(The last page of the 241st Session, containing the personal material omitted in the regular notebook copy.)

The appointment made but not kept refers to the fact that you all said you would get together again in the near future, and you did not.

(As has happened before, I remembered this as soon as Seth mentioned it. As did Jane, even while she spoke in trance.)

All in all, hardly our best. However the color and the initial— the initials particularly, were quite specific. *(Results of Jan'es envelope-ESP test.)*

I wanted to add a brief note, to the effect that neither of you have any health worries at this time. You may insert this in the record or not, as you prefer.

("What's the deal with my right foot?")

This is something different, representing on your part an impatience, an urge to step out strongly as far as your own work is concerned. To finish the painting which you have begun . You would like to have it finished to take to New York. There is also another connection here, and a rather amusing one. It is connected with the apartment house. You would like to kick the downstairs tenants out, and you would like to kick your poor landlord, because you think that Ruburt would like that apartment, and you cannot afford it; and he would not, you believe, come down on his rent.

We will end this evening's session. My heartiest regards to you both. You see then why these various concerns focused themselves on the foot; a motor expression for inner desires in this case.

("That's what the pendulum told me a few months ago.")

If you wish we can continue, or end the session as you prefer.

("We'll end it then. But we should discuss Ruburt's sinus condition soon.")

We shall indeed.

("Good night, Seth." End at 10:48.)

SESSION 267 (DELETED PORTION)
JUNE 13, 1966 9:42 PM MONDAY

(From the 267th Session. Second delivery from 9:42 to 10:04 PM. Omitted from regular records, and so noted there. Jane's manner very active; her eyes were wide open and very dark for about the whole delivery.)

(9:42.) You may, or you may not, include this in your notes as you prefer.

I did you see make my earlier suggestion to Ruburt, also in the hopes that it would initiate the sort of discussion in which you have just been involved.

I am thinking of you both. However there is also a fine psychic balance upon which our sessions rest, and this balance must be maintained. Domestic tranquillity is highly important to it. The psychic partnership that exists between you and Ruburt is absolutely necessary to our sessions.

Now within certain boundaries, and taking certain circumstances for granted, Ruburt is more flexible than you may think he is. I am simply not going to waste time by telling you that you have nothing to worry about financially, for neither of you believe me. This is quite all right. *(Smile.)* Were I in your circumstances I do not know if I would believe me either. The hard work of the last few years will indeed pay off, and shortly. It does not matter whether or not Ruburt gets a job because you are both simply unable to wait. It does matter if you worry too much.

In some ways you see you must both operate as a closed unit against the world, but you must also operate as an open unit, receptive to the world. You must close yourself off from some stimuli in order to fully utilize the stimuli that you do perceive.

Physical reality is noisy, and complicated, and riotous and contradictory. Nevertheless there must also be balance, for to close yourself off too much robs you of any abundant expansion of spirit.

The sense data is important, you see; the new balances that your separate personalities achieve lead you both to new expansions. Each expansion however must also be accompanied by a deepening security of necessary inner isolation. For from this inner isolation, you achieve the strength to expand psychically outward. When the balance is a good one, then the outward expansion leads to inner expansion.

You should have spoken quicker. When you do not you build up inner resentments that mitigate against your welfare. You are then tempted to see trivial disturbances as large ones, and to cut off all heads indiscriminately, in order to get rid of one or two main disturbances, because you can no longer tell one from the other.

In any case, your *(smile)* faithful companion, and so-quiet partner Ruburt, picks up your disquiet whether or not you speak of it. Now he reacts you see by bothering you all the more, peeking in on you, to discover whether or not you are really upset, or rather, if his own imagination runs away with him.

When anyone is disturbed chemical changes occur, as you know. Now these changes affect the ways in which you perceive sense data. You know that you create physical matter. It is extremely important that you know your own emotional climate. For changes must come from the inside, and in that way you will change your environment.

I am to some extent an affectionate but detached observer here. Most of your personal recommendations were valid ones. If you had made a stand earlier however you would have saved yourself time and effort. It would be most beneficial for you to do some painting outdoors, or to walk outdoors.

I have said much of this before, and undoubtedly I will say it often again.

You may take a break before our Instream material. *(10:04.)*

(From the end of the same session— page 1924 of original notes.)

Now if I gave a note to Rob, I give one to you. You would do much better by being frank with him, for he becomes irritated and resentful when he feel you are upset, and is left to guess at the cause. For often he is not sure...

Now I could and will whenever you wish, discuss your personal situation, whenever you want me to do so...

SESSION 367 (DELETED)
OCTOBER 1, 1967 9:15 PM SUNDAY

(July 14, 1971: When sessions resume, check with Seth about what Jane might have blocked in this session—as well as what she revealed. My part, principally—see pendulum of this date. This session appears to be basic, but perhaps parts pertaining to me were blocked, to spare my feelings?

(This session is not included in the records since it deals with personal material. I asked for it this evening because Jane was not feeling well, and indeed had seemed to decline since the New York trip in August.

(This afternoon while painting the thought came to me that Jane's trouble was that she was avoiding success; and success was looming ever closer with the advertising campaign planned for her ESP book, the near-completion of the dream book, etc. In the 350th Session for July 6, 1967, is a sentence which has stayed with me—when Seth said: "Ruburt has an unfortunate sense of unworthiness, without which the situation [Jane's symptoms] could not have developed." I wondered if the unworthy feeling and the fact of success could be linked through the symptoms.

(Jane did not volunteer this session; I had to ask for it. She has never volunteered a session re her symptoms. She began to speak rapidly, in a somewhat odd-sounding, almost muffled voice, and with her eyes closed.

(See the deleted session for November 26, 1972, in Volume 2 of these personal sessions)

Now, good evening.

("Good evening, Seth.")

What we have here is a deep struggle between various needs, a struggle between various portions of the personality, each with their own demands and interpretations of reality.

If the possibility of success had never emerged the problem would never have emerged. It was unfortunately a cue point, and itself the time bomb of which Ruburt spoke. *(Before the session tonight.)*

There is one part of the self, confident, assured of its abilities, and somewhat demanding, rather powerful. It has to this point driven the personality onward despite all obstacles. It never admitted the possibility of failure, but only worked toward success.

Now, to the other portion of the personality however, success was failure.

This part of the personality remained relatively quiet until the other portion began to achieve its ends. This portion considered itself not only unworthy but evil. It *(The "sinful self" May 10, 1982)* is basically an overgrown and almost cancerous super-conscience that applied brakes in the past to some extent, and now has largely taken over.

It believes it works for the good. It mistrusts all spontaneity. It believes the personality must be toned down, held in bonds, slowed down, or else the wrath of God will descend upon it. It is not rational.

The physical not-being-able-to-run, the slowing of motions, are all physical manifestations. This is the Irish grandmother, the mother, and the neighborhood shouting: Jane, do not run. Though consciously disobeying as a child, the suggestions took deep root. Spontaneity was evil.

The spontaneous ran out of control. This has something to do with the mother's talking to the child about the father. He was uncontrolled— uncontrollable, lax, slow, and yet evil. The father had money and was evil. The poor were virtuous and on the side of God. The rich would never attain heaven. This is Ruburt's penance, you see, put upon him by this other part of his personality. If he succeeds he must pay, for if he does not pay, if he does not willingly submit to his own punishment, then there is eternal damnation.

There must be self-sacrifice, to some degree self-mutilation. And even hence you see the loss of weight. The dark side of the mystic, I am afraid.

For every act he considers uncharitable or sarcastic he must pay. The Harriet poem: for that you see he believes he must pay. The irony of course is carefully chosen— that he choose those symptoms that reminds him of his mother. For she flaunted the neighborhood and the Irish background physically in her youth, and paid, and Ruburt fought it intellectually, and feels he must pay.

The whole psychic framework is against the Catholic training. This also has something to do with this.

The Crowders representing money, you see, appall him. He expects the wrath of God to fall upon them at any time. He hates them because he considers them evil because they are wealthy. The old car *(our Ford)* is a badge of virtue to Ruburt since it is old and decrepit. It is a sign of safety.

(Yesterday, Saturday, September 30, Jane and I visited my parents and the Crowders, up from Norfolk, Virginia. Since the old Ford—1955—was in the garage with gas tank trouble over the weekend, we were given a ride to Sayre and back from Elmira by the Crowders in their Cadillac. Vivian, Mrs. Crowder, is my mother's neice.)

Ruburt's student Venice must have her weight, or she fears destruction.

Ruburt must have his failure, and relative poverty, or <u>he</u> fears destruction.

If this were the whole personality this would be no problem. He would avoid success like a plague. He would have been successful long before this. However the other portion of the personality <u>is</u> spontaneous, highly gifted, creative, intuitive, and <u>loves</u> luxury. This last being deeply hidden from the conscious personality.

Scrounging about, taking secondhand items, allows him to accumulate some extras with impunity, because they are not new. He is deeply afraid of finishing his book for fear it <u>will</u> sell. He sends out messages pressing for the success of his original book, and sends out equally strong ones urging that it not be accepted, that it is not a huge success. This is the original book. *(The ESP book.)*

He fears destruction in the terms of being a complete cripple. To avoid this he adopts the symptoms, hoping to cheat his idea of the gods, or fate. To have the disease, or punishment, and still not have it, to satisfy both demands.

The New York trip *(in August)*, his response to it, was largely responsible for the setback. He believes also that he must therefore accept any disability and discomfort because it is just punishment. The <u>other</u> portion rises up in arms and forces him to demand success.

When you did not expect success, really, then you did not threaten him. Now you expect success, and he feels even beforehand an added threat. Then he will have to suffer for you both, he feels.

Running is symbolic. He could run, his mother could not. She was evil. But if he is successful, then he believes he will be successful when he does not deserve it. Therefore evil also, and so he shall not run; running being symbolic of spontaneity. If he gives himself emotional and psychic freedom, then to compensate he will deny himself physical freedom. I have been a safeguard, for I was between him and complete spontaneity, you see.

I was enough like his Father Traynor to be safe, and without me his psychic abilities would not have matured at all. I will not be dispensed with. He cannot afford it. Also I am legitimate enough and independent enough in my own right.

He has no use for women, and women are not supposed to succeed. I am legitimate. His needs and personality were the reason, however, that he could communicate with me. He would never have communicated with, say, any female counterpart of me. I have literally held his personality together for some time, in relative balance. He has never been mentally unbalanced, and he has avoided this and any deep emotional difficulty. The physical illness, however, has taken their place. All in all, a much safer arrangement.

The difficulties began with the selling of the first paperback and were accentuated later. The development of abilities and the ESP book represented an effort by the spontaneous self to express itself, for this other portion of the personality was ready then to take over, and it then retaliated with the beginning of symptoms.

When this portion is operating he does not dare enjoy the pleasures of love. No one in his neighborhood did, you see. *(Pause.)* He denies himself then out of fear. When he succeeds he punishes himself. When he fails the other, spontaneous, self rises up in arms. The two warring factions have been beating him apart.

("How come this material is allowed to come through now?")

Wait. The overly conscientious self however is also the teacher, and in the classes the two elements do to some extent combine with some overall benefit. The overconscientious self expounds, you see. These two warring elements are deeply bound up in psychic work because they were deeply bound up early in religious and mystic connotations in Catholic upbringing.

Now. Ruburt's early mystic life was also bound up with priests who were males, with whom one could not have any sexual relationship. He is now bound up with you in these endeavors. While he is so confused, then sexual relationship with you also becomes evil. He also felt compelled to follow the advice of the priests whether or not he agreed with it. This led to his passivity as far as you were concerned. If you were jealous of his success, he should not have it, and it must be plucked out.

The New York trip frightened him by its success. He felt he needed the punishment of the program *(Alan Burke, TV)*, and you helped him avoid it. One remark or circumstance will be a cue to one or the other portions of the personality, which will then take over. He will be free or constrained, you see, until the next trigger point is given.

His mother's letter *(received last week, and containing an old picture of her)*, followed by the weekend visit *(with the Crowders and my parents)*, was the trigger point this time. He is still at the point where he must be saint or devil. He has had difficulties on Fridays because he eats meat on Fridays, and difficulties Sunday because he does not go to church.

You had better take a break. *(9.55.)*

He is afraid of the bed and the bedroom. *(Pause.)* He fears he will die in his sleep and face eternal damnation. There are no windows to escape through, he feels, no available roof. *(Pause.)* He feels freer under all circumstances in this room *(the living room)* because he could run out onto the roof.

The physical symptoms therefore frighten him severely in that he does not run. He thinks you do not want him to talk about his past because you are ashamed of it. Take your break. *(9:58.)*

The material is coming through simply because he is desperate. <u>Both</u> portions of the personality are frightened. One portion fears success is coming regardless of all its attempts to hold it back. The other fears that it is being restrained despite all efforts to escape. The body is the warring point, and it is itself now fatigued.

(10:00. Jane's pace had remained quite fast. Her eyes had begun to open occasionally. Resume at 10:05.)

Now. At times the personality has reconciled these elements and served to express them both. The *High-Low* book of poetry as contrasted to perhaps the idiot poems will explain what I mean.

It is a great help then for Ruburt to write his poetry. This session will in itself be of benefit, for it is the first clear sign you have had of the true situation. Ruburt asked me for help today, and this is my answer and my help.

(I did not know this, in suggesting we have a session tonight. Jane asked Seth for help this afternoon before taking a nap.)

When the overconscientious portion is made to understand that the spontaneous self is good, then the problem will cease.

The psychic classes have been of help for this reason. The overconscientious portion always trusted the spontaneous self as far as poetry was concerned, but distrusted spontaneity otherwise.

Success, tied in with psychic work, can represent his main hope, and perhaps the one main door through which the whole personality can emerge united and intact.

The preaching element was always strong. The poetry went against the church, but here the overconscientious self was able to realize the church's limitations and went along.

Success as a poet would present no difficulties. The overconscientious self was not about to permit the spontaneous self this new freedom, however. The early philosophical poetry represented a philosophy of pessimism. Stripped to its core, it was the good-or-suffer-damnation world.

The later poetry represented joy and the psychic work spontaneity. Yet a reconciliation is possible. The overconscientious self must be shown that the spontaneous self is the God self. If this is done it will <u>add</u> its strength to the purposes of the spontaneous self. Otherwise it will fight the spontaneous self, even to the death. It disapproves of anything it does not consider godly.

There is no reason why it will not listen, however, and gladly. Because of its very nature it wants to attach itself to, and work for, what it considers the good. It has been held within severe limitations and working under a false premise. It is trying to restrain Ruburt from doing that which is wrong. As it realizes through re-education that the spontaneous self is good, the sense of unworthiness will vanish. *(Pause.)*

It has believed from the beginning that spontaneity was sinful. This was the misinterpretation given in early training.

It then set itself up against the spontaneous self, and determined to keep it within bounds. Success is taboo for the unworthy only, you see. When the overconscientious self learns that the spontaneous self is not unworthy, then success is permissible.

If success allows for the furthering of ideas which are good, then success will become a need for the overconscientious self also, and a further reconciliation will take place. Do you see the steps here then that can be taken?

("Yes. Can we have a break?")

You may.

(10:21. Jane's pace had again been fast, and my writing hand felt the effort. She resumed at 10:24.)

We will shortly end.

You are extremely important in all of this, and you can do much to make Ruburt understand. *(Jane paused. She shifted her position her eyes closed. Eventually she ended up lying on her back full length on the couch, where she had been sitting throughout the session. She continued to speak with her eyes closed. Her pace was slower. As far as I could recall, this was the first time she had permitted herself to lie flat during a session while in trance.)* Because of the early training, you have somewhat assumed a position like those of the priests, and your word becomes extremely important, and <u>almost</u> like a law. Hence his passivity in many instances, and his avoidance of sex.

You can use this to advantage however, as you explain the situation to him, for your words have almost magical import at this time. *(Pause.)*

Now that we have reached the true difficulty beneath all else, there should be a good improvement. Steady application will be needed however, and your part as educator is highly important. Do you have questions?

("Can he work along and finish the Dream book?")

With an understanding of this material, yes. And poetry should also be written. I believe the session itself should bring him some considerable relief, but it will not last unless the points given are hammered in.

("Should we keep coming back to this plan in sessions?")

You should. The overconscientious self you see has not trusted me, nor the sessions, and hampered help I could give. It realizes it is in jeopardy however, and the classes have served to open a wedge of understanding.

("*The overconscientious self should be able to see the benefits of the sessions and the classes, shouldn't it?*")

It has largely in the past refused to do so.
(*Question this when sessions resume—July 1971.*
"*It is more willing to see now?*")

It is now to some extent. *(Pause.)* It gave some consent to me in the beginning, but would go no further.

("*I think this is the first time I've seen Jane lay down during a session.*")

He is exhausted, and in a deeper trance than usual.

("*Well, I can think of more questions later.*")

We will then close our session. The very fact that it has been held represents a turning point for the better, you see.

("*Can the overconscientious self literally block material of this kind?*")

It has. When it realizes that the spontaneous self is a god-self, then it will actively help Ruburt.

("*Suppose the overconscientious self blocks this kind of material next session. Is this likely to happen?*")

It may according to circumstances, but it will not always.

("*Then we can keep trying for it.*")

That was my meaning. It should be less inclined to do so as a result of this material.

("*If in a session—*")

It is a relatively new idea to the overconscientious self, that the spontaneous self is good and a part of the god self. When this is completely seen there will be an integration of personality that will result in powerful work, and a definite unchallenged success.

("*I was going to say that if I ask for this type of material during a session, it's likely to come through at least to some extent, isn't it?*"

(Pause.) It should come through more clearly now.

("*Okay.*")

If you have no more questions we will end the session.

("*No more. Good night, Seth.*" 10:39.)

The overconscientious self has blocked many of Ruburt's impressions in the past.

("*In sessions or on his own?*")

Both. Particularly on his own. The Father Ryan influence—and he also had back trouble. Father Doren was seen as a spontaneous but evil man. Father Ryan was seen as rigid and uncompromising, but good. Father Ryan gave Ruburt his first typewriter, and desk, and bed. Now do you see those connections?

("Yes.")

The priests visited on Sunday afternoon. *(Pause.)* The main visits were held in the mother's bedroom.

If you have any questions, now is a good time to ask them. Or we will end.

("Then say a few words about my bent penis.")

This is connected with Ruburt, of course, and you feel your purpose is bent from its main direction, in that you are not painting full time.

("How about the hand tremor?")

Your paintings also represent sons to you. Hence their effect appears in the penis, you see. The tremor, a reflection of what you feel to be a shaky situation.

("We can go into this later.")

We will end. Give Ruburt a sip of wine.

("Yes. Can you give him some beneficial suggestions tonight?")

I will indeed.

("Have his dreams contained any clues to this material tonight?")

He has blocked many of them. Clues were there.

("Okay. Good night, Seth."

(10:47. Jane still lay flat out, her eyes closed. She came out of trance slowly.)

SESSION 368 (DELETED), OCTOBER 2, 1967 9:35 PM MONDAY

(This session is also deleted from the regular records, since it deals with personal material. Jane began speaking at a rather fast rate, with her eyes closed, as she sat on the divan.)

Now. *(Pause.)*

The overconscientious self is also extremely powerful, driven by remarkable amounts of energy. When both portions of the personality are in agreement, then Ruburt's personality is literally overwhelming, filled with vitality and unbeatable.

The energy of the overly conscientious self is as strong as that of the spontaneous self, hence the impasse that had been reached. He can only go full steam ahead when the whole personality is convinced of his course. For the personality knows full well the tremendous force of its own energy potential, and it would be literally disastrous for one portion to go ahead at the expense of the other. Therefore, regardless of present consequences, one portion has been kept down in order to avoid any serious, that is disastrous, cleavage.

The overconscientious self is protecting the whole personality against what it considered evil. It can be reeducated. *(Pause.)* There is a cleavage apparent in Ruburt's distaste of the word God, for example.

In Catholic terms he consecrated himself to God as a child daily. He has done so again but without admitting the fact. There is some difficulty here... *(pause)* not necessarily a blockage, but a misunderstanding.... We shall have to clear it up later.

The message *(the contents of the last session, the 367th)*, so far has reached the super-conscientious self. *(Pause.)* It is not kicking up a fuss so much as hesitating in caution. It was the spontaneous self who kicked up the fuss this afternoon, thinking: hurry, hurry, hurry, see things my way *(when Jane tried to work on the dream book, unsuccessfully).*

Now. When you make love to him, assure him of your emotional love and concern, and affection. In the beginning stress this, and lull him. He needs to be quieted first through word and caresses. Use the word husband often, reminding him of your realistic relationship. And emphasize also the connection between emotional and mystic love that you share.

You, as teacher in this love relationship now, can count oddly enough on the passivity of his nature, and play on this, for then assured, reassured, the super-conscientious self can allow the spontaneous self to emerge in the sex relationship.

He suspended his periods. He is neither pregnant nor beginning the menopause. This was a biological activity he felt he could safely suspend, and in doing so avoid further conflict, the conflict caused by enjoyment in sex, when he did not feel worthy of being loved.

(Jane's delivery was now getting lighter and slower, almost as though she was drifting off to sleep.)

You can be stern here, again counting on his passivity in the love relationship. Reassurances... gentle strokings....*(Pause, eyes closed.)* We will have to add more here, also later.

He feared his mother prowled the house during darkness—this also accounting for some of the sleep difficulty.

Last night's poor sleep and symptoms were simply a reaction to the information given *(in last night's session)*, and represented a <u>momentary</u> (underlined) stiffening of position by both sides of the personality. For both felt equally guilty for the physical predicament, and were acting self-defensively. *(Pause.)*

There was literally a psychological sense of shock.

The autobiographical material produced as novels by Ruburt were also helpful as safety valves. *(Pause.)* An integration is already <u>beginning</u> to take place, however, since last evening's session.

Patience rather than coercion should be used. *(Pause.)*

Ruburt's spontaneous self should not push. Relief will be more immediate if a persistent, soft-sell line is used.

The old neighborhood has enclosed him, and he must now truly escape its limitations while using the psychic potential of his experience as an integrating power. *(Pace slower yet.)* It is also responsible you see for the remarkable potential that he has. He does not feel free to use his full energy until all portions of the personality are convinced of the goodness of his purpose. *(Long pause.)*

There were deeply-significant roots to his relationships with the various priests, that had almost magical connotations to him and his psyche. A submerged mixture of mysticism and sex.

I will myself attempt to communicate with Father Ryan, who is now much less rigid than he was, and this may help. He can himself communicate to Ruburt through his dreams, and clear up many confused issues. Father Traynor will also be of assistance to us, I am sure.

You may take a break and we shall continue.

(10:02. Jane experienced an average dissociation, she said. She felt she didn't get as "deep" as she did last night, and her pace ended up quite a bit slower. She couldn't get the material through in the two instances noted; in the past, she said, she wouldn't have been aware of this, so she considered this new awareness an advancement over the past.

(Resume at 10:27. Jane again lay down on the couch, as last session.)

Now. You see Ruburt has accepted you as an extension of the super-conscientious self, and your word was added to the taboos already set up. Therefore a mystical import, a magical import, was given to your every word.

When your words disagreed with his spontaneous self severe conflicts arose. This is important. You were through your art however also connected to his spontaneous self. Originally you saw Ruburt as the spontaneous self, and your ideas of discipline were quickly gobbled up by the overly conscientious self before you recognized its existence.

The overly conscientious self is the part that will retreat, that carries grudges, that believes an eye for an eye, and is relatively uncompromising. It must be made to understand that the spontaneous self is innately good and can be trusted. It needs to be lovingly protected; but lovingly, not hindered nor fought nor held down.

Both portions however have great capacities for survival, and are each strong, so that the personality has indeed survived. There is a need for the spontaneous self to understand the purposes of the conscientious self also.

Ruburt has wanted you to rub him for the sake of physical contact and reassurance, this being more than acceptable to both portions. He was made to feel unworthy and unwanted by his mother, and it was the spontaneous self who took the brunt of this. He feels therefore rejected by any family group.

The grandfather was as rigid in his way as the grandmother. He was afraid of his own thoughts as a child, believing that thoughts could kill. The unspoken bitterness against his mother built up inside him. He considered it wrong, and could not release it. Hence the Pollyanna attitude at times, a desperate attempt to cover up thoughts that are spontaneous, but that are considered evil by the conscientious self.

(*Again Jane's pace had become slower, with less inflection, sleepier, as she lay on her back on the couch. However her eyes opened occasionally and she looked at me as she spoke.*)

Always a strong trend and ability for high dedication. The conflict mentioned in last evening's session was a barrier to dedication. He felt lost without dedication, and it robbed his days of meaning. He has always seen his daily life in the context of eternal meaning, and the conflict prevented this, robbing him of the previous significance possessed by the most trivial incident.

He was no longer certain of his course. Do you have questions?

(*"Could you address yourself directly to his conscientious self if you wanted to?"*)

I have.

(*"Did it acknowledge your communication?"*)

It has. I am *(pause)* permitted to speak because the super conscientious self is aware of, and convinced of, my moral standing, you see. (*Open eyes briefly.*

(*"Can the conscientious self construct its own dreams?)*

Does it construct some dreams?

(*"Yes."*)

It participates in the construction of some dreams having a more or less important role according to some circumstances. Punishment can be meted out in dreams, you see. But also moral encouragement can be given in dreams.

(*"But these moral encouragements could conflict with the spontaneous self, even in dreams?"*)

Indeed, if as here the super-conscientious self has a limited concept.

(*"Is Ruburt tired tonight?"*)

The two sessions have wearied him some, but will overall be highly advantageous.

(*"Do you think his projections will improve now?"*)

Indeed an improvement has already begun. Some realization has come to the overly conscientious self, even before last night's session, or the session itself would have been much more difficult.

("Has the spontaneous self ever been responsible for any of the symptoms?")

Very seldom. It should be remembered that the overly conscientious self is also responsible for lifelong continuity of purpose, giving direction to the spontaneous self.

("Could you think of the conscientious self as a more basic ego structure than the spontaneous self?")

It is deeper than an ego structure. The ego structure is formed from both, with a surface veneer of superficial characteristics.

The spontaneous self represents basic abilities. The super-conscientious self represents the purposes to which these abilities will be put—how and when they shall be used. The super-conscientious self is the motivation power or purpose.

("Yes. Well, if Ruburt's tired we can end the session now.")

The two sessions, one immediately following the other, you see—both should be highly beneficial however.

("Yes.")

I will bid you good evening, and I will discuss your tremor and some other matters at our next session.

("Good. Good night, Seth.")

(10:55. Jane still lay flat, quite unusual for her; she was not aware of any resistance, she said. Her eyes were closed much of the time, her voice slow and quiet, her manner rather tired.)

SESSION 369 (DELETED)
OCTOBER 4, 1967 9:15 PM WEDNESDAY

(This session is deleted from the record.

(Jane again began speaking rapidly, her eyes opening at times, as she sat on the divan.)

Good evening.

("Good evening, Seth.")

Give us a moment, please. *(Pause.)* Now. When the overly conscientious self and the spontaneous self are working well together there are no difficulties, and Ruburt has the full use of his remarkable energy, and it is well focused.

It is only when a schism develops that the overly conscientious self becomes quite unreasoning in its demands and expectations. The spontaneous self then becomes defiant, and at times purposely needles the portion of the personality it believes would hold it back.

This material coming out through the sessions frightened the whole personality, and there has been some uproar, which is quite understandable. The problem is somewhat one of definition and understanding.

The overly conscientious self defines good in rather narrow terms, and no effort has been made to reeducate it, or very little. Ruburt as a child was highly mystical, and also overly conscientious and overdemanding of himself, and afraid of his own spontaneity and natural appetites.

The church at that point united the personality however, both parts of the personality agreeing on the definition of good. The spontaneous self was the first to break away, and forcibly. It was at the time strong and powerful enough to have its way, and it did not have experience enough behind it. Now a whole new uniting principle has been realized by the spontaneous self, but little attempt was made to enlarge the definitions of good on the part of the overly conscientious self.

Some of the very attitudes considered good by the spontaneous self were diametrically opposed to the ideas of good held by the overly conscientious self. Writing had always united the personality. The direction of the writing changed, and this further seemed to threaten basic held inner beliefs of the overly conscientious self.

What Ruburt believes to be his intellectual skepticism is the voice of the overly conscientious self in quite limited Catholic terms.

The overly conscientious self is afraid of emotion and display, and hence quite terrified of any ideas of communicating with survival personalities. The word God embarrasses it beyond measure, simply because the word no longer means what the overly conscientious self was taught to believe what it meant. It was not the Catholic God. It fears the taking of false gods, you see.

The overly conscientious self is also deeply emotional, though in Ruburt it often hides under the guise of intellectualism. In one way the spontaneous self used the church as long as it could, as an outlet for its own rich emotional extension. The overly conscientious self fears to use the word of God, or the word God. Ruburt thinks this is because he is afraid of being made to feel a fool. In actuality the overly conscientious self has not been educated, and is deeply terrified that Ruburt is taking false gods.

The whole personality knows quite well that the spirit survives and that the personality is capable of communicating with such spirits. To the overly conscientious self however this is not Catholic nor legitimate. At the same time the whole personality is deeply committed and has always been, to such a psychic examination of existence. Even the overly conscientious self is engrossed despite itself.

It wants to know, and it resents the fact that it has been so left in the dark. It is the authoritative part of Ruburt that often takes charge even in psychic matters, and highly relevant. It has been reached. The fact that he has worked without reprisal on his dream book shows this.

At night the two portions have been squabbling, in an attempt to make their peace, hence his discomfort. *(In sleeping.)* His performance last evening showed however a greater participation of the overly conscientious self in the psychic work, showing itself as authority and confidence. It is not of itself limiting in our work by any means, but there has been constant and deep misunderstanding that came to a head last winter, was somewhat resolved, but still continued. As a result Ruburt very seldom relaxed physically, and this has been largely the cause of his symptoms. The muscles fought each other.

(Last night Jane held her ESP class at the home of Ruth Klebert, and was very successful in demonstrating table tipping. Jane told me she really felt a focus of concentrated power emanating through her hands; even when they did not touch the table, the table obeyed.)

He denied himself release in the sex act. The overly conscientious self tried to call a halt to pleasure until the issue was settled. The spontaneous self fought back bitterly. Both sides brought to bear emotional issues from the past that served to illustrate or strengthen their own position, so that Ruburt was pulled willy-nilly.

Aspects from the past were grossly exaggerated, and any normal sensitivity highly intensified by one portion of the personality or the other. Little surprise that he became relatively immobile. The supra-conscious self tried, but the overly conscientious self deepened a preliminary distrust for me, and would not allow me to speak out clearly.

You became an unwilling ally of the overly conscientious self in almost every issue faced by you and Ruburt. This affected the spontaneity of our sessions, and serves to explain the intense emotional climate that pervaded concerning both Fell and the issue of going to work. *(F. Fell, Jane's publisher.)*

Ruburt liked jobs where he was outside and free. The spontaneous self enjoyed them. The overly conscientious self demanded that this was not work enough. It did not pay penance enough for the fact that you were working at Artistic. This, combined with your attitude that he take a normal job, almost literally paralyzed him, for your voice was added, <u>in his mind you see</u>, reinforcing the rigid attitude of the overly conscientious self. It deeply distrusted the spontaneity allowed in such jobs.

The nursery school, in a basement, made him feel imprisoned. The substitute teaching pleased the spontaneous self by its very unpredictability and change of location. The overly conscientious self resented it for the same reasons; and again your voice was unwittingly added in Ruburt's mind.

The desire for punishment led him to contemplate doing the program, but under a guise to fool the spontaneous self. Here very fortunately you refused to be an ally of the overly conscientious self, and half the pressure was relieved from Ruburt. He was free enough to resist. *(The Alan Burke TV show in NYC in August, 1967.)*

The poverty angle reaches in here for you both, but I intend to give you my own ideas and suggestions in the very near future. You may take a break and we shall continue.

(9:46. Jane's pace continued fast, her eyes opening at times. After break, at 9:48, she once again lay down on the couch to resume. This time she was on her side, facing me.)

Now. The overly conscientious self has always seen itself in male terms because of the God concept, of the God being male.

The spontaneous self has seen itself in female terms. When Ruburt imagines that he does not like women therefore, this is the reason. I believe the personality is now coming to terms with itself. Spontaneously the personality always felt at one with All That Is. While he was in the church the overly conscientious self agreed with the terms. Later it became more and more confused.

This deprived Ruburt of the deeply-rooted sense of inner natural unity when he began to rationalize this or examine it intellectually; he already questioned it, and the questioning was on the part of the overly conscientious self. Progress is being made since our first session on this subject. *(The 367th Session for October 1, 1967.)*

I do suggest that you get some enjoyment away from your apartment when you can.

Father Ryan and Father Traynor have been notified. I will myself give Ruburt some additional help while he is in astral form later this evening.

I am going to cover the question of your tremor and other difficulty in one session more or less devoted to those questions. The bedroom window should be opened for him, and for now at least the bed moved a few inches out into the room. Under the circumstances this is enough for this session. We shall take up the matter again however at our next session also. I am keeping this session brief to minimize reactions.

Do you have any particular questions you feel should be covered this evening?

("Just the one; what do you think of the suggestions Jane wrote out the day after the 387th Session, and which she has been reading to herself several times daily since?"

(Interestingly, Jane lost this paper yesterday.)

At our next session I will give him definite suggestions to use. In the meantime what he has been doing is adequate.

("Okay, that's it. Good night, Seth."

(10:00. Jane still lay on the couch, her eyes open often. But she had been restless, and it was quite obvious she didn't want the session to last very long.

(I had written out a list of questions that Jane read over before the session. Some of them were answered tonight in Seth's own way.)

SESSION 370 (DELETED)
OCTOBER 9, 1967 10:20 PM MONDAY

(The usual session time of 9 PM came and passed while Jane and I talked. Finally we used her pendulum to learn that her overly conscientious self did not want a session this evening. Her spontaneous self did.

(In the 358th Session Seth stated; "There are difficulties for Ruburt's associate of last year at the center," meaning Nancy Methinitus. This was on August 2, 1967. Today by telephone Nancy verified Seth, in that her mother is seriously ill at Mayo Clinic; the mother has been ill for some time, but was not, for instance, the last time Jane talked to Nancy, sometime prior to the 358th Session. The two seldom see each other since Jane left nursery school.

(This session is deleted from the record. Jane began speaking while sitting on the divan once more, her eyes opening at times, her pace rapid.)

Now..

For years, literally, it was hammered into Ruburt's subconscious that he was not worthy of any kind of success, and that he would be punished for his treatment of his mother.

The suggestions came from the mother. Suggestions given by the mother are always the most tenacious in any case. While he struggled *(to succeed)*, these did not cause him noticeable difficulty, though they operated underground, impeding his progress. Only when it seemed that success was on its way, or inevitable, did these suggestions show their effects.

He is conscious of some of these in a general fashion. His mother let it be known that she had no use for him, and he thought if his mother could not love him, then certainly there must be something seriously wrong and unworthy about him.

Running away gave him a feeling of security, but he ran in desperation. He stopped running to deal with the problem, to meet it head on. Symbolically then, he stopped running, but he carried this out in physical terms also.

On a few occasions the mother went so far as to say: "I hope you are crippled someday, too." And this became the feared punishment.

Now I strongly suggest, Joseph, one or two hypnotic sessions for a few weeks. You must yourself be cautious, and write down the impressions you intend to give the suggestions. You will de-hypnotize him, you see, to the effect that he is good, his basic instincts can be trusted, and he can therefore be free to move and act in a spontaneous manner.

He can and <u>should</u> have excellent health and flexibility, in order to carry out the work that he was meant to carry out. This will also get the overly conscientious self on your side. You can take it as slowly as you like to begin with, but the step should be taken.

He has made advances in understanding since our last sessions. You must also be patient with him. The overly conscientious self was angry *(today and tonight)*, and he projected this anger at you, so that he thought he was simply a bother to you, and of no benefit. Understanding this is necessary, but if possible in small ways show him that this is not true; for it can amount to an emotional conviction on his part, and an emotional assurance from you will work far faster than the use of words, though both are necessary.

He did arouse himself for battle yesterday *(at my parents', especially noticing the poor condition of my father)*, and this was effective, but this state of battle should not be maintained as a daily thing. He understands your need and right to security from all this. You have it. Therefore you can afford to give emotional assurances. If these are withdrawn he has a tendency to panic, although now he deals with this in a much more effective manner than he did.

The inner security that you attain is also a reassurance to him, for you can then be relied upon to operate with some objectivity, and he knows this. You can afford gestures however that are meaningful.

Even the third class will be of benefit to him, regardless of finances. Now, he does feel that you have purposely cut yourself off from any interest in the classes. You can clear that up. Regardless of his condition, he does offer an emotional bridge to your mother, though he is frightened when he does so.

In his efforts to understand and help your parents he has more than made up for any failure with his mother. He should understand this. Others more capable have taken over the same role with his mother. *(Pause.)*

The suggestions he has written down should be read twice at a time, three times daily, morning, noon and before retiring. Some excellent work has been done lately while in the dream state. For a while when he feels tired, or when he feels a definite resistance against work, he should do something that he enjoys doing. Never mind resenting the lost time. He will be refreshing himself, and the same amount of good work will be produced in any case, possibly more.

He should work on the dream book each day, whenever possible, but not all day. The spontaneous self dislikes the spelling chores and the bare typing, and the overly conscientious self fears the books success. Two, at the most three, hours daily is sufficient for now. Possibly two hours unless he feels like more. When he does, this is fine. The rest of the time for poetry. This is the most reasonable and attainable goal for the present. The book will be finished, but not too many demands will be made of either portion of the self on a daily basis.

Now, indeed, his upset over your intimate life is a good sign. The anger, for there is anger, is against the overly conscientious self, and he should know this. On the other hand on your part, all signs of affection will be of great benefit. Do not press overly, for sexual response. Give the affection freely without demand, and you will need no demand. You will know when a demand is the right thing under the circumstances, however, and this is also important, for he will on occasion yield gladly. The affection without demand must first lull the overly conscientious self, for it needs to be quieted and relaxed.

I suggest your break. This will be a brief session, and you did well to see that it was held. It was needed.

(10:50. Jane was well dissociated, retaining little memory of what Seth said. Her pace continued fairly fast. Resume at 10:55.)

Now. All so-called spiritualistic literature should be avoided at this time, simply because the overly conscientious self misinterprets it, and sets up further standards of perfection.

Ruburt did take a good step this evening in talking out to you his feelings. In the past he would have tried to ignore them. The overly conscientious self however tells him that you do not want to be bothered, and so he hesitates and interprets your words, sometimes, in that light.

Now he questions his own attitudes, however, which is good, and helps him avoid the full brunt of such pitfalls.

I have a small suggestion. Temporarily (underlined), you could open and read his mother's letters and inform him of anything he should know. Then he can answer them. For the present this would avoid some difficulties.

A very small point, but interesting: he resents ironing, this because his mother was overly particular. This resentment is on the part of the spontaneous self in the main.

Unless you have any questions we will end the session. These last sessions should be read several times weekly however.

("Did I know Jane was going to have this trouble when we married?")

You did indeed. Again, the spontaneous self opens and warms to affection, colors, movement, you see. The overly conscientious self is overly orderly.

("Do you think he should continue with the book he's reading?"—a self-help book on auto-analysis.)

He has finished it. It will do neither good nor harm.

("How about similar books in the future?")

Each book is an individual book. The question cannot be answered in those terms. The spiritualistic books however he will manage to misinterpret at this time. Short trips out of the apartment are beneficial. Walks, rides, people. Casual encounters as of this evening are good for him.

Do you have other questions?

("Is the overly conscientious self less alarmed now?")

Yes.

("Is it cooperating more?")

It is cooperating more. Its overconcern arose as the result of the suggestions given over the years. *(Jane again lay down on the couch, flat on her back as she continued speaking.)* As they lose their power it will be able to relax.

("Then it has learned more?")

It has.

("Can the same be said for the spontaneous self?")

They are learning to communicate.

("When I hypnotize Jane, am I apt to encounter you?")

Not under the circumstances.

("You will be aware of it though.")

I will indeed. You can call on me if you want to—

("That's what I was wondering about.")

— to take over at any point. I will not interfere with the process.

("Then you could speak if I asked you to while Jane is under?")

Indeed. But I would not suggest that you interrupt.

("No.")

Unless you have good reason.

("If we hit upon something touchy, could I ask your help?")

Indeed. If Ruburt were under hypnosis you would then command him to let me speak. You could try the permissive request first, and if this failed use the command technique.

("*Well, what's the difference between the state he's in now, and the state I would put him in? He's in a trance now.*")

Yes, but a different sort, leapfrogging to the desired level. You would be dealing with the personal subconscious, and there is a tremendous difference. The subconscious for example would speak, and the ego would then allow this direct contact. I must pass through the subconscious, but I am not directly concerned with it. And from me you get knowledge of its feelings and attitudes when you request them.

I can perceive them. In hypnosis as you are planning, you would directly contact the subconscious.

We will now end the session. These sessions should not be too long.

("*Okay.*")

I am like a doctor, able to describe the condition of the patient, or the subconscious. In hypnosis the subconscious, as the patient, speaks for himself, or is spoken to.

("*Good night, Seth.*")

(*11:21. Jane was still reclining on the couch.*)

SESSION 371 (DELETED)
OCTOBER 11, 1967 9:27 PM WEDNESDAY

(*This session is deleted from the record. Once again Jane spoke for Seth while seated on the divan. Her eyes opened often, were very dark; her voice was average, her pace again fast.*)

Good evening.

("*Good evening, Seth.*")

Now, we will have a fairly brief session, simply because I am adjusting my techniques of therapy according to Ruburt's reactions.

For a while however none should be missed, except for very good cause. The reaction following sessions has simply been the arousal of antagonism. The symptoms have been a defense against the sort of self-enlightenment that I am now giving in the sessions. There is then a natural reaction at times, as those tendencies in the personality that adopted the symptoms actually struggle to retain them.

A dislike of me for ripping away the veil of secrecy, for with the veil down the symptoms must disappear. I will judge therefore the duration of any given session in this light.

Now the late affairs with the table have been good training on Ruburt's part, and given him a release of energies that is acceptable and beneficial. It has also opened up a new line of inquiry for him, and much more will come from this, both on your part and Ruburt's.

("Well, I see you're still being allowed to discuss these matters.")

There is no serious blockage now. He has forgotten the peanut oil however, and this is a good aid, for the arms particularly. His abilities have been developing rather rapidly of late, and this shows a basic inner improvement—a lack of previous blockage, that will soon be more distinguishable in physical terms.

This evening's explosion on his part did represent an advance. He would not have let himself spontaneously express his anger in so direct a fashion earlier.

(When Jane got mad at me after supper tonight.
("Is a part of his personality still actually trying to block this material?")

Not actively. It is difficult to explain. The symptoms themselves cause certain chemical changes that have an effect, then, on the personality itself. If the self accepts the symptoms, and in all cases of illness to some extent or another this is true, then paradoxically a portion of the self identifies with the symptoms.

To rip away the symptoms becomes a ripping away of a portion of the self, even if a most disagreeable portion. The procedures immediately call for new growth on the part of the self, to replace what is being taken away, and to replace it in a more constructive fashion.

This necessitates finding the causes for the symptoms, backtracking, really, to the point before the symptoms' appearance, and facing problems now that would not be faced then. The symptoms represent in all cases one attempt, one method, of solving the existing problems. The personality must become aware of the inefficiency of such a manner.

Now in some cases a physical illness is the best solution for various reasons having to do with reincarnational influences, and the inner lack of balance of the personality. In Ruburt's case this is not so.

We are trying to make him see the basic difficulty, and give him a solution that is acceptable. He should make every effort to understand them consciously as well as emotionally.

("Is he?")

He is progressing. The desperation caused by the symptoms became greater than the problem behind them. This alone showed him that his solution was wrong. The nature of his own individuality makes it impossible for him to accept such a solution. Therefore he had to seek others. This is a case where his curiosity stands him in good stead.

("Is there any large area of this material that he's relatively opaque to, consciously?")

Give us a moment on that question. *(Pause.)*

He must fully understand that while thought is action, thought cannot hurt nor help another without the consent of the other person involved. Their decision has to do with their own problems and solutions. He had nothing to do with making his mother a cripple, nor does his fear, hatred or scorn of her <u>keep</u> her in that condition.

He is not responsible for the fact that his father left his mother. Now he did contribute, but no more than many others, and the main circumstances were chosen by the mother and the father.

Ruburt's birth did not cause his mother to become an invalid. These facts have not been blocked, but withheld. There is a difference.

(Jane was now beginning to recline on the couch once more, while speaking. In each of these recent personal sessions she has ended up laying flat on her back on the couch while in trance—something she hadn't done until recently.)

He believes strongly in the power of thought. The Catholic Church judged evil thoughts as evil deeds, and to some extent this is valid. But every man has a <u>strong</u>, domineering and definite voice in his own destiny, and he accepts and reacts to those influences of his own choosing.

(Jane lay out flat on the couch.)

Ruburt did not therefore destroy his mother, break up her marriage. He is not responsible for the death of his grandmother, or for the death of the maid. He has always been a creative rather than destructive personality.

He has done already more good than he knows. He must realize all of these points.

("How about his recent projections to Saratoga? Are these a good idea at this time?" Saratoga Springs is Jane's home town.)

In these cases so far, they have been beneficial.

("Could he control the destination of his projections?")

He can.

("How about those vivid dreams he's had lately. It seems he's been getting instructions concerning his symptoms, etc.")

They were not vividly <u>remembered</u>. They were definite experiences, and I was instructing him, as I have done recently. *(Pause.)* I was trying to correct certain errors. They are not egotistical errors and so I bypassed the ego.

("Were you successful?")

I was partially successful.

(I was about to ask Seth what the errors were when the phone rang, inter-

rupting the session. Jane came out of trance without shock. I answered the phone and it was a wrong number. We took a break at 9:55. Jane resumed, sitting up again, at 10:00.)

It is advisable that you not discuss Ruburt's condition after a session of this nature, but turn your minds to some other interest before retiring.

If, and whenever possible, another brief, perhaps half-hour session, could be held. This is only a temporary measure.

("You mean before next Monday?")

At your convenience. This is merely a suggestion. The material is rather highly charged. *(Pause.)* The short session allows him to handle and dissipate effectively any reactions. This is done as we go along, and therefore does not build up.

Not only how much material you get is important, but how and when. It must be assimilated and digested.

("Can I ask a question off the subject?")

You may.

("What do you see when you look at me?")

(I asked this because Jane's stare at me had been especially noticeable; her eyes had been very dark and luminous, I thought.)

When I look at you, or when I look at you through Ruburt's eyes?

("Well, first when you look at me.")

When I look at you, I see a multidimensional form in motion, a geometrical collection of highly intensified energy, with a nucleus that is your whole self. The self that you know is only a small portion of that self, boxed in, so to speak, by its limited perception.

Now, through Ruburt's eyes, I see you as Ruburt's physical eyes must, wrapped in your particular time and in your particular place, held in a unique spatial arrangement.

(During the above two paragraphs Jane's eyes had been open. Now they closed.)

Now, with my eyes closed, the physical matter of Robert Butts vanishes, and the Robert Butts is seen as one unit in all these other forms. The physical matter of course continues in a different fashion.

("Very interesting. While you're looking at me through Jane's eyes, how much of her are you aware of?")

(Eyes open.) I am aware of Ruburt to some extent in the same way that he is aware of his astral form when he is traveling within it, though my awareness is much stronger, and my control is more deliberate. My sense of participation is more vivid.

("Does his poor eyesight, for instance, influence your perception of me?")

I use the mechanism as I find it, and do not tamper with it, for any tampering would be reflected either in advancements that he was not prepared for, or in alterations for which he was not ready.

("Do you want to say a few words about the table last night for Jane's ESP students?")

(Last night Jane had a very successful table-tipping session with her ESP class. The table appeared to move and tilt although her hands barely touched its top. I too sat in on the session, which lasted until midnight.)

You are involved again in the further development of Ruburt's abilities and confidence. He has already learned a lesson, in that that same concentration can be applied to change the condition of this own psyche and physical body.

(Last night Jane was especially aware of her success at concentration in getting the table to move.)

It was an excellent display of intense focus of energy and utilization of materials. I will go more deeply into the whole affair—perhaps our next session can include, as this one has, a section on Ruburt's condition first, and then a discussion of other matters.

We will go directly then into the whole table affair, how and why it is done, and give the source of the energies behind the phenomena. For that session you may also include a few questions on your own.

We will now close this session. My heartiest regards to you both.

("Good night, Seth. It's been very interesting." 10:20.)

SESSION 372 (DELETED)
OCTOBER 16, 1967 8:50 PM MONDAY

(This session is deleted from the record. Jane began speaking a little ahead of time, while sitting on the couch once more. Her eyes opened often, her pace was fast.)

Good evening.

("Good evening, Seth.")

Now, my best to you in a difficult time.

Ruburt is learning much to his advantage in the present circumstances regarding your own parents. The affair allows him to make comparisons, to compare and evaluate present events with past ones. To discharge, and then examine, emotional responses that have lain latent.

In a new crisis situation, in facing a present crisis squarely and dealing with it in adult terms, he may indeed free himself largely; for the present situation through association brings up highly charged emotional energies that have been stopped up and causing difficulty.

It is highly necessary then that his present course be maintained, expressing his emotions honestly to himself and to you; and examining them, if he prefers, afterward, then taking with you whatever steps are necessary in your family situation.

This is the adult's chance to understand and emotionally exorcise parental ghosts from the child's past. They will be viewed in the light of the present, brought up because of your family's dilemma, to the light of day.

Ruburt should not brush aside any emotional connections then, but understand what is happening. For this process is releasing him already, and operates like a catharsis. His development allows this to happen. The situation, you see, somewhat earlier, could have had far different connotations, and he could not have handled them. This is very important, the above.

I will try this evening to help you on both of these levels. On Ruburt's part he is finding himself able to handle a parental situation with you, along with you, even though the crisis evokes long repressed, highly charged emotions from his own past.

Even the welfare considerations enter in here. He sat on the family porch Sunday to escape the house as he did as a child in Saratoga. In his subconscious your father and mother become two aspects both representing his own mother. The father, nearly crippled, to be cared for, and therefore frightening. Yet he spontaneously kissed the father, and tried to give him strength.

The father, your father, represents to him, Ruburt, the helpless portions of his own mother, directed so to speak where he can see them. Your mother represents to him the destructive, unreasoning energies of his own mother, and in the pull and conflict between your mother and father, he sees the tortured connections of his mother's soul.

He can run without being compelled to run away. *(Slowly.)* He has a free choice, now. In facing these problems, he is releasing himself through highly traumatic inner psychological dramas. He is not using the situation in a derogatory sense. He is able however, now, to face realities, allow himself motion, and not fear that motion will automatically mean cowardly flight.

In facing the situation in your parent's house, he faces and conquers the situation once existing in his mother's house. There is some resistance, but he now recognizes it as such, and is able to overcome it. The situation does not gobble him up. He was always afraid that it would.

The parents are not all powerful. They now need support. They are people, they are not magic monsters out to devour him.

Now, if you will forgive me, he sees your mother's stupidity in important matters. If she is destructive, he sees that this destruction is the other face of love never truly given. It is not aimed, it is a rage, enveloping like a storm of nature, enveloping even the personality from whom it emits, so that the mother becomes a victim also.

Ruburt can see this then objectively. Your mother is not out to kill him personally. His mother was not out to kill him personally. He was simply there.

(Pause.) I am letting your hand rest a moment.

("Yes." Long pause, eyes closed.)

These realizations free him. The realizations themselves release him. Now give us a moment.

They, your parents, are done with each other, your mother being more honest than your father in this respect. *(Long pause.)* Her rage, you must understand, is the other face of life, vitality and love, and she will not give up her demands. She will try to shove him out, and he will cower before her strength. He always resented her vitality.

Her heavily applied, overly feminine characteristics, were donned by her to hold him in the early years. She had more strength than he. She pretended to be dominated by him, but both of them knew. *(Pause.)* He would have preferred daughters. She gave him sons hoping to pacify him, but he always felt that the sons challenged his vitality and position.

He gave up years ago. Her energy made him keep up appearances. Her vitality fed him, but it could not <u>rouse</u> him. Now he in his helplessness pays her back, and she rages against him. The sons left early, but he refuses to leave. She feels betrayed by the sons who left, and the father who stayed.

She will not listen to reason, because reason would rob her of her rage, and all of her vitality is now in her rage. There are reasons in the reincarnational background. Some have been given *(in early 1964)*.

Your father fulfilled his main purpose in this existence, and was satisfied, sometime within five to seven years after his marriage. He wanted to leave then. The main portion of his personality, the integrating functions, the strong core, left, and rejoined the entity years ago. A fragment, the shell that you know, remained.

She could not let it go. She demanded that some portion of your father remain. They made a bargain, all without knowing. Her vitality would not permit her to leave. She was tied too strongly to earth through physical connections. More than half of your father's personality has been vacant, and this portion has been with the entity. It has grown and matured. It stepped out.

(Jane's pace was now quite slow, with many long pauses, some up to a minute in length. Her eyes were often closed.)

There was no inner need nor purpose in its remaining. There were reasons why the two personalities, your mother and your father, met. These reasons on your father's part were consummated. He did not feel that he could die. *(Pause.)* He left what she wanted. *(Long pause.)* She fears the presence of her husband's other self, but does not know this consciously.

She feels cheated, and has, for *he* has gone. In a last life she died fairly early, and she would not face life, she did not want to hold on. This time her vitality, chosen by her, forces her to do so. She wants the man she once knew but her rage forces her, and has forced her, to stay alive, with the one part of the man that remained.

In each of her three sons she sees portions of the man she knew. *(Long pause.)* He will be reborn, and his abilities of inventiveness will play a large role in the 21st Century, where he shall be born in Egypt. *(One minute pause.)*

She is young in her dreams, and cannot see herself in the old woman. She is expressing a rage that she would not express in the past, and it will purify her and leave her free. Otherwise it would have blemished innumerable reincarnated selves, and prevented any of them from achieving fulfillment.

You may take your break or end the session as you prefer.

("We'll take the break.")

(9:52. Jane said she had been far out, but was aware she had spoken for a long time. She resumed at a faster pace once more, half lying back on the couch, at 10:04.)

Now. Several things.

Your mother tried to change you into the image of the man she had known. You were to take his place, and she enjoyed it when you supported the household. Every bill you paid, or small item you purchased, had erotic connotations, and on two levels: on your part subconsciously, because you felt her strong emotional pull, though it terrified you; and on her part because you took the place of the father.

You nearly fell into disaster, living in the house. You knew you would meet Ruburt, however, and she tried to prevent it, for she knew it also. The shell of your father rejoiced. You recognized your predicament, and henceforth refused to take the main responsibility for your mother, which was the responsibility of a man for his wife.

This also has something to do with Ruburt's fears if he is not financially contributing to your establishment. Do you see?

("Yes.")

(Pause.) Your brother Dick was meant to be a female. He was to have been a little sister. Give us a moment. *(Pause.)* There will be a separation of the mother and the father. The father's shell will feel pushed out initially, but then will

find peace and contentment, for it is passive, and has been pushed to exhaustion. *(My parents did end up separated)*

Other elements of it will rejoin the main personality. It stayed as a counterbalancing influence in the family, for the sons' sake. What is left will enjoy the sunlight and green grass, and be peaceful. *(Pause.)*

Give us time. The house eventually will pass into other hands. Perhaps an A.K. The mother will to some extent find release, staying I believe near Betts and Loren, or very strongly connected to them. The aggressive social outlook would be good for the mother. Betts and Loren must help others, for they cannot find peace within themselves otherwise.

This is quite legitimate. They are not developed enough to <u>have</u> peace within themselves. Helping others turns their aggressions into beneficial action, a transformation of sorts.

Your mother needs action, physical vigorous action. Your kind of life would drive her mad. She could destroy your other brother. For a while she will stay at home. *(Pause.)* Your father's ghost or shell waits to be reunited with the other portions of itself. In the meantime it will roam through the old house, seeking what is lost, and <u>finding</u> recreated scenes that bring him peace.

The existing personality shows delusions, for what the ghost knows the physical self does not perceive.

Do you have questions?

("How about Jane and the large table moving the other night?")

Ruburt is developing his abilities, and I helped him on that occasion. He overintellectualizes when he works the table alone. Let him get his results, and do his critical work afterwards. His abilities are <u>being</u> released because energy is now <u>being</u> released.

The suggestions he has written down are also taking effect. Your intimate life and his biological periods will also improve now, but he must continue what he has been doing in connection with your parents. A portion of him <u>is</u> quite deliberately using that situation—that is, as a catharsis, so the honest emotional attitude must be maintained.

He is slightly worried about the social-worker appointment. Let him acknowledge it freely, you see. Then any old fears become present, and are subject to solutions that the adult finds.

("Yes.")

His classes will continue well, and within six months they will be completely filled, which will substantially aid your regular income. Good sales on the ESP book <u>will</u> materialize. Within a two-year period definite substantial gains, well above expenses, will be seen.

(This session was held on Monday, October 16. On October 17, Jane got a letter from her publisher, outlining details for the first full-page ad that he has placed in a national publication for the ESP book. F. Fell added that he expects to sell a lot of books.)

He will be freer now to continue and complete his dream book, without feeling coerced. That is he will be spontaneously inspired, I believe, to continue it.

The old panic is being dispelled through the present situation with your parents. At a lesser degree of development this would <u>not</u> be the case. Both your father and your mother subconsciously know your position and Ruburt's. Subconsciously they both know that this good is coming from their own situation.

Once more: Ruburt begins to realize he can have full freedom of motion, without feeling that he will be forced to run away. He has a the choice of motion now. He can stay and face a situation through, and have full freedom of motion. He will not use motion in a cowardly manner, as he feared. He can also use freedom of motion to help.

We will now end our session. My special regards to you both.

The table experiments will lead to more highly developed interests.

("Is there any point in using heavier tables?")

We will have to discuss that issue at another session. I intend to discuss it thoroughly. Ruburt's corner *(Jane pointed to the west corner of the living room, where her working area lay)*, is of help psychically.

Tell Ruburt to answer our friend's letter concerning his wife, and we shall have some material shortly.

("How is she doing?")

There has been some marked improvement, but worry over the mental temperament, and increased irritability. This is natural however as I shall explain.

("Okay. Good night, Seth." 10:38.)

SESSION 373 (DELETED)
OCTOBER 18, 1967 9 PM WEDNESDAY

(This session is deleted from the record. Before the session Jane and I held a general discussion re her improvement, my parents' serious situation, Jane's recent days of writing poetry. Including one she wrote today involving her grandfather.

(Once again Jane sat on the divan, and began speaking for Seth, in trance, at

a rather fast pace, with her eyes opening often.)
Good evening.
("Good evening, Seth.")

Ruburt's poem <u>is</u> of help to him, springing as it did from both levels of his personality. The "no" being rejected is rigidity.

The overly conscientious self also wants freedom of motion toward goals with which it agrees. It operates in a restricting fashion only when deeply suspicious of goals, and this suspicion is usually generated by a lack of communication.

The overly conscientious self is life-<u>sustaining</u>, however. It gives a steady abundance of energy when it approves of overall commitments. It must so approve for any advancements to be made. This gives direction to the spontaneous self. It does not limit the <u>fields</u> of endeavor however. It simply attempts to keep the self united and the energies clearly focused.

It is cohesive. It can become highly stubborn when ignored. It is a rock-bottom portion of the self, a Taurus characteristic *(Jane is a Taurus)*. Of great benefit when it is not ignored, it needed reeducation, and is being reassured now.

It <u>was</u> somewhat overdeveloped in function because of early experience. It can be placid, peace-giving and very agreeable when it does not feel crossed. Because of its distorted ideas it was roused into a frenzy. It is now withdrawing to a more normal position.

It is more than reassured now. It is somewhat astonished to discover that the spontaneous self is no enemy, but a friend and ally. Already it has released energy for the use of the personality. The energy was bottled up in symptoms.

The suggestions Ruburt has written down are excellent, and are helping considerably. He is expressing his salvation now through his poetry, which is natural for both portions of the self. This will also be felt in his dream book, however.

The overly conscientious self has distrusted frivolity. This still somewhat concerns it. This comes from the Irish grandmother. A suggestion that gaiety and frivolity are also natural aspects of life, and joyful celebrations of existence, harmless, in fact beneficial play exercises on the part of the soul, will help here.

Before bed this evening let Ruburt read his suggestions twice. This will take care of any lingering doubts on the part of the overly conscientious self concerning the success implied in the Fell letter.

(In the last session, 372nd, October 16, 1967, Seth predicted good sales for Jane's ESP book. The next day Jane got a letter from F. Fell in which he outlined plans for the start of a national ad campaign to promote the book. First ad already

scheduled in a national publication.)

For Venice, a small note: I believe AA was indeed a family friend when she was very young in this existence.

(This re an entity, AA, received when Jane practices table-tipping with one of her ESP students, Venice McCullough.)

Ruburt should continue as he has been, and further blocks of symptoms will drop away. At the same time larger amounts of energy will be restored for the personality's beneficial purposes. The experiments with the table only represent a beginning for Ruburt. He is in other words at the beginning of a new venture.

Give us a moment. *(Pause.)*

Your own symptom, the hand, representing uncertainty in your work. You felt a shaky foundation. You felt that your talent was giving you but a shaky foundation or basis within economic and social realities.

(Jane now began to pause more often. Her delivery slowed somewhat and her eyes were closed much of the time.)

Anger that your art did not bring you more money. You felt that if your hand were surer you would be better recompensed. You were angry at your talent, wishing it were one that was more quickly recognized in financial terms in your society.

("I still do, I suppose. I still have the tremor.")

The attitude itself helps cause that reality, to which you then react. When you were attempting to take your father's place, you used your talent as your mother wanted you to. She had no use for your father's talent of inventiveness, because he did not use it to make money.

You were a commercial artist to make your mother happy, and to take your father's place as breadwinner.

You were guiltily aware of this, and punish yourself by refusing to allow yourself to make money with good paintings now. This is that key to understanding, Joseph.

("Yes." Jane's delivery was emphatic, her eyes open.)

To paint paintings for joy was an act of defiance against your mother, and so you have punished yourself in several ways; by being overly concerned with their quality, insisting upon perfection, and by not making strong efforts to sell them or to work for recognition in that field.

To search for perfection within your art is good. The drive is good. But this is something different. Each painting has a spontaneous reality that you have often refused to acknowledge. *(Pause.)* Carried to extremes this could smother the spontaneous spark that is the heart of each painting.

Had you continued engrossed entirely in the commercial field your painting would not have developed. Your father would not have worked as a photographer. You could have become all but sexually your mother's husband. This was avoided.

(Long pause, eyes closed.) This session itself should aid your understanding enough to allow some improvement almost immediately in the condition itself. Two issues are involved. The painting was an act of defiance against your mother, an act of independence. She approved of the commercial art because it made money. Therefore if you made money through your paintings, then subconsciously you thought that your mother would still be getting her way. You see?

("Yes." Again, Jane was very emphatic.)

Not allowing yourself to make money through paintings also allowed you to punish yourself for what you considered this act of defiance. Two purposes in the main were served. This also affected your work itself to some degree, in that you sometimes inserted qualities in the paintings to hold people off, a remoteness.

Now all of this operates at varying degrees, you see. The symptom was the recognition of conflict. *(Pause.)* Rest your hand a moment.

(9:50. Jane's pace again slower.)

Commercial work also still rankles. Beside other considerations you feel, subconsciously again, that you still serve your mother's purposes: art for money, and that therefore your initial act of defiance and independence is not complete.

Working as you have also rouses associations with your father. *(Long pause, eyes closed.)*

We will take a break or end the session. We will go further into this material, but have reached some that is difficult to get through clearly.

("We'll take the break, then.")

(10:04. Jane said she had been well dissociated. I thought that perhaps Seth asked about an end to the session because Jane was blocking material about me she thought I might not like to hear. We now had a discussion about my motives in painting; I hoped it would release any blocks Jane might have set up. Seth then broke in at 10:15.)

Now.. We shall discuss this.

You made large attempts to close yourself off from deep emotion, in reaction against your mother's emotionalism, and largely because you felt emotionalism was false. With her, emotionalism was often an excuse.

You therefore believed all emotionalism to be of this nature. Ruburt was of great benefit to you here. In the beginning feeling and emotion sparked or initiated your paintings, but you worked it out of them to some considerable degree, not trusting it, and therefore not trusting the particular painting. So you did not feel justified in accepting money or payment for it.

Give us a moment. *(Pause. Head down.)* Now hear me. Using what you have learned here tonight, you can use your ability more freely. *(Pause.)* You can step out, so to speak, you can allow yourself to rely upon the integrity of spontaneity as it applies to your painting and to your talent.

What you want is not a perfection which *is* rigid, but the ever-balancing action of spontaneous motion, a balance precariously maintained for a moment through ever-approaching and receding imbalances that result in objects.

The perfection that you seek is not ever a finished, but a becoming quality. The technical ability gives a poised point through which these realities can emerge. The technique that *is* yours and *is* excellent should be the point of departure that sends the spontaneous action into new reality, and not a rigid mold to contain it.

Your potential is now. It did not exist as you conceive of it *(Jane, lying back on the couch, turned to face me)*, until you felt free to let it emerge, and you did not. You should now. *(Pause.*

("Well, what do you think of these temperas I've been working on then?")

Wait. *(Pause, hand raised.)* I am concerned over your arbitrary idea of age and advancement in terms of what you should expect at your age. *(A point I rather deliberately made during discussion at last break.)* This is limiting in concept, and rather uncharacteristic of you in larger respects.

("I think I'm quite aware of these larger aspects. I usually think of it in that way."

(Jane nodded, eyes closed.)

Your artistic abilities, <u>because</u> of their power, demand other abilities for their fulfillment, and you are now just becoming free enough to develop these other abilities. Your career should be ahead of you.

("Well, I think of it that way. It just makes me mad to think I could have been doing some of this in the past—with the use of hindsight."

(Pause.) We will have more on this subject. You may now take a break or end as you prefer.

("We might as well end it then, I guess.")

You are heading in the right direction. Only faith in your own abilities will allow you to be daring.

(After a long pause Jane came out of trance at 10:28. She said she had been much farther out than usual, and believed this was due to tonight's material; she was afraid of hurting me. For this reason my questions and comments bothered her, she said. We discussed my abstract paintings briefly, speculating on the reasons people

were attracted to them, and Seth came through briefly at 10:30.)

Now. For you the abstracts also represent excellent exercises in the free flow of spontaneity, and this benefits your other paintings also. The other questions that you have in mind, and such material, will be discussed in our next session.

("Okay." 10:32.)

SESSION 375 (DELETED)
OCTOBER 26, 1967 9 PM THURSDAY

(This session is deleted from the record.

(This afternoon Jane and I took my parents to the hospital in Sayre; mother for an ear examination, father to be admitted to the psychiatric ward. Tonight Jane assumed I would want Seth to talk about my parents, but I told her Seth could discuss anything he wanted to. I planned only a couple of questions to ask.

(Jane began speaking at a slower pace than she has used recently, with her eyes opening often.)

Good evening.

("Good evening, Seth.")

Now give us a moment. *(One minute pause, eyes closed.)*

The man that is left, your father, will be agitated, but then he will feel peaceful. It is almost like a reflex habit, a mechanical one, that keeps him now connected with your mother. *(Pause.)*

There are very dim memories still lingering, confused. These are ghosts of memories, not this man's memories really at all—ghosts of those memories that still linger because of the physical connection, the relationship between the man who remained and the main personality who did not stay.

On the one hand the woman takes pleasure that he now seems to need her so desperately. On the other hand she knows subconsciously that the need is actually counterfeit, and she resents this bitterly. *(Long pause.)*

In each of her three sons she sees portions of the man she married. They are not however open to her. She cannot find what she is after in them, and because of this she is also angry. She did not want children. Your father did.

Now, in a few of his delusions he was quite content. He imagined his sons as children sleeping. The whole personality who left is <u>aware</u> of the situation, but <u>he</u> is not vitally concerned. Your father began in this life as a whole personality. Various goals were set by him, and these were reached. He left a fragment of himself to satisfy the few lingering requirements.

He wanted to be the father of boys. There is some matter here not clear, not distorted or blocked, simply not <u>clear</u>, concerning the actual desire for the birth of males, however. He wanted to be the father of <u>three</u> for his own reasons, rather than the father of one or two children, you see.

Now, and no distortion here from our friend *(Jane)*, your mother was from the beginning a fragment, an offshoot actually, from the personality that she was in her last existence. The offshoot of fragment had to, and chose to, deal with the relationship that then took place between this fragment and your father.

His part in it was finished early. Her part was not, and she has chosen this road, all without knowing. Characteristics now being shown impeded the progress of the whole personality to which she is attached. The whole personality has to work these characteristics out in physical terms in order to discover through direct experience where they would lead.

The whole personality is a stubborn one, and had to learn in this manner. The vitality of the fragment personality but hints at the overall vitality of the whole self involved.

The characteristics are explosive and seemingly overwhelmingly impulsive, simply because by the nature of a fragment there are few balancing features, usually instead a one-sided explosive offshoot. These characteristics have in other lives held the personality back. Now the personality will realize the detrimental nature, and has <u>purged</u> itself, so to speak.

The whole personality will be much more free to progress. The characteristics were allowed to run their course. It had been agreed between the mother and the father beforehand. The whole personality of the father did not need to be involved after a certain point however, and withdrew. *(Long pause; one of many.)*

There has been a certain release given on the part of the mother, who has taken joy from lack of restraint. There are of course reasons why the three sons were born within the family. The vitality of the mother was of great benefit in many ways to the sons.

The fragment also knows that this life is being lived for the particular reason given. A duty is being performed. Certain characteristics and qualities incorporated about a fragment identity for a definite purpose. The fragment is always aware of this, and it is always aware of its inner identity with the whole personality.

The analogy is perhaps an old one, but the fragment is like an actor playing a character role, partially lost within it, perhaps disliking the character he plays, and yet through the part learning lessons that he will use in his own private life with its greater dimensions. Do you see?

("*Yes.*")

At such a crisis point as is now reached, there is great activity on the part of the whole personality of which the fragment is a part. The coming resolution of the drama brings subconscious backflashes from other lives as well.

You are being of strong practical help now, though it may not appear so, by refusing to accept at this point the role that your mother wants you to take. I am not saying of course that you should not be as kind and considerate as possible, but that you not try to take your father's place at your mother's demands.

She would feel quite trapped if you tried to do so, and in a rage, for you would have betrayed her. If you rose to take his place, then she would be driven to do her battle over. Do you see?

("*Yes.*")

This refusal also in many ways represents your own salvation, or the release at least of several important problems at this point. Any weakness on your part would signal to you the loss of inner independence, the loss of a battle that you had thought over years ago.

It could have been a trap, you see. Psychologically speaking, and in these terms only, on certain levels the son desires to replace the father. When the father is vigorous the son is fearful of retaliation. If the son does not understand himself, then when fear of retaliation is removed, particularly if the mother beckons, then a trap is set.

You have literally turned over your emotional affiliation now to Ruburt, so you are in this respect free.

Still however out of pity, the trap is still a probable one. It is a probable one simply because it does exist. For your mother it would represent nevertheless a betrayal on your part, for she would immediately realize that she had failed in the bitterest of terms, and to her the most ignoble of terms. This applying to her specifically, for she would win you when she was an old woman.

The betrayal to her would be bitter. *(One minute pause.)* She realizes that Ruburt makes you an excellent wife. She hates her and loves her for this reason. In one way, when you were born, she was quite content that your father vanish. She did not want children, yet giving birth gave her a sense of power, the only sense of power she had experienced in this existence, and so she used this power as a weapon when she felt a weapon was needed.

The overall personality was not so detached as uncommitted. There has on the other hand been a strong commitment to life on the fragment's part.

You may take a break or end the session as your prefer.

("*We'll take a break.*"

(10:00. It had been a long delivery and Jane came out of trance slowly. She still felt its effects fifteen minutes later. She had used many pauses. Resume at 10:20.)

Now. First of all, in the line concerning your emotions, the meaning is this; that you turned the basic emotional feelings from the mother, as is necessary, transferring them to your wife successfully.

If this is not done then the desire to replace the father is a strong inner problem. It exists for <u>you</u>, now, <u>not</u> on your part because of the successful transference, but on the part of your mother. The three sons, incidentally, agreed as to their parents, and with full inner knowledge of the circumstances that would be involved. This is also true in Ruburt's case, and in all cases.

Those who make errors withdraw early, as infants. *(Long pause.)*

Now. We cannot cover all of this in one evening. Your brother Dick has been connected with your mother in the past, as you know. He and she are part of the same entity. His characteristics are a part of those of that entity. He is strongly a part of her, and was born from her for that reason.

In <u>some</u> respects he is a slightly future version of your mother, already having gained from her experiences. He is a larger dimension of her, a different expression, a more adequate and productive one. Now there are twins in time as you experience it. Twins also appears in different times. Do you see?

("Yes.")

As a change of environment affects twins, Twin A becoming something different again through a given environment from Twin B in another environment, so twins born in different times also develop different portions of a basic personality pattern. This is the case here.

This son is basically a psychological twin of the mother, but developing a more spacious personality, and a more giving nature. This one has progressed so well, with indeed little experience comparatively, that he most probably will become an entity of his own eventually.

I have somewhat explained your entity status.

Now give us a moment. *(Pause at 10:33.)*

Ruburt has not worked on the dream book since Fell's letter. No coincidence. The poetry <u>is</u> an excellent idea, and is serving many purposes. Work on the dream book should now be added daily however, and the suggestions read before the work is begun each day.

The difficulty at the drinking establishment was due mainly to the encounter with the college girl, who is connected with the nursery school. Ruburt was caught unaware. Nursery school was connected in his mind with physical discomfort for the reasons earlier stated.

The girl's remark of surprise: "I didn't expect to see <u>you</u> here," was taken by the overly conscientious self as just rebuke. He was in excellent condition before the encounter.

("Why are his arms bent?")

I did not hear you.

("Why are his arms bent?" I thought I had spoken as loudly as usual in asking the question the first time.)

Give us a moment here. The arms should now begin to release. They have been connected with a feeling of helplessness, mainly <u>centered</u> around his feeling that he was not contributing financially what he should. This month he felt fairly satisfied, finally.

Had he been working on the dream book also there would have been some noticeable improvement by now, because of the financial conditions there also. He is finding himself more capable than he had believed also in dealing with your parents' situation. This will add to his confidence in himself, and contribute to an improvement in the arms also.

Again, the peanut oil. And give us a moment again. *(Pause.)*

Strength in the arms and hands has improved considerably over the months. Relaxation again is extremely important. Relaxation of the muscles will help release the arms simply because of the initial mental relaxation and affirmation required before physical relaxation is acquired.

There is also some self-protective device here still operating. The attempt to shield himself, you see, a lack of confidence. *(Jane made a self-hugging gesture.)* He has made increasing gains. They have occurred over periods of time however. *(Long pause.)*

If he works on his dream book daily now, for at least two hours, this plus the benefit from his classes should give noticeable improvement. Remind him to relax when you notice his body is tense, for often he does not recognize the tenseness.

It becomes conscious when you point it out. He will learn to recognize the sensation and try to avoid it. For a week use the peanut oil each morning.

("Just on the arms?")

Mainly on the arms, and neck-shoulder area. Also on any other portions if they give difficulty. It can be applied also when he is working on his dream book.

If you have no further questions we can end the session, or if you prefer continue it after a break as you like.

("I have just one question: what do you think of the painting of the leaf I just finished?" In tempera.)

There is a spontaneity there that you allowed yourself, and it is significant.

("I found myself thinking it wasn't too good a painting.")

It is a good painting. There is simply a reason why you are not satisfied.

("I thought there would be, yes.")

Give us a moment. *(Pause.)* Also, do not forget your sketching work. This allows for both spontaneity and discipline.

You are close to releasing yourself in a particular way through your painting, through your work, and you will find this way intuitively. By close here, I mean very close. It is this very nearness that made you dissatisfied with what you had just finished, an inner comparison of this with work you will do in the very (underlined) near future; and no reflection on the leaf painting, except by future contrasts. Some hint of the new appeared in it.

("I thought that something like that had happened.")

I believe that by February, you will be involved in a new concept in your work, and engaged in a new series of paintings, that will carry you creatively through winter, spring, and perhaps a portion of the summer.

You may then take a break or end as you prefer.

("We'll end it then.")

My heartiest regards to you both. A fond good evening.

("Good night, Seth." 11:02.)

SESSION 377 (DELETED)
NOVEMBER 6, 1967 9 PM MONDAY

(This session is deleted from the record.

(Sunday afternoon, November 5, I devoted to a long pendulum session, concerning my attitudes as related to Jane's symptoms; it was most beneficial and rewarding, and we were anxious to have Seth's comments on it this evening.

(Complete notes made during the pendulum session are on file. This afternoon, incidentally, Jane and I spent in Sayre, visiting my father in the hospital, eating supper with mother, etc.

(Last Thursday, November 2, Jane received her first royalty payment from Frederick Fell for her ESP book—a substantial sum, over $250, much more than we expected.

(Jane's pace was on the slow side this evening; her voice however was good, her eyes open often.)

Good evening.

("Good evening, Seth.")

Now give us a moment. *(Pause, hand to eyes.)*

You see, now, more clearly than you have, that your problems are the results of unfortunate personal reactions and interactions, that two are involved here rather than one.

You must realize however that in your interactions you and Ruburt work together in <u>some</u> areas very effectively. You will be pinpointing those areas where negative interactions are involved.

Now. You did indeed see your father *(as my pendulum told me)* not as a man who failed in several important areas, but as a failure in all areas: as a husband, breadwinner, father. *(Pause.)* You identified with him however out of fear of your mother's emotionalism. You did not dare identify with her.

She always had strong sexual desires. She considered these as beneath her, and wrong. She was unable to relate to her husband in this way. You were aware of her sexual energy however. It was a current between you, for she did not recognize her feelings toward you when you were a child, as sexual. Therefore she permitted herself to show more affection toward you than she did toward her husband.

You identified with your father because he seemed free, in that she did not direct actively these strong affections toward him. To be like him then represented safety, for she did not like failures.

She was an activist, so you tried to become the opposite. Now then: on the one hand you attempted to be virile by identifying with your father, yet he was also to you the symbol of a failure. To be a failure therefore was virile *(as my pendulum told me)*.

Any push toward success became a threat to your virility; a push from a woman became to you a double threat to your virility. You felt as if she threatened to castrate you. Ruburt has been aware of this. This is one of the main reasons that he suffers from strong feelings of disloyalty whenever he allows himself to wish that you were more successful in your work, artistically or financially.

He fears that you will interpret this as a threat of castration. Because of his own background you knew that he would not push you in this respect. He has an innate talent for making money, that has not been developed nor used for these reasons; and all suggestions made by him to you have been regarded by you as threats, and he felt that the suggestions were mistakes on his part. *(One minute please.)*

I have told you that you can change the past. In doing so you change the self, by choosing from past experience those elements to which you shall and shall not react. This you can do. *(Long pause.)*

I have several points along these lines to discuss with you this evening.

There is one point however, an important side issue, that I want to mention first. It is this: your ideas of the daily amount of time being limited—these ideas are limiting you and your work far more than time is. This attitude automatically suggests that progression in your work takes a certain amount of time, and limits your intuitional insights, confining them to your idea of time.

You can, in other words, intuitively progress within an hour a year's work, if you allow it. I am not saying here that you should not set aside specific hours for yourself. I am saying be cautious, for while certain periods of time seem necessary within your system for the development of your work, that the ideas of limited time on a daily or weekly basis can slow down the intuitional qualities of your work and growth.

You deal then with a single-line type of within-physical-time development, and tend to ignore the value fulfillment kind of development which is entirely independent of a time structure. To be fearful for time is to neglect its full use.

You may take your break and we shall continue. The last on time is connected, incidentally, with what we have been speaking of, for it can lead to an insistence upon outer realities, and result in a lack of inner intuitional development, which alone is the fountainhead of true art.

(9:27. Jane's pace was rather slow throughout, with some long pauses. Resume at 9:47.)

Now. There are specific steps you can both take, and we will get to these.

The book Ruburt is reading *(Psycho-Cybernetics by Maxwell Maltz)* offers a good approach. Following those directions I will give you specifics.

Here are some general points, but I will fill these in and add to them at our next session.

(Long pause.) Ruburt has been adding to the strength of the negative influences of his past. The more he reacts to them the more thoroughly he convinces himself of their strength. His background was unfortunate. It was not as unfortunate as he supposes. Many of his most redeeming qualities and characteristics were formed by it.

His vitality was formed in that environment. The passive qualities in him would have been far more predominant, overly so, but for the adversity he faced. His mother's colorful, emphatic and mystical characteristics gave him incentive, and generated mental and psychic activity. *(Long pause.)*

She was highly imaginative. At times she did not know fantasy from reality. Ruburt was literal-minded in many respects. He took her hysterical and desperate threats literally, when many children would not have done so. The background of Ruburt's personality was unfortunate, and fortunate.

("His personality chose this background, didn't it?")

The overall self chose the background. Now. Ruburt has <u>always</u> been primarily driven by a desire to write successfully. His mother encouraged the writing. At the same time he felt guilty that he was free and the mother was not, and he blamed himself to some degree for her situation. The mother did blame the child in this respect.

The mother wanted success for the child, and yet Ruburt felt *(pause)* that success would also be resented by the mother, that the mother would be jealous of it. The mother wanted success for the daughter so that the daughter could share the fruits of the success and provide for her. While Ruburt had no money there was no fear of this.

Financial success was put off, you see. It was not to be denied but put off. *(Pause.)* He did not want to share it with his mother, for to Ruburt this meant having his mother live with him.

Now these feelings served to put success off. They were not strong enough to deny it entirely, and he was working through them, although this took considerable energy.

These hidden feelings however made him susceptible to your own fears. He must indeed, completely, rid himself of his strong resentments at his mother. The above paragraphs should help him. He cannot resent the environment nor his parent, since he chose both. *(Long pause.)*

Now. You can change the past, and in doing so change the present and the future. You can change the present, and in doing so change the past and the future. You can change the future, and in doing so change the present and the past.

The exercises in the book Ruburt is reading are excellent. With our added instruction they shall be even better. You will change yourself in the future by vital imagining today. You will put high expectations to work at once in this manner, and project a new image into tomorrow.

This projected image will of itself already alter the past and the present. You will change the past, your reaction to it, by vividly imagining happy hours that you refused to focus upon. These pursuits in the present will automatically change the nature of the present.

A complete reversal of attitude can take place, and <u>will</u> if you persist. I am giving you a rather general outline here, and I will fill it in.

There is also much yet to be said concerning why you and Ruburt chose your particular parents and early environments. Being an artist and being successful were opposites for your inner self. You could not therefore have both. *(Pause.)*

I should make this more clear: being a <u>fine</u> artist and a success were opposites.

We will fill all of this in for you. If some of it seems disconnected it is simply because I want to outline the main areas to be developed. Ruburt saw himself as a writer, and not as a psychic. He knew intuitively that he <u>was</u> a psychic. He was also highly anxious to succeed, and knew that he was not doing so.

The psychic abilities appeared precisely when he needed an extra drive toward success, and a way toward success that would not be instantly recognized as such.

His own past fears of success were finally set aside with the acceptance of the ESP book. Not so much set aside as driven back. He saw instantly that you resented the publication of the book, as he had seen earlier that you resented the publication of *The Rebellers*. You resented <u>that</u> book very much.

("The Rebellers?")

(Jane nodded yes. Pause, eyes closed. She held a hand up.) He was frightened then at your reaction. It was this fright that prevented him from finishing all of those projects he began, or from selling them.

You both became involved in the psychic work. He felt therefore that you would feel his success was yours also. He thought at that time that you were simply jealous of him. Your reaction to the ESP book quite literally terrified him. He then realized that you did not want either of you to be successful.

("Was any of this conscious on his part?")

Some was, but when it became conscious he became panic-stricken. His drive toward success had been quickened by its taste, however. He wanted more. He felt hampered by you. At the same time he felt the need to contribute financially, and he felt that you were tying his hands by forcing him to make money in ways in which he was not particularly equipped to do so, while forbidding him to be a success with books.

The dream book was an attempt to try again, a desperate attempt for independence on his part to succeed in spite of the negative influences. *(Pause.)* He felt that you rejected it as a whole, and completely. His impatience and panic did impede his judgment, causing him to send it out too early, and for this he blamed you.

The book became a sore point, and the focus in his work of the inner problem, a symbol. Finally he had to force himself to work on it, and at times he could not work on it. There was an inner refusal to make concessions. You both maintained your positions, and would not communicate.

His symptoms represented his problem. He felt literally paralyzed, and unable to move. Now he can move, but he still cannot run, you see. He moves much better. He is partially released but far from fully.

At the crisis point you were both alienated. He was completely bewildered. He was doing what he felt you wanted him to do, yet the results displeased you, and he felt you found him physically repulsive. In desperation you both began to question inner attitudes, and <u>you</u> then broke the ice with a pendulum session. *(See the 350th Session.)*

The affair can be cleared completely, and free you both and your abilities. Again, in many areas, you work together very well, and this inner closeness which does aid your work and make the psychic work possible, is the same closeness you see that opened you to these other interactions.

You may take a break or end the session as you prefer.

("We'll take a break."

(10:42. Jane was farther under this time, she said, kept there rather cleverly by Seth. She wanted to resist the material about her mother, at first, but then went along with it. Resume at 10:50.)

Subjectively, when you were jealous *(see the 350th Session)* you were actively jealous of Ruburt for being successful, and wished to strike out in retaliation. When you feel envious now, you envy his success, but you are not jealous of him as a person.

(Here Seth clears up a point in Sunday's pendulum session, in which the pendulum told me I was not jealous of Jane, but envious of her success. I wanted to be sure I wasn't confused on the jealousy-envy terminology; I also wondered if there was actually any difference.)

It is the success you envy.

The father identification can be tackled. Vivid imagining of yourself as a success will automatically weaken it. It will also be weakened with the emotional understanding that you are an individual, identified with no other.

The uniqueness of your art will also weaken it, for your art could not ever be produced by your father. Your art is indeed an excellent defense, used in this manner, for it is an anthem of individuality, and a statement of uniqueness.

Now my dear friend—*(staring at me, Jane tapped with her foot on the coffee table between us)* your hats, your caps... Do you see any connection?

("With my father?")

Indeed.

("Well, I guess I do. He wears a hat, and I stick to caps...There must be something here I'm missing, though.")

He has worn caps much like the one you wear, and for many years they hung in the back porchway. This is an unconscious item of identification that you have donned.

(I now remembered father's caps, once Seth mentioned them. But I felt somewhat in a dilemma, since father also wears regular hats.)

Now let me see. *(Pause.)* Both of you should read the book Ruburt purchased, carefully, and follow most of its instructions. *(Psycho-Cybernetics).* I will give you specific material to use along with the book, and will add my own explanations.

Another note: Ruburt's letters, business letters. He allowed you to take spontaneity and friendliness from them. *(Pause.)*

All of this can be cleared, and no blame is to be attached to anyone. This would only compound the problem, and indeed there is no blame. There was simply ignorance.

You have both avoided many problems that could have arisen, because in those areas you were not ignorant. Ignorance implies a refusal to see, or rather an inability to see at a given time, for various reasons. Never underestimate what you have, for you have much. I shall enlarge on some of these topics at our next session.

Now all of this affected our sessions. My ability to help is determined by many issues. Ruburt's overall condition has to some extent impeded us, *(pause)* and because of a distrust of his own abilities he will sometimes doubt my legitimacy. Such doubts then impeding his progress and limiting what help I have to offer. *(Pause.)*

His distrust of his abilities was partially a result of the basic conflict, and if he could not trust himself how could he trust me when I spoke <u>through</u> him?

You may again end the session or take a break as you prefer.

("We'll end it now.")

My heartiest wishes to you both, and my best wishes for your success.

("Thank you. Good night Seth.")

(11:07. Jane said she was far out again, and it took her a few moments to come out of trance. Her pace had been faster.)

SESSION 378 (DELETED)
NOVEMBER 8, 1967 9:39 PM WEDNESDAY

(This session is deleted from the record.

(Today while relaxing, Jane received two impressions, both somewhat worrisome, that we hoped Seth would cover tonight.

(Last night Jane woke me up shouting in pain, because of a cramp in her back, momentarily. We wanted Seth to discuss this also.

SESSION 378

(It will be recalled that I had my excellent pendulum session last Sunday, November 5, pinpointing the part I played in Jane's symptoms. Using the pendulum each day since then, I have been surprised to note a rapid change in some inner attitudes. I wanted to know if these changes, from negative to positive, were legitimate, and possible in such a short time.

(Jane began speaking in trance this evening at a slower rate that usual.)
Good evening.
("Good evening, Seth.")

Now. There is a point when you can take advantage of certain information, understand and perceive it. You always have the information but you must grow up to it, so to speak.

You are both at such a point now. You had both gone astray, and you are making necessary corrections. A complete overhaul was necessary of your attitudes, emotions and goals.

The book I recommended will be of great benefit *(Psycho-Cybernetics)*. However, it would not have been nearly as helpful earlier for you would have accepted it in a surface manner.

Much of the inner meaning would not have registered. You would have thought it a surface book, because you would not have understood clearly the premises beneath. This means obviously that you must be at a particular stage of development before the author's suggested techniques will be of any great benefit.

At your point of development now they will be extremely helpful, and do not be deceived at their seeming simplicity. This also means of course that the author does not realize much that must go on underneath <u>before</u> his suggested techniques <u>will</u> work.

Ruburt is particularly now ready and able to start anew, and he has already done so. It should be realized however that this starting anew is also a relative term, dependent upon other beneficial initiations that have been going on for several months, and that make this final—in this phase—start possible. *(One minute pause.)*

The steps given in the book for activating the aid of the inner self are excellent. Make certain that your idea of success is not merely financial, or concerned overly with the acquisition of the material objects that you do not now have.

It may seem to you *(Jane pointed to me)* that this would not be the case, and that the caution is unnecessary. A part of you, however, does strongly resent the material benefits that you did derive from your early commercial work. There is a bitterness picked up from your family, working here. It is so well hidden that it has gone almost unrecognized. This is apart from your conflicting ideas concerning success, but colors them.

At times it masquerades as a distaste for material possessions, but often it is simply also resentment. In secret parts of yourself this does cause some considerable bitterness that works to your disadvantage. *(Long pause.)* You have been afraid of success for the reasons stated, yet resentful that you did not have the material acquisitions that go with it. *(Pause.)*

This resulted in an active resentment against such symbols, which actually prevented you from acquiring them. Although at times you would consciously want them, the hidden bitterness intruded. You know, I am sure, that if you are successful as a person and as an artist, then financial success will follow.

I am trying to tell you that you have concentrated as strongly <u>at times</u> in a negative manner on success symbols *(pause)*, as others might in a positive manner to acquire them. In either case the focus upon success symbols was there. I do not believe you were aware of this. Instead of course the concentration should be upon fulfilling your abilities, all of them, and financial success will come.

Indeed, you should expect it. You were almost putting the cart before the horse, but in a negative manner. The outflow of energy, the freeing of energy, into your work, automatically is determined by a general outflow of energy through all facets of your personality, that will automatically bring many different kinds of benefits, including financial ones.

Again, the particular methods given in the book are excellent, as applied processes to release your abilities. You will both literally be astonished at the changes for the better in your situations, if you follow the book's instructions, with the variations and suggestions given by me. Once more, those methods would not have worked for you in the past.

Much work has been done, you see. The author does not realize how much is necessary before his methods will have the effect that he expects. You have been able to reason with your subconscious, of late, and get through to it, because with the pendulum and through our sessions we have been able to unscramble the uncertain state in which it found itself. This is the point missed by the author.

You have made strides since Sunday. The communication system has been cleared sufficiently. The author you see does not completely understand the work that must be done in this respect before his methods will have <u>great</u> value. We have cleared the communication channels both privately in your individual cases, and your joint communication systems as you operate together.

In any relationship that must be done.

Now. Ruburt was simply kicking up a fuss last night *(with Jane's back cramps)*. Physically, he had begun to use muscles in a more normal manner, and to activate some muscles that he had hardly used for some time.

On a physical level only, there were then some strains and tensions, fairly normal under the circumstances. On deeper levels however there was conflict, and normal enough rebellion considering the situation. *(Pause.)* The part of the self who considered the symptoms necessary, you see, has realized they are no longer necessary, but still some habit persists.

An unfortunate grouping of habits operating through the body are breaking up. Originally they had a purpose. It now no longer exists, but they still resent the breaking up; and Ruburt's yells, quite involuntary, represented in fact the death throes of the symptoms, and the part of the self who had accepted them as an attempt to solve problems.

It was a rather frightening experience, but without it or without something very much like it, complete recovery could not occur.

You may take your break.

(10:22—10:23. Jane said she had a peculiar feeling of sadness at the above information. I then wondered aloud at the apparent suddenness of the breakup of symptoms, just three days after my pendulum session of last Sunday, and two days after the session with Seth on Monday, November 6. This brought Seth back at once.)

You can hardly call this rapid.

That grouping has been disintegrating since the crisis point last winter. The death of that grouping is now a fact. The body must still stabilize itself however, and consolidate its gains.

There are still some lingerings of mourning, for the grouping was indeed vital, and adopted initially to help the personality. The grouping was doomed to failure, in that it could not succeed in helping the personality, you see, but hindered it.

When it realized this, then all nourishment was cut off. Not only did other elements of the personality begin to deny it energy, but it—this grouping—also committed suicide, so to speak, sacrificing itself for the whole personality which it tried to serve.

Now you may take your break.

(10:28. Jane had delivered the above dialogue with her eyes wide open and very dark. She had been farther out, she said. Now she felt "real weird," she said, understanding, sad, yet glad also. The feeling was like the feeling she had experienced last night when she had cried out because of the back cramps, she said.

(10:36.) Now. The death of the old grouping now allows for the birth of

a new grouping, this time a grouping that will effectively deal with the problems at hand, and that will allow the personality to develop and expand. The instructions in the book will help guide the formation of this new grouping.

Give us a moment. *(Pause, long.)* The telegram impression is legitimate. The telegram may or may not be received by you, but having to do with family, yours or Ruburt's, I am not sure. Or it will be received by one of your family or Ruburt's. *(Pause.)*

The uterus *(pause)* impression had to do with Vivian *(Crowder)* I believe *(pause)*, and Ruburt picked it up from your mother, who is not consciously aware of the knowledge. *(Pause.)* A harmless cyst. Perhaps six months involved here. It's importance simply being the result of a previous operation. No danger involved.

(The above are the two impressions Jane received while relaxing today.)

Ruburt is doing well with the exercises *(in Psycho-Cybernetics)* and will improve. You may now as you like end the session or ask any questions as you prefer.

("In the light of the recent information, do you want to say something about the role of the conscientious self?")

What we have said concerning this is still legitimate, as of the time we gave the information.

Communication has improved, and this portion of the personality has changed the direction it followed previously, and is highly active now in initiating this new program. The sense of direction pleases it, and it takes off with all the energy of a convert. *(Smile; much amused.)*

This is all to the good. It is relinquishing its former rigidity. It approves of this new book because God is taken into consideration, and yet it is not cultist in its terms.

(In the terms of the overly conscientious self, Seth said in answer to my question.)

It is aiding in this new impetus, and will find itself rejuvenated. It always releases the spontaneous self under such conditions, and experiences a refreshing new spiritual birth itself. *(Pause.)*

Within a very short time now the two will be joining full energy, with fresh purpose. The body experiences more and more release. The pressure is turning swiftly off. Energy is being released for constructive action.

This will automatically build up Ruburt's resources and inner psychic defenses against negative influences. We will have more to say concerning your *(meaning me)* symptoms at our next session, and offer specific suggestions; the exercises and the book should now help you rid yourself of these.

("I now expect them to disappear.")

If you have no more questions we will end, though I am willing to continue if you wish.

("Did Jane know about the death of Otto Binder's daughter?")

She did know, and so did you. Ruburt will not therefore experience another episode like last night's. My heartiest wishes then *(smile)* for your joint success.

("Good night, Seth."

(10:54. Jane was fairly well dissociated, etc. We learned about the death of Otto's daughter Mary, on a conscious level, this week when we bought a recent book by Otto on flying saucers, and read the dedication. The book was published in March 1967. In the "old days" I drew many a comic-book story by Otto.)

SESSION 379 (DELETED)
NOVEMBER 13, 1967 9:05 PM MONDAY

(This session is deleted from the record.
(Jane began speaking in trance in a voice a good bit stronger than usual.)
Good evening.

("Good evening, Seth.")

Now. With Ruburt we should work toward the development of contrasts —deep relaxation and fast <u>heating</u> motions. Motions that induce a feeling of warmth.

These need not be necessarily violent motions, but they will induce a feeling of freedom and spontaneity, and increase blood circulation. He should in his exercises imagine strenuous exercise, running very fast for example, until in his mind's eye his muscles are fully relaxed.

Running until he feels himself out of breath, or dancing to the same degree. The system should be fully activated, you see, and flushed out through such activities. Now. Strenuous exercise, not necessarily overdone you understand, but strenuous exercise physically and imagined, will in itself lead to the kind of deep relaxation that he also must learn now to achieve, and which is needed by the system.

He is indeed too careful of his motions out of habit and fear of the consequences. Physical work or activity, <u>almost</u> indeed to the point of exhaustion, will be good for him, for the muscles will react with deep spontaneous relaxation.

His imagined exploits should definitely include such vigorous pursuits with the accompanying relaxation. His physical day should include as much of this as possible. The rope jumping is a good idea from this standpoint. So is fast dancing and most physical activities. Running would be excellent.

He can do more now physically than he realizes, you see. He should try jumping rope in his mind, and then perform physically. Running as quickly as he can up and down your staircases is another suggestion. I do not mean that he overdo, but he is doing none of these things.

Let him use his arms and hands more. He has thought of returning to his habit of sitting on the floor. Let him begin doing so. The attempt and the willingness will bring results; and let him picture himself in these activities.

I suggest the exercising images be executed in the time now given to the relaxation exercises, and replacing those in the book *(Psycho-Cybernetics)*. Let him imagine himself performing varied vigorous activities until he is nearly exhausted, and then imagine the ensuing deep relaxation.

He was right. There was too much passivity involved. This applies to him only. Now give us a moment. *(Pause.)*

Your own symptoms have been caused also by an inner indecision, a refusal to come to terms with yourself and your work.

There was also an implied threat involved. You were trying to force yourself and yet punish yourself. Your mother was in the background here. You were trying to punish yourself for not making more money as an artist, since you still felt her old demands.

At the same time you threatened yourself with the possibility of complete failure as an artist, almost in retaliation. *(Pause, one of many through here.)* You would not (underlined) be a full time commercial artist, regardless of any old demands, though you felt still somewhat guilty at your refusal.

The tremor represented guilt here, but also a threat, for you thought: before I will do this full time for money, my hand would fail. The tremor served two purposes in this respect. Your mother, incidentally, has largely given up focusing upon your artistic career in any way. She now simply wishes, as Ruburt knows, that you had taken up another profession. *(And as I know now.)*

She does not understand your goals. To her they are nongoals, for money is the basic one to her, the magic charm which in her mind makes all other benefits or comforts possible. She no longer considers your art either as a potential ally, as she did in earlier years, nor even as a threat as she did in later years.

It is simply a portion of you that she does not understand. To her it is a weapon that you have to force money from others, and a weapon you will not use. The word weapon is important here, for she believes that money must be forced from some unfriendly source.

On her part, you see, the demand has vanished. Your tremor was to this extent a response to the past.

This does not mean that she does not consider such ideas now and then, but she is not actively concerned with them.

Your exercises following the book should be much concerned with images of spontaneity, exhilaration and freedom. The free flow of intuition. You should make the effort *(smile)* to speak before thinking on occasion. I did not recommend that Ruburt particularly follow this suggested practice.

You may take a break and we shall continue.

(9:36. Jane's voice continued good, eyes open often. There followed a very funny discussion—to me at least—of Jane's propensity to talk at our gatherings of friends, even to the point of ignoring their creature comforts, such as drinks, snacks, etc. Resume at 9:50.)

Now. The exercises in spontaneity on your part will help to improve the hand condition, for you have been tampering here.

As far as possible, take your conscious mind away from the condition. On occasion, imagine both hands in vigorous motion of one kind or another, until they become tired and at complete (underlined) rest. See them motionless and beautifully relaxed. Do not overstress this exercise however.

Within your allotted time schedule try to give yourself more freedom. Again, also speaking before thinking. Do not be afraid of making errors in your paintings, but trust your inner self. This will also help your hand. *(Pause.)*

Your painting technique is excellent. Further important developments here will be intuitive flashes as to how the technique may be used. Trust yourself to plunge fully into large endeavors in your work, and do not be afraid of making errors.

Ruburt's "Be Careful in Nothing" sign *(on our hall door)* has deep implications along these lines. You will do beautiful work, and your technique can be flawless. You know enough now so that you do not need to be overly concerned with it on a conscious level. Now that it is developed let the inner self guide its use, and it will serve you as it was meant to serve your intuitive self.

Now these exercises will also help your intimate lives, particularly on Ruburt's part, with the combination of vigorous motion and corresponding depth of relaxation. This is natural to him—spontaneous exertion and relaxation, and he must again let it return. *(Long pause.)*

Give us a moment. *(Pause.)* Let me emphasize the author's point: state your goals. Do not be overly concerned with the methods by which they will be accomplished however, for the inner self will take care of these methods. Be alert for intuitional signs and ideas however that come to you.

Sometimes they may not appear to be directly concerned with your goals, but underneath there may be connections that you cannot see on a conscious level.

Now and again, do not overemphasize this next exercise, for the condition with the penis is after all but a symptom. Imagine it limp and soft, and then hard and straight, you see. The overall concentrations should not be on ridding yourself of any particular symptom, but on directing yourself properly toward your goals, for this direction and proper focusing will automatically result in the disappearance of symptoms.

While the exercises having to do with symptoms are good, they should not be overly emphasized, for your purpose must be much larger than the disappearance of any symptoms. *(Long pause.)*

You may take a break, and ask me any questions that you have, or you may ask me questions now, or end the session as you prefer.

("We'll take the break." 10:07—10:16.)

Now, Ruburt, follow through on the program, but do not be overly concerned on a conscious level. Give the inner self spontaneity and freedom to work out solutions. Leave your subconscious alone for now. Just for a time, and let it rest.

Your renewed work schedule will automatically refresh it, and it is already gathering more energy and vitality.

You, Joseph, are doing well with your pendulum work, and your attitude is good. *(Pause.)* Let Ruburt follow the program faithfully, yet with a more carefree attitude toward it, with a more relaxed attitude, He should reread the book, yet in his free moments he need not concentrate upon the program. Follow the suggestions and let it rest. Now, did you have questions?

("They deal with symptoms, so maybe we'd better forget them now... When are we going to get started on some more theoretical material?")

I have been dealing with our present material at your request—

("I know it.")

—and because you *(smile)* needed it. At our next session we can have some theoretical material, and I shall add any other personal information that I think necessary. It is a good idea however for you to request such personal information.

("I guess we'll always be doing that.")

I will then close our session. You should also follow the program outlined in the book. If you find it difficult to take a half hour for each exercise, then take what you can, but <u>do</u> each exercise. My heartiest wishes to you both. My congratulations on your progress.

("Good night, Seth." 10:28.)

SESSION 380 (DELETED)
NOVEMBER 15, 1967 9:14 PM WEDNESDAY

(Jane said she felt somewhat tired before the session, and almost decided not to hold one this evening. However, as has happened before, results were excellent even though she didn't seem to be in the mood at 9 PM. This session is deleted from the record.)

Good evening.

("Good evening, Seth.")

Now. You must understand, in our discussions of late, we have been dealing with your current problems, and treating them in those terms for your convenience.

We have been dealing with the condition of the immediate self in its response to environment and situations. This immediate self is not isolated however from other portions of the entire personality. The very fact that you have <u>me</u> here is the result of past experience and development

On the one hand all of your questions have their answers. The inner self knows, but the immediate self does not recognize their answers. The degree of your understanding and development is the result of past endeavors in other lives. The degree represents your practical ability to use inner knowledge to solve problems.

On the one hand, again, you know the answers. On the other hand you must learn to recognize them and apply them. Each succeeding reincarnation finds you in a better position to do so. The inner self must therefore be recognized by all levels of the personality.

The inner self must <u>become</u> the immediate self, you see. This unity then puts you in a position to begin a truly fulfilling existence in other realities after physical death. You are solving many problems therefore now, since this is to be your last reincarnation in physical terms.

You must know enough to speak <u>nearly</u> as an equal with your inner self in order to do this. The process had finally to become conscious in your terms, with the ego highly involved. The intuitive portions of the personality had to have the full cooperation of the intellectual and conscious self at this point in your development and I am speaking of you both here.

The conscious had to appreciate in quite real terms its dependence upon intuitional wisdom. There had to be agreement and unity. The conscious self was not to be left by the wayside, wondering while the intuitional abilities led to fulfillment. The conscious intellectual faculties had to realize what was operating in order that they themselves be fulfilled.

True questioning and true use of the critical faculties will always lead, Ruburt, to intuitional truths, so there is no reason to fear them. Those who do not understand their abilities intellectually must one day be led to question them. The intuitions and the intellect are meant to challenge and develop each other, and intuitional knowledge and intellectual knowledge will ultimately lead to the same answers.

It is only when you do not carry through in either that there appears to be contradiction. An excellent example presents itself in the manner that Ruburt utilizes intellectual and intuitional knowledge in his poetry. This same spirit should be used in approaching our work, and in his general living pattern.

An alternate example is your painting. These are the most fruitful ways for both of you to approach all problems. The same qualities and spirit that you bring to your work should be extended to your life pattern, for they are correct for you both, and you operate at prime efficiency then.

Otherwise you utilize some qualities at the expense of others and do not as quickly attain your goals. As Ruburt thrusts ahead, trusting his ability in his poetry, so he should in his psychic work, and now in vigorous physical activity. The idea of restraint therefore must be banished.

He does indeed often speak without thinking, and when he does he often influences people most. Now he must trust himself to move physically without thinking, and as much as possible to let his body act in a spontaneous way. Do not keep checking. This does not mean he should ignore discomfort particularly, but he should take his conscious mind away from his physical body and let it operate alone.

And I repeat, he should indeed stay away from spiritualistic literature. Not because there is anything basically wrong with it, but because it presents <u>him</u> with a dilemma. He knows intuitively what he knows. Intellectually he will catch up with this. The spiritualistic literature causes a needless conflict between his intellect and intuitions.

The intuitions will clear this up for him if he lets the matter rest, and again trust his inner self. If <u>you</u> trust your inner self, the penis difficulty will vanish.

You may take a break and we shall continue.

(9:42—9:52.)

What you are after is the recognition by the immediate self of the larger inner self of which it is part. This is always the direction of development. Until finally the immediate self and the inner self are one.

This does not occur in the course of usual reincarnations, but it does occur ultimately in all. Christ had such a recognition, for example, and this recognition is merely the beginning of another phase of development.

Problems are methods of learning, set by the inner self. This is a particularly important statement. They should always be faced in this light. Other existences also involve these challenges.

(*Smile.*) I must help <u>you</u>, for you are brothers left behind. You are therefore challenges to me. Your progress is my challenge. Ruburt's condition now is his challenge, for in overcoming it he overcomes limitations of which he was not aware before. Only when they became physical was he acquainted with them.

Looked at in this light, you see, they become methods of learning. Without them there would be little progress. I am not saying that without illness as such there would be little progress but in your system you materialize your strengths as well as your weaknesses, and deal with them.

Ruburt's recovery will be the symbol of a far greater recovery and of inner development that will never fail him. He must now push himself to physical activity, into vigorous action, and in doing so he is expressing the inner decision that he will no longer tamper with intuitional spontaneity. He has learned what happens when he does, and he has <u>unlearned</u> the false and distorted lesson that was put upon him in his early years.

He will have finally learned intellectually and consciously, that he need not fear the spontaneous self, which has always been his strength, for it sustains him. He was made to deeply fear it, and it was a strong, dominant part of his personality. The psychic work made him fear that he had allowed it to go too far.

The ego found poetry acceptable and never challenged it. The psychic work was something else entirely. This, with other problems mentioned earlier, led him to a deep mistrust of the intuitional self. He felt he could not go ahead.

He needed time to get his bearings. He felt psychologically paralyzed to some strong degree, and this was reflected in physical terms. Luckily the intuitional self did not retreat to any large extent. The developments were already fact, and worked to good advantage.

They were held in abeyance however. All of the other reasons given of course also applied, yet the intuitions could not be allowed to operate at the expense of the conscious self. The conscious self had to learn to accept and welcome them, and to unlearn false lessons.

All of this was worked out through the symptoms. There were other ways that could have been chosen. Some easier ones. However there was no more <u>effective</u> way, considering the personality's makeup.

The final stages are unfolding, and now both the conscious and intuitional selves are joining forces, and will bring about the body's release from symptoms entirely.

You may take your break.

(*10:15. Jane's pace had been good, her eyes open often, her manner emphatic. At break she stretched out on the divan, eyes still closed, instead of sitting up as usual. She breathed deeply. It was several minutes before her eyes began to open; she struggled to open them, but gave up finally.*

(*She did not recall the material. I thought it an excellent summary of the problems we have been facing for the past year. Jane began speaking at a slower pace; oddly enough, when she did she sat up again, and after a few paragraphs her eyes were opening as usual. 10:21.*)

The arms will open completely when there is complete acceptance of what I have just now told you, when both portions of the self are completely accepted and embraced. You need have no doubts of this.

I recommended peanut oil, and it has not been used.

Ruburt is entirely over the block with the dream book now. His monthly periods have also straightened out. His chemical and hormonal systems have now normalized themselves.

His body is utilizing in-taken vitamins now. The circulation <u>is</u> slightly poor still, due to the <u>relative</u> (underlined) normal (?) underactivity of the extremities. Exercise will help here.

The program outlined for the 21-day period is an excellent incentive, and serves to give his conscious mind some place to focus, so that the inner self can complete the healing process.

All activities are good for him, mental and physical. His classes stir him up, you see. It was fear that slowed him down. Faith in his abilities and in himself as a part of All That Is, will now set him in motion. He picked up restraints from you because he was open to the idea of restraint so strongly.

Before, he used his intuitional abilities but always intellectually mistrusted them to some degree. Now he will trust them consciously and intellectually, and this development had to occur for his fulfillment now. It was a prerequisite for other developments and work that will come.

You always recognized and envied his spontaneous nature, without realizing consciously that it operated despite his intellectual disapproval of it. Through his difficulty you are saved considerable problems, for through his experience you understand the dangerous inhibiting nature of overrestraint. It is because his spontaneous self is so strong that the conscious self had to learn to cooperate, if the personality was to achieve full stature.

I bid you good evening.
("Good night, Seth.")
(10:38. Jane was again very well dissociated, and a long time coming out of trance. Her pace was quite slow last delivery. Her eyes opened very slowly, and she went to bed when she finally did get up.

(Her trance was as deep as any she has had, she said later. It seemed obvious that Seth used this extreme in order to get the material through tonight without distortion. I thought it an excellent summary of problems we seem to be surmounting.)

SESSION 382 (DELETED)
NOVEMBER 27, 1967 9:15 PM MONDAY

(This session is deleted from the record. Jane began speaking in trance while sitting on the divan. Eyes open often, voice average.)

Good evening.
("Good evening, Seth.")

Now. The events of Friday evening have literally changed the lives of those present, yourselves included.

The others present will always remember what happened here, and my explanation was a necessity if the affair was to be successfully concluded.

(I spent quite a few hours over the weekend putting the broken table together.)

You are both learning new methods and approaches, whether you realize this or not. You are learning to utilize energy in new directions. The affair that evening will affect others who were not in the room. Limited concepts of the nature of reality have already been broadened in those present, in some of their descendants, and in others to whom they will speak.

The event has ripples, you see; and yet though in your terms the event is over, it is not over, merely the first movement has begun. The energy used that evening has not begun to complete itself. *(Pause.)* AA *(the personality inhabiting the table)* is also learning. You will discover in practical terms how you move and affect physical matter before we are finished, and discover quite practically that you create it.

The nature and focus of your energy as you learn will be important in other areas. You will be able to help apparitions appear, for example, on occasion. *(Jane stretched out on the divan.)* You will have sufficient control over energy to make very successful projections. You will have more direct evidence for the survival of the human personality.

I will help you in certain areas. Others will help you in other areas. The energy generated continues to generate more energy, and more will be available for you both to use. The spontaneity was excellent, and Ruburt has learned to give his spontaneous self more freedom in our work.

Your recommendation to him earlier was excellent, having to do with his exercises, and the book. *(Psycho-Cybernetics.)*

The work with the table will continue and develop into other areas. It is a necessary preliminary, where the effects are definitely seen in the material universe. You will have no difficulty in finding tables to work with.

(We are concerned about replacing the twice-shattered table used so far in the experiments. It will be recalled it is borrowed from Ruth Klebert, one of Jane's ESP students. Although repaired, we feel it is too fragile to withstand any great amount of banging around.)

Ruburt and you can practice by touching various objects, getting the feel of them, so that you can recognize their psychic makeup, and feel it as strongly as you feel the physical composition. This is only one of the surprises in store for our friend the Jesuit, incidentally. *(Bill Gallagher.)*

The energy that showed itself the other evening appeared in peaks of activity, rushes in like waves, and is always present. You were tired the following evening, so that the energy seemed withdrawn and used up.

(Pat Norelli, Claire Crittenden, and Carl Watkins ate supper with Jane and me the next night, Saturday, Nov. 25. The supper, spaghetti, was a heavy one, but all of us felt a lassitude other than that possibly caused by a heavy meal. We speculated about the lack of energy for earlier in the week we had planned to go dancing Saturday night .

(Later in the night the five of us stood around the heavy library table in my studio. We have wanted to try moving this table for some time. We felt vibrations in the table at times as we kept trying, but no other movements were obtained.)

You learn to take advantage of the crests. Psychically you are still in that ebb, but the energy is there. Do you understand?

("Yes."

(Jane sat up as she spoke.) Ruburt was able to direct and use a strong amount of this energy that evening, and he was also aided by your participation. A A originally needed the emotional contact with Ruburt's student *(Venice McCullough)* in order to activate within your system.

He has learned however to operate without that crutch, and has set up a different kind of bridge with Ruburt. Now. Some personalities, survival personalities, because of their personal characteristics, are more able to directly manipulate physical matter than others, more temperamentally suited to it, and consider it in itself a challenging endeavor.

To move an object in one universe, in one field of reality, from another field of reality, is hardly child's play. Such personalities must learn at their end, and this learning is often accomplished along with corresponding learning on the part of a developing medium. This is what you have here.

I am the mentor in all of this, pointing out the implications and the lessons to be gained. <u>As a rule</u>, (underlined) I leave these practical lessons to others, for the mental considerations have always intrigued me more. On occasion I will assist you, but I will assist you far more through our sessions. And by carrying through in other aspects of your education.

Ruburt's clairvoyant abilities need farther development, and I will help here, for instance. Much of your own energy has been used in the situation involving yourself and Ruburt and your joint problems. His energy is now, incidentally, normal— that is, his <u>energy</u> is at the point where it was, but now its emergence will not be blocked as it was at that point, just before his symptoms.

It is unblocked, and will grow. To some extent you have been waiting to see how his condition would develop, and you will soon feel some release and emergence of energy on your part. Some did come, and you used it well Friday evening.

Your own psychic development came to some <u>comparative</u> (underlined) standstill, as did Ruburt's, for a while during the darkest periods last winter. You shut your own down, partially feeling guilty at your part in Ruburt's dilemma. His slowed down simply out of fear. Now both of you will move.

Are your hands tired?

("No." 9:45.)

Ruburt's abilities began to expand again when he realized he <u>would</u> regain his health in the late spring. *(Pause.)* The book *(Psycho-Cybernetics)* will do you every bit as much good as it will do Ruburt, and I recommend it heartily, with some variations, as a basis upon which to build the rest of your days.

Its suggestions will give you a good framework within which to grow and develop, and a yardstick so that your progress is always kept before your mind's eye.

(Smile.) I will write such a book for Ruburt, but this is for your future. It will be a famous book, and it will help many.

("Very good.")

You may take your break, and we shall continue.

(9:47. Jane reported that she was pretty well dissociated, but recalled the last few sentences with a smile. I suggested some titles for the book: "Sethenetics," "Sethgestions," etc. Added later: Seth Speaks, in 1972. Resume at 9:55.)

Now. Here is something else, and you almost hit upon it a moment earlier.

Ruburt could have solved his problems, as we have said, without such severe symptoms. He is returning to health. Neither of you need have any doubts here.

Now listen. Because of his background with his mother he had built up in defense a strong dislike, not merely for illness, for <u>this</u> *(Jane, eyes open wide, pointed at me for emphasis)*, is beneficial, but a strong dislike *(pause)* that amounted <u>almost</u> (underlined) to hatred, for <u>anyone</u> who was sick, particularly crippled in any way, or hampered in motion.

He was terrified of anyone in such a condition, and he could not allow himself to be compassionate out of fear. I did not give you this material earlier; quite truthfully, I believe you would have misinterpreted it.

Earlier, he had no understanding nor feeling for the weaknesses of others. He would never imagine himself in their place. Do not mistake me. It is not good to imagine yourself ill, but it is not good to condemn the <u>person</u> who is ill, for that reason.

He was in no position to help others, for he hated their vulnerability. For his own development therefore he needed to face this on his own and conquer it. Otherwise he would never be able to look upon the sick with a compassionate or understanding eye.

Again, he was too terrified. He will completely recover, and then his story will have meaning. You both knew this. You had your own time of it, partially for the same reason, but he had to face the depths of his own terror, and rise and walk away from it, if he were ever to help others do the same.

There was no easy way therefore, really, though easier ways were available. Had he chosen them, there would have been other problems to face in their stead that would have greatly hampered both his development and your own.

Now, do you have questions, or do you want me to end the session?

(Pause.) The material just given also helps to explain, you see, the dark emotional depths he traveled, for he followed this very far, spiritually to the depths, and then began his way out. I was a light, but I did not want to help him too much or I would have hampered him. Do you see?

("Yes.")

It was difficult for me then also, even though I knew that he would indeed recover.

Now. There is no distortion here, Joseph. The recovery is secure, the hang-ons simply the result and indication of the severe storm that has been successfully vanquished. The debris left that is still being cleared away, and cleared away it shall be.

He breathes a sigh of relief, knowing it is indeed over, simply waiting now for the new growth to come.

You may ask questions or end the session as you prefer.

("What do you think of my painting now?")

You are coming along well, still in a transitory stage that is necessary. The book *(Psycho-Cybernetics)* will help you as an artist. I will help you more in the near future, when we devote several weeks to the subject. I am also getting advice before I hold these sessions, from someone who is much more of an artist than me.

("A survival personality?")

Indeed.

(As far as I can recall, this is the first time Seth has stated such an approach to a problem, explicitly; although in the past he has referred to various subjects by saying he was not well informed about them.)

Your development as an artist however, given your particular abilities and personality, was not possible in your early years. The qualities for which you shall become known will be somewhat the result of your psychic development also. This much I do know.

You were not spontaneous enough as a personality to allow fulfillment of your abilities at an earlier age. Overall this is beneficial, since you were saving your power until you were ready to contain and express it. Earlier it would have frightened you.

Ruburt aided you by helping to develop your spontaneity. Now you repay him by showing him how to rediscover his own. The question of medium will end up as relatively unimportant.

("I thought it would.")

Color, meaning and form will predominate, though perhaps in an unexpected manner. Your hand symptom will disappear entirely as your accomplishment grows in your mind, and later grows practically in your work.

("I thought it was interested that I picked on the two Bills for models—Bill Gallagher and Bill Macdonel."

(Two days ago, on Saturday, November 25, I took a few exploratory photos of my two friends, preparatory to beginning work on portraits of them.)

You will do a painting of the Jesuit *(Bill Gallagher)* that will become well known. It will be the outgrowth of a conception in the painting sold to Sonya *(Carlson, of Johnsonburg, Pennsylvania)* of the idea, I believe.

("Did you expect my father to go back home?" I meant: what did Seth think of my father going back home to live under mother's care, from the hospital, instead of going to a nursing home, as we had all thought quite possible.)

I did not particularly focus upon intermediate stages.

(Jane stretched out on the couch, eyes closed.

("How come I've had trouble remembering my dreams lately?")

She will now *(pause)* give him full attention, you see, that he has craved. *(Pause.)* What was your next question?

(Repeat.) This will pass, as it will in Ruburt's case. You have lost the intent, afraid to have dreams about your parents. This is also the reason, the main one, why Ruburt has not recalled his.

("Jane's getting ready to send out a book of poetry."

(High, Low and Psycho.) He can trust himself to write to his parents now incidentally. I have nothing to say concerning the poetry this evening, and I suggest we end the session unless you have pressing questions.

("No.")

My heartiest wishes to you both. It is good for him to sleep without a pillow for a while. The personal contact last evening was good for you both. Your hands upon him— this is of benefit, and to some extent you can direct healing energy to him in this manner. Keep this in mind when there is such physical contact. This is of more benefit now than it would have been in the past, and I recommend it. I did not suggest it in the past because your own inner feelings were so confused. You could have done more harm than good, but that is over. There is a healthy interchange of energy now between you both. This is merely an impression: have Ruburt send the poetry book to a company beginning with a V or an L.

("Good night, Seth." Jane seemingly ended at 10:35, but at 10:37:)

Ruburt should endeavor to forget his arms. He is overly concerned with them now, and this holds the image of them in his mind. This clouds the image of his arms in their normal healthy position. Let him <u>forget about them</u>, and they will return to normal. His attention is directed too much toward them. *(Long pause.)* As for your earlier comments let him focus upon his general goals. He is not having success with the exercises I suggested because he is trying too hard. *(Seth's suggested motion exercises, instead of passive ones.*

(End at 10:42.)

SESSION 384
DECEMBER 4, 1967 10:15 PM MONDAY

(This session is deleted from the record.

(Jane and I engaged in a long discussion this evening, covering a lot of ground

concerning her symptoms, my role, her lingering and bothersome symptom hang-ons, etc. Much of what we talked about is developed in the brief session that followed. For the first time, however, Jane gave voice to some doubts about the sessions that I had not realized she entertained. The purpose of the discussion was to unearth any reasons for the symptoms that we hadn't touched upon, and we struck pay dirt here. These discussions are uniformly beneficial.

(*I did not expect a session to follow the discussion, but at 10:15 Jane announced she could hold one. She began speaking in trance in a quiet voice, with a few pauses, eyes open often.*)

Now—I shall be brief, as you are tired.

This was not the whole problem. It is merely the portion of the problem that still remains. It has been there since the first.

(*Jane's intellectual reluctance to wholeheartedly accept the sessions and all they implied.*)

Ruburt was strongly committed to the sessions on the one hand, and highly skeptical on the other. Your own illness did literally terrify him, and he feared that if he faced his true doubts concerning my existence, that he would hurt you.

(*Pause. Jane gives the sessions credit for ending my own serious illness in 1963.*)

His own inner belief in the sessions was strong, and is still strong, but the other conflict continued. He misused such abilities in a past life, and this time he is having to work for them.

The spontaneous self is learning to manipulate and maneuver within the somewhat rigid ego limitations. Yet the ego has also expanded, and has allowed channels to open. The classes *(ESP)* are a means to that end .

We will have a freer hand since Ruburt has vocalized some of his doubts. Before he was reluctant to do so as clearly as he did this evening. Had there been a strong or powerful overall threat to Ruburt, I would have discontinued the sessions. These are growing pains, that are already passing.

Now, if you have any questions I will answer them. I simply wanted you to have my statement on this evening's discussion.

("*How much of a part is Jane's past-life misuse of her psychic abilities playing in this life?*")

Simply that this time he must work harder to accept the abilities that last time he took so for granted, and misused.

("*Was this in Boston?*")

This was.

("*In what way were they misused?*")

He used them indiscriminately. *(Pause.)* Wait now... He let them run away with him, and is doubly afraid now. He used little common sense, and was overly emotional, reading signs where there were none, and ignoring the fine intellect that he had even then.

("Was he male or female?")

This is an overcompensation, you see.

("Was he male or female?")

This is also the reason for his strong reaction concerning spiritualism. He fears <u>over</u>indulgence. *(Pause.)* He operated as a professional medium on Guinnip Street, perhaps 451, or any sequence of those numbers.

His own mother in this life had, and has, abilities. He was frightened of <u>her</u>, you see, and therefore frightened of the abilities. There is a growing acceptance on the part of the whole personality now; as he sees these abilities help others, his students for example, he grows to trust them more.

He was never afraid of me. He was afraid for portions of himself, for reasons having little to do with me, per se. *(Pause.)* The spontaneous self he was afraid of. The conscientious self becomes much more pleased as time goes on and others are helped.

It is Ruburt's nature you see to accept heartily or to disagree heartily, to plunge headlong into, or to run from, and the psychic developments made it impossible for him to do either; or rather his reactions made wholehearted acceptance or rejection impossible. This put him in a nether land, to him highly unacceptable.

(And here, probably, is the key to the whole dilemma.)

Periods of belief would be followed by periods of skepticism, and the wavering nature makes it most difficult for me to give him the very assurance that he needs. This was one of the reasons for the table developments, and these will be followed by others.

He is highly skeptical of AA, when he tries to consider him as an individual person, but is perfectly content to think of him as a <u>force</u>. *(Pause.)* It is not his early complete acceptance of the Catholic Church that is a block here. It is his disillusionment with the church that followed. For this led him to skepticism. And to a distrust of spiritual matters.

You are tired. You may end the session or break as you prefer. I have said what I felt necessary, so do as you wish.

You feel my presence, you see, because you allow yourself to do so. *(One of the points we discussed before the session.)* Ruburt feels my presence now, and during many sessions, and he knows it well. Often he simply distrusts what he <u>feels</u>, but the feeling is primary. The help that the sessions afforded you has been given. It has happened. It is not reversible. *(Smile.)* You have taken it and used it and made it a part of yourself. Ruburt need have no doubts there.

For himself he knows that he will continue, that his improvement is definite. Though the decision is his, I have never come when I was not wanted, nor would I.

I am with you now, though our voice is mild enough, very strongly this evening, and I am making an effort to make my presence known quite definitely to you and to Ruburt; and I shall do this more frequently to build up Ruburt's confidence.

He does not realize the full strength of his psychic acquiescence, you see, which is far superior to his egotistical half-denials.

Now do as you prefer.

("We'll take a short break.")

(10:44. Actually this was the end of the session. I had asked for a break only in case Jane had any questions she wanted Seth to answer.

(She had been far out. Her eyes opened quite slowly. She had, she said, been quite aware of Seth's presence, but when asked could not describe it.)

SESSION 385 (DELETED)
DECEMBER 6, 1967 9:46 PM WEDNESDAY

(Tonight Jane and I had another rather long discussion before the session, as before the last session, and once again our talk proved to be very beneficial. Once again Jane gained insights into the problems behind her symptoms, and we planned a course of action as a result; the course merely concerns a way to think about her psychic abilities, with some suggestions given to this end in a specific way.

(As we talked Jane herself made the intuitive connection that her "intellectual skepticism" about her psychic gifts is really a fear, an emotional masquerade that prevents her from being really objective in considering her abilities. Jane made valuable connections here about the honesty necessary in evaluating her psychic gifts, linking this same honesty with that she uses while writing poetry, etc. Both of us felt we were on strong solid ground here, and that our insights this evening probably concerned the last problems to be dealt with in the banishment of symptoms.

(Jane began speaking in trance while sitting on the divan, using a quiet voice, a direct manner, with her eyes open often.)

Good evening.

("Good evening, Seth.")

Your presession discussions are valuable. Ruburt's intuitions are strong then. You have come a long way in understanding this problem this evening. Now give us a moment. *(Pause.)*

He is strongly accusing toward anything he regards as religious deceit, because of his experience you see, with several priests in the past. There is some connection here. He is deeply committed to his idea of truth and goodness. When he could no longer believe in the tenets of the Catholic Church wholeheartedly, fervently and completely, he divorced himself from it as thoroughly as he had once embraced its tenets.

He would make no compromises. He still finds it most difficult to understand those like the Gallaghers, who remain in the church while not rigorously believing in each dictum.

His loyalty, once given, is under most circumstances irreversible, unless deceit is involved. At the time he believed deceit was involved in the church hierarchy.

His potential for commitment is truly powerful. He is committed to you for example, in this way. He is being overly cautious, realizing the strength of his commitments. He makes few of them. It has been all or nothing until this point.

Here he has tried to hold back, and yet not hold back. One very large portion of the personality is totally committed to our endeavors. Another portion has so far withheld complete commitment, though the rejection seems greater by contrast. In others the rejection would come close to commitment, but for him this is not enough.

A definite strain therefore developed, particularly painful since it involved his work also, to which he has always been strongly committed. He recognized the value of our endeavors to his work. On the other hand he still was not <u>completely</u> (underlined) committed, and therefore mistrusted.

He did not want to use his work *(pause)* to place his work, at the service of a cause to which he was not indelibly committed. *(Long pause, eyes closed.)* He has always been concerned with teaching, as I have been. The conscientious portions of the personality are of great benefit in that area. *(Voice quiet but firm and emphatic)*. He must believe completely in what he is doing, in what he is teaching, or he feels himself deceitful.

His energy was very purposefully restrained and held back last winter. He denied himself its use to anything like full capacity, for reasons given earlier, and also because he refused to use it rather than misuse it. He had to be more certain of our cause before he would allow himself to direct energy into it.

He could not do this in one area, and not in others. Therefore the energy was held largely in abeyance. *(Pause.)* The inner self grappled. Large portions of the self were won over, and the symptoms began to lessen, and the energy to return. The classes were of great benefit, and are. *(Pause.)*

You may take a brief break and I shall continue. His mother, incidentally, was deeply terrified of faith healers. *(Pause.)*

Now, I could not give you this material earlier, for he would not allow it. It would make no impression upon him had I given it, nor would my appearance have convinced him of anything more than what he would consider his own duplicity. The session itself therefore is an indication of his progress.

Your own attitude <u>now</u> (underlined) is most beneficial, and you are doing him a service that no one else can do; partially of course to help make up for harm that you did unwittingly. He let you *(smile)* do the harm, but he would have let no one else do it at the time. *(Smile.)*

The <u>survival</u> personality in itself does not automatically make one wise. Survival personalities are individuals. The god concept is a valid one. This for Ruburt. It will be explained by others according to the limits of their own understanding.

Take your break.

(10:12. Jane was far out, etc. Resume at 10:22.)

Now. Le Cron *(Leslie Le Cron, author of Self Hypnotism)* was a help at a time when he needed to reexamine his past.

<u>Now</u> however Maltz *(Psycho-Cybernetics)* is called for, and his idea of reacting only within the bright focus of the present. This alone, when Ruburt realizes its implications, will be of great help.

The muscles in the arms work against themselves. *(Pause.)* Again, massage on your part will benefit. Because of the idea behind it. There is little need to go into various symptoms however, for as he begins to feel at one with himself again they recede and will vanish.

Even if he takes a conscious <u>neutral</u> stand, this will be of great benefit, for as he overreacts, he overreacts to his own doubts. They are not as severe as they appear to him. Even a neutrality here will be a step forward on the part of consciousness, you see.

In any case he must realize that <u>no</u> fraud is involved. He is not lying, as the child is accused of doing when he describes something his parents consider outlandish.

(Again a very quiet, positive, emphatic delivery for the nest few paragraphs. Jane's eyes were wide open and very dark, and she pointed continually at me as she spoke. I consider these paragraphs to be the key that unlocks the symptoms.)

He is involved in a search for truth, and he must be prepared to follow wherever the search leads him. <u>The intellect cannot, because of its very nature participate fully in the actual trance experience</u>. He must realize this. (Pause.)

Let him remind himself that he is fearless in his poetry, and commits himself to it fully, and his ability here has always led him onward to further unfoldments and never into betrayal or deceit. It is precisely this same kind of ability he is using now. *(In trance.)*

He must trust it. The intellect follows when and to what extent it can in the poetic experience, <u>but does not directly participate in the initial moment of revelation or intuitional insight</u>. It follows on from there, <u>translating</u> the experience in terms of physical reality. Let it serve the same purpose here.

Ruburt does not mistrust himself because he plunges headlong, literally, into the poetic experience. He does not feel guilty because he does not intellectually question the moment of poetic revelation. He should therefore allow himself to plunge headlong with the same commitment into this experience.

The strength of the intuitional insight itself convinces the intellect of its validity <u>after</u> the poetic experience, <u>because</u> Ruburt allows himself full freedom to encounter the revelation. In our work, if he allows himself this same freedom, <u>the intellect will also be convinced of our validity</u>.

(The same quiet, intent delivery all through here.)

The very freedom will give me more leeway in making my presence known to him. I am so a part of him during sessions you see *(smile)*, that he cannot observe me or my presence, and this is a source of irritation to him. *(Pause.*

(Emphatically.) I am now you see so a part of his system at this moment that no part of his consciousness can sit aside and isolate me. He would like to isolate me and observe me. When he allows himself more freedom, he will be able to sense me in definite terms, though as a rule not <u>during</u> a session.

He senses my presence then, but not in terms outside of himself, you see; you can do this during sessions.

You may take your break or if you prefer you may end the session.

("We'll take the break."

(10:43. Some of the time Jane lad been flat on her back as she spoke to me. She resumed this position now at 10:46.)

We will close the session. It is however a fact that I am so a part of him during sessions, that makes him doubt my <u>independent</u> existence. He feels the closeness, you see.

Yet, I cannot completely be myself while within his system, since I am using <u>his</u> nervous system. It is the mixture of strangeness and familiarity that confuses him in this regard. It is not possible for me to speak through him, now, without using his physical structure.

He is so used to its feeling. He recognizes the existence of a different psychological personality and pattern however. *(Pause.)*

If your situations were reversed he would have had instant belief in my independent nature. Now, unless you have questions, we will end what I hope will be a most helpful session.

("No questions.")

My heartiest regards to you both, and Ruburt should definitely continue with the Maltz exercises. The "be careful in nothing" advice is just what Ruburt needs now. *(Pause.)* And tell him to smile as he goes to sleep, and if he wakens to relax the facial muscles and smile. Also on awakening. The jaw should particularly be relaxed. There is a tendency to grit the teeth.

(10:55. Jane was far out, etc.)

SESSION 387
DECEMBER 11, 1967 9:35 PM MONDAY

(This session is deleted from the record.

(Before the session I described to Jane my dream of Wednesday, December 6; and the second vision I had, of another painting, on the evening of Thursday November 30; the first painting vision being the one of Bill Gallagher on November 28, 1967, and discussed by Seth in the 382rd session.

(I also described to Jane a vision I had upon awakening on Saturday morning, Dec. 9, and sketched in my dream book.)

(Jane said she was a little tired this evening. She began in trance while seated in our rocking chair, using a quiet voice and pauses, eyes open at times.)

Good evening.

("Good evening, Seth.")

The visions will continue on your part. There is a continuity of growth in them that I do not believe you have so far perceived. *(I have not.)* This will become apparent.

You are being given directions and suggestions. *(Pause.)* You are of course amiable to inner visual stimuli, and used to interpreting reality in highly specialized forms, through visual data.

Your inner perceptions will often come in this manner then. The information must impress the nervous system, and it will take the most highly developed physical channel. Ruburt's inner perceptions often take the auditory, you see. His hearing is exceptionally keen. Therefore inner data is directed, often, into that channel, for it will impress him vividly.

Now he is used to dealing with words, and you with images. That does not mean that all inner perceptions will be restricted to these particular channels. They will carry a strong weight, however.

Ruburt should read more in his Maltz book, definitely, and concentrate on achieving relaxation, not only in periods set aside, but in his normal daily hours at work or whatever.

He did very well with his class, not only by holding our session *(see the last session, Jane's first without my presence)*, but by releasing and vocalizing his deep inner convictions. This helped his students immeasurably. He was helped, for part of himself was another student, listening.

His success practice is coming along exceptionally well, much better than the relaxation exercises. These have a strong therapeutic effect also, and will increase the benefits of all else that he has learned.

The paintings you saw are realities, already created by you in other dimensions, and existing as potential forms in this dimension.

One has already been painted in this dimension in your future, I believe this is the first, mentioned somewhat earlier. *(Of Bill Gallagher; 382nd session.)*

Another point here on Ruburt. The relaxation exercises will help short-circuit his tendency toward overreaction. Maltz's telephone episode should be imagined by him in place of all unpleasant stimulus. Let him—again and again I say this— focus toward his work and classes, and pleasant daily activities, and <u>away</u> from symptoms.

This does not mean he is expected to pretend they do not exist, but he is to give a <u>minimum</u> amount of attention to them. They will completely dissolve that much quicker. What he is doing now is correct. *(Pause.)* An inner trust is developing. He must avoid being overly concerned on a conscious level.

Maltz is quite correct, in that an <u>overly conscious</u> (underlined) attempt is harmful. There has been improvement in his attitude since Wednesday's s session *(385th, December 6)*, and with you I recommend that he reread it several times a week for a while.

<u>Pleasant</u> relaxation is the key, as opposed to a retreating, drugged-like mood, or an overly tense, overly conscious worry, as to the degree of his improvement. *(Pause.)*

The success exercises are also teaching him how to focus his energy without strong conscious deliberation. Often he tries too hard to relax. Now give us a moment here. *(Pause.)*

Your dream was a psychological drama. *(See my dream notebook for December 6, 1967.)* The water did represent the streak of life. *(Pause.)* The rocks represented in the past a desire for aloofness. Not only did they lead back to the water, but all other routes along them that you followed were perilous. The water, despite all, was safer than the rocks.

The man who threw in his burden ahead of time was your father. *(Smile.)* He did this years ago in effect, hence you passed him by, while recognizing his gesture and deciding against it. The packs represented abilities as well as burdens, you see. He was afraid of his abilities and his burdens. He could not go along with them on his back. He was afraid they would drown him. He leaped into life, denying himself the use of his abilities because of the responsibilities they entailed, hence the separation.

Instead, you tried aloofness but kept intact and with you your abilities and responsibilities. You saw that the course could not be pursued, for all the roads led to involvement with the water. *(Pause.)* You still did not want to enter in however. It was Ruburt who drew you emotionally into participation.

You saw that she still carried, as Jane, the abilities and responsibilities while in the middle of the stream. Had the dream not ended you would have made your way across to him, in time *(smile)*, to help him up when he fell—this symbolic of his difficulties in the past year. The others were individuals that you have known.

You may take your break and we shall continue.

(10:10. Jane was dissociated as usual. I believe the dream discussed above might have been interrupted by the alarm clock. As Jane spoke I became aware that I had felt quite sleepy at times. She resumed at 10:22.)

Now. Deep relaxation is necessary for Ruburt.

The main difficulty with the arms now is an absence of relaxation in the shoulder area, a tension that is physically demonstrated. There are two main physical ways to approach this. One is through exercise which flexes and moves the muscles so that they become relaxed. The other is through direct relaxation.

Exercises so far have been too intensely entered into. He was so intent upon performing all given, either exercise or posture, that he became discouraged and pessimistic. The dancing, you see, he considers pleasurable. Its exercise function is secondary. He forgets himself, uses his body, and at least creates the climate in which muscular relaxation can occur.

Housework is in the same category usually. *(Pause.)* The exercises you see should have a joyful, gamelike atmosphere, or a nonchalance. He makes them a combat zone: his will versus his symptoms, and this defeats his purpose.

He did this even in the mental exercises I suggested. I now recommend all endeavors that combine enjoyment and exercise, where the exercise at least to his mind is incidental, or at least secondary.

Again, massage on your part will help. In this case pleasure on his part supersedes the purpose, and therefore reinforces it. He enjoys your touch, regardless, and therefore allows himself to relax. This is of paramount importance right now.

If Maltz is followed, and our last two sessions, a deeper state of relaxation should be possible regardless, this coming from inner peace. We should like to work it from both angles, however. One generates the other.

Pleasant thoughts and images will help as he falls asleep. The suggestion that he has pleasant dreams will benefit. We want the condition completely healed, and for this joyful relaxation is definitely prescribed.

In the same way that he has lately caught himself tensing his jaw, so has he tensed his neck and shoulder muscles for some time. We want him to be able to recognize tension in the shoulders, as he can <u>now</u>, but could not earlier, recognize the tension in the jaw.

You may take a break and I shall continue.

(10:36. Jane was out as usual. During the delivery I had become increasingly sleepy— so much so that at times I had to struggle to keep my eyes open; at times I let them close briefly in relief. I felt as though a trance state might be trying to intrude, rather than being aware of any general weariness. As I wrote, I looked about the room in hopes I might see something unusual— Seth etc., but noticed nothing.

(At break I got up and walked about, explaining how I felt to Jane. I cleared up a little during break, but when Jane resumed at 10:50 I found myself back in the state, fighting to keep my eyes open, etc.)

Now. A definite exercise schedule should be set.

I will at least counteract some of the muscular tension and dissipate it. The activity itself will encourage him. Fifteen minutes at the least. Some exercises where he can see his own progress. These not to be picked up and dropped, but continued. They need not be the same.

He need not decide, now, whether these be yoga or other exercises. He can do one one day and one another if he chooses— but fifteen minutes minimum of any kind of exercising activity.

Now. The paintings have come from other portions of your personality, who know better than you what you can do. *(Long pause, eyes closed.)* These will be, I believe, a series of visions, extending over some time. You will see various ways in which your abilities can be used, various possibilities. Progressions along <u>various</u> lines.

I will have more to say here at another session. *(Long pause.)*

Your possibilities will be clearly shown, in the various works you can produce. You will choose among them. Some paintings will automatically negate others. If you do some, you will progress along certain lines rather than others. The various lines however all represent full use of your abilities, merely pointing out various lines of focus that you may choose.

They are meant to enkindle you, and program the self that you know in line with the purposes of the inner self. In themselves they represent greater development on your part, or you would not be able to perceive them. Our next session will deal with this.

I will now close. Now you *(Jane pointed to me as Seth)*, for a very brief time, close your eyes and see if you experience anything. My best wishes to you.

(11:02. Still in trance, Jane sat quite still in her rocker until 11:07. Her eyes were closed, and she was Seth for the next five minutes.

(I had felt just as sleepy as before, but had managed to keep writing, although I had a strong urge to merely lay down and sleep. I now did as Seth suggested, feeling a trance on my part was probably involved. If anything I felt a little less tired now, but with my eyes closed tried not to "try" for any effect too hard, less I block it by conscious effort.

(Every so often I deliberately opened my eyes to check on Jane, but she sat quite still. Later she told me she opened her eyes briefly, once, just before 11:07. At first I perceived nothing unusual, and felt my own relaxation wasn't what it might be. Finally, very briefly but rather clearly, I visioned internally the hanging sculpture sketched below. I knew it was mine. The piece was in cast iron, with a soft mottled black-brown patina, densely conceived, and I liked it very much. It was perhaps two and a half feet high, hanging from a ceiling by a chain.

(See my dream book for Friday, December 8, 1967, for a sketch of the first vision I had that involved sculpture. The seeing of sculpture is most unusual for me, since I have never done any; though feeling all along that I was quite capable.

(My sculp shows on the next page.

(Jane told me that during this experiment she was aware of a "cone" of energy being focused in my direction from herself, with the wide end of the cone at her end—she could not really describe this feeling, she said, any better than this.

(I closed my eyes again after visioning the sculp, hoping to see more. This was just before 11:07, and the session's end. This time, before I realized it, I was "far away" in a fashion I cannot really put into words. Suffice it to say I was seemingly miles from my physical body, briefly, without being aware of any sensation of seeing anything else— no location, etc.

(I did not feel alarm, but could have been alerted. I suddenly straightened my head up as I sat on the divan and my eyes popped open. I discovered that I was now fully awake and alert— the drowsiness was fully gone.)

FIRST HYPNOSIS SESSION, JANE
FEBRUARY 12, 1968 9 PM MONDAY

(Tonight I hypnotized Jane for the first time.

(These notes are not included in the Seth material, for obvious reasons, although Seth may refer to these sessions. The notes are a summary, written from memory; later a tape recorder may be used.

(I had wanted to hypnotize Jane for some time, but had been hesitating even though my pendulum told me I had nothing against the idea. I was still aware of resistance, however, and so thought I would wait until the intuitive moment arrived to begin. That moment came today, from an almost casual remark Jane made this afternoon, and which I am not even able to quote. I believe her remark fell upon ground well prepared by a book I am currently reading: Many Lifetimes, by Grant and Kelsey.

(Joan Grant is evidently a well-known English medium, and her husband, Denys Kelsey, a practicing psychiatrist who tells of some remarkable successes in treating patients, while keeping in mind the role reincarnation can play in present "living" personality patterns.

(I believe Jane was a little nervous at the idea of being hypnotized, since I mentioned it at supper time. I was also as 9 PM approached, but not overly so. I felt I had read enough about the subject to know intuitively how to proceed once the time arrived. The fact that Jane was a willing, even eager, subject was of course a great help.

(We chose our bedroom because it would be more private and comfortable than the living room. We each had a glass of wine before starting. Jane lay on her back with her hands crossed. I began to induce a general relaxation, following techniques I had read, and which Jane had used with me several years ago. I began with the feet and worked up to the head— generally at first; then each time I started again at the feet my suggestions for ease and relaxation became more detailed.

(One thing caught me unprepared, and perhaps came close to interrupting the session. As I began talking steadily my voice began to become very dry. I am not used to speaking so steadily, although Jane later said that she too had noticed a voice stain in her first session with me, until she became more relaxed and used to the idea. Luckily there was a little wine left in one glass; as I finally became so hoarse I could hardly talk, I began to sip this, and it helped a great deal. A glass of water handy, I thus learned, will be standard in sessions after this. At one time I simply had to stop talking because my voice gave out. Jane said she was aware of this, and that the break almost snapped her out of the relaxed state she was entering.

(All in all, we believe things went quite well for a first attempt, and we are pleased with the results. I spent perhaps half an hour by the clock inducing the first general relaxed state, including the suggestion that Jane's eyelids were quite heavy and relaxed. I did not definitely tell her that she could not open them, but believe that had I suggested this she could not have done so— this in the light of later events.

(I told Jane before we began that we would not stress tests to prove hypnosis, that these could come later if we chose. I was confident that I could induce a good sound relaxation and at least a light trance state, and we achieved this and more. Especially in the beginning I did wonder at times at my progress, but continued following my ideas without allowing any doubts to become bothersome. Once Jane's eyes closed at the start of the session they remained closed until I told her they would open at the end.

(After the first half hour I felt we had progressed enough to try various things. My recall here may not be in strict order. One of the first things Jane told me, after I asked her to speak, was that the bathroom light bothered her. This, even though a closet light in the bedroom itself was on, and brighter. But I turned the bathroom light off.

(At my suggestion Jane began to flex her feet, then her hands. For a few moments she let her hands lay at her sides, but since there is tension in the upper arm muscles, her arms cannot lay fully relaxed upon the bed when she is flat on her back; after a few minutes she again crossed her hands, and told me later that this was more comfortable. Of course I noted that even after my suggestions, her arms did not fully relax, but I had not stressed that she would achieve any great or startling improvement; this first session was more to learn how to proceed, and during it I tentatively tried several different approaches.

(One was to regress Jane to a period of two years ago, chosen at random. I counted to ten backward, with appropriate suggestions, but when the count was completed she told me she could see nothing. I thought then that I had been premature to try this idea, and attempted to talk around it and change the subject, so to speak, rather than say that it was a mistake. Jane appeared to accept my way out without question.

(By now I had learned that she could speak under hypnosis without difficulty, a point we had wondered about to at least some extent. I thought she was in a light trance state and Jane later agreed that she was, that she felt very relaxed. Often as I spoke to her I told her she would have full memory of what transpired when the session was over. When it was over, she told me her memory of parts of the session was somewhat hazy— reinforcing the idea that she was hypnotized, if somewhat imperfectly, and that my control was not all it will be in future sessions.

(I began to tell Jane that she was now going into a deeper trance. This proved effective, I soon learned. Jane said she had no particular feeling of entering a deeper state, but when I brought her out of it at the end of the session she had a very definite feeling of rising, of leaving it to return to full consciousness.

(Previously Jane had spoken the one word "four" without elaboration, even when I asked her to explain. She now repeated it again, still without explanation, and later told me that she was aware of resistance concerning the word. Next she said "1961", and "Florida."

(We have lived in Elmira since 1960, and were in Florida before this, so the discrepancy is apparent. I did not correct it, for it seemed we were getting to some material that was emotionally strong for Jane in recall. By now I had begun to tentatively mention the symptoms, and to ask Jane what she could say about their origin. It was almost as though she had been waiting for these questions; she quickly spoke the word Florida, and after this I had no doubt that she was at least fairly well hypnotized.

(Before the session I had reminded myself that if we came upon strongly emotional material I would attempt to guide Jane through it, by helping her to express it but not become overwhelmed by it should it prove very painful. This is why I had earlier told her she could remember what transpired during the session. I also had in mind that should it seem necessary I could suggest that things too strongly charged could be temporarily forgotten upon awakening. We did not reach this point however.

(Quickly now, Jane began to talk, and I encouraged her to do so. At the same time she turned on her side toward me and drew her legs up, almost in a fetal position. She also began to cry. Her voice however never became loud. Her eyes did not open. She said two things, close together, that I at once recognized as important.

[Both of these were elaborated upon later.]

(The first was that her troubles began in Florida; that it was her fault we left Sayre to join her father in Florida, and that I had not wanted to leave my parents. *[I had cried in the car as we drove out of Sayre on the way south, but had, I thought, regarded this as natural enough at the time.]* Jane told me that it was her fault we had chased around the country, that her spontaneity had done nothing but get us into trouble. Jane described how she had become very frightened in Florida over the job situation, and that I had been forced to get a job anyhow even though I had told her most emphatically that I didn't intend to do this. *[When we went to Florida it had been agreed upon that she would hold a job while I tried out some painting ideas. Her father was to help us out financially also, but did not do so.]*

(Then, Jane continued, still crying, we had returned to Sayre, then Elmira, where I had worked full time for three years, then became very sick for a year. *[It was during this period that Jane's hypnosis sessions with me had proved most helpful.]*

(It was, I believe, after my own recovery that Jane's first symptoms, unrecognized by us as to their potential severity, began to show. And now under hypnosis Jane said the second important thing: she told me that if *she* got sick, *I* wouldn't be sick any longer. It is true that I have been in generally very good health since my own illness in 1963. However I have two symptoms carried over from that period, that still must be dealt with, and I feel these are directly related to Jane's symptoms. That is, I believe there is a close interaction between us that is responsible for the bulk of symptoms upon either side.

(One thing I would like to explore in these sessions is what effect past-life memories can play in present personality patterns, and my attempt to get Jane to regress a couple of years was a first halting step in this direction, that was not successful. But already I can see several other ways to approach this, and expect no trouble.

(The balance of the session tonight after these two important revelations, consisted of an interchange between us that stressed reassurance upon my part,; including the statement, repeated often, that Jane now understood she didn't need her symptoms any longer, that they could begin to disappear. I made strong efforts here to tell her of my love, and to impress upon her that our travels had also been enjoyable and adventurous along with their hazards, and that whatever we had done was done together; no one should feel blame. Yet it was now apparent that Jane felt a sense of blame, even shame; at the start of the deeper trance state she told me she felt I was mad at her all the time because I had worked full time at Artistic, etc; I tried to counter this by pointing out to her the benefits we had both obtained from this.

(The course of action evidently succeeded to some extent at least, for Jane quieted as we talked. I gave her no suggestions that her symptoms would disappear at once, for they involve some physiological changes and I didn't know just how quickly her body could chemically return to a fully healthy state. Here I count upon the repeated suggestions that her body can clear itself. I did tell her that her physical improvement could seem like magic, and repeated this several times. Later Jane told me that my reassurances were most welcome, and that she "drank them in" like water.

(I was more open and reassuring with Jane during this session than I have been for some time, and I told her I realized this was a fault on my part, and that I would do my best to remedy it.

(The session ended at about 10:45 PM. Since Jane was by now much more relaxed I thought it a good time to end. After beneficial suggestions as to her state of well-being, I told her that when I had counted to ten, slowly, that she would be out of trance and could open her eyes.

(As stated, this worked well, and as I counted Jane felt herself rising or lifting toward waking consciousness; the effect here was much more pronounced than when I had suggested she enter a deeper state, as described earlier. After the session Jane said she felt she had been in at least a good light trance state, and possibly a little deeper. I agree with this.

(I think that more suggestions would have induced an even deeper state with her, and that probably amnesia could have been induced in this deeper state had I so desired. After the session Jane said she felt very relaxed, although I believe she has induced as good a state in some of her self-hypnosis sessions. I did not give her a key word, for instance, to speed up future inductions, but plan to do so when I have more experience.

(When we retired Jane said later that she dozed off quite easily for perhaps an hour. She then woke up, took a couple of aspirin, and slept through the night— in fact until about 9 AM. The following day she felt generally fairly good, although the symptoms were not banished.

(We believe the session a success for a first attempt. It seems Jane has strong emotional energy blocked up behind the symptoms, and that we released a little of it this time; the crying certainly was of benefit here.

(Two additional points now recalled: When she began talking about Florida, Jane told me "I got scared in Florida"; she was also sure I would leave her when the job situation got so bad and things didn't work out as we'd hoped they would. [I remember her telling me this in Marathon, when I returned to the trailer after driving out to get a job painting signs.]

(The second point grew out of the above: Jane told me, crying, that if she got sick I'd feel sorry for her and wouldn't leave her. During the period of reassurance that followed these revelations, I stressed to her that at no time since our marriage have I thought of leaving her, in Florida or anywhere else.

(I repeated often that her spontaneity had been very valuable to me, that I

needed this, and that I had never once doubted her loyalty or love.
(Jane also blamed herself for the death of Mischa & the cats.)

SESSION 393 (DELETED)
FEBRUARY 14, 1968 9 PM WEDNESDAY

(Just before the session Jane said she felt unusually relaxed. On Monday, February 12, I had hypnotized her for the first time.)

Good evening.

("Good evening, Seth.")

Now Joseph *(pause)*, neither of you should overlook the fact that in one way or another, and regardless of the psychic development, such a crisis point *(Jane's symptoms)* would have appeared in Ruburt's life as a result of personal characteristics, present-life background, and past-life characteristics.

The crisis would have developed on the condition that Ruburt tried to use and develop his spontaneous and intuitive abilities on an adult basis. The cleavage between discipline and spontaneity had long existed; given the all-or-nothing attitude of the personality, there was bound to be a swing, a complete swing from one to the other until the personality learned to combine the two and become more thoroughly integrated.

As long as he acted with relative abandon, as in the early years, relatively unreasoning, then there was no point of conflict. When he tried on the other hand to act in a more reasoning and disciplined manner, when he became convinced of the necessity for discipline and this was in Florida, then he attempted to stifle all spontaneity.

His necessary job was to combine the two, for in him the intuitions and intellect are both strong. To use his abilities fully both had to operate smoothly and simultaneously, and give each other freedom and elbow room. Old fears would make him gyrate, panic-stricken, from one method of operation to the other.

His abilities, to be used fully, would inevitably have led him to such a crisis point, or better to such a challenge. Any work of art of his, not an apprentice work, would have led him to the same point. Poetry is the exception, for here the necessary integration happened early in his career.

The poetry was not seen as threatening to the disciplined self. Any work of fiction in which his abilities were at all fulfilled would have brought him to this point, and any endeavor such as the psychic work, which was adopted. In other words, for the personality to use its abilities fully that challenge would have had to be faced in every instance but the poetry.

The crisis would have occurred according to the circumstances and a variety of probabilities, but many of these led in that direction, you see.

It would have been a mistake of the most tragic order, however, to shy away from the full development of abilities. Otherwise there would have been an extremely rigorous personality, with intuition very strong but firmly held at bay; or a highly disorganized spontaneous personality frittering away its energies without direction.

The development of abilities, your introduction to me and the sessions, came because both of you realized that a rigidity was settling in upon you. The pendulum had swung too far over in both of your cases, to a discipline that became static and frozen. There was a boomerang effect on Ruburt's part.

This would have occurred however on the introduction of any strong spontaneous action. *The World as Idea Construction* came to him, beside its extrasensory origin, subconsciously, with an exploding effect to save him, because he had so put the lid upon his creative activities after *Rebellers*, that he had effectively blocked the intuitive self.

Of course you played a part. He felt relatively free in his spontaneity in the beginning with you, for he granted you super-human abilities, relying upon what he thought to be almost absolute strength and stability. He did not have to reason, for you would reason for you both.

You therefore would protect him from the results of his own spontaneity, carried too far, for he never thought in terms of a spontaneity tempered by self-discipline. In Florida he saw his father as the epitome of unreason and uncontrolled spontaneity, which had actually become a hodgepodge of unrelated emotional acts, and he felt you then deserting him symbolically.

Here, when you became ill, he saw you were not omnipotent. You could not basically protect him from himself. You had been his in a basic manner, and he saw that you, his director, did not know where to turn. The hidden and bedrock, latent, strong conscientious self then rose up and took over control, and would not give the spontaneous self then back any of the reins.

A strong breakthrough was needed if the personality was to develop its potentials. The spontaneous self, relegated to the underground, then used all of its strength and forced the issue through opening up the psychic channels, which are very legitimate, and in the past had been an unsuspected deep portion of Ruburt's personality. The challenge and the conflict were then set.

But without the challenge and the conflict the personality would have had little chance to develop its potential, particularly in terms of understanding. Your own relationship would indeed have deteriorated to some degree.

The spontaneity of Ruburt's nature otherwise would have nearly dried up, and you as well as Ruburt would have sorely missed it. This brings us nearly to the present.

It goes without saying that all of this was fueled by past symbols and associations that then emerged. As the psychic development appeared the overly disciplined self reacted strongly.

Now, you reacted strongly though your activity was not physical.

The overly-disciplined self could not be hidden now. One part of the self could no longer be dominant at the expense of the other. The physical symptoms represented the conflict as the overly disciplined self again tried to take over the reins. It has gradually let itself fit in now, let itself integrate, and in so doing the body has been relived of symptoms.

As complete integration takes place the body will be restored to normal. If the process seems slow, you can be assured that it is a legitimate and steady integration, for nothing but a complete integration would suffice if the personality is to achieve its potential.

If the personality settled for less, then, true, the conflict would not have arisen. The conflict would have arisen however in whatever field the personality chose, except for the poetry. Even in that area however it is highly dubious that full potential could be reached.

You may take a break and we shall continue.

(9:45. Jane took a very long time to open her eyes, and when she succeeded they were very heavy and bleary. Throughout this extra-long delivery I had thought she was in a deep state, and she now confirmed this; she had but a vague memory of what she had said. "I was out." As stated, she had been unusually relaxed. "If Seth ever came through undistorted, this was it...."

(Her manner had been forceful, eyes open at times. Resume in the same fashion at 9:51.)

All your parents frightened him, for he saw them as he saw his own father. Often what passed as spontaneity and emotionalism were often unrelated acts of instinctive nature. What seemed to be freedom or free acts were instead the result of unreasoning propulsion.

He feared his own spontaneity then was the result of unreasoning propulsion, and in his early years certainly some of it had been. He could not differentiate, and feared his spontaneous self the more, and he saw you fear your parents' behavior.

He doubled his discipline, and tried to put the lid upon the spontaneous self. For some time he confused true spontaneity with acts caused by blind propulsion, so he could not trust his spontaneous nature. Your mother for example says what she thinks often. Ruburt therefore thought she was spontaneous; for a while he did not see the blind panic behind the words or acts.

Your father seemed to be, earlier, highly disciplined. Ruburt did not see that the discipline was the result of terror, and <u>was not</u> true discipline. He saw both personalities as frozen, finally, and he thought: if spontaneity and discipline are both false roads, then where do I go? There is no road, and no escape, you see.

He identified strongly with both of your parents, for each of them seemed to signify the warring aspects of himself. He identified with each, hating and loving each for that reason. He did not trust you when you told him to free his intuitive self, now, when the symptoms were bad last year, because he felt you did not trust yourself to be spontaneous in your dealings with him. This is just before your own pendulum sessions.

Now, the overly conscientious or disciplined self is letting go as the integration takes place. The inner psychic in terms of psychically psychological activity has been constructive therefore since the process of integration began. He should, as he realizes, avoid dwelling on the symptoms consciously. This does not mean that he pretend they do not exist.

There should be a conscious letting go now also. This life sees this integration as necessary. <u>Past lives</u> have involved him with personalities either strongly intuitive or strongly intelligent, highly overbalanced in one category or the other. The full potential therefore should be seen in this, the last reincarnation.

You may take a break or end the session as you prefer.
("We'll take a break."
(10:15. Jane came out of trance a little more quickly this time, but still took quite a bit longer than usual. She became more alert at break however, and waited to see if Seth cared to resume.
(10:30.)
Some of the confusion was the result of Ruburt's attitudes toward spontaneity and discipline, toward the spontaneous and strongly conscientious aspects of his personality.

The erroneous attitudes had much to do with the difficulties. He thought of the spontaneous self, <u>his</u> spontaneous self, as joyful, free, intensely creative, but also as somewhat evil, frightening, unreasoning, and liable to lead him to disaster.

He thought of the overly conscientious self as stern, good, boring, constricting and uncreative, but very safe. He never made any serious attempt to integrate his personality, or to understand these portions of himself until recent years. He did not understand that discipline can be an aid to creativity, and that the spontaneous self is good. These erroneous attitudes were built up in this life. They echoed however experience in past lives also.

Only the poetry represented neutral ground. On other areas of life the spontaneous became highly suspect in both social and work areas. In his gallery work experience he did his best to disguise his spontaneous nature, out of his own fear and also as a result of your attitude at that time.

An out-thrust from the spontaneous self was a necessity then. The integration that is taking place will insure an end to such teeter-tottering. *Psycho-Cybernetics* <u>faithfully followed</u> (underlined) will insure the best possible conscious circumstances to enable the process to come to its speediest conclusions.

I am not saying that the personality will then become static, obviously, but the basic psychological framework will be such to allow the fullest development.

Unless you have questions we will end the session.

("No, I guess not.")

One word. I do not see any tragic circumstances surrounding the sister of Ruburt's student *(Shirley Bickford)*, of the kind told to Ruburt. *(Pause.)* A change of environment would be good, not in an overly permissive atmosphere but one in which some personal freedom is tempered with the expectation of definite achievement of some kind. *(Pause.)* Any sort of a school meeting that requirement would suffice.

We will then end the session, and at our earliest convenience take up the other matter before us: the ill woman and her husband. *(Peggy and John Pietre, of Louisiana.)* A good portion of a session should be given there.

My heartiest wishes to you both. I leave at your convenience but will continue if you choose.

("I guess not. Good night, Seth."
(10:45.)

SESSION 458 (DELETED PORTION)
JANUARY 20, 1969 9:47PM

(Continuation of Session 458, January 20, 1969, after break at 9:47. This material is not included in the records.)

(Resume at 10:01 PM. Point at Sue Mullin [Watkins].)

Now, give us a moment. Some information for you....

Your child, in a past life, this child was an uncle and in an accident you killed him. You were in a carriage, driving it. He went to adjust a bridle.

England, 1451. Give us a moment.

James. He was James Talbert. You were his niece. Matilda Montage. You were from a side of the family with French connections and at that time flighty, easily upset, with some ability as a musician in piano, but without the discipline or drive to use the ability,

He was taking you to a concert. I do not know now, or see now, what initiated your reaction, but something happened that frightened you. You yelled at the horses and screamed. Your uncle fell. The horses panicked, and he fell beneath a hoof. You never forgave yourself, and now in your first reincarnation as a woman since that time, you decided to be the vehicle through which he could enter physical reality again, and so became his mother in physical terms.

This was the extent of what you felt to be your responsibility.

You had not been a mother to a male before.

Now. While the inner self is aware of this connection, the present self has been fooling itself to some degree, for it did not accept the intuitional knowledge. Regardless of what you thought consciously therefore, you still inwardly blamed yourself for letting the child go, and therefore the difficulty with the womanly organs.

You blamed yourself for financial reasons, though consciously this would be the last thing to come to your mind. You think yourself quite free of financial conditions, and as an adult now in independent terms set yourself free of your parents. But subconsciously you wondered what social environment your child would really (underlined) encounter,, and whether or not you deprived him of the social and economic benefits that you have convinced yourself, consciously, you do not need.

You also wondered about depriving your mother of a grandchild now, for though you tell yourself she would not understand, still you wonder if interest in the child would not give her additional impetus and interest.

Now these are the things, some of the things, that you do not want to face consciously. Your uncle did not blame you for the accident at the time. While there was a past family connection, you were not the closest of friends, and there was no need or desire on either of your parts for a family connection of any duration in this life.

At one time you and the child were also brothers. He was impatient with you at times for he remembered you as a companion in male pursuits, and bitterly resented your femininity.

For various reasons, and because you did not understand, you held it against yourself that once you accidentally killed him, and then when he was a child you gave him away. You gave birth to him however when you did not have to, in order to give him this reentry. There were other entries available, but he understood your purposes, and accepted you as a mother to show you that he held no grudges. *(Humorously:)* There were two accidents, then.

Even the first had its psychological applications, for the uncle at that time was dissatisfied with existence and with his accomplishments, and the carelessness that helped result in his accident was also partially his own. But the fact that the conception was accidental, and the death was accidental, has its own intuitive logic.

There is in other words no need for you to punish the organs of your body that were involved in that birth.

You may take a break.

(10:24. Jane was out of trance easily. She said she could see horses' hooves and cobblestones beneath them as she talked. And possibly stone-type houses, close together, on each side of a street, crowded houses. This was not country settings.

(As Seth talked the witness felt a series of intuitive jolts that led her to believe the information was good. She likes horses this life. Jane resumed at 10:37.)

Now, I cannot give you your entire reincarnational history in an evening.

The father of the child however was a sister of yours in that life. Give us a moment. *(Pause.)* Your mother died when you were very young. The sister was older than yourself, and you felt, favored over you by your father.

You were also fascinated by her clothes in particular. You felt that she had taken your mother's place in the affections of your father and she lorded her position over you. She was not that much older than you, you felt, to be put in charge of you, since there was only a five-year difference.

You used to wonder what there was about her that so captivated your father, since he had an obvious preference for her, and you would watch her secretly trying to find the answer. You disliked her heartily but the fascination kept at you, so that you studied her mannerisms, and even at times tried to copy them.

You used to stand in a mirror and copy her expressions. *(Pause.)* She married a man whom you also have known in this existence. Your father simply preferred her because she did remind him of his wife. In a past life you had no use for women, and therefore chose an existence in which you were feminine; not only feminine but endowed with those qualities that you had particularly disliked; because you feared those qualities you therefore lived with them, and to some extent learned to understand them, though you are still left with some impatience when you see them in others.

Your sister was also fond of the uncle, and therefore was instrumental in this life in allowing him new entry; but you joined for that purpose only. The fascination was an expression of a past fascination of a different kind, though you were pleased that this time you were older.

Both of you realize this intuitively. *(Long pause.)* As personalities however you have worked out your relationship. When you come together, one or the other insists upon domination. You have decided not to work out any further relationships together. Often problems with one personality are worked out by relationships with another, different personality.

You felt that you wanted to give a life for the one you accidentally destroyed, but it need not have been the life of the same personality, had you chosen otherwise. You also still remember that the father of your child was a woman, and your sister, and so in this life you have found the relationship ambiguous.

Now you may end the session or take a break as you prefer.

("We'll end it then.")

(Pause.) If you take this information to heart, you should intuitively realize that by giving birth to the child *(pause)*, you performed a kindly gesture, and opened a door. The system should then realize that there is no need for the symptoms, and release you from them.

("Good night, Seth.")

(10:58. Jane left trance easily. The witness said the data contained many intuitive insights, etc., citing especially the material re ambiguous relationships, etc.)

SESSION 471 (DELETED PORTION)
MARCH 31, 1969

(There is more on the symptoms and related material in the session than is included below.

Now it will help if you take it for granted that under <u>some</u> circumstances, dealing with Ruburt's idea of authority, he has difficulty expressing dissatisfaction, or any normal impatience… It would help if you simply remind him of this when such occasions arise… for this would be enough now to let him make a suitable adjustment at any given occasion. You need not force an issue, but remind him.

You fear overinfluencing him, but since your influence is considerable in any case, this is a good time to use it. His intellect will then begin to take over. When you say nothing he uses this as an excuse, thinking, "Rob has said nothing, therefore he must agree with what I am doing."

You have not forced Ruburt into paths where he did not want to go. What seems to you like inner difficulties or problems, or lack of success, like Ruburt's desolations, serve as the very impetus to development. *(In my art.)* Ruburt should be open about the symptoms *(etc.).*

You know, I know, that your compliments quite go to his head, when they are real ones, and this also sends his symptoms running.

(There is more to the session.)

SESSION 472
APRIL 2, 1969 (COMMENTS)

(Very good.... [See session 472 in Volume 9 of The Early Sessions.*] Material on Jane's symptoms, interior and exterior illness, inner-self constructions and challenges, recognizing problems, etc. The viewpoint of the inner-self. Jane's despondencies. Therapy in the symptoms, etc. Reread periodically.)*

SESSION 473
APRIL 7, 1969 (COMMENTS)

(An excellent session, deleted from the record. Read the whole thing often. On Jane's childhood, fear of aggression; religion; my role, etc. Ego and health and illness. Illness not natural, etc. Psychic abilities and fear of ridicule.)

SESSION 473 (DELETED)
APRIL 7, 1969 9:05 PM MONDAY

Good evening.

("Good evening, Seth.")

Now. No personality chooses a life situation of illness. It chooses the best method it can to aid in overall development.

(This data is apropos of what Jane and I had been discussing before the session.)

It uses illness as a teaching method, and discards the method when the lesson is learned. In entire life situations—I am speaking in terms of a lifelong illness now—the illness is not predetermined by the personality to last the length of the life. Many severe illnesses disappear miraculously, it would seem, though an individual has been plagued since birth.

Here the lesson has been learned and the illness as a method discarded.

The ego's desire for health and the organism's impetus toward health, are constant balances, and are always present. The illness is not to be regarded as a natural (underlined) event, but the reason for it sought. The reason is often a lack of a quality. The realization of the lack and the mental, emotional and psychic acquisition of the quality, brings the illness to a close.

Now this is highly simplified, but the problems set are open problems. There are usually several different solutions or contexts within which the personality can find the solution. The individual does not set himself problems for which no answers exist.

I will try however to give you this as an example. A personality is born in a particular environment that is not clear and straight but crooked, as in a maze. The angles, corners and curves of the maze he has cleverly formed himself, before this existence. To get out of the maze automatically means that he has developed the abilities necessary. The flexibility, spontaneity, persistence, what have you, none of which he may have acquired had the "road" in quotes been absolutely straight from start to finish.

Obviously he must forget that he constructed the maze to begin with. This does not prevent the unmazed portion of the self from watching, giving helpful hints of a kind to ward off discouragement. The helpful hints are themselves lessons, reminding the personality that only a portion of it is involved in the maze.

Has this generally cleared the matter for you?

("Yes. But what about the cases where the personality does die from its illness; the illness never clearing up....")

In those cases the personality has done one of two things. It has solved one problem and decided to use the method to solve another, or it has decided that from its particular vantage point it would rather close the books and begin anew.

Death is not nearly as disagreeable, you see, as you think it is. Illness is far more disagreeable in many cases.

("That's about what I meant.")

In other circumstances, though the problem is solved, the physical body, being physical, is in such poor condition that the personality decides it much better to discard it completely.

("Does error enter in here on the part of the personality, or the inner self?")

Now in many cases of coma, the personality simply leaves before the body's actual death. Errors can be made, but in the overall they amount to little. Now give me a moment. *(One minute pause at 9:25.)*

I want to give you some personal material this evening, but we shall wait a bit longer. *(One minute pause.)*

Many of the points you have made to Ruburt lately have been well taken, and were more important than you realized. To you they seemed rather obvious, and trivial, almost. Now Ruburt's ego had been hit over the head, so to speak, so many times in his childhood that it became very sensitive, developing a rigidity out of self-protection.

It was afraid that psychic endeavor would leave it open for further scorn, and it would not for a while allow ordinary motion, until it was somewhat assured that it would not meet with contempt for its efforts. It was particularly afraid of ridicule, rather say than of hatred. *(Long pause.)* The affair with the school psychologist, and the class here, infuriated him, and he hid his reaction. The school was the college again, you see, and the academic community that had already rejected him as a student in the past. For a while he should have nothing to do with the college.

He also remembered that they had turned him down when he looked for work. Give us a moment.

He should also, for personal reasons, stay away from the monastery. The monks coming to the house subconsciously rearoused old fears and resentments. This does not mean he is not rising above them, for he is. It does mean that until he is in control of his organism such episodes are not helpful.

("How about Jane's speaking to the Unitarian Church later this month?")

That affair should not bother him, nor did the Methodist group. You see, he is really working in new religious frontiers. He has no hang-ups with Protestant groups.

("Do the Gallaghers bother him?")

Give us a moment. *(Pause.)*

In the overall, no. There will be later comments I will make here however. There are strong sympathies he has in common with the Jesuit, and also strong disagreements that he does not recognize.

("Concerning episodes like those with Elmira College, and the monks and the monastery: How come Jane doesn't take steps to protect herself in advance from such implications?")

He likes to take it for granted, in quotes "that he has conquered" such matters . In actuality the term conquered in itself is a poor one. Now give me a moment before another question here.

Many of the elements of his religious background have been creatively used and built upon, and this involves the complete transformation of potent, unconscious material, from potentially destructive to creative centers.

What you see as symptoms are those that have not as yet been transformed. Now this is a creative process where the personality uses for its advantage and development those elements in its background that it <u>seems</u> (underlined) could have destroyed it.

Give us time. *(Pause.)*

Now regardless of the nature of our sessions, their legitimacy and my own reality, only certain peculiarly gifted personalities would be able to make consistent contact, to obtain such information over a period of time. Only a certain kind of personality could find balance between spontaneity and discipline. Literally, as you recognize, a tremendous creative endeavor is required. A personality embarking upon such pursuits had to allow for various emotional and psychic elements from early childhood.

These elements would then be put together in such a way that they would give the impetus and the psychic challenge, the need to know, that could result in work like ours.

The personality for best purposes would have to be a woman, for the intuitive nature is more easily developed. I do not want to go tonight too deeply into other connotations, for they can lead us astray right now.

It was no coincidence however that Ruburt's Father Trayner read him poetry, inspired Ruburt's love of poetry, and that Ruburt would feel that he had to use poetry to express ideas with which his mentor did not agree.

The psychic influence of the other priests was far more creative than he realizes, and it was always in the realm of ideas that he rebelled against authority. That is important. He did not leave the church, literally, until long after he had left it spiritually. Yet all of his religious background gave him an immersion in a strong organized religion. Inside that framework he learned what was wrong with it, and from his experiences was born the strong inner, barely conscious, desire to help his fellow beings emerge into some kind of lucidity. There were strong pressures operating. All that remains is for him to realize that he is indeed now on the right track. Do you want to rest your fingers?

("Yes, I might as well.")

Take your break then.

(10:01. Jane's eyes opened quickly. I was quite upset by the material given, even though we had already talked a lot of it over before the session. Both of us were looking for ways to break the cycle of symptoms. I suggested a pattern of protective measures we could take. Resume at 10:10.)

Now. When he is requested to speak as an authority, as at his next engagement, this is something different.

He felt that the professor was bringing his students to show them he was a fraud. His sense of duty was actually a coverup. He knew he did not want the people here, and thought he was a coward. Now give us time.

Legitimate response, legitimate aggressive—*(It is interesting to note that Jane stumbled over the word aggressive, even speaking as Seth)*—response, is no problem, for there is no buildup behind it. It clears the system, and the other person can handle it. This Ruburt must learn. Often in such situations he will hurt himself because he has an <u>exaggerated</u> (underlined) idea of the hurt any normal aggressive reaction, from a frown to a verbal one, can have.

He wants to help others. On the positive side this leads into new frontiers, and it expands and develops his abilities. It is a basis for his ethical and intuitive achievements. On the negative side he can go overboard, fearing to cause another the slightest hurt, and hurting himself instead.

There is still an exaggerated idea of the <u>power</u> of aggression. It is not nearly as powerful as he imagines. Only when it is not allowed <u>normal</u> (underlined) outlets. Now give us a moment.

The girl from the monastery is perfectly all right, as long as she comes here unaccompanied by a monk, or met by one. The Friday episodes should probably be discontinued therefore. There is no harm in her coming to classes, or in the simple fact that she lives in one of the monk's cottages.

Now when I gave the session for our lady of Venice, I spoke as an authority, as myself, and there was no representative of the college present. This did not bother Ruburt therefore.

Now on one occasion he did very well, although he picked up strong ideas from you of a negative nature, and this incident, in time, was connected with the college affair. He spoke to Mrs. Stein and her friend, and picked up your ideas concerning the gallery. He did surmount them you see, and the interview was creative.

("I'd like to ask you about such things in the future.")

You may. Give us a moment. *(Pause.)* The religious area is tricky, because it contains high potentials for his development, and also sore points, you see. If he is asked to speak out of sincere desire, he can do his best. If he feels he is on trial in the religious area, then this has negative connotations.

I am trying to get at more material here. <u>When</u> (underlined) you can manage a trip it will be advantageous because of the literal bent his mind often takes. To him a change of environment is a change of mind. *(Smile.)*

There is more here. See if we can get at it. *(Pause.)* When he feels he has stumbled he does not walk right. When he cannot look to the right or the left it is because he is afraid to. *(Very rapidly.)* When his ankle bothers him it is because he fears he might fly off in the wrong direction. When his fingers are full it is because of accumulated bitterness, unspoken. When his periods are late he is "holding out" in quotes until he is certain of his direction.

Now all of this serves to impede constructive and creative spontaneity, and when this does find its way though, it is in such an explosive manner that he fears it because it seems undisciplined. If he lets go creatively he fears his aggressions will also be expressed spontaneously. But spontaneously released aggressions are not only natural but beneficial.

Others recognize them as legitimate, and are geared to handling them. When they are withheld others intuitively fear an explosion, and react accordingly. You had better take your break.

(10:35—10:45.)

Now. We will end briefly. *(Long pause.)*

When Ruburt finds himself concentrating upon his symptoms, then let it be a sign that normal aggressions are not being recognized, that he is afraid of hurting someone else, and that this is blocking his normal enjoyment of daily activities.

("What could he possibly do, that is so terrible, that would hurt others?")

I explained earlier his exaggerated notion of aggression and also the reasons behind it. The smallest aggressive jerking of his mother's bed could cause her pain, you see. Tremendous self-control was exerted. Do you follow me?

("Yes.")

So there was an exaggerated idea of the effect of normally expressed aggression. A normal child at times can slap its parent back, and the parent is obviously immune. The child's strength is nothing against the parent's. In Ruburt's case such normal reactions were out of the question.

("I get it." In answer to a questioning look.)

This caused him to withhold his strength under such circumstances. Those who felt it were obviously hurt out of all proportion. Now he did not realize this completely earlier, and this should help. It is more important than I can say.

(Long pause.) Do you have questions?

("I have often wondered: why do such childhood experiences have such lasting effects through an adult life, that may be many years longer?")

The effect is also positive. Again, it leads to Ruburt's desire to help others, and to look for a way to do so.

On the positive side to some extent it even led to our sessions, for he knows that my material, the material, can help prevent people from hurting each other. On the negative side, for him personally, it can lead to an exaggerated idea of the individual's vulnerability.

You have told him that life is far more generous, that there are built-in mechanisms of defense. He magnifies the terrors. He imagines, with the stray cats, you see, for the same reason.

You can help lead him to an understanding of the fact that life is far more vigorous than he realizes. It will also help to point out that he has positively used many of these elements creatively. He must not project an exaggerated idea of the power of aggression. At some time or another almost every child wishes that his parent or parents were dead, and the parents manage to survive quite well, until they are quite ready to leave your sphere of activity.

Normal aggressive acts are like microscopic chunks of ash that barely fly very fast or far. It is only highly charged and repressed aggressive energy that turns into bombs.

Have him read this session at least several times. And I wish you a fond good evening.

("Good evening, Seth, and thank you very much. It's very good.")

Your prayer efforts are an excellent idea.

(11:02.)

SESSION 474
APRIL 9, 1969 10:02 PM WEDNESDAY

(Jane and I had a long discussion before the session, etc.)

Alright. Now you are both afraid of making a move, but it is much easier for Ruburt to adopt the physical symptoms of immobility, because of his own background.

I told you in our last session that one member of a family could accept the symptoms for the whole family. Some of these are of course his own. In your particular circumstances, because of Ruburt's background, you see the physical manifestation of both of your fears—an incapability of motion.

Now in your discussion you released some emotions, and this is beneficial, but you have not discussed such problems together in some time. You feared upsetting Ruburt, and Ruburt would immediately insert desperately positive statements out of a panic to find that you were so disturbed, and this would anger you.

An inability to face or admit, or solve, physical problems, can also be reflected in the physical condition, and reactivate earlier sensitivities, leading to a sense of hopelessness. Then you come to an impasse where there is no motion of a positive nature, either in the physical realm, or the mental or spiritual one.

The very attempt to solve the physical problems brings out inner abilities.

The very attempt to solve the physical problems often solves the inner problems that are being projected upon the physical reality. You cannot stay within a physical condition you consider hopeless and not change it, and expect any kind of creativity or help. You must either accept the situation wholeheartedly, or reject it.

When you can into longer accept it then you must change it. Otherwise the feeling of hopelessness builds up. Ruburt has been afraid, because of his background, to accept the negative aspects of your exterior circumstances. He loves you so deeply that he never wants to admit that you are hurt, bitter or sad. He has always thought that you were used, mainly by your mother, but he was afraid that his statements would be misinterpreted because of his own relationship with his parents.

He feels you are being bled, money-wise. Now your physical situation is not entirely unbearable. Think what you have in comparison to what many human beings on your planet have, and you are kings. Remember that.

("I do think of that.")

However Ruburt has also picked up your feeling of hopelessness. Both of you have refused to come to grips with it and have been afraid of making any physical moves, or upsetting the apple cart. Ruburt is only too aware of the fact that he pushed to leave Sayre, and that your circumstances afterward in Florida were negative. He felt you blamed him for this, and thought it was an undisciplined action on his part, forcing you to make changes you did not want to make.

You would not have left your parents so <u>far</u> behind at that time, he felt, except on his behalf. He felt also that you chastised him and held it against him bitterly. He has therefore never pushed you really to make a change since that time, and has pushed such ideas away from him, although he feels that the longer you stay at Artistic the more unhappy you will be; and there is also in him, and in you, a fear of making a move in physical terms. You are afraid of the consequences.

When you are afraid to move you are creatively constricted. Ruburt is acting out your situation as a family and as a unit. You did this at one time. <u>That</u> (underlined) terrified him more than the present situation.

All of the material given concerning Ruburt's background and motives is highly legitimate, but it shows clearly why he was willing to take on this role. He thought it would free you. In late months he has seen that it has not.

He would do literally anything to see you relieved and happy, and working productively. He thought, or felt, that by taking on the symptoms of your joint problem, he could free you creatively, and was bewildered when it did not.

You were willing to let this continue, feeling that it was temporary, and that you had done it for him before. You have a deep distrust of moving, because of your parents' stationary background, and because of your father's distrust and fear of the outside world.

When you do move you have a tendency to feel that Ruburt should pay for the inconvenience. Here you associate him with your mother, and Ruburt feels this unfair. Except for our sessions there has been little freshness in your environments because you would find it, both of you now, threatening. In other words you have preferred to place the problem, both of you again, upon Ruburt in physical terms, rather than face the inner issues with initiative and daring.

You, Joseph, have been afraid of daring in that respect, and so have closed your mind to solutions that are possible. Ruburt's own affiliation and identification with a place has allowed him to burrow in here and thus go hand in hand with your fear, your own fear, of initiative movement.

You do to some extent identify with your mother, in terms of a husband rather than a son, now that the king, father, has been removed. Ruburt feels that the mother acts as a center from which you will not move, but feels guilty of this feeling. To some extent out of misguided loyalty, all of the men in your mother's life have kept her from using her own strength.

Her happiness is not dependent upon your activities however. She has far more vitality than any of you give her credit for. She will make out, in Ruburt's terms, no matter what you do, or your brothers do. You have used this as an excuse.

You may take a break or I will continue.
("We'll take the break.")
(10:32—10:35.)

Now you both thought that Ruburt's symptoms were a solution. You thought they bought you time. This has been a cooperative effort. You felt your physical problems insurmountable, that you had not the energy to face them. Ruburt's symptoms you thought gave you both time. You had moved so often in the past you were afraid of making a false move, and so you chose to make no move at all. You became afraid of challenge.

Ruburt was terrified because his early efforts seemed to have left you nowhere. You seemed to have no initiative to make a physical move on your own, and he was afraid of making another false suggestion. You simply became afraid to act in the physical universe. For a while you adopted the symptoms of immobility then Ruburt accepted them.

The thought of the Seth sale revived you. Then the old ideas of hopelessness settled back in, particularly when Ruburt discovered the taxes. You have both been resentful against your landlord, and particularly against Leonard Yaudes, and he had something to do with Ruburt's latest (underlined) symptoms.

Your attitudes are entirely wrong, and causing much of the difficulty. Properly applied, the book Ruburt's student brought from New York could be invaluable to you, and I mean invaluable. It does not mean that it would relieve you of personal responsibility, however.

Now take your break.

You have also picked up your father's bitterness. Some of your ideas are legitimate interpretations of the facts, but other are exaggerations. You must make an effort to face these other problems head on.

(10:43. Seth returned almost at once, after I said that I wasn't interested in solving our problems by simply changing jobs for more money — the problem was that I wanted time to paint, etc., and time for Jane to write.)

I am not speaking of the physical challenges of other jobs. You misinterpret me. I am telling you that when your entire physical circumstances appear hopeless to you, then you must change them, or honestly admit that these are the circumstances within which you must work, and not fool yourself. And when you do not feel that the physical circumstances are worthwhile, that you are not getting enough out of them, that the disadvantages outweigh the advantages, then you must change them. Here again attitude is all important.

Now. One note. You both felt that since you were the one who had the part-time job, Ruburt would accept the physical symptoms of your predicament, and you felt this was just.

You did because you felt that you were facing physical reality to that extent, and he was not. And he did for the same reason.

We are speaking of inner values; not inner self values but subconscious values.

One note. You would both do better nearer water.

(11:07. This was the end of the session, although Jane started out to merely take a break.)

SESSION 475 (DELETED)
APRIL 14, 1969 9:10 PM MONDAY

(Before the session, in line with our new way of thinking, Jane and I said that we could have six main categories in our lives: work; finances; living quarters; health; mobility; spiritual contentment, which would include helping others. The idea being that positive thought within these broad outlines would pay rich dividends.)

SESSION 475

Good evening.

("Good evening, Seth.")

You might recall that I have been giving you the same sort of material for some time now.

("Yes.")

As a unit you operate in certain ways. As individuals you operate in certain ways. When two individuals with strong negative thoughts are together, then their reality has strong negative aspects.

Remember that all of your behavior was not negative however, and give thanks for those abilities and accomplishments that are your own. Now, <u>imagine</u> (underlined) how you will feel when your paintings sell, the joy that they will bring others, the joy that you will feel knowing they are wanted. Imagine what you will do as you sell so many paintings that you need more time to produce them, and how you will then leave your job in order to paint, and the sort of place you will live, and the feeling of contentment and creative challenge that will fill you.

But do not imagine this in future terms, but in present terms. In other words, it is already accomplished, and it will then be fulfilled in physical reality. Do not then look <u>anxiously</u> (underlined) about for buyers, to check whether or not this is working.

Your own intuitions may suggest acts for you to take that will be beneficial. Be alert to the inner voice, so that if this is the case you will hear. Consider all of your contacts as possibilities, all of which may unfold, but do this imaginatively rather than <u>willfully</u>.

Now I tell you that if both of you use these methods, you will indeed completely change for the better not only your physical environment and reality, but your inner, creative, psychic and spiritual environment. Already because of belief, a massive healing is taking place. The thoughts themselves cause electromagnetic changes, signifying physical changes deep in the tissues.

But more than this, the fact itself of belief cleanses the psychic and spiritual channels of negative debris. Often in the past you worked against each other unwittingly. When one managed an overall psychic change for the better, the other would negate it through discouragement or negative patterns. Now as a unit your separate realities obviously form a larger combined unit in which you operate. Two of you working together can do seven times more than one operating alone. Do you follow me?

("Yes.")

Your trip *(Sunday, April 13; we drove to Cortland, NY)* was beneficial, but it was impeded by negative thoughts of Ruburt's, and also to some degree by the fact that you pointed out his symptoms without reminding him that the inner self <u>could</u> and <u>would</u> minimize them. You need to remind him when he forgets.

("I didn't even think of it that way." And should have, of course. This is one of those instances where the mere mention of what you have been doing makes the action glaringly obvious.)

It is helpful to point out that he is holding himself stiffly for example, but not in that manner. The approach should be "You can be flexible, you can relax. Remember your inner self is helping you relax, and be flexible." Or touch him as you say this and speak directly to the neck or shoulders or whatever is involved.

Otherwise he simply feels the weight of his errors, and becomes angry at himself. You may say "It's all right, you are learning. Now feel the inner self remedy the condition." But do not say "Your shoulders are stiff," or "You are not walking well," for you reinforce the condition. Say instead "You will find you can walk easier. Feel yourself flexible. Give your inner self a chance."

Do you understand the approach?

("Yes.")

In your own case, with paintings.

Now. Imagine your paintings in homes, in different environments, with people enjoying them. Imagine what you will do with the money. Settle upon a reasonable amount and expect it, knowing it is just. Do not think in a negative manner "This is good work. I won't let it go unless I get a good price. People owe it to me. Why should I let it go otherwise?"

("I don't seem to think that way."

(But upon reflection, I see that the part about "letting it go otherwise" is all too true, etc.)

Think instead, "This is a natural talent I have, and it is natural that it appeals to others, and as I have an abundance of talent, so shall it bring me abundance. It will help others, and it is natural that it help me."

Now you are learning these laws. It is simply a matter of applying them correctly. I have told you how they work, and how precisely your thoughts and feelings form the universe that you know, and your own reality as physical creatures.

It has taken you some time to understand this in practical terms. Ruburt gave you some good images when he said that thoughts were like the colors and the lines you use to make a painting. Except the painting, which is physical reality, has more dimensions, and you must experience it quite directly.

Your thoughts and feelings instantly reach out and form the objects that surround you. Calling upon this inner power, for it <u>is</u> power, will bring about the fulfillment of many other abilities and strengths that are within you. Do not limit it therefore. Do not insist for example that money come to you only through painting or writing, or that this power show itself only in health; and remember always you own relationship with others, so that the energy that flows through you and is used by you to your benefit, is also free to flow through you to others.

Do not dwell upon the physical inconveniences of your immediate environment, for this only brings about their continuance. Think in terms for example of space, and you will have at least a feeling of space within your present environment. You will also find that the idea of space is a part of you, and it will be given to you in this environment or another. And as long as you continue to think of Artistic as a poor-paying organization, so shall it be for you. It is your thoughts you must change, and these will bring about the changes you desire in physical reality. Telepathy operates.

The idea of financial abundance and of an abundance of the good things in life will not limit you, nor limit the means possible by which they will come to you. In your imagination therefore do not limit the means. See yourself enjoying the abundance.

If you reread much of the material you will again discover truths that escaped you; for I tell you precisely <u>how</u> the ideas in your book operate. But neither of you took me to heart in practical terms. You had the means and did not use it.

("We probably weren't desperate enough.")

(True. At break I took pains to explain to Jane that with the new approach I was using, I was quite aware that Seth had said it all before, and planned to go back over portions of the material thoroughly.)

I knew you would learn. Now. It is basic patterns of thought that help you or impede you, psychological colorations of thought that form the general overall pattern of your physical reality. One thought alone seems to matter little, and yet it is part of a characteristic pattern of inner behavior, and as such has its place either in bringing you freedom and abundance, or in denying you freedom and abundance.

Now when Ruburt tried to apply these laws in the past, he often did so erroneously out of a fear of action. As mentioned earlier, he exaggerated the power of aggression, so that the simplest self-protective act frightened him, and resentments built up.

He still believed in the fantastic ability of destruction, and he tried to cover it up. He did not believe that strongly in the creative function of his own being, and in the natural abundance of life itself. He was more pessimistic than you realized. A sick kitten was a dead kitten, not one who might recover.

He did indeed fear destruction so that he saw it everywhere, and therefore in himself. Nevertheless his creative functions continued. In one frown of yours he saw ten, and imagined all kinds of dire thoughts were going on within your head. A myriad of negative thoughts paraded and were exaggerated.

If he could not reach out to comb his hair correctly then he was no good, a cripple for life, and useless. Much of this has fallen away, but some patterns remain, though he is now alert to many of them.

Now you did the same sort of thing in financial terms. You simply picked different areas. Drawing upon this energy in one area also releases it on other areas. The poor do get poorer, the rich do get richer, because the poor become entrapped by their projections of poverty.

Using such abilities to obtain money only can be highly disadvantageous however in the long run, particularly if there is no thought given to the help of others. This is why you have miserable rich men. You can also have happy poor men. It is (underlined) possible, but in these cases limitations are put by the individual, closing off other channels, and this in unnatural.

Unless you place limitations these released powers will operate in all channels of your reality. (*Humorously.*) I did not realize that I had to speak to you in such simple terms. Now you may take your break. This is a read-along session...

(*"Oh yeah?"*)

... to attach to your book.

(*9:52—10:06. Jane's delivery was fast, etc.*)

Now, think of it as already accomplished, in the same way that you see the image of a painting before you paint it. Otherwise you are adding time limitations needlessly.

Imagine your surprise, delight and gratitude, as if the events had already occurred. This is not lying to yourself. It is instead forming the framework of your physical reality. Imagine it also in the future, and it will be in the future.

Imagine your reactions as if the events were already accomplished physical facts. Embellish them as much as possible. Then forget them. The feeling of expectancy is all important, that in the end all good can come today.

Now again, these thoughts actually form reality.

In your particular circumstances it was understandable that a while would elapse before you would put these truths to work for you in physical terms. To do so however increases their spiritual help also, for you see the results and then you have to realize that the truths are real.

Yet you must feel the truths are real before you can put them into effect. Do you follow me?

("Yes." This is about our present stage.)

As long as you felt that unfulfillments were a part of your lot, because of your backgrounds, then this came about as a result of your belief. Change your belief and the lacks vanish.

Form your new reality with as much trust and love and confidence, creativity and joy, as you do a painting, or Ruburt a poem. You have denied your powers. No one has closed you off. You had closed yourselves off. On the other hand, once you realize this there is no failure. You have your own abilities to work with however. This does not mean that Ruburt should expect to go off and make great money as a musician. But expect abundance and the release of all your abilities.

Again, do not limit. Ruburt should not forget the idea of some money from his painting, or you from writing. This does not mean any change of careers, it simply means that you should keep yourselves open. Otherwise you are saying that money and abundance come in this corner of my yard. And no other. Do you see?

("Yes.")

Now. Ruburt of course must work on his own attitudes along with the healing process. The knowledge that you are helping him however is of great import, and you can often help him when he needs it most. Health is not your hang-up. Because of your love of him, and his receptivity to you, you can be of great benefit; and touch on your part is far more important than either of you realize.

However Ruburt can be of great help to you as far as thoughts of abundance are concerned. With a few changes in his attitude, which I will try to bring out in our sessions, he can help bring about a definite change for the better in that regard.

There he <u>can</u> (underlined) be very free. Abundance is a good word to use, for it signifies a free and easy access to all pleasurable things, including creativity, mobility, both mental and physical, and easiness in <u>flow</u> (underlined) of any kind.

The word itself is the antithesis of restraint, and it is an excellent word for you to use—you—*(pointing to me)* and understand. It sets you apart from your father and mother, and serves to sever any negative suggestions. It will also release you in your paintings. It will serve to release your abilities in any direction, both of you.

The book you are reading is excellent for your purposes. Ruburt should watch feelings of restriction when he does your grocery shopping. This is negative. There is a difference between gluttony and abundance. Now you may take your break.

(10:28—10:39. Jane didn't recall any of the data.)

Now. The main point is the acceptance that all of this is as natural as rain or the seasons.

It was only your idea that this was <u>not</u> natural that prevented you from using your abilities fully. Ruburt thought it was natural for him to become ill because of his background, and to overreact for the same reason. He thought it was natural for him to be afraid of life because his mother was.

You thought it was natural and inevitable because of your background that you should not have money, even that you should be a loner for the same reason, and deny yourself natural companionship. Part of this you circumvented. The rest you did not.

You did not want to give of yourself to the world because you felt that this was a natural reaction, picked up from your father. You would paint, but not share. When you realize that health and abundance are natural, and illness and limitation unnatural, then you are free, free to develop, to use what you have, to give and take.

Now your attitudes for example toward this apartment formed your reality here from the moment you walked in. Both your positive and negative attitudes toward it seemingly were justified, because the exterior conditions mimicked perfectly your inner attitudes.

Did your attitudes cause the traffic then, you may ask, and I tell you that they did.

They exaggerated the sensory stimuli. Had your attitude been different the stimuli would have been so minimized that noise never would have bothered you. Literally, your environment would not have included it.

This does not mean you cannot have a home where there is no traffic, and where it is still. If you persisted upon focusing on noise rather than quiet however, you would find no quiet regardless of the circumstances. It would obviously be ridiculous to settle in the middle of a city like New York if you valued quiet above all things, so common sense operates. Yet even in the midst of that noise you could find quiet if that was your reality. There are several more points I want to make, rather important ones.

I will give them to you this evening or at our next session, as you prefer.
("You can at least start now." 10:48.)
Give us a moment then.

In his imagination, let Ruburt feel the sense of joy and release he would feel if he had run down the back stairs easily and joyfully. He need not see himself do so, but feel his emotions as if this had already happened not once but many times.

He need not concentrate upon images. Now he has been imagining himself happy in and out of the windows to clean them, and had some trouble with the images. Have him instead simply imagine his joy and freedom with the <u>performance</u> completed, and forget the means.

He is sitting inside looking out at the clean windows he has just washed from the outside. Have him imagine his feelings with the full realization that his entire strength and flexibility <u>have</u> returned. What will he say and what will he do—his joy and release, and forget the how.

And with your paintings, imagine the result, not the means. Your feelings with the accomplished facts. You are making a living as an artist at last, your triumph. How you spend your time, the galleries that want your work; and <u>divest yourself</u> of negative ideas regarding galleries. Do not limit yourself. Take that sentence to heart. Do not close doors.

Do not, from your experience with one gallery, project a negative attitude toward all galleries, any more than Ruburt should do this with publishers. This is highly important and represents a block in your progress.

Ruburt should definitely send some poetry manuscripts out, and work at his poetry. If he does not, then how can he complain that he has not written much lately? Galleries are a way of selling paintings. If you automatically view them negatively you are setting limitations. Let <u>all</u> doors be open.

Now because of your <u>latent</u> (underlined) interest in the medical profession, you have sold to hospitals in the past, commercially and you have sold paintings to dentists. There is a connection here. <u>Accept abundance in whatever way it comes</u>, and underline that entire sentence. Let this abundance express itself creatively in your work, and it will automatically bring financial abundance. For you particularly, use this word.

Ruburt's word should be flexibility in all aspects of his life. Now he thinks he punishes his body for being ill by not allowing it pleasure with you in intimate relations. He is now realizing that there is nothing to punish it for.

The intuitive realization came this afternoon, though he did not realize it, for it is natural for his body to bring him ease, pleasure and satisfaction.

Now I will end our session. My heartiest good wishes to you both. Your individual psychic work will also improve as a result of these efforts.

("Good night, Seth, and thank you." 11:03.)

DELETED SESSION
APRIL 15, 1969 TUESDAY

(These suggestions are based upon the reaadings by Jane and Rob in Psycho-Cybernetics. *We think they are excellent-we can identify with them because they*

"fit" our particular psyches in what we think are ideal ways. We plan to refer to them often, and trust that they will help others also.

(My body and all its organs were created by the infinite intelligence in my subconscious mind. It knows how to heal me. Its wisdom fashioned all my organs, tissues, muscles, and bones. This infinite healing presence within me is now transforming every atom of my being, making me whole and perfect now. I give thanks for the healing I know is taking place now: Wonderful are the works of the creative intelligence within me.

(April 15, 1969. Page 49.

(Infinite intelligence leads and guides me in all my ways. Perfect health is mine, and the Law of Harmony operates in my mind and body. Beauty, love, peace, and abundance are mine. The principle of right action and divine order govern my entire life. I know my major premise is based on the eternal truths of life, and I know, feel, and believe that my subconscious mind responds according to the nature of my conscious mind thinking.

(Page 41-42.

(The infinite intelligence which gave me this desire to paint leads, guides, and reveals to me the perfect plan for the unfolding of my desire. I know the deeper wisdom of my subconscious is now responding, and what I feel and claim within is expressed in the without. There is a balance, equilibrium, and equanimity.

(Page 42-43.

(My subconscious knows the answer to this problem. It is responding to me now. I give thanks because I know the infinite intelligence of my subconscious knows all things and is revealing the perfect answer to me now. My real conviction is now setting free the majesty and glory of my subconscious mind. I rejoice that it is so.

(Page 43.

(This prayer is for my wife, Jane. She is relaxed and at peace, poised, balanced, serene, and calm. The healing intelligence of her subconscious mind which created her body is now transforming every cell, nerve, tissue, muscle, and bone of her being according to the perfect pattern of all organs lodged in her subconscious mind.

(Silently, quietly, all distorted thought patterns in her subconscious mind are removed and dissolved, and the vitality, wholeness and beauty of the life principle are made manifest in every atom of her being. She is now open and receptive to the healing currents which are flowing through her like a river, restoring her to perfect health, harmony, and peace.

(All distortions and ugly images are now washed away by the infinite ocean of love and peace flowing through her, and it is so.
(April 15, 1969. Page 84.)

FROM CHAPTER 11

(From Chapter 11, page 128:
("Infinite intelligence attracts me to the buyers for each of my paintings. These buyers want the paintings and will enjoy having them. Each buyer is sent to me by the creative intelligence of my subconscious mind, which makes no mistakes. These buyers may look at many other paintings, but mine are the ones they want and will buy, because they are guided by the infinite intelligence within each of them. I know the buyers are right, the time is right, and the prices are right. The deeper currents of my subconscious mind are now in operation bringing the buyers and myself together in divine order. I know that it is so."
(Remember always that what you are seeking is also seeking you, and whenever you want to sell a property of any kind, there is always someone who wants what you have to offer. By using the powers of your subconscious mind correctly, you free your mind of all sense of competition and anxiety in buying and selling.)

SESSION 476 (DELETED)
APRIL 16, 1969 9:10 PM WEDNESDAY

Now, good evening.
("Good evening, Seth.")
We will continue along the lines begun, since *(humorously)* you seem to need this particular material now.
Remember that your present reality is the result of years of positive and negative thought patterns. It is good that you have begun to recognize some of your own negative attitudes, for it is highly important that you do so.
Realize that each time you replace a negative thought or feeling by a positive one, this is like making a correction in a painting. Soon you will be able to do this automatically, but in the beginning conscious effort is needed.
If Ruburt has the full plan for a book in his head, then this is real. It may take him a while to put it on paper. It may take him a while to receive the money when it is sold, but all of this is dependent upon the first and basic reality—the idea for the book. Therefore know that your positive ideas of health and abun-

dance are the basic realities, the most important.

Thoughts of abundance immediately begin to work for you, at their inception. Again, always consider the thing desired accomplished and projected in <u>present</u> reality, present physical reality, and so it shall be. This does not mean that a wish today for five thousand dollars will come minutes after. It does mean that it will come shortly, in your terms, according to your belief.

You must be systematic until your reactions become fairly automatic. You must therefore replace negative patterns with positive ones. As you know, the negative patterns bring results. Now give us a moment.

Do not overemphasize however in intellectual terms, but use imagination and feeling. An overemphasis implies a fear, and will impede results. Intensive concentration along these lines should be followed by several days when you simply do your prayer experiments and then let the whole thing drop from your mind, and give the creative inner self an opportunity to work for you. This will insure success and you will not be overhammering the point. Do you follow me?

("Yes.")

This doesn't mean that in the interim you allow every negative thought freedom however. Now you are beginning a most significant venture here. I want to impress upon you its importance. I want to make sure in these initial stages that you have the correct ideas. If you do not sell a painting by next week, for example, I do not want you to say "This does not work." You have many negative patterns to conquer.

It is quite possible you see for you to have results tomorrow, but it takes time to paint the picture from your idea. You <u>know</u> you will do the painting in physical terms, and you <u>know</u> you will have results in this endeavor, and excellent ones. It is very important that Ruburt, here, change his attitude toward his physical body – his own image of it.

He must think of it as lovely, flexible, quick and responsive. It has not done anything to <u>him</u>. He must think of lovingly recreating it, of helping it. He knows this but lest he forget I will remind him. He must think of it as a joy, a comfort, an aid, rather than a rigid bony thing he must put up with. He should consider it a thing of joy to himself and to you.

Now it will help him to some important degree if he considers his arms and his hands in the following manner.

"My arms are straight and flexible. And through them the creative energy moves freely, released and free, down to my hands and fingertips. Blessed are my hands and fingers through which creative energy translates intuitions, poetry, and knowledge to the typewritten page. Blessed are my hands and fingers which translate my ideas onto paper."

"As my mind and spirits are now flexible, so are my fingers flexible. Straight and free are my arms, so that intuitive knowledge can flow freely through them, out through my quickly moving fingers to the page. Open, straight and free are my arms to search for truths, and to embrace the magnificence of nature. My mind is open and clear, therefore my arms and hands which translate my thoughts into printing are open and clear, channels through which my creative energy may flow."

Give us a moment. *(Pause.)*

"I am free to stand or kneel, to run expectantly forward, for there is nothing ahead of me that I need fear, and the way ahead of me is clear and open. I am free to express my joy, for from it springs my life. I am free to bend. I am free to move easily and well, for I am composed of motion, and I move with the motion of my thoughts, which are free and open."

"I can see easily and well, for within my sight there is the freedom and joy of the universe. My spirit is free, and my body reflects its freedom."

You may take your break.

(9:46. Jane's trance had been good, her pace fast. Before the session I had asked that Seth give Jane a prayer that she could use for herself; I would say from the above that he responded in excellent fashion, as usual.

(Resume in the same manner at 10:00.)

Now. Give us a moment.

Your creative energies have always been highly beneficial and positive, and worked for you in ways you may not have known. Their energy has attracted other people to you both, and with all of your negative attitudes the overall impression others received from you, generally speaking, was of creativity.

Many do not know how to use their creative abilities. Many do not have specific abilities. Such people have often given you items for your household gladly and openly, because it made them feel a part of a creative endeavor.

Now you often projected negative thoughts, not being able to accept the items in the spirit in which they were given. You felt it made you inferior to accept such gifts. This is negative to begin with. You *(pointing to me)* wanted to feel aloof, and I tell you, superior. There is a knack in accepting and receiving. Your attitude was a rejecting one in general—that is, it was a reflection of a deeper pattern of negative thinking.

Some of this had to do with your own background. There was also a feeling, "Since you do not buy my paintings, do not hand me your junk." But these people did not feel you wanted them to buy your paintings. You did not project that thought.

In fact, you often stated that you wanted them as studies. They felt they were laying gifts at the altar of creativity, in their own way. I want to point out however the negative pattern behind this, on your part.

Give us a moment. *(Pause.)* To some extent there was a bottling up of energy, in that you could not take or give freely. You projected your own negative patterns of thought upon those who gave joyfully. This does not mean you look for alms. I did not mean they gave and therefore placed themselves above you. These were quite simply offerings, and they considered them little enough.

You mentioned this to Ruburt recently. I wanted to point out the important point however, the rejection on your part, as well as the attraction or the reason for the offering. Remember what I said about limitations. There is more here. Give us a moment. Behind it a fear of being taken advantage of when you accepted anything from another. But the habit of rejection, generally applied, (underlined) is a limiting one.

Specific incidents may be reacted to freely. But an overall pattern of rejection should be watched. It can extend to ideas, and limit both creativity and abundance. Its basis is fear. When you realize you have freedom, there is nothing to fear in this way. Do you follow me?

("Yes.")

Automatic rejections therefore should be avoided. In your thoughts of finances, also avoid limiting ideas, both specifically and generally. If a bill arrives do not think "How will we ever pay this?" or "This will make us short," for you are painting your picture of poverty, you see. Instead say to yourself "Money to pay this bill is coming to me." You will instantly set up currents of activity that will bring it about. With the other reaction you close them off and deny them.

Now Ruburt did follow through here with your car, and he simply saw you paying the last of the money, without any idea of where the money was coming from, but believing it would be there while not draining your own account.

You must still realize how practical these ideas are. You should realize it, for you can see their effect when they are used negatively. This is the way you build your life, whether you realize it or not. This is one of the main purposes of my material, that you construct your own physical reality, and that it is a replica of your ideas. For this does not apply within your system only, but beyond it.

Now you may take your break.

(10:26—10:36.)

Now. You do give to others. Those with whom you work, and those who come here. You give what you have to give. You receive what others have to give. You have helped broaden the horizons of many of the people that you know.

When some of these offer you a physical object for your home, they give in their way. You give to some. You may receive from others. You follow me?

("Yes.")

It is not I give you a spool of thread, and you give me a spool of thread, and we are even. You give to one in your way, and something may be given to you of a different nature by an entirely different person, and yet it is a result of your own giving. Therefore do not limit the flow of energy in such circumstances.

Now this will be the end of the session unless you have questions.

("I guess not.")

If you do have any on this evening's material to you, then I will answer them at our next session. My heartiest wishes to you both. A fond good evening, and success in your ventures.

("Thank you. Good night, Seth.")

(10:43. I told Jane that I did have a question but hadn't asked it because we both seemed to be tiring. It concerned the best general approach to establish our new attitudes, since we had many different desires at hand to deal with.

(Thus Seth returned at 10:45.)

That is why I told you that the word abundance was such a good one. Give us a moment. *(Pause.)* In your prayer episodes deal with Ruburt's health, and do not divide your efforts. Generally speaking however see a free, abundant flow of energy between you and your environment. I will need to give you more specific directions however, and for these I will wait until your next session.

You are mainly concerned with overall patterns of thought, <u>replacing</u> those that you already have, replacing negative ideas as you are aware of them. This does not take much additional time, you see.

("I was wondering about confusing the rest of the personality.")

Concentrate on the health issue in your exercises for now. Let your thoughts flow naturally during the day. They will of their own accord touch upon various issues such as work, finances and so forth. When they do then correct any negative thoughts with positive ones.

The <u>feeling</u> (underlined) of abundance, spiritual, psychic and physical, is what is important, and the avoidance of thoughts of limitations. I will have more to say in our next session. You are making it more complicated than it is. Give me a moment.

In the normal course of a day your thoughts dwell to some degree on the issues that you have mentioned, and about which you are concerned. Now in the past such thoughts were often highly negative, and they have resulted in negative conditions. No special efforts are required, save that such thoughts are now made positive.

The healing exercises will automatically increase spiritual abundance. When you feel you are ready, then the two daily prayer periods should be retained with a change of focus, that will take care of other issues. You need not concentrate them upon one issue or another. I will give you suggestions to use, and affirmations that will show results in all aspects, financial and otherwise. The change in your attitude will automatically begin to bring results in any case, and in all areas. Now does that answer your question?

("Yes, very well.")
Do you have others?
("Yes, but they can wait.")
I will bid you a second good evening.
("Good evening, Seth. It's been very interesting."
(10:58.)

SESSION 477 (DELETED)
APRIL 21, 1969 9:55 PM MONDAY

(The session was late in starting because we were visited by Curtis Kent from 8 to 9:45. He's an artist I work with at Artistic Card Co.)

Good evening.
("Good evening, Seth.")

Now. Since you have already been through one monologue this evening *(humorously)*, I will not keep you overlong with mine.

("I feel all right.")

I have some suggestions however. First of all, the "prayer" in quotes that I gave for Ruburt is tailored to his own needs, and will therefore be quite effective. I suggest that he use this during your prayer periods. In the morning it would be good for him to say this aloud, or even sing it in an exuberant manner.

Care then should be taken to concentrate on the daily matters at hand—his writing, and to avoid conscious concentration upon the state of his health or the progress of healing. Any positive improvements that you notice, Joseph, or any positive statements concerning his appearance or performance, should be stated. If possible spontaneously when you note them.

This will avoid any overemphasis such as might occur if only negative situations were mentioned. Do you follow me here?

("Yes.")

Now as to your noise episode, here are some suggestions for future use in <u>any</u> episode where irritation is involved. Followed, these suggestions will help you answer the demands put upon you when you feel the need for certain responses. When you are annoyed, if possible state your annoyance to the person involved, <u>reasonably,</u> (underlined) but at the time of the annoyance. When you do not respond in this manner the annoyance builds up and you are then tempted to respond to one incident as if many were involved, because the others were not responded to adequately at the time.

In the particular case for example you should have called your neighbor while you were being annoyed. That would be a healthy and reasonable response. Had this happened in each such case the annoyance would not have continued. Even if it <u>had</u>, you would then be justified in taking more firm steps.

On your part also then there was a reluctance to react to annoyance in a normal natural manner, and this is why the situation built up. By not reacting you gave your neighbor the license to further activity. By reacting normally you would indeed teach her respect for the regards of others, and <u>she</u> would have felt your reaction quite justified.

Your irritation would have been understandable and in proper proportion to the annoyance. When you do not behave in such a manner, bitterness piles up, and generally speaking you are not helping the other person involved. You may end up doing them harm through repressed reactions that suddenly explode.

When reactions seem emotionally out of proportion to one event then it is usually because of inadequate reactions to the same kind of event in the past. I am speaking now of reasonable reactions. I am not speaking of flying off the handle, say, at each small upset. Violence for example is the result of such repression.

Give us a moment. For you again now the word should be abundance. I would like you when you have time to meditate on the various kinds of abundance that you do presently enjoy. In terms of air, water, how freely these are available to you, sunlight, even the abundance for example of emotional energy present in your friend who just left here, for he makes it available to you also, and gives of it freely.

Think of abundance in terms of ideas also. In terms of color. I want you to feel easy with the word, and whenever you feel a sense of limitation of <u>any</u> kind, (underlined), then try to get the <u>feeling</u> (underlined) of abundance instead. Ruburt can also follow this advice. It will serve him well.

It would also release new ideas in your paintings and give you a sense of freedom in dealing with various techniques and media. You are not limited to

any media. You <u>choose</u> and have the freedom to choose. Do you follow me?
 (*"Yes."*)

You understand the abundance of energy possessed by your young neighbor. You simply do not want it expended at your expense. She does not know where to draw the line for her own good. She will be quite satisfied if someone she respects helps her draw a line of adequate behavior. She expected this from both of you for some time.

When you did not firmly or adequately express your displeasure then she wavered. She was not pleased with her own behavior, yet needed support that your reprimand would have provided, and can still provide.

Now you may take a break, end the session—
 (*"We'll take the break."*)
—or ask me questions. We will take our break then.
 (10:27—10:37.)

Now. To begin a program of reasonable adequate response, to annoying stimuli, is your best insurance against overreaction and repression.

Always ask yourself "Am I reacting to this present event only, as I should, or am I reacting to this event and five others in the past to which I did not react?" Soon you will find yourself with responses in proportion to present events, and will be free from old habits.

Now these are hardly your habits alone. I am using the present case but it has general implications. Your nervous system is prepared to act when you are annoyed. Left alone and operating naturally, you can trust its spontaneous response. It <u>will be</u> in proportion. It is only when you overload the nervous system by such repressed action that it then begins a cycle of overreaction to what seems to be one event.

For a while then you must closely watch your reactions by making sure that you are only reacting to a present episode. Soon automatically the system becomes adjusted to normal action, and the process becomes automatic again. It is also important to react <u>when</u> you feel an annoyance, rather than postpone action, whenever this is possible. Your system is cleared. When you are beginning to learn you may find yourself overreacting initially, simply because of the accumulated, unrecognized charge of past repression.

This applies to you then in your way, as well as to Ruburt in his way. It also applies to all of your reactions. It is the spontaneous nature of emotional creatures, and it frees the self and opens the channels of creativity. When you are pleased or joyful or have a pleasant comment, then these should also be expressed <u>at the time</u>, and in the fullness of those emotions, for such expression satisfies and pleases your own system, and also pleases others.

These things should not be postponed either. Do you have questions?

("No, I guess not. Just continue as you are.")

The system then enjoys its own spontaneous expression, and is flexible and therefore more receptive. Postponement of reaction can then lead to a pattern of rejection, for you are rejecting the expression of your own emotions. Again, this does not apply only to you personally.

The suggestions I have given you here can be of great practical use to you personally. If you do not have questions then I will end the session. I am trying to get you both straightened out, but this material, directed to you, can still be of great general use. Ruburt can interpret it for the help of others. My fondest wishes to you both, and a hearty good evening.

("Good evening, Seth.")

(Humorously:) I would stay longer, but out of the goodness of my heart—

("You can stay longer.")

—I give you rest. *(Pause.)* I can stay longer. You fought a battle with yourself however over the noise issue, and this more than the lack of sleep leaves you in need, now, of that refreshment that sleep can bring.

("All right then.")

(10:55—10:58.)

One note. It is extremely important that your dissatisfaction be expressed to your neighbor, and by <u>you</u>. Ruburt may join in, but it is important that you personally express this irritation, and feel its release for yourself in so doing.

Whenever possible such reactions should always be expressed directly by the person involved to the person who causes the irritation, regardless of whatever steps may be taken. The self feels cheated otherwise to some extent. Also with such expression there is a direct involvement with the offender, and such involvement can lead to greater understanding on both parts that otherwise might not result. The interaction is important to both parties. Do you follow me?

("Yes.")

Your neighbor has no <u>real</u> conscious knowledge of the nature of your emotional reaction. You projected negative attitudes upon her because you had not reacted adequately in the past. She would feel hit by a sledge hammer if you followed through on your plan. *(Pause.)* She is looking for direction.

Now, sweet dreams.

("The same to you.")

(11:03.)

SESSION 478 (DELETED)
APRIL 28, 1969 9:05 PM MONDAY

Good evening.

("Good evening, Seth.")

Now, as for Ruburt's upset Saturday... It was caused by a fear of fear.

He became so aware of fear's destructive energies that he panicked, thinking there was no way to keep fear away. It was quite beneficial that he spoke to you about the brief depression, for this helped relieve it, and your reassurances helped rouse his confidence.

He was frightened at the amount of negative thought that he encountered in himself, and recognized. Now you are not actively to seek out negative thoughts, but to find positive ones. Otherwise you concentrate upon the feared result rather than the desired one.

The negative thoughts can and should be recognized and plucked up as they are encountered, but you do not need a shovel to pluck up one weed at a time, nor hit yourself over the head with a sledgehammer for finding a weed in your garden. This does little to help the gardener but put him out of commission for a while, and it does not pluck any more weeds.

In other words negative thoughts can be recognized and plucked out with no more rancor than you would pluck out weeds in a garden. There is no need blaming yourself that in the past you allowed the weeds to grow, sometimes in your ignorance imagining them to be flowers. Your job now is simply to remove them, and as you remove each one, <u>easily</u>, to drop in a seed of positive thought to replace it.

A few fond prayers, such as you have been doing, are fine. But a watched kettle, if you will forgive the mixed metaphors, does not boil. Let the subconscious bring the seed to fruition. It does not need to be watered with tears, with pledges, or told ten times a minute to grow. These things put a shadow over the seed.

Fear of any kind, including fear of fear, is destructive. <u>A negative thought gains in power to the extent that you fear it</u>, and you had better underline that whole sentence. A better attitude is "Well, there is a negative thought, let's get rid of it." Now, mentally, have Ruburt pretend it is simply a weed, and mentally throw it over his shoulder after he has plucked it from the seed of his consciousness.

Now we will throw in something better. Even the word "peace" will do. He need not go about at the time searching for an antidote, you see. "Those aren't the kind of thoughts I want," that mental statement is a help. If the negative mood persists a while he should not think "Oh now this will be reflected in symptoms, what can I do?" This adds more negative connotations.

He should instead think "Well, this will pass, and I let it pass." Minimize its importance, if necessary, rather than overstate a projected negative reaction to an already negative mood.

Now tell him he has learned, for in the past he would have allowed this to continue, and he did not. You help him pluck out the mood. The whole idea is not fear of the symptoms that you have. He must not build them up by comparing them with the state of health that he desires. This builds up the wrong end of the equation.

Instead imagine the desired result, the health; and his methods in *Psycho-Cybernetics* do serve him very well in that regard, firing his imagination. One of the main problems however is any undue emphasis on the problem. The emphasis should be on the solution as already being known, and being (underlined) realized.

One of the gravest errors he makes is in thinking "How far from health I am," when he compares what he wants to present physical conditions. Then self-pity enters in.

I will give you a prime example, and it is one of the reasons why difficulties are sometimes encountered on weekends, often the situation when the two of you plan to go downtown in the morning. The night before he worries, and often consciously, that he will not be in good condition, and imaginatively then as a result, sees himself in poor condition. Because of the force of the imagination this does sometimes then occur. Then he compares your health and vitality to his condition, and imagines you are impatient with him, since he quite literally drags his feet.

He drags his feet because he does not want to go, because he is afraid that he will be in the poor condition that his imagination has gotten him into. The more urgently you want to make the trip, you see, the better he wants to feel, to make it with you. His mistake has been in letting his imagination work against him, thwarting his desire, rather than for him.

His mental attitude should be "Of course I can feel fine in the morning," and instead of imagining himself dragging down the stairs, he should playfully imagine himself ahead of you, as if he were playing a game. The pity of the world's present situation is that the methods people use often to achieve their desires, are those specific methods that will bring them the opposite.

Now I have mentioned this because neither of you realized it. Ruburt was furious in the store, and felt abandoned. He was furious at himself however, not you, that he could not follow you quickly enough. He was angry at the salesgirl, whom he likes, for her remark about his weight, and he was sore at himself for being sore in body.

Now I have given you suggestions that will work to clear up the difficulties I have named. In the overall with your methods, he is doing well. The specifics showed their results, and as more specifics arise, if they do, I will mention them.

On <u>occasion</u> only, there is some difficulty with the grocery store, and he suspects this. He berates himself for not being able to help you more in the carrying of the bags, and in any ordinary chores with which he would normally assist you. This includes the carrying of the wash. You forget how conscientious he is toward you.

Your assistance here will be of help. Remarks such as "Soon I'll let you carry all the bags," or "Soon you can carry them all," will help. It is also good to remind him that he carried the bags for you when you were ill, and that you regained your strength, and that he is regaining his strength.

The problem is obviously distressing, but help is not to be found by discussing its distressing aspects. It does not serve as an impetus any longer, now that the problem has been faced. Now concentration should be upon the desired solution. He must not grit his teeth and think "<u>I will get better</u>." Both of you should look for, and mention, any new freedoms. A feeling of expectancy on both of your parts will be of great benefit, and must in fact be a part of your prayer activities.

Now generally he has made strides, particularly in the morning. He should not spend any day entirely inside, as you know. He should imaginatively see himself using his body properly, for these thoughts alone activate it. But the whole idea should be "I am free, to clean the cupboards, to get down on my knees, to get up." Feelings of mobility are highly important.

Now out of mercy for your fingers you may take a break. I presume you need one.

("I guess so.")

(9:50. During break I made several remarks about the poor quality of the pen I was trying to take notes with, and of our difficulties lately finding the brand pen we had been used to using, and which worked so well. I intended to add more to my remarks, but Seth broke in at 9:58.)

Now. By such a statement you effectively make sure that you will not find the pen you want, and it is a small example of the use of the wrong method.

("I expect to find one in another store, though." This is what I had intended adding to my statements.)

The remark that you just made was the kind of a remark that put an impediment between the desired end and… *(Here the pace was too fast for a couple of sentences. Here, again, Seth refers to my remarks at break.)*

Instead, you should see the pen you want in your mind, know that you will have a steady supply of them, recognize the statement you just made as leading away from your desire, and replacing it with a statement like the one you just made.

"I know I will find a store that carries the type of pen I desire." This is a small illustration but a good one. You should study it, for it applies to everything, and any desire. You have within you a readymade method of achieving desire: positive visualization, positive imagination, and confidence.

Negative visualization, negative imagination, and the feeling that the result will not be achieved, leads to the opposite of your desire. There is no other way, nor answer. To affirm is to receive. To deny is to lose.

Now there have been some definite accomplishments since your prayer period, and if you had the proper attitude of expectancy in the beginning, both of you, you would have added gratitude in your prayers for what has been received. The overall condition is looser. The spirits almost immediately began to revive, outside of the few errors. The arms have dropped down once again from the very uptight position they held at the beginning of your venture. The aching and pain has disappeared, and the soreness is beginning to disappear.

Do you want a break while you look for a proper pen?

("No." 10:05.)

To some extent, (underlined) you have still been concentrating upon the symptoms that remain, hardly noting those that have been relieved. This could have a tendency to undermine your confidence. Here I am pointing out adjustments to be made, but I do not mean to say that you have not been meeting with success.

With these adjustments made there will be a very noticeable change for the better and an acceleration of healing.

Your apartment-hunting ventures have added to a sense of freedom on both of your parts.

Now apply what I have said tonight about Ruburt to yourself, in terms of your desire for abundance in all things, and examine yourself to see what negative attitudes you have, that you may not have recognized. Take the pen example, and apply it to other things that you want; and remember again, imagination as a valuable tool used correctly. It is your paintbrush, with which you form your reality. Do you have questions?

("No, I haven't had a chance to think. I'm concentrating on selling paintings.")

This is indeed beneficial. Think of selling them with love, and you must love the people you sell them to. I do not mean a false Pollyanna-type love, but you must feel that the paintings will bless them, and that you in turn accept the abundance in terms of money which will return to you.

Give me a moment. *(Pause.)* The idea of the ad *(to sell paintings)* is a good one. There is a reason why you have done nothing about it. For one thing, remembering what you are reading, there are several attitudes that you should change, for while you believe them you work against your desire. And physical events <u>then</u> (underlined) seem to prove the attitudes true:

"Society does not give a hoot about the artist. We could starve for all most people care. People don't want to buy a painting. They'd rather buy a TV set. People come in here and look at my paintings, but I don't see them buying any. People don't want to pay good money for paintings."

Now these are merely a few ideas that come to mind, and while you hold them they form the reality in which you exist physically. Change the ideas around completely, and I tell you, you will sell your paintings. While you hold these ideas you are telling yourself that your desire cannot become fact.

Now do you have any questions?

("I've been working on those attitudes.")

Then I suggest we end the session, although I will answer any questions you have in mind.

("Why did our landlord sell this house?")

Give me a moment. *(Pause.)* One point, not having to do with the sale: he feels that you and Ruburt have no time for him, since he moved away. Telepathically he picked up your envy, and it hurts him because he is afraid of his own driving concern for money and security. This is why he plies you with food and drink when you do see him there. *(At his dine-and-dance club.)*

He is always afraid because he feels lost in disorganization. He feels guilty for his daughter's difficulty. He sold the house on the one hand to make money, and on the other hand he sold it to do penance because in his own way he loved it. He talked of selling the land and tearing down the terrace as a projected act of self-mutilation, mutilating something that he loved, to do penance for his sins, in his light.

He felt driven to do so. He is filled with a great love that he can never fully express, and is gifted with an intuition that he cannot follow but cannot close out. His intuitional abilities are considerable. It was not because he did not care for the house, but because he did care that he sold it.

Now take your break or end the session as you prefer.

("Well I guess we'll end it then.")

My heartiest wishes to you both, and a fond good evening.

("Good night, Seth."
(10:29.)

SESSION 479 (DELETED)
APRIL 30, 1969 9:10 PM WEDNESDAY

Good evening.
("Good evening, Seth.")
Now. While the emphasis in our last sessions has been mainly on Ruburt's condition, there is a definite overall general application, and this portion of the material will someday be used, though not verbatim, in a book having to do with my ideas on health.

Now it is true that two individuals in particular who have left physical reality have been trying to help Ruburt, particularly in the dream state. These two initially were contacted by Edwards. They carry on conversations with Ruburt and on an entirely different level than the normal conscious one.

They attempt to straighten out his basic ideas. They also give directions for him to his own supraconscious, so that suitable physical adjustments may follow. It will help if Ruburt remembers this fact, and does remind himself that he is indeed being aided, although the work is not being done <u>for</u> him.

If he reminds himself then he will have memory of some of these encounters, and this will be of help. The word exuberant is a good one for him to use. He should create the feeling within himself, and it <u>will</u> be physically materialized.

The added monthly count on his part was the offshoot of the work he has done thinking of abundance. Granted the effects were not large, but they were definite. He did not overconcentrate, you see. He sent out the thoughts with full confidence, but in almost a playful manner, thinking merely of extra money.

He did not think of what he <u>lacked</u>, but of what he wanted. And this is what must be done in the health work. His dental appointment today in a way amounted to the same thing. He wanted brilliant teeth *(humorously)* for the visit of your Aerofranz *(Tam Mossman)*, and he gave a quick but direct message when he made the phone call, that an appointment would be available before your friend arrived.

(Tam arrives this weekend, May 2. Jane's original dental appointment was for later in May. The receptionist told Jane she would notify Jane of any cancellations that developed.)

He did not think "How miserable my teeth will look." He thought instead briefly, effectively and playfully, "When Tam comes my teeth will be cleaned. No matter what she says, there will be an appointment for me this week."

Tell him then again, easy does it. The imagination is all important. Even be ridiculous with the use of the imagination. Have him imagine for example pillow fights with you, or wrestling on the floor with you. Now it is extremely important that his conscious attention be elsewhere after he has given his suggestions. I suggest the following: that he worked at his writing certainly no less than four hours a day, preferably five; and that a portion of this time be given to poetry.

This will effectively have him concentrate his attention where it belongs, while the inner self follows through on the suggestion which he has given.

Now this is a necessity: the *Psycho-Cybernetics* for at least fifteen minutes, no more than a half hour, in which time he allows his imagination full imaginative play, positive play, where he is writing well, enjoying his body, where his pursuits are succeeding. He does very well at this, but during this time have him concentrate on the imagination, and not give conscious suggestions to himself for he then becomes too heavy-handed.

The prayer series should be continued. In this period let the conscious suggestions be given with emotion and feeling, and then have him forget all about them. He does not need to give himself conscious suggestions every fifteen minutes. This is too much like clock watching.

The before-bed suggestions, given lightly and with feeling, are fine. He has done better in that area. Again, any signs of progress should be encouraged, noticed, and concentrated upon. Now this is the plan that I recommend.

You have already sold a painting, and will learn of it shortly.

Now give us a moment. Your feelings toward the parking lot have gone out from you, and from others, to bring the proceeding at least to a temporary halt. Your landlord is extremely suggestible, and your own feelings fell on fertile ground, the ground of his misgivings.

I believe that the garage will be torn down to provide extra parking in any case—the doctor's garage. The affair is highly plastic at this time. There is a good possibility that your land will not be touched.

(*This may be so. However on Saturday, May 3, 1969, the landlord and a helper tore down three-quarters of the terrace extending outside our living room windows. The land in this area would be used for any parking facility.*

(*This session was held on Wednesday, April 30. On Thursday and Friday, May 1 & 2, surveyors were at work on the property, laying out the dimensions for a proposed parking lot that would run from W. Water St, in front of the house, to the back fence of the property, some hundred feet.*)

There is also a good possibility that your Dr. Levine and another doctor, or dentist, will combine their finances and share the lot on the other corner. There may also be an arrangement where Dr. Stamp's garage is torn down, and the two driveways combined into a small parking area. At this time however conditions are very plastic.

("How about the deal for the house itself?")

Give us a moment. A period of time where the issue is uncertain on both the part of your present landlord and your prospective buyer. *(Florence Halliday, who was once an ESP student of Jane's.)* This, again because of the psychic conditions involved, is highly plastic. The woman wants the house badly. She is stronger because of this desire at this time.

("Did she know about the parking lot?")

On the other hand her lawyer may say something to your landlord that will make him make an angry retort that will <u>then</u> cause the buyer to hold off. She may not buy, believing that a parking area will be set up to drive off the sort of tenants she wants; and then after this proscribed time of contract the parking area itself may well fall through, as I told you. These are the probabilities now, in which case your landlord will still own the property, and it will be relatively unchanged.

There was deception in the terms of half-truths, not completely explained, in answer to your question. The truth was stated in such a way that it's implications were not understood.

(This statement of Seth's has been more than vindicated. First a mutual friend of Jane's and F. Halliday explained what was intended by the parking lot. This on Thursday, May 1. F. Halliday could not believe the parking lot idea, saying she had been told a "circular driveway" was all that had been planned, curving around the doctor's house next door, and not disturbing much property. She had no idea that much of the yard on the side of the house, from the street to the far back fence, had been earmarked by our landlord for sale to Dr Levine for a parking lot.

(On Sunday, May 4, Jane spoke to F. Halliday by telephone, and was so informed by the prospective landlady herself. She is to see her lawyer, "to see what can be done, if anything," etc.)

Now you may take your break.

Put in the letters P A L here. I do not know if this has to do with the house situation, or to your painting. When more comes on this I will give it to you.

(9:50—10:05.)

Now. Your expectations are initially emotional.

They pulsate. Their force is dependent upon their intensity. When enough of these in a given area congregate together a strong field of activity and attraction is formed *(long pause)* a highly plastic first draft or underpainting model for future events or physical reality.

As this field is further activated through imagination, emotion and expectation, it becomes more highly charged and attracts to it those elements which it needs to give dimension to those elements already present in the basic version. Do you see?

("Yes.")

Once begun it contains its own motive power then, repelling those elements that do not fit in with its sense of unity, and attracting those that do. All of this goes on before any event appears in physical terms, in the same way that much creative activity goes on hidden in your mind, behind each movement of your hand as you apply paint with a brush to a painting. You see the color and the brush strokes but you do not see the inner workings that led you to produce those particular brush strokes. You know they are there, the inner meanings, but you do not see them in physical terms. You see instead their effects in the color, the brush strokes and the painting.

Now you give yourself conscious direction by taking it for granted that you paint well, by trying to see the completed painting in your mind. This is the function of the conscious self, to use the emotions and expectations to bring about a desired result.

You then let the motive power within take over but you do not try to bully it. If your conscious mind is to be a foreman he must be one who is easy to get along with, and not so authoritative that he is yelling demands all the time. He is to be a gentle director and not a bully.

He is only a bully when he suspects that his in quotes now "subordinates" are in rebellion. The inner self is not a subordinate to begin with. It is the power that has been given to you as an identity, its services available to you—that is, available to your present personality, for its use.

It does what you want it to do, in other words, but it still contains abilities of which you have little knowledge, and sources of information that belong to the entire entity of which you are but a part. It <u>is</u> a protector. It will even protect you despite your own wishes, keeping the physical system going for example.

It is your contact with All That Is, but it is up to the conscious mind of the present individual as to how much its abilities will be used and in what manner. The present individual is to learn. The inner self therefore does not overstep the boundaries of the ego, go against the ego's wishes, or try to <u>force</u> (underline) the ego. It is up to the ego to learn how to use these vast potentials that lie within the inner self, how to use them to help itself and others.

If the inner self took over completely therefore the present personality would not learn on its own. The inner self does offer advice, intuitional help, inspiration, all of these things, but it does not force the ego to accept them.

When the ego is using its abilities in an unfortunate manner the inner self sets up warning systems, sometimes even bringing the physical organism to a physical or symbolic halt to prevent the ego from doing further damage through misdirection.

Through these maneuvers the inner self does teach the ego the proper use of these inner potentials. The inner self literally carries the ego, and provides life sustenance. Now you may take your break.

The sale of the painting has already taken place within inner reality. I am not sure here, I believe a three-week period may be involved before the actualization. But an individual has already decided to buy; and two will be bought shortly, one by a man and one by a woman.

Imagine vividly an empty space on the wall in place of any painting now hanging there that you wish to sell. Imagine yourself wondering what to put there now that the painting has sold. See yourself discussing this with Ruburt.

Now. Imagine someone asking you if you have sold any paintings lately. See and hear yourself telling them *(long pause)* that you are selling more paintings than you ever believed possible. See an envelope marked with painting money and see it stuffed full of painting money that you have received from your paintings. Imagine how you will spend it.

Think how thankful you are to have such a talent. This is most important. Never think that perhaps you would be better off without it, or that it presents more difficulties than those encountered by other men. Be thankful for the talent, be thankful that others appreciate it. See how natural it is that it should be appreciated. Think in terms of the intuitional help your painting gives to others.

Be careful of the suggestion "I will sell all the paintings that I want to sell," for you are setting up conditions and limitations. Either say "I will sell all my paintings," or "I will sell these paintings," referring to specificness. Do you understand the difference?

("Yes.")

Give us a moment. *(Pause.)* Do not say "so-and-so will buy such-and-such a painting, he has the money," if there is any touch of accusation in the statement "He has money." Do you follow me?

("Yes, but I don't believe I do that.")

Now do you have any questions?

("No, I guess not.")

The feeling of freedom on both of your parts has increased. Do not overwhelm yourself with suggestions before sleep, but it is a very good time to give yourself suggestions concerning your painting in terms of creative intuitions to help you use your abilities.

("Yes.... Why haven't I put the ad in the paper about selling my paintings?")

Why did you not?

("Yes." Seth mentioned this recently.)

For several reasons. Give us a moment. *(Pause.)*

You do not like to advertise. You feel that people should come to you. This is a method however to bring them to you, and a legitimate way of gaining attention. You have held off, also negatively, not wanting strangers to come and disrupt you. Buyers however would help your ability and not hinder it, and make it possible for you to devote your energies to your work.

There is some connection here that you can easily dislodge, having to do with your father's reluctance to sell his photographs, his attitude, and his reaction to clients when they entered the house. You have remarked that your mother did his selling for him, or he would not have done it.

These, again, have no power over you if you counter them with positive suggestions. There are some other reasons and I will discuss them with you at our next session. An understanding of them will be of benefit.

You must share your talent, that is why you have it. Underline that.

Now you may take a break or end the session as you prefer.

("We'll end it then.")

My heartiest good wishes to you both, and a fond good evening.

("Good night, Seth, and thank you very much.")

(10:55. Jane said she was "really out," etc.)

SESSION 480 (DELETED)
MAY 7, 1969 9:08 PM WEDNESDAY

(Jane and I sat for the session as usual on Monday, May 5, but it was not held. Jane at session time was in an extremely relaxed state, and she could not bring Seth through, although we waited until 10 PM.

(Tam Mossman and his fiancée Eve had been our guests over the past weekend, May 2—4; he had heartily approved the work Jane has completed on the Seth book and we thought that this belief might have something to do with Jane's very relaxed state. Jane said no conscious suggestions, that she was aware of, had been

involved today or this evening. Tam is Jane's editor at Prentice-Hall, Inc.

(Jane said the sensations were "like a loss of tension," and I thought it was a general release from her symptoms, at least temporarily, plus a dissociated state. While sitting in the usual rocking chair she uses during sessions, Jane said that at times she felt as though she were outside the house, enjoying the spring air, grass, flowers, etc. She told me that at various times Seth was around during the evening while we waited, but never did come through.

(Jane experienced a remarkable release from symptoms, but even so her neck was not fully released, as she determined by testing. She had done some yoga this afternoon, but she didn't think this had anything to do with the present state.

(The next morning, we must note, the symptoms had returned; Jane was tight and stiff, though as the day wore on they lessened.

(The session on Wednesday was held as usual, and of course we asked Seth for an explanation of Monday's events.)

Good evening.

("Good evening, Seth.")

Now. If our friend feels fully productive, exuberant and free to use his abilities, then he will be entirely healthy.

He has overemphasized limitations in the past, of all kinds, and this has led him to deny many of his own positive characteristics—this concentration upon the negative. Now some of this he picked up from you, and then exaggerated. Much of this attitude in passing now.

I suggest however that you continue your own prayer periods, as you have been doing them. Ruburt during his period should imagine feelings of exuberance, energy, and inspiration, general feelings of release and freedom. Let him play a game with himself however as to how long he can honestly <u>forget</u> (underlined) his symptoms in daily activity. Do not give them extra energy through concentration.

In his prayer periods emphasize that his full attention can go into his work and creative endeavors. This automatically takes energy away from the symptoms.

("Have the prayer sessions been doing any good?")

They have indeed. Now give me a moment, *(pause),* and a long moment. *(Pause.)* Concentration should not be upon feeling well enough in the morning to do something he wants to do. It should be upon the thing he wants to do, and away from the physical condition. When he feels his full enthusiasm bubbling up in his work he will not need to give himself suggestions that he will feel well in the morning.

The inner self will see to it that he does. Health should be considered then

—and this is important—as a means to a desired end; full productive creative work; full use of abilities; daily enjoyment; helping others. When he focuses upon health itself as such, he overconcentrates. Health as a means to excellent performance in fields that are important to him; health as a means to use those abilities with which he has been honored; health as a means to bring joy to himself and hence to others; health as a source of strength that is available always to help him use those abilities and to fulfill his destiny here, now…

Now this information will help in the most important way—to help him get over those blocks still operating. Health as a means of allowing creative energy to flow through him.

Give us a moment. *(Pause.)* This will drastically reduce his concentration on symptoms. *(Long pause.)* He can imagine health as a means also of showing others, of setting an example.

Now. He was frightened to some degree of the sudden reduction of tension. This refers to Monday and Tuesday. He is used to being armed for battle. There is no battle, and that is the secret. In the past the reaction would have lasted much longer however, and considering that he had it at all, he did not succumb to anything like the same extent.

The focus again now therefore, in his prayers, should be on feelings of peace, tranquility, safety and joy in creativity. He need not fight invisible enemies nor brace himself against them. This sort of focus, <u>for his personal</u> makeup, will bring about a quicker complete recovery. Now, you have the season on your side. Give me a moment. *(Long pause.)*

Now if you will touch him affectionately, or speak in such a manner, when the two of you first awaken, this gentle reminder of our love and affection will be of great help. <u>Particularly</u> on awakening, and you have helped him immensely through such gestures and affirmations. It is safe for him to relax. This is the important point. *(Long pause.)*

I am trying to delve into questions concerning the bedroom. *(Two minute pause.)* Try this: now a north-south direction is still best, as I told you. But with the bed now out further toward the center of the room, with space on either side of it you see, so it is open and is not against the wall. The doors open so that the light from the other rooms, from the windows, is available.

(Long pause. For many months now our bed has been in an east-west position.)

He should put into the bedroom objects that have particular value for him. I do not mean furniture necessarily. But the bedroom is devoid of the favorite objects he keeps about him in this room. *(The living room.)* He feels that such objects are protective, and since he is without these he feels more vulnerable.

(9:41. We were interrupted by a telephone call. It was from Bill Macdonnel, in California. After I hung up we decided to make it a break time. During break I voiced a question.

(My question had to do with the various kinds of experience sought by the inner self. I wondered, with some apparent irritation, why Jane's inner self would permit such a detriment as the symptoms to continue for so long. Once the experience of the illness had been gained, it seemed to me, it made better sense for the inner self to terminate the particular experience and move on to others. I thought there were many more valuable kinds of experiences to be had in many kinds of healthier, more creative endeavors, instead of letting the symptoms interfere with Jane's attempts to perform such creative endeavors.

(Resume at 9:50.)

Now. I told you in our last session that the inner self will not take over entirely. In this particular case built-up negative attitudes of years' standing set up negative patterns that prevented the most creative parts of the self from using their natural potential.

Now there are distinctions to be made. The negative patterns, many of them, came from conscious deductions made about the nature of reality. They seeped down into the personal subconscious layer, causing blockages here that prevented even deeper areas of the self *(pause)* from giving necessary help.

The subconscious—personal subconscious layer – became blocked with debris that seeped down from the conscious layer. The personal subconscious then acted like a lid, blocking off the healing energies that came from below. Now your book uses the term subconscious to cover the whole inner self. Those healing abilities, that exuberance and love of life, is from a deeper layer of the self.

There is no doubt in this deeper layer that full abilities will be used, and potentialities carried out, and there is no time to this portion of the self. There is no desperation there.

(This also irritated me.

("Well, it knows part of the personality is involved with time though, doesn't it?)

It does indeed; and it continues along all lines available to it. If it is cut off in one area it will find another. Now the reversal of the negative trend has already taken place, so openings are available. But <u>both</u> of you are overanxious, and even you concentrate too much upon what seems to be the enormity of the difficulty, or Ruburt's present predicament.

("It's rather difficult to avoid"

(More irritation on my part. I felt, and still do as this is written, that Seth gave only a partial answer to the original question, concerning the purposes and awarenesses of the inner self; I intend to press for a more complete answer.)

It is exactly what you must avoid, and what you tell Ruburt he must avoid, for it does reinforce the present condition. You both have a tendency to concentrate upon remaining symptoms, or intensified ones, and to give little attention to the improvements. It is as if the improvements did not exist, and they do.

That is an important sentence. You are both concentrating on the remaining symptoms, and the improvements escape you. You do not give energy to them, nor look for them. You look for the remaining symptoms. You do not add reality, physical reality then, to improvements as they first show—you do not nurse them expectantly as you would a seed. You concentrate on the part of the plant that is not doing as well.

("What are you supposed to do in a case like Tuesday morning?")

(When Jane's symptoms were intensified following the exceptionally relaxed state of Monday night. No matter what improvements may have taken place, as Seth states, during such times it is very difficult to be aware of anything but the present.)

Now. There will be more improvements as you look for them and notice them. This is as important as any information I have given you.

As far as the Tuesday episode, in such a case recognize that negative attitudes entered in. Take it for granted they are already dissolving, and the impediment was temporary. Do not let such an episode throw you into panic. Ruburt is aware of certain thoughts that helped cause the episode, and he will tell you.

(Panic is not the right word exactly—anger would be better. I felt the episode was unnecessary. This is being typed on May 10—three days after it was held. So far Jane hasn't said anything about what caused Tuesday's episode.)

It is extremely vital that you look at him for signs of improvement, and that this takes your interest. *(Long pause.)*

You have told him not to concentrate upon his symptoms, and yet you also have a tendency to do so. There is nothing that can work against your desires more. This leads to a sense of desperation, and undermines your confidence.

I cannot stress this too strongly. If you find yourselves doing this you would be better to drop any emphasis on health specifically. Do you follow me?

("Yes.")

Now you may take your break or ask me questions if you prefer.

("No."

(10:00. This was the end of the session. I was not happy, one thing led to

another, and we did not resume the session.)

SESSION 490 (DELETED)
JUNE 25, 1969 9:08 PM WEDNESDAY

(Before the session I asked a question that Seth answered as soon as the session began.)

Good evening.

("Good evening, Seth.")

Now. There are no karmic influences that necessitate the particular physical condition *(in Jane)*.

There are tendencies and conflicts that have been with the personality in other existences, that have influenced his nature as he vacillated between spontaneity, usually exaggerated, and overdiscipline; in some lives a great lack of concern for the welfare of others, that could be called an innocent callousness, a joyful, utterly spontaneous personality with little idea of practicality. He died once simply as a result of acting without thought, forethought, on the impulse of the moment.

He was murdered for an act of pure thoughtlessness, of impulse. He determined to discipline himself much more carefully from then on, but from this point he threw himself wholeheartedly, for two lives, into lives of great restraint and overcontrol.

Fear of course was the motive behind this iron discipline. In the last life, as a medium, he had swung somewhat to the other side again, deliberately not using his intellect and giving the spontaneous portions full play. He was open-hearted, rather childishly vain, the emotional pattern quickly moving from joy to tears.

With all of this he helped many, and died at an old age.

Other portions of the personality, while recognizing this, still felt that the personality as a whole needed to impose some restraints upon what it regarded as flamboyantly spontaneous qualities. Therefore it chose a highly restrictive early environment. It chose a parent whose emotions were highly unrestrained, so that the parent's action could serve as a constant reminder of its own flamboyant emotions.

It chose an environment where hardship would automatically teach a certain discipline, and yet one in which the psychic nature of the circumstances would also permit intuitive creative growth. In fact the controls were applied precisely in proportion to the intuitive gifts. The purpose was to set up a situation in which both strong facets of the personality could emerge; the intellectual, reasoning, rather practical and controlling aspects, hand in hand with the highly volatile creative spontaneous portions.

Now give me a moment here.

The religious element in one way or another has always been a strong one. It has at one time or another in various lives been on the side of the strongly disciplined portions, in which case it was greatly given to dogma, and concerned with cultural problems of punishment and law; or followed the intuitive side, in which it emerged as mediumship, and high mysticism.

So these important elements merge at this point. It is the first time, so to speak, that the personality, seriously tried to merge them, and yet for prime development and fulfillment this had to be accomplished. The personality regards this as a challenge of the highest order, but strains naturally develop.

Give us time here. I will at your request, at any time, give you the details of these lives. This evening I am answering the question I believe most important, and details will follow. I will not put you off on this. Now. In this life until very recently the personality has been involved with highly charged, volatile emotional personalities. He worked up a proportional degree of energy to ward off their influence. It was necessary that he learn how to do this. Do you follow me?

("Yes.")

In so doing he learned to understand his own emotional nature, how to direct its energies, and how to use it as a source of creativity and psychic and spiritual accomplishment.

Now we are going to give you a short break, but we will leave our friend in abeyance. Half in and half out. *(Humorously.)*

(9:34. Jane's delivery had been fast and emphatic, her eyes open often. Now she came partially out of trance easily, her eyes still darker than usual and somewhat glazed. At first she said nothing, but eventually we carried on a brief conversation, without any emphasis.

(Jane stayed under all right, sat quietly most of the time, and resumed at 9:40.)

He has used his symptoms to some degree as a checking point. Before, the presence of his mother and those surroundings acted as both restraints on <u>over</u>-spontaneity, and as aids for the growth of creativity. Do you follow me here?

("Yes.")

Now. When these were released, when he left the initial environment, he ran willy-nilly, he felt. He tended to be ruled more than he would prefer by emotionalism. *(Pause.)* At this point he began to rely upon you somewhat as a controlling factor, since he felt you were more given to reason and control. When you became ill, he realized that no other human being could be used in such a way.

He also felt, as mentioned earlier, that emotionalism on his part brought you ill fortune in Florida. The part-time job at the gallery for a while became a controlling factor, preventing him from dealing with the creative self on a full-time basis.

The psychic development was one of the main issues of importance he had been waiting for, and several circumstances had to be met first. He had to be in fairly dependable circumstances, fairly permanent surroundings. There had to be a strong need to propel the development, as impetus. These were met.

Once the development occurred however the personality knew it would mow have to face the main issue: how to handle its own creativity, and find a comfortable balance between spontaneity and discipline. It could have been clear sailing from there in.

Unfortunately several episodes frightened him enough so that he felt again the need for controls. Now here is one nice little point. Ruburt's mother, as mentioned earlier, had often told him that if he kept on as he was going he would lose his mind; and contacts with psychologists, when he feels they are testing him, brings up this old issue.

Now I could not tell you, for the personality had set up its own guards in the realm of personal material. The old Instream data enters into this. Now Ruburt's mother was not there to serve as a restraining element. You would no longer act in that role. Moreover, Ruburt did not feel it proper to project that role upon you any longer.

Therefore the symptoms were adopted, mimicking the mother's symptoms was the next best thing to having the presence of the mother as a control against the spontaneity.

The long series of Instream tests were involved here, and yet they were also necessary, since the issue had to be met and faced in one manner or another.

Bernard did not operate as a psychologist. Ruburt thought of him as being on his side, and there was no hint of accusation in Bernard's attitude.

Now I was not able to give you any information, particularly at that time, but this did have something to do with my rather vehement recording, which I hoped would have the effect of discouraging Dr. Instream. I could not however shield Ruburt in all of his activities in any case. He would have to face the problem, and if it was circumvented in one way it could have returned at a later date.

You have I believe the reason for the symptoms now as clearly as it can be given. Give us time.

Ruburt interpreted Instream's final attitude to mean that the psychologist had more or less by implication justified the mother's frequent warning. The affair was not to be taken seriously as a psychic phenomena, and Ruburt with his either/or attitude then decided that it was time to apply controls.

The symptoms had begun however before that time, but lightly. He also felt that you had adopted symptoms earlier, somewhat that as a system of controls—that you were so emotionally upset you didn't know what to do, and therefore put yourself in a position where you could do little of importance: you could not make errors.

Since he had temporarily put you in the role of a controlling factor, this was also in the back of his mind. You emerged whole and hearty, and so should he. The issues were not identical, you see, but similar enough in his mind.

Do you want to rest your fingers?

("Yes."

(*10:02. Once again Jane stayed under during break. She moved about but didn't talk. Resume at 10:07.*)

Now. We are going to keep on with this to get all the important points out while conditions are good.

The symptoms initially were clamped on in panic. One or two poor test results frightened him. This of course added to the other issues. The purpose however was two-fold again, the development of an environment in which controls would be there: the symptoms taking the place in this case of the mother's restrictive presence, and the comparative isolation in the house, the comparative solitude that he felt was necessary then for the emergence of the creative abilities—both of these you see existing in the child environment.

Otherwise he felt he might fritter his energy away. At the same time he was afraid of it for the reasons given, and felt it was best to handle it in an environment of applied controls.

Give us time. He did not count upon the body's response. He was terrified of the vulnerability to pain, and yet he felt the ability to face and handle the pain was something he would run away from otherwise; that he had done everything to avoid it, and that it was one of life's physical realities that he had refused to admit. So he felt a taste of it would not hurt him.

He also felt it would help him understand to some extent his mother's actions, and rid him of the hatred he had of her. Now give us time. The problem as he set it in the framework he made for it, was quite literally huge. He also wanted to understand the effect of mind on matter. He did not really believe, intellectually, what I told him, that you form your own reality, and he felt that the symptoms would also help. He did not get his symptoms to test my theories, understand. Do you follow me?

("*Yes.*")

Give us time. He was quite appalled at the conditions once he had set them up. He did not realize until he went through it, how this kind of strain reacts on the body. When he began to realize this the inner plan had already been put into effect, and at the time of worst symptoms he literally could not withdraw quickly. Many processes had to be reversed.

This realization then threw him into panic, reinforcing the symptoms. Now give us time. Your father's condition frightened him because of the mother's old suggestions of losing the mind, and of course the nursing home environment that represents to him the mother's environment.

I am searching for pertinent information, so bear with me. *(Long pause, eyes closed.)*

The matter of speaking the opposite of what he means to say: this always occurs then he makes an innocuous remark that is meant to cover up a repressed feeling. The remarks are again harmless ones, usually a line or two of pointless conversation, chatter meant to cover up a thought that has briefly come into consciousness, and been repressed.

(Just before I sat down to resume typing this session, Jane made such a remark, about the food she was giving one of our cats for supper.)

The use of the opposite is simply to tell him that he is not meaning what he says, that the remark, usually a pleasant one, is covering up an unpleasant feeling.

What you have now is a residue in the body of conflict representing mental conflict, when at the same time the muscles are being given signals to let go completely, and also signals to tense, signals of control. They work against themselves then. Give us time. *(Pause.)*

In the arms this causes knots, as if you knot up a cord it becomes shorter and pulls, so that the arms are pulled upwards. The tension and the lack of relaxation causes a lessening of lubricating fluid in the joints.

Now, this also causes a lack at times of lubricating fluid in the female organs, which is why Ruburt will turn away, as you mentioned.

The *Psycho-Cybernetics* that I have mentioned, when he does them properly, make him smile, reducing tension in the facial and neck areas. Good relaxation is extremely important, where the muscles are let go as far as possible. Physical activity of a fairly steady variety is good. Both are needed.

One evening dancing, he tried consciously too hard, so that he tensed the muscles as he was trying to use them, and there was a physical result then. Now, the point is, he no longer needs the controls. *(Pause.)* Understand that the whole situation, on a very deep basis, was protective as it tried to reproduce to some extent, though to a far lesser extent, those early conditions that allowed for the controlled and disciplined growth of strong creative abilities. He chose a mock version of those early restraints. Now. The controls are no longer necessary. The reasons as given in this evening's session should make him realize that. The physical symptoms now remaining are a direct result of these contradictory messages being given—one relax let go, the other wait, now, not so fast, slow up.

The controls were actually adopted in fear against the insanity threatened by his mother, and the implications that he felt implied in the Instream affair. He did not for example fear he was insane, but he felt the need once more to control the spontaneity. Your father's condition as always had these implications, and it did not escape him that your father, in his mental condition, is put in a wheelchair and restrained forcibly. In other words Ruburt restrained himself ahead of time.

Give us time. He has been letting the symptoms go, as he has become aware of emotional stabilities. He has let them go slowly: "Now how will you behave if I give you this much more freedom? And a little more?" You see. Give us time. *(One minute pause.)*

For him now the idea of a long trip is a daring adventure: does he really have the freedom to go so far?

("Is it okay to go to Saratoga this weekend?")

Earlier this evening when you were speaking of the weekend he mentioned two days, and you said Sunday. He interpreted this to mean that you did not think he had the freedom to travel as far as a two-day trip.

(This was not what I meant by my remark. I was, rather, briefly considering expense. Actually we did go to Saratoga, on June 28-29, 1969.)

Again, we are trying to search for all pertinent points. *(Two minute pause.)* There are still a few issues, and I am trying to get at them. *(Long pause.)* His writing schedule, as he knows, should be maintained. He punishes himself with symptoms when it is not. The symptoms then become an issue for the next few days, that prevent him to some extent from carrying out the schedule. It can be flexible, but he operates well within it and can use it as an aid.

The depressions are also caused when he overemphasizes control and smothers spontaneity. Now the writing schedule provides two needs, both control and spontaneity, and is therefore comfortable. A circle is set up: an overemphasis on control leads him to a depression, which interferes with his writing schedule. This bringing on symptoms which further impede the schedule.

He feels then that he is accomplishing nothing, and this period ends this cycle with a depression like the one in the beginning of the cycle, in that he usually manages through discussion with you or *Psycho-Cybernetics* to break the cycle and initiate a period of fair balance; and symptoms are minimized and decent improvement shows.

Continuing the writing schedule regardless would automatically break the cycle in half even if it began, for the resulting feeling of lack of achievement would not result. Do you want to rest?

("Yes. Now about our going to Saratoga this weekend?")

We will get into that. Tell me when you are ready.

(10:55. Jane stayed in trance during break. At 11:00:)

Are you ready?

("Yes.")

Now the difficulty in the morning follows those days when he feels he has not put in his writing time, and he does not realize this. He projects that day of relative failure into the next day, and experiences symptoms and feelings of hopelessness upon awakening.

Now, some practical suggestions: one I mentioned earlier. Remember that many symptoms have vanished. He should be on the alert for restrictive statements, vocal or mental—I can't, for example; I'd better go slowly; or mental pictures of that nature. Such thoughts automatically tense the muscles. If he is consciously adding instructions to relax on top of this he worsens the situation, for the muscles cannot relax and contract at once.

When he says to himself "This arm or whatever is tight," while he consciously tells it to relax, he is also confusing the muscles. Do you follow me?

("Yes.")

His conscious mind, when he is not writing, should be anchored on something. There is too much unrecognized free brooding, when he sits doing nothing consciously, waiting perhaps for inspiration but not in a positive way. He will know to what periods I am referring, now that I have pointed it out. He should have a painting in progress as a hobby, or several for such times, or do household activities. His mind, his conscious mind, is the type that should be anchored in such a way, for it is overactive, otherwise, and when he is not at his best it will leap to brooding. He lets this go by.

Now. The Saratoga issue is clear. If you drive past his old house he should tell himself that he no longer needs it or what it stands for, that he can retain good memories of it. *(Long pause.)* It will be very easy for him to think of the town as the place where his grandfather lived, and this will bring about the beneficial aspects. It reassures him however to know that the town is still there, that he is free to go to the town and free to leave it. Symbolically this is important.

It is important to go so that he is free to leave. Do you follow me?

("Yes.")

It is also good for him to see that it has changed, that it exists in the present, along with his own adulthood, and you can remind him of this. Even his mother you see has left the town. Now do you have questions?

("No, I guess not.")

We will then close the session, and my best wishes to your fingers. The information should prove quite valuable. Ruburt did not feel he was mature enough to handle his abilities. Tell him that I am saying that he is. He can quite literally relax with them now and with himself. He can quite literally let down. And a hearty good evening.

("Good evening, Seth.")

(*11:18. The trip to Saratoga was a great success, and Jane did experience many of the ideas, realizations, feelings, etc., detailed above by Seth. Both of us enjoyed seeing the town again immensely, and Jane without doubt has now put Saratoga in proper perspective, both as to her past, present and future. She met some schoolmates, saw her old house, etc., and thoroughly enjoyed herself.*)

SESSION 503 (DELETED PORTION)
SEPTEMBER 24, 1969

(*This data deleted from the 503rd Session, September 24, 1969*)

...You may leave in the record or not: temporarily at least there are several connotations in the private aspect of your lives.

Ruburt held back from the recognition of desire, physical desire, for many reasons, and subconsciously now that he has begun listening to his inner feelings, he has been using this as a sort of test case.

Dare he let himself be aware of these feelings when he feels them, give expression to them, since they also involve you? Will you feel threatened, how will you react? The feelings of desire therefore are symbols also of other inhibited feelings. While legitimate in themselves he watches your reaction to them very closely.

Is it really safe for him to let go entirely? Will you accept him as the emotional creature that he is, as you accept the intellectual creature that he is? I thought I would cue you in here.

("Yes.")

The desire then becomes a symbol, and is in any case, of spontaneous feelings and energies. (*Pause.*) They bring release in themselves, and the system also clears itself in other ways as a result. But if he seems afraid it is because he fears, in an exaggerated manner, that if given freedom he would want you, and you would consider this disruptive, of work and schedule.

Behind this you see is the fear that simultaneous release of feelings can be disruptive. There is more here. *(Pause.)* I do not believe I have the point across to you clearly.

("I think I see what you mean.")

He may then in the beginning want you particularly when you are working, to prove the point that he will not be rejected.

("I understand.")

I wanted you both to be aware of this. He is saying, really, is it safe to admit all feelings now? *(I nodded yes.)* He is at the point you see where he is beginning to do so. The practice is good for him. The roof will not fall in.

("I hope not.")

This matter is extremely vital however. He was afraid of himself so he could hardly give himself. Do you follow me?

("Yes.")

Now you may take your break, or I will continue.
(End of this data.)

DELETED SESSION
MARCH 11, 1970 9:10 PM WEDNESDAY

(Personal session, not included in the record.)
Good evening.

("Good evening, Seth.")

Now. I am going to give you some comments on the situation you have been discussing, and I am going to do some more work on my book. Now which would you prefer first?

("Your comments on the personal matters.")

I suggest, quite seriously, that Ruburt make up a list of his accomplishments; that he make a list of his good points; that he write down a short list of those things he thinks he is doing right *(humorously)*, and the things he enjoys; and you add to these lists. I want him to concentrate upon his accomplishments rather than any failings, and you also. In a determination to do better, he has begun to concentrate upon failings. Your loving endeavors toward him have indeed helped, but until very recently you also fell into the same trap.

He began to think that just about everything he did was wrong. His reader's report *(for Prentice/Hall)* pleased him however, as did your reaction to it.

Now I think you will agree we need to build him up—

("Yes.")

—put some weight on him. Now think of it this way. He has been tearing himself down psychologically in an effort to find out what has been wrong, that the symptoms persist. He has simply gone overboard in that direction. So to build him up psychologically and not artificially, we remind him of his accomplishments and those areas in which he is doing very well.

Now there are several, and they are being bypassed and to some extent unrecognized because of this other emphasis. Some of this also applies to you. For example, Ruburt is doing very well in his classes, enjoys it, and closes his eyes, relatively speaking, to the improvement he has worked in the lives of his students, and to the freedoms he has allowed himself in class in using his abilities. The class before last is a case in point. Both of you do not realize the exceptional impact you have on others in personal relationships.

I should mention that it is because Ruburt asks so much of himself that he so often fails in those requirements he has set for himself. Yet both of you should realize that those failures still give you an overall performance that few people can achieve, in terms of the quality and overall endurance.

Often Ruburt's failures would still be successes by other standards. Do you follow me?

("Yes."

(Pause.) The achievements therefore must be kept in mind; not only are they not focused upon, but they are often forgotten. To some extent this also applies to you in your own endeavors. Reminding Ruburt of these achievements, of the things he does right, will put some weight on him. For when he concentrates upon his failings, for whatever reason, he sees himself as a person of <u>no substance</u>.

(Seth was quite emphatic here, and half humorous. In spite of our seriousness I had to laugh. I found myself doing this in many spots through the session, though half of it, I believe, was in frustration. Jane's delivery throughout was fairly rapid.)

Now, some of these problems are simply those of the creative personality emerging, in Ruburt's individual case, in their own way. They should not be overemphasized however, for the creative personality, by the very standards of creativity that it adopts, becomes a focal point for varying conflicts that in many other kinds of personalities are never allowed to emerge. Therefore they are not resolved.

They are however conflicts that are deeply a part of the human condition, and that must be faced in one life or another, both for the sake of the individual and for the sake of humanity at large. The creative personality does indeed have the potential use of greater amounts of energy, the latent capability for emerging psychic insights. The creative personality is striving to be born in new dimensions, to release entirely original concepts, regardless of the field of activity chosen.

This in itself arouses conflicts, again, that the majority of individuals have not yet taken upon themselves, though they do, to whatever lesser extent, partake on a much smaller scale.

The conflicts however are also points of impetus, explosive elements that propel the creative individual from the, in quotes, "ordinary" dimensions of consciousness into another. Now you have experienced this in your own way, and so has Ruburt.

Now. While these conflicts appear highly destructive, and you shake your head at what appears to be some stupidity or stubbornness on Ruburt's part, the conflicts themselves are creative, and will be used creatively. Do you have questions?

("I'm afraid that Jane's symptoms lead her to concentrate too much upon them. They overshadow her other accomplishments. I also get irritated at them. Then we try different things in an effort to get rid of them, etc.")

In an attempt to discover the reason for the persistence of the symptoms, he began to concentrate upon those in quotes "negative " aspects of his personality. The overconcentration continued the symptoms, and the symptoms themselves became exaggerated in his mind. Do you follow me?

("Yes.")

I suggest that you take your break, and we shall continue. Some of the material tonight on the creative personality should help you understand other points that we have not discussed. The determination to attempt so much, the responsibility to use potential, helped make our sessions possible. It is two-edged therefore. It helps bring about Ruburt's greatest accomplishments, and yet at the same time, overemphasized, it can become a source of failures.

(9:44—9:58.)

It is a matter of concentration.

In the back of your minds, your main point of concentration has been "What is wrong with Ruburt?" Now, I gave you this information a while ago, and I have said it in various ways at different times.

You should concentrate upon creativity and health.

("I know it, we know it. But he [meaning Jane] doesn't.")

In your efforts both of you often put the concentration upon the things that are wrong. Now I cannot put it more simply. Both of you concentrate more upon those symptoms that remain, forgetting the improvements that he has made. It is a method that is wrong. Your loving attitude has been of great help, and of a creative nature.

Overconcern however is negative. Ruburt has physical symptoms. This is not good. They are not the worst symptoms in the world however, and while there is much room for improvement, they should not be concentrated upon. They are not a stigma.

("I believe he thinks they are, though.")

That is why I am giving this material in this session. Tell him he does not have to be spiritually, psychically, or creatively perfect in order to have good health, in the particular way I gave that statement; remind him, for he is equating perfect health with inner perfection, and no human being attains inner perfection. He is holding off *(emphatic)* on good health until he feels he deserves it. Now this is a point that has not come up before, and he does not realize this consciously.

("When is he supposed to deserve it?")

With the attitude that he had, he would never achieve it.

He has the idea that good health is a reward for excellent inner performance, and part of this attitude is because of a literal and uncompromising misinterpretation of my remarks that the physical body is the direct materialization of the inner condition.

In other words, he felt that unless he was using his abilities fully, and was spiritually, creatively and psychically perfect, he should mar his physical performance. His idea of honesty and his literal interpretation led him to the idea after the worst part of his difficulties were over, that he should keep some of the symptoms to show he was not a hypocrite to others.

(Consider the whole page underlined. It's important!)

Now, I did not say that you had to be a saint to be healthy, and many saints were not healthy, and this had nothing to do with merit. Until he used his abilities fully, he did not feel he could use his body fully, for this would be hypocritical.

("How come he's letting you say this now?"

(Seth-Jane looked at me, pausing, with a half-comical, half at-last expression that again made me laugh.)

He is so confused about the reasons for his condition that he literally did not know where to turn, and so he turned to me.

("At last.")

Now if you please, tell him that despite any misgivings, overall he is using his abilities rather well. Tell him also that good health is free. He does not have to pay for it, by being a saint on earth; and that if this were true no man or woman alive would be in good health.

Tell him that good health is as accessible to him as air. He does not have to work for it. It is indeed his right, and natural heritage. It is a means toward using his abilities, not a reward for using them. It is not something given to him when he is good, and withdrawn when he feels he has been bad.

According to the standards he set, no man alive would ever be healthy. Tell him also that he need have no worries about my book. It will progress.

You did not get the full information from the pendulum. It was not so much that Ruburt was jealous of my book, as it was that he felt he should distrust anything that came so easily.

You may ask whatever questions you have, or take a break as you prefer, or both.

("Whatever questions we have will come up during our conversation at break.")

I trust I have been of some assistance. *(Amused.*

("Yes, very much so, a tremendous help."

(10:25—10:31.)

Now, I am not finished with you yet.

Both of you set up problems for yourselves to be faced in this existence, challenges to be met. You do not realize that you could have solved the problems and met the challenges adequately, but without the satisfaction of strong creative endeavor. You are managing the problems, though it may appear to you that you are not, in such a way that enduring creativity results.

This is all to the good. <u>In any creativity there must be a magnification</u>. Underline the statement. An intense focus, even an exaggeration of normal tendencies. Without this there is no creativity. You draw the most out of yourself, or out of an event. The same event could be quite flat by contrast, to others. Certain personality characteristics are exaggerated quite purposefully by the creative personality, to act as a lens to intensify experience.

(This is highly evocative material.)

This in itself puts a strain on the personality that is not felt by other kinds of personalities, though they also have their own kind of behavior. The desire for perfection is meant to lead you onward, and to make you discontent enough so that you will attempt new creations. There must be a gap between the desire for perfection and the physical result. Now and then the desire for perfection gets out of hand.

Now, in your good intentions you told Ruburt lately that he was using only a tenth of his abilities, meaning that most people only used a portion of their capabilities. *(I also explained this meaning to Jane at the time.)* He took this as an accusation, however, and further concentrated upon his lacks. Neither of you should expect perfect performance in your work, and I say this to you as well as to Ruburt. To some extent there has been a weaving in and out, so that at times Ruburt's symptoms were personal, and at times they were symbols for both of your attitudes.

His symptoms would become then at times symbols of your joint lack of perfection, mainly in your works. His symptoms became a hanger upon which you could hang your joint dissatisfactions, his physical condition an easy mark to stand for what both of you considered inner imperfections; again, connected mainly with your creative endeavors.

It was like having a handy whipping-dog around. Now if the whipping-dogs were not connected with Ruburt, this would be a handy family mechanism. Another point I would mention: Ruburt knows quite well your own progress in your own work. He has always been psychologically and psychically attuned to your work. He knows for example when you are doing well and when you feel you are in difficulties, even if it seems to you he does not look at a particular painting, or take, notice.

He knows how long you work at a painting before you are satisfied, and he felt that you might be hurt by my book, seemingly so effortlessly written. So he had to make it more difficult. Do you follow me?

("Yes. I think I've thought of that."

([Jane:] "I _don't_ feel this way. I'm eager for you to do the book. I _know_ it will be a fine thing, should you decide to do it." RB.)

You work mornings outside. He feels guilty that you do. He feels how you would enjoy and appreciate painting in the same way that my book is being presented, so spontaneously and quickly, comparatively speaking. He thinks this should be granted to you rather than to him, to make up for your job, and so he has felt somewhat guilty about it, and punished himself by holding off. He was afraid you would be jealous of the book, and hurt, and his panic was of your reaction.

(Already I am at work on Jane to disabuse her of any ideas like these. I could only be hurt by her feeling this way any longer.)

He long ago made a pact with himself, that he would not hurt you. Now, none of this material was known to him. It has all been beneath the surface. So when you said to him "use your abilities fully," he was in a quandary, for to use them might be to hurt you in that particular manner.

Also, to some less extent, and at different times, he would know that the symptoms were a whipping-boy for you both, and so he was afraid at times to dispense with them completely. (Of letting them go, for fear they would be needed next week.)

(This last statement came through from Seth during next break, just this one emphatic sentence, when Jane and I were discussing the material given.)

Your own loving endeavors of late have been very helpful, again, however, and helped bring about this session this evening, with this material.

Incidentally, the parsley is good for him. Make it a part of your salad diet, for his periods. It is an old, valid recipe. Take your break, for your fingers' sake.

(11:00. Jane could remember none of this data except for the reference to parsley. Resume at 11:12.)

Now. You are tired—

("I'm okay.")

—I'll shortly close. A few more points however. Discuss particularly the early portion of this session with him, and get it through his head that health is not dependent upon perfect performance, creativity, psychically or spiritually. This is extremely important, for this is a strong belief with him now; and he did not see the humor when he heard what I said—it made perfect sense to him. This is an area where you can help him.

(This is very important. Seth is right. Jane didn't see the humor, at first, and was still questioning me about this several days after this session was held. But we are making progress now.)

To him, because you are in good health, he took this to mean that you were therefore better than he was, closer to perfection. When you felt at your best he felt accused. Do you follow me?

("Yes.")

Another point. To some extent he has always felt guilty at the work involved in your writing up the sessions, and when my book began he felt this twice as badly, you see.

(Seth's delivery was very friendly here. I've told Jane before that typing up this material has always been a job I do gladly, since I believe in it and regard it as having a vital part of a work that is both highly creative and original. It also gives me an opportunity to do some writing on my own in conjunction with Seth's own data and this I enjoy greatly.

(If Jane cares to, she can excerpt Seth's book from these sessions, typing up her own copy for personal use; but I think also that the book should be included in the body of the regular sessions, whenever it pops up—part of the regular record, as always.)

Now I can laugh with you, but he will not when he reads this. He felt he was not worthy of the healing ability because he was not perfect. Again, do all you can to convince him that his good health is not dependent upon his performance or perfection. This is extremely important.

I intended to do some on the book, just to set <u>him</u> at ease this evening, but when I found him open enough to get this material through, I decided this would be the greater benefit. Now, I will take a moment to see if there is anything else, and you may use the time to think of any questions, if they come to you. *(Pause.)* On certain evenings he does not feel he deserves to sleep if he has not produced.

("Is this material tonight related to all those earlier sessions you gave us, on Jane's early background, etc.?")

It is all connected. The trouble is that when the early environmental conditions, which helped set up the episode, ceased operating <u>strongly</u>, the pattern of behavior was set, and used then for other psychological purposes as noted. *(Important!)* Past environmental episodes have little now to do with the symptoms. The data given this evening relates to the present situation. Now, the cat lover's attitude has a healthy effect on Ruburt, regardless of its basic legitimate nature. Do you follow me?

("Yes." 11:25. The rest of the session is taken up with Seth's analysis of some arm trouble Peggy Gallagher has been having; this material is on file. None of this session is included in regular records. I think it all excellent.

(11:25 PM. March 11, 1970.

("Can you say a few words about why Peggy's arm is bothering her?"

(Jane didn't know I was going to ask this question. Nor had I planned upon doing so; the idea came to me a few minutes ago.)

The immediate causes reach back for several years.

For one thing, she is afraid that the Jesuit will get more severe symptoms of his own, as a result of work pressure, and in a protective way she is trying to say "Bill, do not get sick. See, I will get sick myself instead, for you."

She also feels guilty at being in good health when he is so unhappy in his work, and has adopted symptoms out of sympathy.

She also feels that because he has been so busy he has been away from home more often, and because of his worries, less attentive. The symptoms also serve to say "Remember me. I need your care and attention also." Quite simply, she is saying "I hurt because you hurt."

Beyond this the symptoms are a protest. She thinks that he could get out of <u>some</u> (underlined) obligations connected with work, if he really exerted himself to do so, and was not afraid of doing so.

She is saying "You are not only hurting yourself, but you are hurting me also." Symbolically, the malady is expressing her attitude perfectly. She is strongly dependent upon the Jesuit, even while she appears, and is in many ways solitary and aggressive; and she is afraid that their intimate life might suffer if the acceleration of his work experience is continued, and if his attitude toward it does not change.

She is ready to combat the symptoms actively and aggressively, because she does not feel that she can actively and aggressively combat the Jesuit's attitudes that are causing her concern.

It is the Jesuit's attitude, and not the conditions, and he can (underline) change those attitudes once he realizes the effects they are having not only upon himself but upon his wife.

The cat lover will not want to admit some of this, for it seems to accuse the Jesuit, and she feels he cannot stand any more strain. She does not want to add to it, so she takes the strain upon herself. This is undistorted incidentally, and as valid a diagnosis as could ever be given.

Do you have any more questions?

("No. I'd like to read over the material about Jane and me first.")

I will meet with you then at our next session, our regular session.

("That's nice.")

My heartiest regards to you both.

("Thank you very much. It's been excellent.

(11:36. Jane was slow coming out of trance; it had been deep. She remembered little of the material after last break, except that I'd asked a question about Peg.

(The entire session is deleted from regular records.)

DELETED SESSION
APRIL 1, 1970 WEDNESDAY

(This is the regular Wednesday session, for April 1, 1970. It is deleted from the record since it deals with the excellent results Jane achieved using the pendulum today.)

Good evening.

(Good evening, Seth.")

Now. This is not for our book. And give us a moment.

Ruburt's insights this afternoon were largely correct. Tell him that he does not need the symptoms as a set of checks and balances. This is extremely important. Behind the attitude is still the feeling that he needs to whip himself on in certain areas, and check himself in others. That spontaneously, left alone without such checks and balances, he will go to the extremes.

The symptoms have been kept therefore in case they are needed. A method of discipline that he no longer needs.

Now give us time. He is feeling more secure, and this feeling will grow as it sinks into his mind that he will not have to "worry" about his money productions for the next year, for example. He has also undergone in the past few months another level of development where he trusts his psychic abilities more than he ever did.

The symptoms are now like guards that he sets about his behavior. The spontaneous self is being given more and more freedom, yet under a cautious eye, and with the symptoms in the background, again just in case.

It is a habit of cautiousness, that is translated of course into muscular cautiousness. <u>Remind him, for the 100th time, that he can trust his inner self implicitly, and does not need to set up guards against its spontaneity, for spontaneity is his life, and the source of his creativity</u>; and underline that sentence.

Now, he realizes this much more than he did, but the mental and muscular habit of cautiousness carries over. Now this can be handled in several ways. The mental feelings have caused mental images that in turn hamper physical motion. The body is therefore affected physically, since certain portions of it are not normally used or exercised, and other portions are kept in a state of strain.

Some of these mental habits can be cured rather easily, comparatively speaking. When he felt joyful yesterday, the sense of release was translated, as it should be, into physical expression – he sang, for example. This automatically released, exercised and relaxed areas of the chest, shoulders and back. He felt like running, and made a halfway respectable attempt to do so.

Feelings of spontaneity therefore automatically release the body mechanisms when they are allowed expression. When this occurs and he sees himself for example running, to some extent this makes the mental image of a nonrunning self less vivid. The body and mind are so connected that the mind remembers, say, muscular spontaneity as the muscles remember mental spontaneity. And the <u>will</u>, now, can be used to <u>initiate</u> a series of actions that <u>will be</u> spontaneous; and the motions now, the physical motions, in turn set up mental images of spontaneity that become self-generating. Do you follow me?

("Yes.")

I suggest therefore at this point, that you encourage Ruburt in spontaneous physical activity as divorced, say, from a discipline exercise. Often, out of habit now, though not always, the muscles are restricted. Let him try as he once suggested, running in the apartment, or outside. The motion is associated with joy and spontaneity. Do you see?

("Yes.")

Give us a moment. When he feels mentally happy, and he does often, have him in his imagination translate the feeling into spontaneous physical motion. We are trying to initiate some small exercises that will encourage freedom, both mentally and physically.

The hands are quite improved over what they were even two weeks ago—let this not escape his notice. The last few days he forgot to put his corn pad on *(smile)*, with no resulting difficulty—another improvement he should notice. His period is on time again.

(On the evening of April 2, while brushing her teeth, Jane got this flash from Seth: "You need to relearn the joy of physical achievement.")

I mention these because again they would go by the wayside, lost in the concentration upon the physical problem. *(Quietly:)* A fear of retaining the symptoms could result in maintaining them longer. This is very important. Anything that is done to minimize that fear is highly important, beneficial, and significant.

One reason, you see, that I suggest the running is that any running at all prevents him from projecting into the future a nonrunning self. Once he runs he can improve on the running, but he can no longer consider himself someone incapable of running. This is extremely important from both a mental and physical standpoint.

Now the same applies to getting down on the floor, and up from it. He thinks of himself as someone who cannot. Doing so will prove him wrong, and break up still another annoying mental image. At the same time—I do not mean simultaneously—in spare moments, playfully and not seriously, he should see himself performing any number of activities on the floor—from painting as he used to, to talking or reading. These are simply practical but important sideline exercises that will help break down specific detrimental images that he has. Many from the past have been completely destroyed.

This jumping off the radiator the other day, in one stroke disintegrated one such detrimental image that had impeded physical motion. Now it is true that initially the motion was made in his mind, and accepted, but the will can also be used to initiate such actions. Particularly as long as the imagination is allowed to function in the same direction.

These may appear to be minor suggestions, beside the point, and yet they will initiate greater feeling for spontaneity and motion, and represent breakthroughs that will also have symbolic significance—which is of course why I suggest them.

Now you may take your break and we shall continue.
(9:45—9:53.)
Now. Each time Ruburt finds himself making a movement that he

thought he could not perform, then one of the blocking mental images loses strength.

It is true, again, that an initial corresponding inner freedom makes the motion possible, and that the motion itself already means that the mental image of new motion is replacing the old one. The physical motion is obviously the materialization of inner willingness, but you must also set up the opportunity for this to happen. Do you follow me here?

("Yes.")

Hence the suggestions I have given. The session itself, with these suggestions, automatically will set Ruburt's imagination going along these lines, you see, and the idea of freedom is generated both mentally and physically.

Now he has been improving, but now we will work at this from both angles. Earlier we could not have done so. A sense of play must accompany this however. We do not want for example a desperate attempt to run, which is self-defeating. The same applies to what I said about getting up and down from the floor. And these should not be overdone.

We simply want to remind him again of translating the idea of motion into physical motion. These are merely techniques to help along particular lines. Now, basically, spontaneously he is sympathetic and understanding. The feeling of contempt he had for the sick or crippled has long vanished. Tell him indeed that annoyance with his own symptoms could now prevent him from helping others as well as he might, because the energy devoted to maintaining the symptoms is not being used for such constructive purposes.

<u>He can help other people better now by being completely healthy, and with his full energy at his command.</u> All of that should be underlined.

The specific exercises I gave are to break up lingering habit patterns, both mental and physical, and to encourage spontaneity. Give us a moment. Underline the following sentence: <u>It is safe for him to let go completely now.</u> *(Pause.)* There is more here that I am trying to get at. It is not a matter of Ruburt blocking, necessarily. I do want him to initiate some fast, quick physical motion, you see, so that the muscular memory is imprinted in this direction.

I am still trying to get something more for you. *(Pause.)*

He has been tensed for so long that he has been afraid to let go all at once, in his terms. Much of this had to do with his career. The contract from the dream book will work a great beneficial change. *(It is in the mail but hasn't arrived, due to the postal strike.)* With his literal mind, he wants to see it in black and white.

I suggest your break while I see if I can get at this other material.

(10:12—10:22)

SESSION 4/1/70

Now. In all of his endeavors Ruburt should adopt a more playful attitude. Even to imagining throwing the symptoms out the window.

He is at a point where they are ready to break up entirely. I want to see that he takes advantage of this. The mental patterns <u>are</u> beginning to break up, and I want to be sure that this is translated into physical behavior, completely. The spring and the recent good news are having an effect, and the knowledge he gained this afternoon has given him a conscious understanding that he did not have before; and this will automatically minimize the symptoms, in a way that is not at once apparent.

The point was completely unconscious earlier.

Give us a moment. Tell him that the inner self <u>has its own</u> system of checks and balances. He does not need to reinforce it with physical symptoms now. <u>He does not need</u> to fear he will be carried away through spontaneity. Age and experience provide checks and balances of their own that he did not have earlier.

There are some final connections that have not been made this evening. You will see why when I give them to you. I have given you however information that will be highly valuable. Ruburt may also suggest that more insights come to him, for you are close to a final and important breakthrough.

I am not going to dictate on the book since it is too late for what I had in mind for the next installment. Do you have questions? One point: I am glad of your good news, but it was not what I had in mind.

("That was the only question I had.")

(In my original and unpublished notes in Session 520 in Seth Speaks *I listed three chances for the fruition of Seth's prediction: The mention in* Cosmopolitan *of Jane's ESP book for April 1970; Tam's news about New American Library being very interested in the Seth material book; or Jane's contract for the dream book being in the mail from Prentice-Hall.)*

My heartiest wishes to you both, and a fond good evening.

("Good night Seth, and thank you very much.")

(10:37. Jane said she felt funny—that there was something there that she didn't get; it was frustrating, she said; she thought it might be a final bit of necessary data for a last breakthrough.

(Seth returned briefly at 10:39.)

One additional note: have him plunge now into his new book—and stop concentrating on the problem of the symptoms. With his energy in the book he will have less time and energy to think of them.

DELETED SESSION
APRIL 15, 1970 WEDNESDAY

(This session, for April 15, 1970, Wednesday, is deleted from the record.)
Good evening.
("Good evening, Seth.")
Now a few notes, not pertaining to the book.

Ruburt's poetry this evening did represent a breakthrough of sorts, both in the ideas presented and in the poetry-writing itself. The feeling of ease and release is a magic quality here—for health can come as naturally and easily.

You know that physical symptoms are the materialization in the body of inner dis-ease. They are apparent and easily recognized. Now, not writing poetry was also a symptom of inner disease, not so readily recognized as such. While the intuitional abilities first appeared in poetry, and while the poetry in one way was a channel into other areas, the poetry was not meant to be shut off because new areas were opened.

Any work blockages are also symptoms. Seldom therefore do physical symptoms appear alone. They are usually studied almost in isolation, but wherever they appear their counterparts will be found to one extent or another, in all the activities in which a personality is involved. It is only when these less visible, less apparent symptoms are ignored, when the causes for them are not sought or found, that physical symptoms show themselves.

The nonphysical symptoms will also appear in various guises, often symbolically within the dream state long before any physical symptoms appear. Behind any kind of symptom, regardless of its nature, or the specific problem, there is usually a blocking off of spontaneity that is caused by fear. Either the individual no longer trusts the <u>purpose</u> toward which his energy is being expended, or perhaps worse, he feels that there is no reason, or that he has no purpose, and does not <u>know</u> in which direction to turn his energy.

In Ruburt's case therefore the distrust of spontaneity was indeed reflected in all areas of his life, particularly in spontaneous activities in both physical and creative realms. The sexual portion of his being also reflected the blockage in spontaneity. No problem therefore will be expressed in one way only. You are highly creative creatures. As the joy of life is reflected in all of your acts, affecting your work, bodies, environment and the people you meet, so your problems are also faithfully reflected in all of these areas.

Sitting down at the desk to write poetry, the act and intention automatically reminds Ruburt of all the times that he has written poetry before, and primes the pump, so to speak. When this is done, as it was this evening, easily, getting up and down from the floor does the same thing physically, reminding the body and the mind of successful performances in the past. With each success, the <u>failures</u> fade away. The same applies to running. Ruburt does not need his conscious mind to perform as a guardian. It is indeed the spontaneous self, as he is now realizing, who is the guardian.

I will have more to say for him to read, but I suggest a short break. Some of this material will be quite pertinent, generally speaking.

(9:32—9:49.)

Now. Tell him to leave his body alone with his conscious mind in the same way that he leaves a poem alone with his conscious mind when it is forming—to think of his body as a poem.

Give us a moment. It is not now so much a matter of relaxing, as going joyfully <u>along with</u>. Now this is what I have been after. The position *(emphatic)* of the arms has symbolically represented the degree of resistance to spontancity. At his worst the arms would be like this, you see, as if to hold back—

("Yes."

(As Seth, Jane held out her arms with them bent at about right angles.)

As they have dropped down they represent the dropping of resistance, and strength returns to them. They were not at all strong, but weak to an extreme at their worst, because they were denying the source of strength.

I have told him that concentration on his work will dissipate the rest of his symptoms, but he adopted a <u>too-conscious</u> (underlined) deliberation here. He should write his book the same way that he writes his poetry—not demand of himself, but simply and quietly and joyfully expect.

He learned, or relearned, something quite important this evening with the poetry—the <u>feeling</u> of spontaneity and creativity, and will be able to apply some of this now to the physical condition. A more playful attitude should be adopted when he gets up and down from the floor, and in the running. Have him see himself on the floor, for example, and get there without too much concentration upon the method or the muscles used, as this will take care of itself.

Now his contract *(for the dream book)* is assured, and tell him I said so.

(The day after this session, Jane received a letter from her editor at Prentice-Hall, Tam Mossman, asking if she had received her contracts through the mail; there has been a worrisome delay, due at least in part to the recent postal strike.)

Tell him also to trust his feelings in regard to Mary Sharp or anyone else, even when they are contradictory. That is quite natural.

Contradictory feelings can also be expressed through the body, tell him. Remind him. Tell him also to <u>shake</u> his arms downward from both the elbow and the shoulder, and in a playful manner, as if he were a rag doll perhaps. His idea about the morning symptoms was correct—knowing this will minimize them.

The depressions have virtually disappeared. Several symptoms in both the hands and the feet have also disappeared within the last three weeks. The Friday syndrome is just about entirely gone—so again, do not concentrate upon the symptoms that remain. They will vanish as well.

He has actually been trying too hard on the dream book—his mental set. The spontaneous attitude of a joyful endeavor will release him here. His attitude has been "I have to start my dream book." Tell him that his dream book will start itself if he leaves himself alone. The attitude has impeded his dream experiences also.

Tell him that he produces books as naturally as a tree produces leaves. He does not have to try so hard then. When he lets himself alone this happens naturally. Now this may sound redundant, but he has been listening to me rather well of late, and I know that there is significance even behind the obvious words I speak.

Some of all the difficulty in the past few years has been the result, simply, of Ruburt's coming to maturity, and the episode could have been far worse. His system now has more than stabilized, and is now in the process of complete recovery. Therefore I want him to understand how best to help himself along by letting himself alone.

Again I make the recommendations about the bedroom.

(The next day, Jane changed the bed around to north-south.)

When he allows himself spontaneity his true vitality returns, and the feeling of joy, active joy, that he has so often missed. My word to him now then, for the 100th time—but now he will take it—is to allow himself spontaneity on a daily basis, the feeling of playfulness. A clue incidentally that his vitality is returning: he has not been nearly so tempted to nap, particularly in the afternoon.

You may take a break.

(10:16. During break I said I hoped Seth would discuss the episode Jane experienced during the 523rd session for last Monday, April 13, 1970. While speaking for Seth, Jane realized later, she evidently had a brief out-of-body, seeing herself from a position near the bookcase in our living room, as she sat in the rocker delivering session data.

(Resume at 10:26.)

Now. We hope to do more along those lines, for even though *(smile)* I am doing my own book, I will help Ruburt on his, and he could use a few projection episodes during sessions. *(Humorous and emphatic.)* It was also a way of getting him out of the way the other evening, so that I could work in peace on my book. It was rather a displacement of consciousness rather than a projection, for his consciousness was in a trance state, and then displaced to the bookcase area. *(About six feet away.)*

Now the last time I told you that a period of excellent improvement could be expected in his condition, it followed. Do you remember?

("Yes.")

I tell you this now again, except that the improvement should be far more startling: the time and the season and Ruburt's psychological state are right. This is why I have taken the time from my book for this session, and the other recent ones for him. Therefore see that my suggestions are followed.

The hints on spontaneity that have been given this evening, again, may sound simple, but they are highly significant, and Ruburt will know when, subjectively, he is being spontaneous. At one time he could not tell the difference.

He is to forget thinking of the dream book as something he must do. It will come from him naturally. He has been using the idea of the contract as a club, and this is why he has been so sensitive about it. The contract is his as naturally as the book is his.

The next time we try a displacement of consciousness, we will put him on the other side of the bookcase *(as Seth, Jane pointed)*.

Now, do you have questions about your painting, or of your own?

("No. I guess not.")

(Smiling:) Some other night we must have a session that is recorded. Ruburt can transcribe the tape, and you and I *(voice abruptly louder)* will have a pleasant conversation.

("That would be good.")

(Seth's voice again stepped up in volume—louder than I had heard it for some time.)

<u>Now the energy that I am using now is also being made available for Ruburt *(louder)*, and now he is no longer afraid to use it joyfully, and it will straighten out his arms and release some of the crooked ideas that he has in that head of his.</u>

Consider the whole paragraph underlined. *(Seth's voice still boomed out powerfully.)*

You can also use some of it, it is yours for the asking.

Now I wish you a fond good evening, and this has not been a recording. *(Still loud and strong.)* I intend to speak with our beloved and sometimes knuckle-headed friend this evening in the dream state, and make some points that I have not made this evening. It will serve him well, and we will not need session time to do it. *(Loud.)*

And I never was a daemon.

(10:38. Seth's humorous, emphatic ending referred to a passage I had come across in Blavatsky's book The Secret Doctrine. *The passage referred to a biblical Seth, and to a Seth who was an Egyptian god, who ended up as a daemon, etc.)*

SESSION 525 (DELETED PORTION)
APRIL 22, 1970 9:14 PM

(From the 525th Session, April 22, 1970. 9:14PM)
Good evening.
("Good evening, Seth.")

At our next session I will do your tape for you. I would not even tell Ruburt ahead of time *(humorously)*, but even I need the tape in the recorder.

(This is a reference to Mary Sharp's attempts to record "spirit" voices, etc.)

I also have some comments before I begin dictation.

Ruburt has made advances today, partially aided by the receipt of the contracts *(for the dream book)*, but also for reasons given by me recently. He should indeed now learn to become aware of those immediately denied impulses toward motion, of which he spoke this evening. And of course to follow through with the motion, rather than to check it as he has often done.

Now I tell you that he has been checking such impulses a good fifty times a day, this including impulses of which he has not been consciously aware. He is ready now to become aware of these. They are just beneath consciousness, and will yield readily to his attention. He must obviously make an attempt to accept them, and that at least is a step in the proper direction. What he is becoming aware of clearly and consciously is the residue, the checks and balances, that he has been using to restrict physical activity.

I told you that he was ready for a <u>giant</u> (underlined) improvement, and a necessary requirement was and is his recognition of the impulses that he has been denying or restricting. Getting up and down from the floor, as I knew it would, reawakened muscular memory, you see, and this in turn knocked at the door of his consciousness, jarring him into new recognitions. He will know that he is accepting these impulses, and they will become points of triumph now, and can serve as gateways to achievement.

I expect then a concentrated effort to spontaneously accept impulses toward action <u>and</u> immediate performance of the act. The checking and subsequent blocking occurs three or four times usually at your meal. Several times both morning and afternoon when he is at his desk. Now these are simple impulses to get up. Other impulses involve leaving the apartment, going down the stairs. He checks the impulses—now, he checks the natural impulse—to throw his arms out straight away. *(Gestures; emphatic delivery.)*

He is seldom aware that that impulse is even there, so I want him to look for the impulse whenever a situation would seem to call for that motion, and he will find it… other impulses he is now becoming aware of. At one point they were buried. This includes the impulses to sink down upon his knees when the occasion warrants it, and to rest upon his hands when the occasion would warrant it.

It is his fingers that want to grasp firmly, and he out of fear, fearful habit, has blocked the impulse. Reading this will remind him of that; but again here, when he is about to open something, or to grasp it, I want him to try to feel the impulse to do so, and then go along with it.

Even in his experience today he has gratified portions of the body by allowing them proper motion. This automatically improves such things as circulation and distribution of nutriments and energy throughout the organism. It reassures muscular memory, and again, he can no longer accept himself as someone who cannot perform a certain motion.

These activities also open up nerve sources and make more energy available to him, because he is not using so much energy in blockages. He quite surprised himself this evening, and there are more surprises to come. Tell him tomorrow morning I expect him to begin writing his book. He is simply to write even if he only produces five pages that he does not use, or that he ends up throwing away.

This material should be placed with the other recent sessions for him, on the top. I am keeping up with his progress, and these hints for him are uniquely tailored for his present development. He will do well with his book. He sees himself as not having begun it however, even though he has a chapter done, with which he is not entirely pleased.

He is to begin writing, and to continue each day, and the book will take care of itself. It makes no difference where he begins to write. But I expect five pages tomorrow.

Now this impulse business is highly vital. When you see him checking an impulse to move, and it is often obvious to you, then handle it in this way. Simply remind him that it is natural for his body to move. That is, do not be critical, but <u>firmly</u> encourage him. Following this advice will have far more reaching and far quicker beneficial results than either of you now realize, and will also release energy that will be quite obvious to the both of you.

Now you may take your break.

(9:43—9:53.)

Now. I have a few more remarks, and then we will resume dictation.

He also blocks impulses to eat during the day, or sometimes before bed. He does not do this at meals, but the small snacks that he would ordinarily want, he does not take. He has not been tying to run, as I specified. This is important, for to him running is a happy, spontaneous activity, and he has blocked the impulse at times rather consciously because he feared he could not do it, that it would hurt or that he would look silly.

Here, for his own reasons, as given much earlier, he latched upon what he considered and interpreted as cautiousness on your part. You <u>used</u> to tell him (underline used) not to tell everyone his good news, for example, perhaps lest it did not develop. In his own way at that <u>time</u> (underlined), he picked up the habit of checking happy spontaneity, and he felt you were accusing if he displayed it, and in small ways began blocking. Later he himself did not trust any good development, and so felt unsure in expressing it. He also interpreted a habit of "natural secrecy" (in quotes) on your part quite literally. To keep a secret was not to express it. This is simply background that did apply however to the running aspect—either running physically or running off at the mouth. So it is important that he begin showing himself that he can run, and now he knows that you will heartily approve. Now give us a moment for our dictation.

(End of personal data at 10:03.)

DELETED SESSION
MAY 6, 1970 WEDNESDAY

(This session, for Wednesday, May 6, 1970, is deleted from the record, since it is a personal one for Jane and me.)

Now, good evening.

("Good evening, Seth.")

I will have a few remarks before dictation.

For the record, again, I suggest the running and the up and down movements. These are imperative, and tell him I said so. Now I have two simple exercises. I want these done every day. They take hardly any time, but will be most effective.

I want first of all Ruburt, quite simply, to imagine your penis straight. This is to be done once at a time only. Do you follow me?

("Yes.")
Then he should think, it is done—that is, straightened, and let it go at that. Have him do it out of the corner of his mind, as it were, and whenever it comes to his mind.

Now I want you, in the same way, to picture his arms straight in normal position, and follow the same procedure. Is this clear?

("Yes.")

Now each of you may do the same exercises for yourself also if you want to. The important thing is to do it easily. Ruburt can picture, mentally, your straight penis, more easily than he can his own arms. When you do this sort of thing, one for the other, your love is added, gives extra force; and the love between you is relatively uncluttered, and can be directed well in this fashion.

Any impeding subconscious ideas are bypassed. Now. The book that you have just received from Prentice *(Psychic Discoveries Behind the Iron Curtain)*, will have an important effect upon Ruburt, and a beneficial one, helping to increase his confidence in his own abilities.

The present notes he has written to himself are highly effective, and he should follow them and the procedure they suggest. What he felt this week, and in beginning his book, was the rousing of his energies. Then he can direct them. Now when he feels a sense of exhilaration—he knows the subjective feeling I refer to—then have him direct it, that energy, to his arms.

You have been holding on to your own symptoms while Ruburt still has his. They are like notes to yourself, reminding you that things are still not as good as they should be. Tell yourself that you can help yourself and Ruburt far better without the disease caused by the symptoms. Once they were reminders that you also had a part to play in the entire situation. You accept that fact now, and therefore no longer require them. The need for them is over. Once they were meant to promote your psychological understanding, but now they can only impede your progress; and you are also slightly resentful at Ruburt, feeling that he is somewhat responsible, by still maintaining his symptoms, for your own.

("Yes. I know that.")

It is somewhat for this reason that you do not <u>more actively</u> (underlined) use the positive encouragement of which Ruburt was earlier speaking. You feel you are helping him sufficiently enough through all your efforts, and withhold this more positive approach out of that resentment. Do you follow me here?

("Yes. All of this verifies what I've learned on my own, through the pendulum.")

(True. This material is a fine example of communication between two people without words being used. I have been periodically using the pendulum to get at my

own situation, and did not tell Jane. Of course she knows I use the pendulum, and with excellent results; but I hadn't told her about this other inquiry.

(*More of what I had learned with the pendulum is verified by Seth in more material throughout the session.*)

This also serves to punish you for the resentment, since by not giving this more positive support, which incidentally is far more effective than you would imagine—you also to some degree help to hold back that which you both want so badly.

I thought I would unravel this little puzzle, though I see from what you say that you had already arrived at some of these conclusions.

You are also, as you know, <u>relatively</u> (underlined) of a solitary nature, and to some degree, and because of misinterpretation, distrustful and resentful at the thought that suggestion is so important between individuals. You would still like to believe in the importance of suggestion and telepathy, but only when it suits your purposes, and to minimize it in those areas that are somewhat touchy.

(*This I didn't know, not having explored it with the pendulum.*)

You do not like to believe that an individual can be so influenced, because of your background. This makes you want to isolate yourself, and also prevents you from benefiting from suggestions yourself, and benefiting others through your own suggestions in certain areas. In other areas you accept and utilize the nature of suggestion. (*Pause.*) Now give me a moment.

A small remark: The resentment of which I spoke earlier caused some overreaction on your part when you would have <u>visited</u> (underlined) your landlady over the dog episode—when a call was sufficient. These are simply pointers. You may take your break.

The good news however, has been hinted at but not yet completely developed. It has to do with the paperback rights, and a good price for them.

(*9:44. Jane's pace had been fast. I explained to her at break what I had been trying to learn on my own with the pendulum. Seth's information will prove to be very useful.*

(*The good news data refers to Seth's prediction of same in the 520th session for March 25, 1970: "I believe there is also some good news for you that you do not expect." I asked Jane for a comment about this before tonight's session.*

(*10:01.*)

Now. You are working toward several breakthroughs in your own painting—actually a three-way breakthrough.

One intuitional discovery will open into two others. Dissatisfaction, creative dissatisfaction, triggers in you new intuitive developments, and this one will be fairly important. On your relationship now, yours and Ruburt's: unconsciously you inspire each other.

The inspirational aspects however can be strengthened and magnified on both of your parts. The positive approach on your part, mentioned earlier, can indeed be interpreted in such a light. You feel with some justification, that Ruburt in his own concern forgets your lingering symptoms; and he should make an effort now to use his abilities to help rid you of these.

Often you can help each other quite effectively, direct your energies toward the other, and bypass those impediments that help prevent you from using your own psychic energy as well as you should in your own behalf; so that you can help Ruburt in some areas where he is weak, and he can help you in some areas where you are weak. You get a full concentration of healing energy in this way, and directed through love.

In last night's session *(for Jane's ESP class)* rather extraordinary amounts of energy were released here, to the benefit of all concerned. Psychic and spiritual peaks are experienced by those in the room during such sessions, and the subjective experience of the students can then be used by them as a reminder of moments of psychic understanding that they seldom achieve.

Now I do not mind your chasing the cat *(Seth's voice was suddenly loud; I had taken a swipe at our cat Willy with my notepaper, when he was about to jump up into Jane's lap)*, but chasing my foot is another matter… this energy is then picked up by the families of the students, and their lives indirectly benefited.

Ruburt's own system is charged at such times. The negative ions are multiplied in the room itself.

I did want to remind him that many of his classes, and our class sessions, have this effect, and again remind him the notes he has made himself are excellent for <u>him</u>.

The notes particularly about energy, and with his small experiment *(smile)* about arising this morning. He immediately showed himself that such was the case. I decided to give you this material this evening because it is important to both of you, and also because I will probably finish up the chapter I have begun in one rather long session, though it may run into another.

If you have any questions please ask them.

("No, I guess you've already answered the ones I had in mind.")

I had intended to chat with you for a while. Now that you are back with steady sessions once more, I need not use <u>every</u> session for dictation as long as I know my book is doing well. I thought you might perhaps miss the more easy give and take, if every session was dictation—though of course most sessions will be.

But if you have nothing to say to me, how can we chat?

(10:20. Seth and I did have a chat until 10:38, without notes. Our talk covered quite a few topics and was very enjoyable, although I was in a somewhat quiet and depressed mood this evening. I wasn't at my best but did rouse enough to have a good exchange with Seth. We will have to do this more often. Habit is strong, too: there were some points I would have liked to make notes about....)

SESSION 527 (DELETED PORTION)
MAY 11, 1970

(This material was given us by Seth at the end of the session for May 11/70 —the 527th; and is deleted from the regular record.

(11:28.) I want to get our friend *(Jane)* into motion, with this running, even if you have to chase him through the house. Or take twenty minutes when you can, with those rackets *(badminton)*, so that running is combined with the idea of fun.

I would like you <u>kindly</u>, not sternly, when he moves slowly, to remind him that he can move more quickly, for in almost all instances he can. The two exercises I gave you both—do not forget them, either of you.

(There followed, here, two predictions related to Jane's forthcoming book, The Seth Material. *These are listed in the 527th session.)*

If <u>all</u> of my suggestions are followed in line with your general circumstances and Ruburt's health, there will be <u>vast</u> (underlined) improvement.

I hesitate to repeat myself, and yet remind Ruburt of this playful attitude I have spoken of. It is very important. The responsiveness, physically, is beginning to show appreciably in your intimate relationship. He does not need to protect himself physically from any experience, nor hold up the arms to ward off the blows of fate. *(Gesture; emphatic.)*

Lift up his rib cage area *(gesture,)* so that he gets the idea of that up and down easy motion. The body will remember it.

Now. Do you want to have a pleasant evening of conversation, or do you want to go to bed?

("I think I'll take bed, if you don't mind. How about Wednesday?")

I will be here Wednesday.

("Good. I'll look forward to it.")

My heartiest wishes to you both. Now give me a moment. *(Long pause. Jane's eyes were closed; she sat quite still.)* I sent some energy to your member.

("Good.")

One more point: if you will excuse the pun. *(Humorously.)*

("Yes.")

(Pause.) For a while you did not feel that the way was clear, psychologically, between yourself and Ruburt. In the beginning this was on your side. Then however you felt a cleavage on Ruburt's part, and continued the symptom. Do you follow me?

("Yes.")

Remind yourself that the road between you now is clear and straight. I sent you considerable energy, and transposed a clear image of the perfect organ. And now, good evening and a good night's sleep.

("Good evening, Seth, and thank you very much. Very good.")

(11:35. Jane's trance was good. She said she felt "something" go out to me from her body while Seth paused during his delivery... I would like to report that the next day I noticed a considerable improvement in the condition, physically.)

SESSION 528 (DELETED PORTION)
MAY 13, 1970

(Deleted from the 528th session for May 13, 1970.)

End of dictation. And now give us a moment, if you please.

(10:51. Jane sat quite still in her rocking chair. A one minute pause, eyes closed.)

We are directing energy toward your member. *(One minute pause.)* And toward your hand. *(I was surprised at this. Another one minute pause.)* And now toward the whole physical image.

(10:56.) Now, from behind you energy is being directed toward Ruburt.

("From behind me?")

From behind you energy is now being directed toward Ruburt, toward his whole physical image. *(One minute pause.)*

Now toward the elbows; and now toward the shoulders... the left shoulder particularly. *(Pause.)* Now the right foot; and now both knees. *(Pause.)* Now toward the fingers, and the arms in general.

With your inner consents, I have been making some adjustments in your own energy fields, that will be more beneficial and allow you both to benefit from the good suggestions given, one to the other.

Now I will end our session unless you have questions.

("No, I guess not.")

My heartiest regards to you both, and a fond good evening.

("Good evening, Seth. Thank you very much.")

(11:00. Jane's trance had been good. She had several things to say. The first was that she was momentarily disoriented when she came out of trance because the chair she was sitting in was <u>not</u> where she thought it was while speaking for Seth.

(Jane was really "fooled" when she opened her eyes and saw her position. She thought the chair was several feet to her own right, closer to our wall-to-ceiling bookcase. "I thought that me, the whole bit where I'm sitting, and me, it seemed to me that I was over there," she said, pointing to her right side. This reminded her of the recent session when she momentarily seemed to be speaking as Seth from near the same bookcase.

(When Seth directed energy at me in the beginning, Jane saw my erect penis straight, then in a pyramid shape, with the end "rising up and up like Pinocchio's nose," she said. It was as though there was a very elongated pyramid over the penis, she said.

(I should add in these notes that the day after Seth first directed energy to my penis in a recent session, I noticed a definite improvement. The next day the condition was as before; and I had described this to Jane today.

(Jane felt the concentration of energy was stronger when it was directed toward me from the rocker at the start of this episode. When Seth spoke of my hands, Jane saw my astral hands upraised—as I was really writing at the time, with the palms outward, toward her. She said energy was particularly directed at the 4th and 5th fingers of my left hand, although energy was going to both hands. Jane said she saw my hands as she had seen her own arms straightened out yesterday. The two fingers mentioned of my left hand were somehow different, and needed the energy, she said. I told her that although the penis had reverted to its original condition, I had been aware of a noticeable and steady improvement in the right hand condition, although no previous suggestions or energy had been sent to the hands before, by Seth.

(Re the energy coming from in back of me: Jane said some kind of projection may have been involved here. Part of her consciousness was at an elevated spot on the wall in back of me. Actually the wall didn't exist, Jane said, merely this dot or spot of consciousness in back of me. Jane did not see me from the spot, nor herself. Yet from this spot behind me there was a part of Jane's or Seth's consciousness with energy coming out like a cone, again.

(Jane felt that part of her was in back of me, that it was some kind of projection, yet she also "saw" this spot from her seat in the rocker, with her eyes closed… At one time, very dimly, Jane felt something was behind her, also, directing energy toward her.

(Again, she felt quite disoriented when she finally opened her eyes and saw the position of her chair, compared to where she had thought it was. Also, the pyramid or cone of energy from in back of me had been directed at the spot in the room where

she *thought* she was—not where she really was.

(*Jane said she had trouble describing some of this data. Nor could she say how or whether she and Seth "worked this" experience(s) together, separately, or just what. These notes may not be in exact order according to developments; they are put together from what Jane told me after the session. End.*)

SESSION 533 (DELETED PORTION)
JUNE 1, 1970

(*This material is deleted from the 533rd session for June 1, 1970. The data came through because of a discussion Jane and I had before the session, in which I expressed a good deal of resentment and negative attitudes, about a lot of things....*)

Now—do either of you mind if we have a session?

("*Nope.*"

(*To me:*) I have a few comments before dictation. Give me a moment. (*Long pause.*) You have a deep love of the land, from your Denmark days. Early in this life you also enjoyed it. You liked working with the land, but because of conflicts with your father you turned against, for example, gardening.

You have ambiguous feelings about Ruburt's garden for this reason. You are pleased with his obvious productivity with plants, underline. You remember how strict your father was however, and methodical, in gardening. This annoyed you greatly, but now to some extent you identify with those leanings, and look down upon the garden when Ruburt does not find his way to follow the gardening rules.

Some of these feelings are also projected upon the apartment house at large, and mask your deep love of your studio, despite all disadvantages.

You have always wanted some land of your own, and have been bitter that you did not have it. Subconsciously you are also bitter because you <u>could have</u> nearly purchased a place of your own with the money that you used to help your father purchase your family home.

Some of these feelings have indeed led you to a strongly charged attitude in <u>some</u> (underlined) cases, a bit out of proportion. (*Humorously.*) This is not to say that one of you is completely right and the other completely wrong, but I will tell you this: you <u>can</u> count upon Ruburt to recognize immediately and intuitively cases of such overly charged behavior on your part.

There is simply a deep difference. Ruburt for example will enjoy and make use of whatever land he has, be it only the dirt in a window-sill plot. He does not have ambiguous feelings to supercharge his reactions in this particular area.

To you this apartment house and its grounds are considered in terms of land, and dwelling. You think of the land you do not have. You have not been able to take advantage of the yard or the ground available as positive things of joy and refreshment, and have therefore been denied an extra advantage from this place, and the conditions that Ruburt <u>has</u> enjoyed.

He thinks of this place in terms of a dwelling rather than as land, but because his attitude is not charged and because he does love land, he is able to enjoy what land there is. Now <u>he</u> compares this place for example to his childhood home, <u>as</u> subconsciously you compare it to yours, whether you know it or not. He comes out far above in comparison. You do not, and this angers you.

To him other apartments, vacant, that you look at, represent automatically psychic probabilities that intrigue him simply because they exist. No land idea is connected. This does not mean he does not notice or dislike a given neighborhood. The lay of the land with you however immediately overwhelms other considerations, and if there is <u>no</u> land you do not even want to step foot upon the property. These are simply variations in reaction that you should both understand.

Give me a moment. A long moment. *(To me:)* You are largely the one to be satisfied, for Ruburt will find joy in almost any environment that he considers his own; you see he <u>personifies</u> in a way that you do not; any place he is in is his place, to his mind, as this is his yard. So any dwelling that you find he will personify and make his own, and therefore your own, if you follow me.

("Yes.")

You should both have learned enough by now however to sense the psychic vitality or atmosphere of a dwelling. There are advantages and disadvantages in living in a house alone. Everyone in this apartment house is seldom in a bad mood at the same time, for example, so to some extent in periods of normal depression you are sustained by others, close by, who are not.

You are also of course open to negative moods of others in the same way. In a house you saturate the atmosphere until the air actually becomes almost an extension, electromagnetically, of your mental and psychic states.

You would indeed benefit from larger quarters. You do not need me to tell you this. I have not mentioned such matters since my early suggestion that you purchase the house you did not purchase. It was a probability that you did not follow.

Do you have any questions?

("No, I guess not.")

There is also in your subconscious the feeling of a land or farm in connection with the one owned by your father's family.

("I don't think I ever saw that farm—did I?")

Simply the idea. Now. To some extent you both overemphasize the differences between you as far as your ideas of a more or less permanent dwelling place are concerned. This has something to do with your lack of action. You can for example find a comfortable compromise between isolation that is relatively complete, and an apartment in the heart of town.

I want you to understand these charged areas however, and some of the reasons for them. You may take a break.

(9:46—9:54.)

Now. I do want to do some dictation, so after a few more comments I will do so.

It upsets Ruburt when you talk of moving, but make no actions to do so, because subconsciously it reminds him of the deep uncertainty and insecurity he felt when he was in the orphanage. Never knowing when he would go home or not, he kept himself in a constant state of readiness to leave. Various dates were given and then his leaving was postponed several times.

He did not realize this connection. It is the indecision and lack of certainty, rather than any decision, that troubles him in this area. He feels he is not living where he is. *(Long pause.)*

While you want land, you also fear that it will tie you down, and to some extent your feelings are ambiguous. This added to the points mentioned earlier, has largely prevented any move; far more, I believe, than any financial considerations.

Ruburt's ideas about a house for example are actually far more positive than your own. He automatically believes that your income would rise to meet the new demands, and he is quite correct, as long as you believe it fully. He also thinks in terms of <u>making</u> such a venture pay, however, of ventures financially rewarding and enjoyable, while yours are negative in this regard.

Now since I am here, you can ask me what questions you have on this.

("You're doing very well by yourself—that's why I haven't interrupted with a lot of questions.")

All right. Ruburt automatically thinks of the productivity of land, when he thinks of land. He would do very well in the future in buying real estate—and there will be money to buy it. He would not do as well with stocks and bonds. They are meaningless to him.

Tangibles are important to him. I am simply trying to explain attitudes. Money in the bank does not emotionally excite him, though he realizes its benefits. It does not bring about his creative nature. Now real estate would, and he could double his investments easily, for he has a good idea of people in relation to dwellings, and of population movement. He is not aware of this.

You need not fear, then, that he would not follow wholeheartedly, say, in moving to a house for example, for the tangible element and the land would rouse those instincts. If you have no questions we will resume dictation, or what was the beginning of chapter 9 *(of* Seth Speaks.

("Very interesting.")

Do you want a short break first?

("Might as well. Yes.")

(10:10. Jane's trance had been good—she was far out, she said. Her pace had also been good. I thought the material excellent. It should prove very useful. I had suspected some points, but most was very revealing, especially my subconscious reasons re land ownership, Jane's very excellent way of personifying wherever she lived, etc., and her unknown ability for real estate dealing, etc.

(I will make the attempt to change negative attitudes. I have often puzzled over our lack of action in seeking larger quarters, etc. My ambiguous feelings re owning land, rather than purely financial considerations, is quite instructive, etc.)

SESSION 556 (DELETED PORTION)
OCTOBER 26, 1970

(Deleted from the 556th Session, October 26, 1970.

(10:40 PM.) Now. We will simply begin on this matter this evening. This is a hysterical reaction. Do you understand?

("Yes." The right hand tremor, etc., which I had explained to Jane in detail at break.)

From your work with the pendulum you understand some points. The affair began however when you first realized that your father would be no longer operative. He had not lived up to your mother's plans for him, and would now obviously not do so.

Emotionally you saw this as the death of your mother's hopes, and felt on the one hand that it was up to you now, so that this reactivated older feelings from the past that you had pretty well handled.

This occurred precisely when you had strong doubts as to whether or not you should stay on the job, and strongly considered it would be best to leave. When you think of leaving you come face to face with the same conflict, for she wanted you to succeed as a commercial artist.

She thinks it far more laudable that you work in an art department with steady wages, and you know this. *(Like Artistic Card Company.*

(Pause.) Give us time.

The condition has meaning on other levels also. It serves to remind you that the issue is operating. Do you follow me?

("Yes.")

It also serves by giving you another message—that you do want to leave, and that your desire to do so has been affecting your work. If you had to stay, and if you will not be given as much money as you think you should receive, then you will see to it that the work will suffer. This is resentment.

Now I am giving you, presently, the picture as seen by your subconscious. The small but frequent breaks in the fine lines represent those times when the resentments break through. The resentment, carried far enough, <u>could</u> affect your work to such a degree that it forced you to leave, which is exactly what one portion of you wants—and that portion does not care how this is done, though it does not want your painting affected.

Other portions are afraid to leave because of the feelings concerning your mother, mentioned earlier. You are also afraid however, to some extent and under certain conditions, of working, even painting, entirely at home because your father worked at home and did not do well.

The job has served to keep you from realizing that. *(True.)* In writing the difficulty shows itself because you are trying not to communicate certain things to yourself. In other words, inhibited material, some that I have mentioned this evening that you have been thrusting aside. You have not wanted to know these things, considering that that they were beneath you, and strongly condemning any feelings that you could not accept as adult. And after your own lectures to Ruburt you should know better.

("I'm ready to accept them now.")

A blockage of feeling in other words.

At work you mar your performance. You did not want to perform well because you are resentful. Then you were resentful over the resentment whenever you became closely aware of it.

You were more affected by your friend's *(Curtis Kent)* departure than you realize, wondering if you yourself should find a better-paying commercial job, and yet angry that you even had such thoughts when what you really wanted was to stay home and paint.

("How come I asked you about this business now?")

The episode also has some connections, again with your father, in that you feel sometimes, and subconsciously, that you will be old and trembly and still at the job. The departure of your friend serves to bring this up to your mind.

("His hands shake too." I suddenly recalled that Curt's hands have an obvious

tremor, a fact I have long known.)

That is why you asked me tonight.

("Wait a minute... Because he left?")

Because he left, and because you knew his hands shook also. At times he wanted to throw his work across the floor.

You need to take a reevaluation of your situation, and to act upon what you learn. This may or may not mean leaving the job, but it will mean a new awareness of all the issues involved, and your attitudes. Take your subconscious attitudes seriously. Consider them.

("Well, I guess I'm beginning to. I have thought often that I'd leave the job eventually. I've especially begun to think this within the past year.")

I have already made comments earlier dealing with that. When you read over the material you will see.

("I intend to.")

You will get further information through the pendulum, and you may try automatic writing. I will help you in any case. It is important for some of this that you work it out through your own system—part of you communicating with another part—

("That's what I've been trying to do.")

—rather than being simply told by me. The knowledge comes from you then. But I will help you.

Now we will end the session but I will have more to say as you ask me.

("Very good. Thank you very much.")

My fond wishes—and you will succeed in working it out.

("Good night, Seth. Thanks again.")

Physically, certain yoga exercises will also be of help.

(11:11. Jane said she was really under while giving this data.)

SESSION 557 (DELETED PORTION)
OCTOBER 28, 1970 WEDNESDAY

(Deleted from the 557th Session, October 28, 1970, Wednesday.

(11:16 PM.) Now. A few remarks having to do with the main reason that your suggestions were not as effective as you would have liked.

You did not rise above the fear that the symptom itself, a part from everything else, gave you. You were in a panic, thinking of the importance of your hand to your work. You feared so strongly that the symptom could stop you, even from painting, that the fear itself became a detriment for positive suggestion. When your imagination operated freely and not directed concerning the symptom, then it ran in those directions. The very charge behind the fear propelled it.

You did not give the suggestions from a standpoint of assurance. They were like thumbs in your estimation, subconsciously, to hold back the dam of feared eventuality. You gave the suggestions out of fear then, not from a strong framework of assurance. You overaggravated the symptoms, overexaggerating their importance because of this fear.

Now Ruburt did the same thing on occasion in the past.

("Do I still do it?")

Give me a moment here. Give yourself suggestions only when you recognize that you have achieved a certain sense of peace within you, even if it is only momentary, the feeling that you have stilled your fears for the time being.

You recognize that feeling. You must not be propelled to give your suggestions by fear of what will happen, or might happen, or could happen otherwise. In your suggestions tell yourself in whatever way you choose that your hand can be steady under any and all conditions.

Do not specifically relate the behavior of the hand with your artistic self or artistic abilities in your suggestions, but in a general manner to the natural health of your being and easy flow of your ideas outward.

The difficulties with the hand were not meant to threaten your artistic self. You feared they were. They were meant, in <u>some</u> instances, to protect your artistic self, if you recall our last session. Therefore the fear was a conscious one, and basically unwarranted. The unconscious was <u>not</u> (underlined) threatening your artistic self. You were afraid that it was, or that unwittingly the symptoms would bring this about.

("Well, I certainly took it that way.")

The unconscious was trying to protect your artistic self. If you wanted to stay home and paint all day badly enough, then it would hamper your hand motions at work. Do you follow that or should I elaborate?

(I was thinking this over. I followed it all right, but at the same time I was wondering why the unconscious, when it saw how I was taking the symptom, didn't get busy and eliminate it and set me at rest. I will have to ask the question, etc.)

It mirrored your attitudes toward your job, not toward your art in that regard. The fear that the artistic self was being threatened led to a certain panic that impeded the flow of information you were trying to suggest to the unconscious.

The understanding that the artistic self was not being threatened should allow you to relax sufficiently for the suggestions to take effect more. You were as a result distrustful of the subconscious, and this hampered the suggestions. You felt, if it were threatening your artistic self, what could you expect from it when you had always supposed previously that it upheld the creative drive? Your deduction you see was false—the earlier deduction that it threatened the painting.

Read that over and ask me whatever questions you want to at our next session, or if you have questions now I will answer them.

("It can wait. This looks like very telling information. Give me the weekend to think this over.")

There was no great diversion. The unconscious was trying to give you what it thought you wanted, in <u>that</u> respect, now. If you wanted to leave your job badly enough and could not consciously decide to do so, then it would force the situation for you in the most obvious way possible.

You did not get your suggestions through adequately because in this important area you misjudged its motives, and this caused a certain panic on your part, as mentioned.

("You'd better stop. Somebody's [meaning Jane] losing their voice.")

(Jane had been speaking very softly, in a very dry and husky voice that I thought was getting worse by the minute. But at my words Seth suddenly boomed through very loud and clear with no voice problem, and quite humorously:)

<u>I have just been keeping it low.</u>

("Oh.")

Now do you have any more questions?

("No.")

My heartiest regards to you and our friend. Have no worries about his voice.

("Okay. And thank you very much."

(11:42.

(Note: On November 10, 1970, pendulum tells me I now agree with this data, where on November 3, I disagreed with it all.)

SESSION 560 (DELETED)
NOVEMBER 11, 1970

(This session, ordinarily the 560th for Nov. 11, 1970, is deleted from the record since it concerns Jane and me.)

Good evening.

("Good evening, Seth.")

Now. A few remarks directed to my friend and yours.

First of all, Ruburt has as you know an excellent intellect. It is <u>not</u> as well developed however as he supposes. He could do far more with it. Now he emphasizes its strictly analytical nature, and in so doing puts limitations upon the ways in which he uses it.

He does not allow it the freedom that he should or set it to work for him as completely as he could. Often when he most <u>believes</u> he is being analytically intellectual, he is instead using the intellect in a surface manner to cover rationalizations.

He has as you know excellent intuitive abilities. In the past in his poetry the intuitive abilities were somewhat isolated. The truths that came through could be considered as creative fantasies and therefore did not have to be accepted literally, or accepted by the intellect.

The intuitive portions of himself he has always considered as feminine. The intellectual capacities he always considered masculine. He relied upon the intellectual abilities therefore as the stronger, because in his own background he believed the male to have the greater strength.

Some of this has to do with the cultural climate that colored his attitudes. He puts his intuitions in as intellectual terms as possible. To his way of thinking this gives them greater acceptability, strength and durability. He will not be laughed at as a result.

One of the reasons why he did not understand that the spontaneous intuitive self <u>was</u> the deeply creative and therefore deeply stable self, was that he identified it with <u>his idea</u> of femininity as he unfortunately misunderstood it. It was therefore second best, undependable, and could lead to byways that were not respectable. He never equated money with respectability or prestige. As a youngster he had no family background or money, and his need to be looked up to and held in esteem could not wait.

He set himself up then as an intellectual, and this became his badge of respectability. It also held a more masculine than feminine image in his mind however, for the reasons as given.

He could not deny the intuitive self, so it became the self who wrote poetry. In his environment this however was an intellectual thing to do. The feminine image meant instability, intuitions that could lead into unrespectable byways, and emotions that were not intellectually restrained.

You, being a male, he felt, would be most alarmed at any undue emotionalisms. This aside from your own reaction to your mother's emotionalism. So there was a good division set up between his intellectual-respectable-to-him masculine aspects, and his intuitive, feminine, private aspects.

The psychic work meant that these would be united. There was strain, as could have been expected. Intuitively and as a woman he would naturally have longer hair, wear earrings and jangly jewelry, which fits the inner feminine image, and also the inner mystical, psychic image of the seeress, the prophetess, and in your own relationship, the mistress.

In appearing on television he wore initially the pants suit to stress the masculine aspects, or tailored clothes, each stressing to him the more masculine, intellectual, respectable qualities of his nature. He is saying, you see, "I am quite normal, quite intellectual, and in my way quite responsible and proper. Do not be alarmed by my wild mystical self, for it is well under control."

He feels also that this image suits your ideas, as indeed it does to a large degree. This also has something to do with your private lives, for the feminine portions of that nature can quite easily be frightened into not showing themselves through the monthly function—that is so utterly spontaneous, so mysterious to the intellect, and the one main sign by which the female monthly shows her difference from the male.

Now to some extent when that began, you acquiesced. For while you were adventurous, you also to some extent feared the spontaneous nature that was so a part of your wife, in those terms. A small somewhat amusing note: whenever, throughout your marriage, you commented adversely when Ruburt was about to throw a scarf about his neck, or perhaps wear an extra chain with others, he interpreted this, and quite correctly, as a hint of caution on your part that he was giving too much prevalence to the feminine love of ornamentation.

Now. In his restrained motion he has to some extent (underlined) adopted what he feels to be the more proper, deliberate responsible characteristics connected in his mind with the symbolically masculine, analytical intellectual.

He is saying "I do not run off half-cocked. I am not feminine, mystical, wild, given to fancies that will take you far from the world you know into unknown territory. I am not the unpredictable and therefore unreliable prophetess or mistress. My slow and deliberate movements should tell you this. They tell me this, and offer me then that security." Thus he interprets these emotions to himself.

They are saying to you: "Once I made you leave your home town and your parents out of my erraticism. I will not irresponsibly lead you into realities that you cannot trust."

He was afraid that as once he felt he dragged you all over the country, you would fear that he was now dragging you all over the inner universe. The symptoms have therefore been an attempt to equalize an inner situation. Now, they have grown less as he understood the inner situation.

The male characteristics he always thought of as stabilizing. The intellect and the tailored clothes went together. The quick motions were always associated with inner intuitive feminine abilities. The symptoms have in part been meant to reassure you that you need not be afraid that he would be driven by his impulses. In the beginning of the psychic work you were concerned at spontaneous sessions, and while you were highly intrigued by the developments. There was one situation in particular that frightened you both—the time that Ruburt ended up on the floor when he picked up the information from your neighbor, Barbara.

You gave him quite a lecture, but it was nothing like the lecture he gave himself, and it rearoused old fears of giving in spontaneously to impressions or psychic data. He considered this dangerous. He began to watch out that such episodes would nor reoccur, and this was reflected in muscular tenseness.

The tests with Instream, and your own, precipitated a situation in which his intellect was constantly checking his intuitive information. Because of his own background this precipitated a situation in which one portion of the self was constantly scrutinizing another portion with a jaundiced eye.

Now you may rest your fingers for a moment, but we are going to get all of this information through that we can.

(10:00. Jane remained quietly in trance to some extent, even though she moved about. She had given the above material at a fast pace, almost without pause. My writing hand was tired. Resume at 10:05.)

Now. Without the psychic development, your combined background could have quite undermined your creative abilities entirely. This was a chance you took, both of you, when you set up this last reincarnational existence.

You had used creative abilities often in the past. This time you had several problems, both of you, to deal with. If the psychic abilities showed themselves, then this would be your last reincarnation. If not then there would have been others, and you knew this.

To some extent illness has been used by you both in a constructive manner. On your part *(RFB)* initially as a very definite warning that you were not to put your full energies into a job. Pressure from your parents could have precipitated such an arrangement. Your illness was then used by Ruburt to bring to the surface of his mind deeply-rooted fears that had been festering beneath. Your illness served this purpose for you also. This further led to a recognition of the basic uselessness of many of the ideas upon which your existences had been based, and upon which your society was based. This triggered the need to find newer answers and to probe into other dimensions.

The very experience however, with all of its triumphs and insights had to bring to the foreground personal problems of development that many people simply do not face, or come to grips with. Strains and tensions developed, but in grappling with these and with the physical symptoms, new insights were reached.

The <u>relative</u> (underline that twice) exile of Ruburt's symbolically feminine characteristics is something that neither of you consciously realized. You did this to assure yourselves that these abilities, feminine in both of your minds, would not so get the upper hand that the responsible, and in both of your minds, masculine or dependable aspects of your life would be threatened.

All of the time of course these feminine aspects were being used as the intuitive, mystical thresholds of psychic activity. I told you once that Ruburt would not have allowed a feminine counterpart of myself to speak, but neither would you have. You would have been afraid of the "unpredictable" in quotes feminine aspects.

Now all of this is highly important. To some extent it was inevitable, considering your backgrounds. The feminine aspects in any case, culturally speaking, were being denied since you did not want children. Reincarnationally this you set ahead of time. If the psychic developments that represented your greatest fulfillment, with all their ramifications in your art and life, had not occurred, then you would have had two children, and continued a reincarnational cycle. There are other aspects here, in that in your last reincarnational life you had somewhat greater freedom within the sexual framework. You can come closer to the ideal identity that gives greater rein within one individual to both male and female characteristics.

When the sexual identity is sound, as it is in both of your cases, this means the need for a greater accommodation within the self. A tolerant attitude, an exuberance and freedom, so that the best qualities of each sex can be harmoniously blended while the personality still retains its necessary overall one-sex identification physically.

So all in all, with the problems, you have managed well. This fits in with your own artistic nature, and with your background in this life. You also identified your creativity with female characteristics or abilities, symbolically speaking, and this has something to do with your distrust of making money with your art.

In your mind making money is a male characteristic, and subconsciously a male prerogative. The fact that you painted and it did not seem to bring you money served further to make you distrust these creative abilities. You identified them to some extent with your mother, the first female of course in your background. She was unpredictable,<u> and so you felt you could not depend upon your</u>

art, nor count upon it as a man. *(Much louder.)*

Now that is the main reason why you have not tried to make a living as an artist per se. You have been convinced that it would never work. Even as you could not imagine depending upon your mother for a livelihood.

This certainty that you could really never support yourself as a fine artist derives its strength from that identification, and in the main from that identification alone.

Now commercial work and the comics meant something else again. It was not fine art but directed outward in obvious fashions in an aggressive sort of thrust, with a particular market in mind, and therefore to you had a masculine quality. You were perfectly free to support yourself in your early years in that way, and your energy was released because in that regard you felt free to use it. When the natural freely creative energies were aroused in you, you instantly dispensed with all ideas of a commercial market, and completely divorced the idea of painting from selling for the reasons given.

The fallacy that neither of you recognized was that the creative, symbolically feminine portions of the self were not unpredictable, given to overemotionalism. They are instead the secure, propelling, and only dependable fountainheads of existence.

You could see Ruburt's errors in this respect to some extent, but you could not see your own. Your feelings then helped feed Ruburt's own misconceptions. You also felt safe when he did not move so fast, when his slower mobility seemed to denote greater deliberation, when in other words he did not let himself go.

Now rest your fingers. I will leave Ruburt as he is. I would have him let this one in.

(10:40. Jane's trance had been deep. She had pointed to our hall door, beyond which our black cat, Ru, had been calling after someone let him in the back door. Still somewhat in trance, Jane let the cat in, etc. Resume at 10:45.)

Now. As noted much of this has to do with the fact that in your last reincarnation both the masculine and the feminine aspects of personality are to be as fully experienced as possible, while the overall present one-sex identification is to be maintained.

This permits the fullest expression of true identity that is possible within the physical system. Otherwise identity is smothered to a large degree beneath a strictly oriented one-sex identification, with other characteristics masked and denied expression.

Your allowing the longer hair is a sign that of late you have become less frightened of the symbolically creative and feminine aspects of the artist. Your refusal in the past to look the part of an artist, per se, reflected your determination to insist upon, to you, the contrasting masculine aspects. As you allowed yourself somewhat more freedom in this regard, you both saw to it that in compensation Ruburt in his appearance allowed himself less.

All of this stems, again, from your misconception of the nature of the creative self. Now logically it may not be stable in intellectual terms, for it knows that one and one do not always give you two, but its great stability lies in its flexibility, its intuitions, and in its unending source of creativity.

In your relationship as a couple then you set up a framework in which freedoms allowed to one were compensated until certain adjustments were made. The creative aspects were given so much leeway, until out of fear one of you applied restraints of a restrictive nature. The painting to you had such strongly feminine connotations that subconsciously you felt your studio was like a womb, out of which the paintings were produced. You felt that this had <u>some</u> (underlined) terrifying implications, many of them threatening your sense of masculinity since, because of your misconceptions you were convinced ahead of time that they would never be used as a means of livelihood.

Ruburt on the other hand felt he could use psychic books as a means of livelihood, for in the books at least he felt the masculine and female tendencies merge; the intellect making use of the intuitive information.

In withholding his periods he also felt he lessened the pressure upon you, for he gave up the biological badge of femininity, and was saying "You will never have to have a full-time job to support a child." He knew full well that you didn't feel you would ever make a living as a fine artist.

The monthly periods unconsciously served as a constant threat by reminding you each of his femininity and ability to bear a child.

Now do you have questions?

(*I pointed to a painting I had just finished, of a male looking up and to my left. It had a strong appeal for me, and was almost a monochrome, done in blues and greens. I felt it had some sort of reincarnational meaning for me, but hadn't yet got around to using the pendulum to see what I could find out on my own.*

("*Can you say anything about that painting?*")

I can indeed. Now in your paintings, many of them, you merge the male and female characteristics—the feminine compassion and intuition often appearing as it does here in a male face.

You do not paint the faces of females as a rule, because of the ideas of which I have just told you. Whenever you show the so-called feminine qualities of insight or compassion, you show them as appearing in the male profile, where they are seen opaquely and not faced full on. You feel they need the male discipline to give them a suitable framework, and to define them. Without this you feel them threatening. This also has something to do with your feelings toward oils <u>under certain conditions</u> (underlined).

(In trance, Jane pointed to the new painting.) The picture is of a man, or rather of a woman who lived in Constantinople in the 14th century. A mystic of some renown who was well-known for looking into the future.

I A N O D I A L A *(spelled)* is the nearest I can come in translation for the name. You painted her as a male for the reasons given.

Do you have other questions?

(I shook my head no. Actually I had several about the new painting, but my writing hand was so cramped I felt I wouldn't be able to continue using it much longer.)

We will then end our session. You will find that I have given you a good deal of information this evening, that you should be able to put to excellent use in your daily life. Now my heartiest good wishes to you both, and a fond good evening.

("Good evening, Seth, and thank you very much. I'm sure it will all be very useful.")

I certainly hope so.

(Actually, I already regarded this as a breakthrough session, in personal terms probably the best Jane has given, etc. End at 11:07. Jane was in as deep a trance as I have seen her. It took her many minutes to come out of it. In the beginning she could not open her eyes for more than a moment at a time, etc. And throughout, the fast pace was maintained.)

SESSION 562 (DELETED)
NOVEMBER 30, 1970

(This session, ordinarily the 562nd for November 30, 1970, is deleted from the record. Excerpts from it, or references to it, may eventually be found in our Reincarnation notebook however.

(This is the first session held in the back-room studio, where we were free from a lot of regular and potential distractions. Both of us liked the new arrangement very much, and plan to continue it.)

Good evening.

("Good evening, Seth.")

I like our new environment, and I have some comments of a personal nature.

Now. Some of this will seem very simple, but often you forget the pure simplicity of your motives when you concentrate upon tangles.

The both of you, individually, have several goals in common, therefore as a couple you are doubly strong in these areas. They are areas in which individually and together you will brook no interference.

As I will tell you, these goals have strong connections in past lives, and in this life you each gave yourselves powerful psychological charges to insure that these goals would be followed through. You chose parental circumstances therefore that would presuppose you toward those directions that you had already decided upon.

In this way you charge your present personalities with subconscious material that will insure your good performance. Happiness and health will be best maintained when you follow certain lines.

You chose ahead of time therefore to be driven along certain directions. Now. Both of you decided that you would give your lives to creative work. Both of you decided that you would have no children, not only because this fit in with the first goal, but because the energy connected with family life would go into your creative productions, would be saved and available when you began to embark upon the psychic work for which you had also planned.

These simple things you know but often overlook. They are forged together. There is a built-in area of adjustment. When you approach either end of this area, automatic danger signals go off, telling you to move in one direction or the other, back to the symbolic center of your energy and abilities.

As you know, again, it is far easier for you not to have children, regardless of all strains. Many people would find it impossible. You are determined not to have them at all cost. You have at different times adopted different methods and adjustments, but your physical relationship has been structured not around mutual pleasure but instead about the fear of having children.

You overreacted, but merely along the lines of a learning process to insure that the main areas were not violated. You went too far, both of you, in that direction. All touch, to each of you now, was not innocent or joyful encounter; it meant "How far will this lead, and is the time of the month correct?" This applies to you both. Ruburt desperately wanted you to cherish him as a woman, to play and flirt with him. He wanted you to show even innocent animal affection. At the same time however, implied in any such touches, in his mind also was the question "How far will this go?"

You both felt that the most innocent of caresses could destroy the foundation of your lives. This was certainly overcompensation. It tended for a while to erode your relationship, and to some extent to set portions of yourselves against other portions. It drove Ruburt at times to try to deny womanhood, to assure you and herself that her body would not betray you both. He would not have his periods—thus he would show both of you, symbolically, that you need not fear his body, since it obviously was not functioning as a woman's should.

This was the reason for his outrage last night. He had done what both of you wanted, and now everyone was angry at him, including himself—but he felt (underlined) that he had done it mainly to reassure you.

These ambiguous feelings on both of your parts have much to do with the penis reaction. It does not dare shoot a straight line. *(Half humorously.)* At the same time that these sexual feelings operated, the two of you have an extremely powerful psychic bond, and a hidden but definite sense of inner identity.

In the physical life this seeks physical methods of expression. Ruburt has strong seemingly contrasting personality characteristics, but seen in the light of the personality's whole purpose, they are not contrasting but complementary, each one woven with the other toward the main goals. The same applies to yourself.

If you realize that unconsciously you both knew of our work from childhood and before, then some of your characteristics will fall into place like mosaic. Ruburt is powerfully attracted to you, and as a woman her psychic center is with yours.

The magnetism is both from past life experiences, and set up ahead of time in this life, so that the both of you would be drawn together and held together, despite the fact of no personal family, no children as a common interest.

Therefore the attraction had to be extremely strong. This applies to you both. Ruburt had to have, and adopted, both strong passive and strongly independent characteristics. The passivity and receptivity as a necessary prerequisite for our work, the independence as a necessary prerequisite to offset the early chosen environment, and also as an aid in dealing with physical communications.

The sense of loyalty was anchored in you, and you both decided upon it before this existence. Therefore you may sense in Ruburt at times confusing inclinations toward high independence in one area, and a self-denying dependence in another. Because he is presently a woman he will react strongly and aggressively if he feels you are drawing too far apart, for this would threaten your life and goals as much as children would—children in your minds being coming too close together. So you have been constantly between the two poles.

Ruburt's physical system has felt the strain simply because both of you feel that it is his body that would be the threat in the child area. You both become panicky therefore in two main areas—both that would affect your primary directives, to devote yourselves to artistic and psychic work.

You feel threatened if you get too far apart or if you come too close together physically. Now knowing this and seeing it clearly in words, you can I am sure make adjustments so that you do not go to those extremes.

Now you may take your break, and if you have questions along these areas I will answer them.

(9:40—9:45. Jane's trance had been deep, her pace fast, as it was throughout the session. The break was short because we had barely begun to go over the material when Jane said "Wow, I can feel him coming back with some good stuff, so we'd better get ready.")

Now. For those reasons you felt most threatened when Ruburt broke in upon your painting time for intimate relations in the past. This symbolically highlighted the whole affair, and brought it too close to consciousness for either of your comforts.

He did it precisely for that reason, although <u>he</u> was not consciously aware that he was trying to bring the problem out into the open. You distrusted spontaneous relations most of all, for those were the ones most likely *(laugh)* to produce the feared results. Therefore when you had relations you nicely and symbolically, with beautiful unconscious irony, made sure that they happened when you wanted them least, either on a scheduled basis or when one or you was tired, or when there was every good possibility to believe that you might be interrupted.

Your before-class activities were decided upon because you knew they could not last too long. Now Ruburt chose, as a woman, to have this strong magnetic feeling toward you, and while the same drives pull you both, because he <u>is</u> a woman this time he is, far more than you, sensitive to the lack or ordinary physical endearment. This leads us to a difference in your reactions to these problems.

He reacts personally and deeply when you get too far in the direction toward noncontact. This noncontact simply is more easily accepted, <u>comparatively</u> speaking, by you. He feels however that his body has been almost cursed by you both, and at its <u>worst</u> reaction he interprets fairly prolonged noncontact in the following terms: the way Christ cursed the fig tree, that it dare not bloom, that his body is forsaken by you both, unwanted, an orphan child, so that even his good looks as a woman are suspect.

He feels therefore a strong division, in that his mind is acceptable, that you both value it, but that his body is unacceptable. On the other hand however, with his womanly characteristics, he wants to be stroked and physically loved, and when he is not he feels that you have divorced his body.

This is the meaning of the dreams he had in the past about divorce. He feels completely uncherished, and therefore he does not nourish his body, <u>because he does not want more of it</u>. Now in that way, and he could not explain it to you because he did not understand it, he did feel completely divorced by you, particularly when he was at nursery school. He felt you had divorced his body, but not you see his mind.

Now <u>you</u> feel more actively threatened when the two of you reach the opposite end of closeness and contact, where you feel that despite all your precautions pregnancy might result. You withdraw emotionally, and it is at this point that Ruburt then begins his reactions. Precisely at the point where he feels pressed enough to practically and symbolically invade your working studio with intimacy in mind, and <u>spontaneous</u> intimacy at that—that is the point that you quickly begin an emotional and physical retreat.

Now Ruburt strongly reacted <u>this</u> time positively, when you massaged his leg, because he interprets your feelings toward his symptoms in this manner: you will not comfort his body physically because you do not like it. You tell him to use suggestion, which is a mental tool, and evade the physical contact which to <u>him</u> is proof of the physical divorce, and a reassertion of the mental being valued and the physical denied.

What I want you to understand is that all of these stresses come about as you learn how to handle the situations that are always under the auspices of your main purposes. There is an old verse, which you need not copy down: "There was a little girl who had a little curl in the middle of her forehead," etc.

Now when Ruburt senses a strong disruption in these main areas he will act up, and strongly. He is trying to see to it, as you are, that your primary purposes are held to. Both of you intuitively realize that your work, both creative and psychic, is bound up in your relationship, for Ruburt helped to bring out in you the freedom to paint, as you knew ahead of time he would.

Now <u>I</u> suggested that we move our sessions back here for the reasons given, but also because I knew that to Ruburt this meant an implied greater sense of togetherness on your parts, and of secrecy. Secrecy is a strong element in Ruburt's personality, and while you recognize this in yourself, you have been very opaque in that you have not earlier seen it in Ruburt.

It shows itself in those matters that he does not communicate with you. It shows itself also in a possessive characteristic that is not as obvious as your tendency in the same direction in your own work. He is deeply offended and outraged at any "invasion" into his own territory—the student who goes into his room at break, or the woman peeking at his notebook. This has to do with his feelings of late, of retreating from the main room. *(The living room.)*

Now too many people enter it. It has become to him a very necessary and important meeting ground between the two of you. Your ideas, our work—and the world at large. It becomes therefore a necessary and important room of communication, but now of communication going out into the world. It loses then that secrecy that has always been important to him.

(*"He can always work back here in the studio on mornings and all day Fridays. I've told him that many times." I work all day Friday at Artistic.*)

The secrecy also enables him to retreat in anger from you to some extent under the conditions mentioned earlier, and also has much to do with all of this brooding in secret. When he feels closed off from you it is then that he keeps important matters to himself. Because he is <u>talkative</u> this escapes your notice, but he often uses talk as a shield.

(*Humorously:*) You may take your break and I will continue.

(*10:15—10:25.*)

Now. When you were working full time some years ago at Artistic your fears that Ruburt would become pregnant became an obsession. You were already breaking one of your directives, you see, in working full time at other pursuits, and so you became twice as frightened that you would fall into the world's familiar mold, have children in which case the job would become indispensable.

In both of you, your feelings toward work and children then are closely connected. Ruburt at that time tried to comfort you as a woman, through caresses, and offering frequent sexual comfort. You repulsed him then, feeling that this would only add to the problem, and he began then to build up this feeling of physical divorce.

A point I want to make: these are small but significant attitudes of his. I suggested frequently the up and down movements and the running, because he must set those legs into activity. I <u>stressed</u> however that he should make a game of it. As you know we have met severe blockage here, and I can now tell you the reasons.

It hurt him of course to perform the up and down motions particularly, and he interpreted this to mean that you wanted him to torture and humiliate his body further by forcing it to feel the pain, and that in doing so he was punishing it further. He interpreted this therefore as a punishment of the body, and a mortification in a way of the feminine self.

In a strange fashion the symptoms also served to <u>stress</u> what he felt you were both trying to deny—his femininity, in that he felt at a very unconscious level that they made him helpless and in need of someone to lean upon—a mute call for support to you, and at that level he was outraged that instead of giving him your hand you would offer mental suggestions.

He also to some degree was angry at me, as a male. He partially identified some of my traits with some of yours, so if he was mad at you for telling him, literally to his way of thinking, to hurt himself five times a day by getting up and down from the floor, he was twice as mad at me.

He wanted you to help him get up and down from the floor, and encourage him. He felt instead that you and I were saying in effect: "You have not hurt yourself enough, now do this five times a day, and you will be a good girl," and this he simply would not do.

I will tell you another of his secrets. In the past, though he knew that he exaggerated, when his legs were bothering him he automatically looked for the nearest available parking place when you were driving. He would never ask you to park close to your destination. He felt it a sign of weakness on his part to even think of it, yet he also felt that on occasion you showed an annoying lack of sympathy or understanding, and at his worst moments he would feel that you purposely chose a place further away—that it was for his own good, you thought, that he face the humiliation in realizing in what poor condition he was. This would automatically cause all kinds of symptoms, needless to say.

He did not feel you sympathized with him at all on a physical level, and he felt that his and your attitudes of dealing with the whole matter mentally through suggestion, was a way of further implementing the difficulty—the physical divorce.

Now give us a moment. I am dealing mainly right now with his attitudes because you did not recognize many of them. Such a physical alienation was bound to have emotional consequences on both of your parts. He did not feel physically loved or wanted by you, but more than this you see, he agreed with the judgment that he felt both of you had made. Had he not agreed, you would have had a different set of problems.

You were actually in agreement to a large extent. Neither of you obviously meant to carry it so far. Understand also, I have been explaining his feelings so that you understand them. I am not saying that you necessarily went to the extremes as Ruburt felt them. Is that clear?

("Yes.")

Now when he felt that physical divorce you made various attempts to come closer, and you have made strides since obviously the symptoms have lessened. But one or the other of you would become frightened for the reasons given, and lately Ruburt felt an emotional separation might occur, and was occurring. Here again the threat to the prime directives, for he feels, and so do you, your work and the sessions quake when your relationship goes toward either extreme.

The class sessions incidentally, served to keep the spontaneity available, for the spontaneity of our own sessions suffers when your own relationship is less than the both of you accept. Then it becomes something you want to do and feel you should do, and a strong part of your work, but the spontaneous fountainheads beneath do not have that easy flow. So that that flow does not dry up when it does not operate as fully as it ordinarily can in our own sessions, then it shoots up and appears in class sessions, as a precaution and simply because the fountainhead as such will not dry up, but seeks its natural release. For this reason to some extent you have distrusted the class sessions, feeling that the strong personal basis of the sessions with you and Ruburt was escaping you.

Symbolically you also compared that spontaneous flow with semen, creative abilities, and were jealous of it getting away from you. Ruburt was aware of this on one level. He also felt that this was the main reason why you had nothing to do with class, refused even once to attend it. You felt it was depriving you, not only of, say, a private session if Ruburt did not hold the following regular one; you also felt that the sexual activity you were not getting from Ruburt was being channeled instead psychically where you were getting no benefit. To use this energy in private sessions was all right because it was a joint performance, a private one, and you both directly benefited.

For Ruburt to have a session without you, and for strangers, was something else. Particularly when you felt you were also being denied in your bed. Do you see the connections?

("Yes.")

Ruburt sensed this feeling, and it was often in reaction against it that we did not have our next private session, and hence the buried connection: "If you do not love me I will not have a session for you." He mentioned the Saturday morning occasions himself lately. He gets better as the day goes on, physically.

He has been much more comfortable when he is alone in the mornings and you are at work, because he feels you do not see him at his worst. This is one of the main reasons why he seems to have such great difficulty in getting up in the mornings during the week; where at least he felt he could arise with some dignity alone, and if he was a mess you would not be there to reprove him.

Weekend mornings you are here to observe. Then to top it off, following his <u>subconscious</u> reasoning here, for he has scarcely been aware of this, you would not only observe him, but to his way of thinking, force him to make a public spectacle of his condition. He went through all kinds of pretenses, smiling when he tried to go down the stairs, trying to tell himself that it did not hurt, and far too upset to make use of the <u>unending</u> line of positive suggestions he tried frantically to give himself.

So when you said "You do not try to help yourself," he was so angry he was nearly speechless. He felt you a stern taskmaster, and the logic as being: the worse you feel the more you should drive yourself. But he felt this also, you see. It was much more important to take a walk when he did not feel good than when he did.

Now this is <u>true</u>. However, he interpreted this to mean "Because I do not want to go, I should," which is not the same thing. I am not explaining this particular paragraph of material as clearly as I would like. There are some fine distinctions verbally that are difficult to make clear.

The spontaneity of action as a result however was extremely difficult. The energy has been blocked. You saw it briefly in his fit of anger. Because of your past-life connections—and I will see to it that you get this material—he chose to put all his eggs in one basket, so to speak, as you did. But he also chose to divest himself of any distracting family references in later life, as far as his own parents were concerned.

He relates warmly to others, but he relates deeply only to you. His nature is strongly emotional, so he becomes more panicky than you when you approach, again, the far side of your safe-contact line, where you become panicky when you reach the close side of the same line.

You have however unknowingly an unconscious supportive relationship simply as a result of the identity of your family. You may dislike it, or isolate yourself from it, but it exists. He has never known that particular kind of belonging, and therefore his sense of belonging in that regard is connected with you alone.

Your relationship exists strongly and validly on many more levels than those between the majority of marriages. You therefore have of course more aspects both for fulfillment and strain to develop. Your work lives are far more intertwined than even you realize, and that is why you cannot isolate one area in your case from another area of activity. This is extremely important, and often overlooked while <u>superficially</u> recognized.

Ruburt would be, and is, susceptible to advances made on your part in the kitchen—the woman's area; also in the living room, which is fairly neutral to both of you; or in his working place, for he has always been aware of the connection <u>there</u>. The bedroom has been an alarm area for both of you sexually, for the reasons made obvious, I should hope, and your studio has definitely been an alarm area on your part.

On one level Ruburt grossly misinterpreted your reaction here; since he was susceptible and knew it in his work area, he erroneously supposed you would be. The fact is that Ruburt, working, attracts you sexually, and you working attract Ruburt sexually. You however, being the male breadwinner as well as artist, feel most threatened by sex when you are working, because pregnancy could threaten the artist. So your attitudes in that regard, and reactions, will be mixed but usually adverse.

Now. Before I close a note: in your combined backgrounds you nicely chose situations in which parents did not have ordinary sexual relationships. Yours did not sleep together for years, and you are quite familiar with that pattern. You could have very nicely decided upon separate bedrooms or beds—it would fit in with your family background, and also with the situation. This is one peril that you did avoid, for it would have allowed you to go even further along the noncontact lines.

There were not even two sexes in Ruburt's early household. Neither of you then had ordinary sexual family patterns that you would seek to emulate, or that would be deeply ingrained—all in line with what you had chosen.

Now I will close. These are important points however. If you have questions I will answer them. I thought your hands would be quite tired by now.

("They are... Let us go over this material, and then we'll ask questions from there. I'm tickled to death to get all the information.")

I will indeed.

("Thank you very much.")

My heartiest regards to you both.

("The same to you. Thank you, Seth.")

(11:25. Jane's trance had been deep throughout the session, her pace for the most part quite fast. I thought it one of the best sessions she has given. It's certain to prove invaluable to us in daily living. Jane hasn't seen it yet as I write these notes. I want to go over it with her, then keep it available for frequent reference.)

SESSION 563 (DELETED)
DECEMBER 2, 1970

(This session, ordinarily the 563rd for December 2, 1970, is deleted from the record.)

Good evening.

("Good evening, Seth.")

Now. I would like to give you some more personal material. Incidentally, Ruburt read the chapter on which we are working, and was newly astonished. *(Chapter 15 of Seth's own book,* Seth Speaks.*)*

Give us a moment here. I want to emphasize the importance of your personal relationship to each other, and mention the ways in which it affects your work. I may as well give you some idea of how these overall patterns operate within your lives, since we have a good beginning, and while we are on the subject.

When your relationship becomes uneasy to a certain degree, then this impedes the spontaneity that you allow yourself in your paintings. You are at that point trying to shove beneath awareness certain feelings of yours, mentioned in our last session. You are, say, close to the point on noncontact. Inhibited feelings therefore are at their strongest on your part. Considerable energy is used to continue the repression as the pressure from beneath grows.

As mentioned, the far contact point is somewhat more manageable for you than for Ruburt, but affects you nevertheless. You do not dare allow your intuitions full reign even when you paint at such times for fear that they will carry up with them these repressed feelings.

The spontaneity is considered safe along certain lines, but these lines become narrowed, and the further the situation continues the more narrowed the area of spontaneity allowed in your work. In the past this has caused a tendency toward overreliance on technique. Do you follow me?

("Yes.")

With Ruburt of course it leads to work blockages, particularly along poetry lines where the emotions appear very clearly. Ruburt saw today that the intellectual portions of the self, and even the literal-mindedness, served an excellent purpose in allowing him to objectify highly intuitive material, and to give it actuality in the world that you know. He did not understand this earlier.

What neither of you <u>sufficiently</u> (underlined) understood was the strong interrelationship between your personal lives and your work. You were aware of it but you did not understand, generally speaking, that your relationship must be actively and positively enjoyable on a daily basis, if both of you are to produce the work that you want.

You were apt to put the personal relationship last, or rather to let it go, so that often it seemed to come after everything else. Now it is true that withheld sexual energy can be diverted to creative aims, but in your cases it was the feeling of daily emotional nourishment that was sometimes lacking.

Now give us a moment. When the point is reached of which I had just spoken, your objectivity comes foremost in your work at the expense of spontaneity. Remember some time ago I mentioned your feeling about oils and the emotions. This is in keeping you see with the fact that you felt more threatened than Ruburt at those boundary-near-contact points. At such times you became more alarmed working with your oils and colors, and wanted a retreat, and sought for greater distance in your paintings.

When you closed off and retreated to compensate, you came closer to the people with whom you work, enjoying their safer emotional contact. It was not threatening, you see. At the same time you adopted a more hard line in your relationship with those in the family, trying to avoid all emotional situations which might trigger a release of the repressed feelings.

You would be grateful then when Ruburt did originate such a crisis, simply because the pressure behind the repressed feelings was more painful then, so that it was defeating its own purpose. You helped initiate these crises in your own way then, by intensifying the noncontact behavior that you knew would cause Ruburt to take steps. On occasion you increased your own noncontact behavior when he did not react when you thought he should.

This would cause considerable panic on your part. On the other hand of course Ruburt also expected you to come up with and initiate the noncontact behavior when he felt that your relationship was getting too close for comfort, that his physical love for you might lead him some time to neglect consciously or unconsciously proper contraceptive behavior.

He would have become instantly alarmed had you not then begun to retreat. This has been a highly formal, ritualized behavior pattern, a psychological dance, so formalized on a subconscious level that it left little leeway for spontaneity, and threatened to freeze you both in highly unconscious regimented behavior. He was to keep you from getting too far apart. You were to keep you from getting too close, and when certain automatic points were approached you both went into your act. For some time the behavior worked. The spontaneity was gradually squeezed out to such a degree that it lost its workability, and both of you were beginning to consider making adjustments. You did not understand the pattern, however. You ran into the invisible danger points and reacted in the old ways.

Ruburt began to overreact more and more, and felt the invisible pull physically. The near and too-far boundaries were uncompromising and arbitrary. A division of responsibility for your relationship was far less satisfactory. The two of you instead now should concentrate your efforts upon forming a generalized, comfortable center, and maintaining that. This will put the concentration of attention in constructive areas, upon warmth and mutual understanding rather than putting the burden of the relationship first on one and then on the other.

(Humorously:) I would make a good marriage counselor.

("You certainly would.")

Within that area you will both find greater freedom, warmth and creativity. Your work will show great advantage, and the energy that has been bottled up can be released. Understanding the issues will automatically help you form this center. It should be flexible enough now for both of you, and <u>not</u> the formation of one rigid point. *(Laugh.)*

("I get it.")

You may take your break.

(9:48—9:55.)

Now. Several more points. Some rather simple, but they should be mentioned.

When Ruburt feels comfortable in your relationship he is much more predisposed to cook and to eat. The kitchen once more becomes a sacred place of nourishment to him, and the food that he prepares is much more nourishing to your bodies, because of his attitude and its results upon the atoms and molecules composing the food.

He has enjoyed your preparing breakfast when you have, far more than you realize. He interpreted it as a sign that you were willing to nourish his body—

("I am.")

—and as a physical reinforcement. Far earlier however <u>he felt that you did it to show him up</u>. *(Louder.*

("I understand.")

Now I want to get to something more involved.

At the risk of repeating myself, your in quotes "role" to one extent was restrictive in the sexual and emotional area; you were the one who drew the line. It was partially a distorted, unconscious understanding of this that led Ruburt to the exaggerated projection of that restrictive role to those other areas of your life.

Because of this role, adopted rather early on both of your parts in your married life, and because of his dim, distorted and hidden perception of it, he was vastly astonished at your permissive attitude when our sessions began.

You were therefore expected by him to keep the sessions from getting out of hand, to help in quotes "police" his spontaneous self here, as you did in the sexual area and in your personal relationship. To him this was logical, if subconscious, expectation.

Instead you see, you felt with some considerable exceptions that in this particular area spontaneity could be safely followed. When you encouraged the sessions in the beginning so strongly, he was taken back for to him you were not fulfilling the implied role. When you urged him onward then he felt that he might be on dangerous ground, for you had been counted upon in the personal area to stop spontaneity, emotionally and sexually.

He mistrusted your permissiveness then. It frightened him. If you could not be counted upon, who could? So he began to build up restrictive tendencies of his own. Before you had handled the spontaneity for him. It was your role. He had handled the other end.

He was unused to setting himself up against his own spontaneity so strongly, yet when you did show signs of drawing the line, say, at fear of spontaneous sessions fairly early in the game, he felt on the one hand relieved, and on the other angry at giving up this new prerogative.

Your inner feelings toward each other have been projected onto your feelings toward the sessions, and psychic work also, then. You became annoyed at him, wondering why the spontaneous woman had suddenly turned so restrictive. You did not understand that this was because you had not carried through the personal pattern into the session pattern.

He of course reacted to the annoyance on your part. The tests from this standpoint were highly explosive, for he did not understand the situation, and found himself in a position highly ambiguous. You were encouraging him to even further spontaneity on the one hand, to intuitional freedom, and yet to his point of view requiring him to exert all kinds of discipline, which he felt was your role—to follow the intuitions so far, know when to stop at the proper target, and it was here that he first deeply felt you as a taskmaster.

The early remarks by the young psychologist had thoroughly frightened him, and he was not ready to go into the deeper implications. He was quite simply terrified. He felt also then that you would give or withhold physical love according to his performance on the tests. But as foolish as that sounds, you see, it was based on these roles that you both accepted.

He then got into the habit of checking the spontaneous self at every point, and setting up opposing muscular reactions and tensions. It was simply not possible for me to give you more information at that time than I could. It was precisely, you see, the relationship between spontaneity and discipline operating between yourselves, that was projected upon the sessions, and inhibited any spontaneous comments I could make.

You had always counted upon him to be freely spontaneous, and could not understand his reactions. When you told him to be spontaneous he was all the more confused. Earlier in both of your minds, Ruburt was the spontaneous part of the relationship, hence for many reasons the unpredictable element. You were the discipline element, the reasoning part. Neither of you were fully willing to work out these <u>seemingly</u> (underlined) contradictory elements of your own personalities. For of course your personality has some strongly spontaneous and intuitive elements, as you now know, and Ruburt also has very definite, now too definite, tendencies toward discipline.

You may take your break. One small point: you both would have denied yourselves strong possibilities of growth had you kept up; do you follow me?

("You'd better say a little more.")

For a while then you were willing, comparatively speaking, to let Ruburt express the spontaneous, strongly spontaneous, elements of both of your personalities; with the joys and perils involved, and denying him the responsibility of learning how to temper and use spontaneity. He was willing to let you express the reasoning, deliberate qualities of both of your personalities—the deliberating elements, and to that extent not permitting you to fully express your own spontaneity. You would not learn to use and enjoy it while he did it for you.

And now you may take your break.

("Thank you.")

One more sentence: this arrangement automatically sets up artificial barriers between spontaneity and discipline, and colorations that were sexual in nature, leading to deductions such as: spontaneity was dangerous, obviously, since it needed such controls.

(10:29—10:40.)

Now. The division was actually an exaggerated projection of the predominating tendencies of your present personalities.

In general Ruburt is more easily spontaneous, for example. Over the years you simply did not allow enough leeway for yourselves, but the overall tendencies are perfectly legitimate. They operate quite obviously, also in your relationship with the world at large. You can put up with noncontact comparatively speaking far better than Ruburt, and will be the first one to draw the line here. As in the other areas mentioned, the more personal ones.

Ruburt is apt to be more adjusting in that area, but here also you see, you have set certain unconscious points, boundaries on either side between what you consider too close contact, and too little. The tendencies operate in all areas, and they provide very constructive guidelines, and are beneficial when they are not carried to extremes, and when the focus is on maintaining the balance between. Because of your fears, both of you had your eyes out instead for the danger points.

In your contact physically with others these tendencies also apply. Ruburt will allow himself to be taken advantage of, for example, more easily than you in personal contacts. This outrages you because your symbolic danger point is brought into focus. It bothers him, but less.

Now give us a moment. Some of this of course can be and has been turned to your advantage. Your tendency toward feeling safe in noncontact situations means that you do not want models in your studio, yet you are highly intrigued by personality. This has led you to develop psychic abilities for creative purposes—<u>that you would not have needed nor sought</u> otherwise.

This in itself has led you away from stereotyped portraits, and you could have fallen into that trap with your background in comics. There you see you avoided facing the ordinary human portrait through figures that were actually not as such individual, but types or even caricature. At that time in your development you were afraid of emotions in art to such a degree that you chose in comics to deal with stereotypes rather than individual characters, to follow rigid patterns.

In later years you loosened up considerably. You still would not want to deal with the intrusive, and to you, immediately disruptive emotions that would be obvious in a sitter. With them you would want to handle the emotion with kid gloves, precisely because of course you are so sensitive to emotion.

Yet human forms and faces intrigue you, hence the development of these creative visions, which are actually often highly intensified emotionally. In that area you were presented with a challenge, and discovered a highly unique way of meeting it.

This noncontact tendency has also had something to do with the fact that you have not attempted to sell your paintings more actively, and all of this fits in with the material I gave you lately along these lines—the male and female connotations.

You feel that abstracts in this respect are neutral, and therefore you feel safe in marketing and selling them. You do not feel that they are as much a part of your self as your other work. You do not feel that they tell as much about <u>you</u>, or that they contain self-revelations.

For this reason you also feel that they are not challenging to produce, as compared with your other paintings. Ordinarily you seldom paint women, feeling that in such paintings emotions would be too blatantly displayed. You may have to watch a tendency to masculinize your women if you seriously begin to do such work, for you may feel, again, that harsher lines are necessary to hold the emotional element in check.

There is no particular reason why you should do women unless you want to. I am not telling you in other words to do so. I simply wanted this evening to round out the discussion, showing how these tendencies operate in various areas of your lives.

For our next few sessions I will work on our book, do a few chapters, and then if you prefer take some time out for reincarnational material, so that it does not go by the board.

("Very good. I would like that.")

Now do you have any questions on the last session, this one, or allied subjects that you want cleared up before we resume dictation next week?

("Not now. I'm too tired to think of any, but I will later.")

I simply would prefer we not stray away from the book too long.

("That's okay. I'll just make a list of questions and save it.")

We will resume dictation Monday, and after the last break present your questions then. I did not want to leave you with the impression that these basic tendencies of yours and Ruburt's were negative, for they have and will serve good purposes. You will be much better able to deal with them and use them constructively now however, for the unconscious material has been brought to the surface where it can be assimilated and understood.

Hopefully Ruburt should have his period within about six days. If he does not, then he will have it at the next regular time.

I am finished with this material. It is too late to begin dictation. Are you sure you do not have questions?

("I guess I'm too tired to think."

(In addition, my writing hand was so cramped I could hardly form intelligible words, etc.)

Then we will close the session. You have both learned a lot this week. My heartiest regards to you both.

("Thank you very much, Seth. It's appreciated."

(11:10. Jane's trance had been good, her pace a little slower than last Monday. I regard Monday's session and today's as two of the best Jane has given. It's difficult to see how the material could be more apropos, etc.)

DELETED SESSION
DECEMBER 14, 1970 MONDAY

(This is the regular session for December 14, 1970, Monday, deleted from the record.

(Before the session I asked that Seth discuss two questions. 1: Why Jane's knees had been so bothersome lately when she was obviously making good progress otherwise? 2: Why I caught a "cold" last week?

(Jane's knees had been poor for some weeks. According to my own troubles, my pendulum insisted that I did not have a cold, even though I had all the symptoms. I

came down with it after asking Seth last Monday, December 7, whether the taped session we'd made for the Claire TV show in Washington had been shown yet. My pendulum also told me that communication problems involving Jane, other than the TV show question, caused the "cold," etc.

(*Since I have great faith in the pendulum, I wanted to know why it insisted that I did not have a cold—when I had felt poor indeed all week. I hadn't tried to do any in-depth probing with the pendulum.*)

Now, good evening.

(*"Good evening, Seth."*)

You will have to let me handle this in my own way—the matter of your symptoms and Ruburt's knees, but for a starter we will begin with you. The pain in your side was a reaction against the first group of symptoms—they gave you a pain in the side. You were angry at yourself for not feeling well.

(*This noon, driving home from work, I pulled a muscle in my right side while wheeling the car around a corner—one of those painful things that you feel when you cough, breathe deeply, laugh, etc.*)

The earlier group of symptoms resulted from several causes. First of all they were in a way, a way of handling a situation. You were not sure that it was safe to communicate spontaneously or easily—emotionally or sexually, with Ruburt following the two personal sessions. (*The two deleted sessions of November 30 & December 2.*) The cold effectively kept you from physical contact.

(*I hadn't suspected this.*)

Now it was on the one hand feigned behavior, but the symptoms had to be bothersome enough or they would not have served their purpose. To some extent verbal communication was also minimized. Your "condition" effectively kept Ruburt from making any demands, or from putting any verbal pressure upon you, for he rushed of course to your support.

You felt to some extent that you had fallen down in taking advantage of the sessions, that you were not putting into practice certain behavior there suggested. (*True.*) There were of course other reasons also. The question you asked in our sessions was in your mind symbolic of a lack of communication still between you and Ruburt, at deeper levels. (*The question about the Claire TV show.*)

There was also, even then, in the back of your mind the feeling that personally you could use the sessions for information in which you were highly interested, and you suspected that Ruburt would not share the feeling, or would even unconsciously block it.

(*"What kind of information?"*)

The question that you asked concerning the *(TV)* program was symbolic

in your mind to other information—
("Oh. I understand now.")
—hence again the question of communication. Do you follow me?
("Yes.")
You were quite struck by the lack of communication between yourself and your mother yesterday. *(In Sayre.)* Or rather, you realized that she communicated her feelings very well, and her lack of understanding, while you communicated less; although your attitude in itself there is of course a communication. And I do know of your outburst.

The last issue had a part to play in the side.

Now. Woven in all of this was the communication issue, and to some extent the symptoms served another allied and complementary purpose. You thought you might be able to understand something of Ruburt's problem, and you were willing to take a day or two out to feel badly.

(This I did not suspect.) Another point. You also felt that the symptoms would take Ruburt's mind off of his own for a change, and also let you see how, if or when your reactions to other people were changed or altered because of your indisposition. *(They were.)*

Beside this you thought sometimes that Ruburt thought of nothing but himself, and you were saying "Look at me, I am no superman," and so actually you were looking for communications that it seemed you did not want in the early part of the cycle.

The symptoms were also meant to frighten Ruburt, to shock him, to shake him up, and then hopefully do him some good, as he saw how it was to have someone around all the time who did not feel very well.

Now you may take your break, for we are going to return along these areas.

(Pause. "Okay."

(Humorously:) When you ask for it, you get it.

("Okay."

(9:32. Jane's voice was soft throughout. She said her trance was good, yet she was aware of wanting a cigarette at the same time. She hasn't been smoking as much when near me this past week because the smoke irritates. Now I wondered how it was possible for Jane to want a cigarette if her trance was so deep, etc. Resume at 9:45.)

Now. We will take a hop, skip and jump to Ruburt.

Briefly, on the cigarettes: it is an automatic part of your session format now—a part of the setting. This is simply for now a brief explanation.

For other material, now: again, some of this will sound simple and apparent. He has a rich emotional nature, and he responds emotionally. Programs, his weekly programs for example, are often a benefit to him, if they are not too extensive, because they give him a short-range challenge which he enjoys.

(Today I had been wondering, after I chanced to see Jane's brief list for the week, which she had made out yesterday, whether she should eliminate such activities.)

His attempt to have you encourage him up and down and running, is a not-too-well disguised attempt for further emotional involvement on your part. He would be as upset as you over a smothering closeness. However often he simply feels lonely—not necessarily for your physical presence, for you are often in the house, but for emotional recognition that you are apt to forget about.

You are apt to forget about it simply because in your childhood home you had to work for emotional isolation.

(I had a brief coughing spell here, which of course hurt the side. This happened a few times during the first part of the session—usually at key bits of material. Finally Seth let me know in a good loud voice, that he hoped I noted the spots at which I coughed. I said I was aware of the connection, etc.)

Your personality structures simply respond at times of course to different stimuli. Both of you can learn to modify these characteristics, but understanding them is basic. Ruburt responds, generally, to people. One reason of course for the classes, and their success. But behind Ruburt's outgoing characteristics you run into some rather restrictive ones that are more on the surface, generally speaking, in your personality.

Once someone gets through your surface restrictive tendencies, obvious ones, then your spontaneity flows to the surface. Once someone gets through Ruburt's open spontaneous characteristics they are apt to wonder what happened, because he will often not let them get any further. *(A very acute pair of points.)* Hence the fact that his students remain students as a rule, and not personal friends. As you know, those who get through all the way find a bedrock loyalty. But the spontaneous emotional character warms up, brightens, and refreshes what can be a morose inner self at times. Therefore your emotional response to him is important for that reason.

You have not been able to ignore him since he had his symptoms. You might be angry at him, in which case there was a definite emotional response, or disgusted; he thought in the past, the dim past, disgusted enough to leave him—but you could not ignore him.

(I had to laugh here. In one way, perhaps hard to describe, it is such a perfect observation on Seth's part—the first sentence of the above paragraph. Jane, as Seth, watched me tolerantly. I had to watch the laughing because it hurt my side, etc.

("I never wanted to ignore him."

I am giving you some good information. Whether you wanted to or not, he felt that you had.

Now. Give us some time on this, and remember we have not given that particular material in that way before. *(True.)* He felt that you ignored him when you became ill—that you were growing so morose that you felt life meaningless. Then the sessions came *(in 1963)*, and he felt they had saved you both.

They also served to see to it that the two of you spent more time together. Then he felt that all he meant to you was contained in the sessions, that as a woman and a wife you found him far less fascinating. Other background information you have been given, and this is background for what is coming.

It was during your illness that he began to watch your face for a hint of your mood and feelings—a tendency he has relinquished only lately. The physical signs of improvement have been most beneficial to him, forcing him to recognize that betterment is not only possible but has occurred.

The knees seemed all the more obvious by contrast, and to some extent then he focused upon them. He sees the two of you together, doing your own thing, but emotionally in rich interaction. This is what he wants.

He has mixed feelings about you and his book. On the one hand he would like you to read it as he goes along, and at times he envisions enthusiastic discussions about it. He thinks you have emotionally closed off from it since you never ask him about it. On the other hand he fears your disapproval and criticism, and thinks you will look for flaws, and so he lets matters stand there.

(There is some element of truth in the above; but also I feel that Jane would rather I wait until she has the book typed up perhaps halfway before I begin to read it. I can change this idea. I had the idea she would rather I didn't interfere with the gestation of her books—at least this is the way my reading of them seems to have worked out in the past.)

The knees are a symbol of the problems of course still remaining. He enjoyed your massaging them, but he did not want to ask you to do so, for he saw it as a sign of emotional giving on your part that must be spontaneous, and not asked for or demanded.

(I agree with this data. I would add however that for me to be asked occasionally would not be a sign that I was emotionally far away. I expect to be asked, I suppose, when I do forget. I forget without attaching any significance to the forgetting.)

Now give us a moment. It seemed to him lately that you did not want to dance when he felt at his best, and you wanted him to when he felt less well. Both of you have been making adjustments since our last two sessions, and in a way Ruburt's knees represented the same kind of problem as your symptoms—

matters brought to the head, and yet not acted upon.

(I think this is very good.)

Now you may take your break.

(10:15—10:30.)

Now. Several other points that we will elaborate on later. In his books he is facing challenges he did not face earlier. Before, a book was a novel. He wrote it through, and that was the end of it. It was all intuitive, emotional and fictional. He did not need to deal with details, the same kind of organization and overall planning.

A draft took him little time. The nonfiction involves him in projects that are of longer duration, and he is handling them very well. He was used to more frequent creative challenges, lesser ones in a way, rather than long-term projects, and he was not capable in the past of the planning for example that is now a part of his creative endeavors.

As a result however he does feel the lack of more frequent, fresh, completely different inspirational material. This can be satisfied through the poetry. Short-term challenges of any kind that are at all practical are excellent to break up for him the longer-term purpose of his book.

Now the ramblings about in your apartment in their own way often serve this end. The emotional quality of furniture appeals to him, and without knowing it the emotional qualities of space do also.

The morning situation can be handled from any of numerous standpoints, but they should be emotional standpoints. He can imagine himself up ahead of you, as he thought of, surprising you with your breakfast already prepared. That is one solution. It would help if you kissed him in the morning, and made some emotional supportive gesture that also encouraged him to get up.

There is more here that we will cover, however.

A concerted effort should be made, either to have him face the issue and solve it, or to avoid it completely. He thought of getting up at four again. What he does is not nearly as important, obviously, as his feelings toward it—and he has highly negative feelings that cause him symptoms when he does not get up and believes he should. I will cover this much more thoroughly however.

At the risk of being repetitive: if he concentrates upon his work, the morning issue will take care of itself, and by work I mean not only his writing, but his own individual psychic endeavors. He measures what he does daily against what you do daily, and feels automatically guilty if you do more than he, or even if he is doing watercolors while you are typing a session.

He still feels guilty about you going to work in the morning, and not getting up just rubs his nose in it further. He is saying "I may not have to go out to work like you do, but I am punishing myself for it, so do not blame me."

(Once again I had to take the time to laugh, or try to, very cautiously. Jane, as Seth, smiled.)

Now we will have some sessions as you would like, along the lines of your personal affairs, and resume dictation as we all see fit. Does that suit your fancy? I do not want you to have a laughing fit.

("Yes...." There followed a short exchange between Seth and me, after he asked if I had any questions. I mentioned the one I'd come up with the other day: what other names has he had in various lives? A list of the names would be interesting, I thought. Seth agreed. He now suggested I ask the question again later, saying the list would run several pages long. He then wished us goodnight in his usual manner, at 10:50.

(Seth returned a moment later as Jane and I discussed her getting up on weekday mornings.)

—and then on weekends, when you do not have to go to work, he feels bad when you have to see him.

(Seth returned again as I read this passage to Jane:)

Also, to keep up the pretense—

("How do you mean?")

If he were in good condition on weekends, he would have to ask himself then why he was not good during the week. The self-deception, you see, could not be so easily maintained.

(Seth returned again when I asked Jane if she could explain why she felt bad on weekday mornings:)

—since he is punishing himself during the week because you have to go to work. *(Emphatic.*

("I wish he wouldn't."

(10:55. I believe the above is new information, and some that we certainly shall explore. After the session, I explained to Jane that my going out to work perhaps represented an unsolved problem on my own part, and that she shouldn't be that much concerned with it.

(Jane agreed to make an effort to think of it this way. In any event, she got up with me rather easily this morning [Tuesday], and told me her knees felt better than they had in some time. It was obvious from her actions.)

DELETED SESSION
JANUARY 18, 1971 MONDAY

(This is the regularly-scheduled session for Monday, January 18, 1971. It is

deleted from the record.)
Good evening.
Good evening, Seth.
Now. We will begin slowly.

You both often lack perspective. When you compare yourselves with others you often do so in material terms. Often it seems to you that you have learned little, that your mental, psychic, spiritual and physical situation should be far better.

Now neither of you know what difficulties are, in the terms with which most people speak. *(A point with which I can disagree.)* Now you are dealing, through your creative endeavors, aside even from the psychic work, with highly subjective material; many people are completely unaware for great periods of time of their own mental and emotional states. These are projected so automatically into physical activities that they are then faced and manipulated as physical events. The connection between the two is never realized. They are not ready as yet to handle their own subjective material or possibilities. Do you follow me here?

("Yes.")

The creative personality encounters his own subjective states in a way that others simply do not. These states are then manipulated, often subjectively, sometimes consciously. Such personalities are in much more immediate connections with their own moods, feelings, the interior climate of their being at any given time.

Now. The persons who are immersed in physical activities must now and then have a counterpoint and an encounter with the inner state. The creative person must allow for sufficient outward-goingness so that the subjectivity is not latched upon too strongly.

Ruburt became frightened in the past, and long before our sessions. He had tried to dissociate himself from unpleasantness because he was surrounded by so much. He led a very active physical life however, and to some degree then could work off some of the emotional feelings that were repressed. He began in our work to become more aware of these feelings, and extremely frightened at expressing any of them, for many of the reasons given by me in the past.

Both of you however have a tendency to dig inward, and to concentrate upon negatives. Now if you were different kinds of people, you see, your own moods would fluctuate widely in the normal give and take with other individuals. You *(to me)* at your job are helped in that manner. Ruburt closed off even from you the expression of his fears; many quite normal fears, dangerous only because he considered them so.

I have told you in the past to make room in your daily or weekly or monthly lives for variety of a quite normal kind. I mentioned for example long ago, short trips. When ordinary measures are not taken, then more drastic ones become necessary. Your greater communication is of benefit, and was of great benefit this weekend. There are cycles, highly individualistic, of emotional moods. Depressions that are communicated allow the feelings to move on, regardless of the reasons for the depression.

An honest acceptance of the feelings is paramount. They must be accepted as real on their own terms. Then the way is cleared for the cycle to move. Resulting inhibited energy is then released. Now in the past Ruburt would brood over the feelings, leading him into a physical apathy. He was ashamed of the feelings. Both of you however still overemphasize the entire situation.

You do not see yourselves as human beings in a quite human environment, but against some perfect yardstick, and this applies for you *(to me)* also. Ruburt blooms like a flower in his classes simply because everyone thinks he is quite wonderful, and he responds.

("Why doesn't he think he's wonderful himself?")

I told you I was starting out slowly.

You both have become somewhat ingrown. The basis, <u>now</u>, (underlined) of Ruburt's situation is not <u>largely</u> (underlined) from the past.

He does have attitudes, as I told him last evening *(mentally)*, that you had some ten years ago, setting up so strongly the idea of responsibility and lack of lifetime *(physical time to live, etc.)*. That spontaneity became severely hampered. The brooding also involves your present situation, the two of you in it, and the future.

You rarely discussed together future plans. He took this to mean you had none. At times he simply wears his body out, and it requires additional rest, but he takes this as a sign of sloth and laziness. Some change within a stable framework is really your answer, with adequate and emotional communication.

Many of the fears have been trivial but he would not discuss them. One worry then would automatically be associated with a pile of other buried worries, and an ordinary unpleasant stimuli could evoke the whole works. A gray day becomes therefore a symbol that the sunny inner self is clouded, and he feared he could not change himself any more than he could the weather.

Above all, the fears could not be discussed with you, particularly if they seemed trivial. He never wanted you to equate him with your mother *(I laughed here)*, and felt that a display of unpleasant emotions would only get your scorn.

You may take your break.

(9:30. The record will show that this is the first personal session for us since December 14, 1970, and is only the second I have sat in on since that date. Jane has had ESP class sessions in the interim however, but our private activity had deteriorated to practically zero. I had demanded yesterday that we have this session.

(Jane had become very frightened a couple of days ago to realize she was becoming quite apathetic. Her legs, the knees especially, had been poor. Yet at the same time we had learned some valuable things on our own, especially over the weekend. I was very anxious that we get all the help we could.

(I felt good when this session began, yet began to feel anger as it progressed. Part of this was probably defensive. I think also the anger partly stemmed from hearing the same things over again in some instances—that is, that we had made so little progress seemingly in dealing with vital points. But the expression of fears was very beneficial, we thought, and surprisingly this was new for both of us.

(At the same time, I couldn't help wondering just what human beings were, why they acted as they did, etc., and why the organism didn't seem able to take better care of itself at least intuitively. Resume at 9:38.)

Now. Pitiful or not, the two of you have been concentrating too much upon your physical problems. This has drained your creative energies, and also led you to overestimate the problems themselves.

If I were telling this to someone else you would think it was excellent advice and wonder why it was not taken to heart. Ruburt needs somewhat more change within a definite framework than you do, but you also need to refresh your own energies. Concentration upon the problem to such an extent does not allow the inner self the freedom to help you solve it, and a condition arises where you expect the worst and bring it therefore about.

The simple measures of going out for example allow a breakup of stimuli, a freer give and take of emotional moods. The conscious mind is fascinated and the inner self free then to act constructively. Encouraging Ruburt to discuss his fears is important, but there is no one reason behind this. Consciousness is not that simple.

All of the sessions Ruburt has on his clipboard are important, and discuss different aspects that are pertinent. Those sessions followed, and the advice heeded, provide you with your answer.

("Then why doesn't he do it?")

Part of the reason is the negative input that you both are responsible for. With the negative and destructive attitudes you had before our sessions, you are both very lucky that you did not run into more difficulty.

Now what are your questions?

(9:50. I had quite a few questions to ask, but since my anger had still been

building up I now did not write them down, or Seth's answers—which were very good, incidentally. I was deeply irritated and frustrated. A sharp exchange with Seth followed, and I ended up furious—which I suppose was a good way to blow off steam. Seth insisted that the answers re Jane's symptoms, and my own contributing attitudes, had already been given in past sessions, but were not being followed.

(Also, I took exception to some statements made in the session this evening particularly that we concentrated too much upon the physical problems—granted that we created the problems, I could not understand how we were not supposed to pay any attention to the difficulties Jane had walking, etc, There was much more, and it's not necessary to detail it all here.

(I did insist that in my opinion the body, including the conscious mind, wasn't doing a very good job of taking care of itself in such cases. I finally asked for a break, since I now could hardly talk. I wasn't sure of the target of my anger, or the reasons—everyone and everything, I suppose. I finally admitted to being completely baffled by the whole affair including the way people lived and behaved generally, etc.

(Jane finally said that my tirade precluded her going back into trance to resume the session. We continued talking however, and at 10:28 she agreed to try to resume. Resume then at 10:30.)

Now. The condition is the result of unhealthy and negative patterns, mental patterns that the young adolescent body managed to cope with through the thyroid condition. This was the safety valve.

Now when I said the problem lay mainly in the present, I did not emphasize past roots, where the patterns originated. It is the patterns themselves, regardless of their origin, that is <u>now</u> (underlined) important.

Ruburt became afraid that the thyroid condition would lead into erratic behavior, and after the Florida incident he slammed doors to expression down. Because he appeared so talkative, you did not recognize the point where he began to hide his fearful thought or feelings from you. This was during your illness when he felt they threatened you.

He felt then of course that erratic behavior was out of the question; and closing that door, he also closed the door largely to emotional expression. He watched his every word and action with you during your illness. The incident in Florida served to frighten him into that reaction.

The pattern had always included a strong tendency of withdrawal superimposed and enforced upon a very spontaneous self. As a child he closed off the expression of emotion from his mother out of fear, and when the fear element becomes strong as it did later for a different reason, with Walt, and much later for a far different reason with you, the pattern was reasserted.

When he felt unwanted, this was also his reaction. Initially there would be no outward change of behavior except for a compensatory additional noisiness of faked gaiety and singing. For some time the organism could take this, and as situations changed the spontaneous self would once again emerge. With a changing physical situation necessitating agile manipulation, the physical stimulations came so quickly that the pattern did not have a chance to jell. It did not become a normal pattern of behavior, but one that was now and then adopted.

When you were ill the incident rearoused his fears concerning his mother, you see. As he had watched her very mood, he watched yours, and for a short time he interpreted your actions in a very accusing light toward himself.

Now running away from problems, literally in space, had always been his answer to everything. One day he could run away from his mother, and he did. One day he could leave Walt, and he did. But he loved you deeply, and there was no place he could run to, nor from the problems presented by your parents.

Now he adjusted very well to these, but an inner portion of his self, you see, is thoroughly outraged, considering all parents enemies from whom one should and must legitimately run. Intellectually, he understood that changes had to be made in his attitude, and he tried to treat your family kindly, and consciously to make up to his mother by being nice to yours.

From that situation be could not or would not run, but in his mind he saw the two of you running free of all of them. He gave little expression to his feelings toward your mother, in a mad rush to get to the respectable and responsible attitude he thought he should have.

These issues are all important, since he could not run in space, and did not, when the pattern of withdrawal began, express his resentment; he still turns off the radio when you come into the room, for fear the noise, which to him will be interpreted by you as aggressive noisy feelings, will annoy you.

It was only too easy for you to accept this withdrawal without recognizing it for what it was, because of your own background, and I mentioned some allied material here in the near-contact session. *(Last night.)* Now these repressions operated constantly in daily life. The effort required to repress such material is tremendous, and the muscular motions affected.

("Are these repressions still operating?"

(As Seth, Jane gestured to me to wait. I asked the question because I thought we had cracked this wall over the weekend, and was anxious for confirmation. I thought we had made a very important start.)

He adopted the symptoms partially out of example, both from his mother and from your own illness. He has made gains, but he had not made gains as far as fears were concerned at all. Some, with aggressions. He was not consciously aware enough of the fears, he had shoved them so far underground.

<u>The body does not have control over the conscious thoughts</u>.

(*This in answer to one of the points I had been mad about earlier in the session.*)

However, when care is taken to relieve the inhibiting nature of conscious thoughts, the body organism sends up energetic emotions that act as physical impetus. That is why a feeling of hopelessness is so destructive.

I understand your problem. You cannot quite get it through your heads that your thoughts form your reality.

(*"No, I believe that. But I get very mad at the way other thoughts interfere with good or healthy constructions. I probably mean that I get mad at the way old habits, bad ones, interfere, or come first. I know what I mean here, but I'm not putting it very well."*)

This is part of the learning process, something that must be understood before you leave your last reincarnation, and it is precisely for this reason that you deal so directly now with thoughts, subjective states, and their effects.

Now. Together at least several times a week, for a month, read the sessions that Ruburt has on his clipboard. At least those portions outlined, <u>together</u> (underlined), as if you had not begun any of this before. Encourage Ruburt toward motion, and have him encourage himself the idea should be "I can do more, and more easily."

Some recommendations I will not give you now. They are in those sessions. Have Ruburt verbalize his fears in whatever way you choose. Feelings of hopelessness should also be verbalized. If they are not they pile up also. Improvements should be noted however. You should discuss plans in Ruburt's terms with each other.

(*Jane has already begun to verbalize her fears since this session was held, and in just two days we have seen good progress. I have also. We really believe now that we have the key to success out in the open now where we can grab hold of it.*)

These recommendations will pay off. Understanding the pattern of behavior should allow Ruburt to take definite steps to alter it. He does not have to creep round the house to be quiet either, for example. Now take a moment and see what questions you have.

(*"I was wondering about the feeling of hopelessness he gets."*)

When he feels that way he inhibits the feeling and does not admit it.

(*"Why the feeling to start with?"*)

Having to do with his condition—that he will not get better, for example. But all of the feelings mentioned tonight, and the unexpressed fears, add up to a formless anxiety that can give him a feeling of hopelessness, and that is extremely important.

(I would say very important indeed.)

There are small areas, quite trivial in comparison, that could serve as counterpoints. As mentioned, any changes within your framework at present that can be introduced. A project in which you can both become involved, that need not necessitate a great amount of time. Painting or furniture. Bright curtains at this windows—any beneficial changes in the environment of that nature.

Now take your break or end the session as you prefer.

(11:05. Jane said she was pretty far-out, etc. I thought the material excellent. Resume at 11:12.)

Now. I am going to end our session. However, one point.

Unrecognized and unchallenged fears cannot be dealt with adequately until they are released. Regardless of their intellectual status, they are highly charged, though they may appear as trivial.

The personality attempts to protect itself from them, for the reasons given, but the psychic energy behind them will leap up and attach itself to events. Because the fears are not accepted individually they have a collective charge, which when properly triggered evokes the feeling of hopelessness.

The feeling then seems to be out of all proportion to whatever current event seems to have evoked it. The personality is then bewildered, feeling the weight of this as a pall. Reassurance should be given then that the fears can be expressed, and not judged intellectually. Often when Ruburt is alone the weight of these unexpressed fears is strongly upon him, then acting like a cloud that holds him down.

("What happened a couple of months ago that touched off this current set of problems through his knees, so that he has trouble walking?")

You understand from what I have said that a strong reaction can be felt from a seemingly insignificant issue. Understand also however that the opposite also holds. An excellent suggestion or emotion taking root, even though trivial, can have a far-reaching beneficial effect. In that case however he expected from the tour much better results. *(To publicize Jane's* The Seth Material.*)*

After the tour, to his way of thinking, there was nothing. He was picked up by the tour and then dropped back. He felt as if Prentice had forgotten him, and that Tam was not interested in his dream book. The visits for example had ceased. He missed the New York calls and the conversation.

("What did happen there?")

With what?

("Well, with Tam for example.")

Tam, for example, is simply in a different position now, with more to do.

He is confident Ruburt will produce a good book, and while busy attempts to keep in touch with him. He has written Ruburt for example more than Ruburt has written to him. But with Ruburt's mind, it had to be more an all or nothing affair.

("What did happen after the tour? I always thought something happened after that, to cool things off.")

(Typically, this was a subject which Jane and I discussed very little, and which obviously must be loaded with hidden fears and angers on both our parts. It will be dealt with.)

Methods mainly of finance having to do with the company itself and with the recession, and with which books they thought would make the quickest returns. Not necessarily the more stable long-run returns.

("Did they figure correctly?")

They were thinking in terms of this year, and affairs of taxes. They tried to play *Psychic Developments Behind the Iron Curtain* for example from a political as well as a psychic viewpoint, and decided to put more of their money into that initially for that reason.

Now I am going to end our session. Please do follow my advice *(humorously)*, and then yell if you do not think it works.

("All right. Thank you very much, Seth.")

(11:35. I thought Seth's advice very good, and indeed that this is probably one of the best sessions we have ever held. I am sure it will produce excellent results.)

(Although we were both tired by the end of the session, I had the feeling that Jane, as Seth, was a bit reluctant to go too much into the affair with Prentice re *The Seth Material*, and ended the session rather abruptly at that point for that reason. Not that I don't think Prentice owes us some explanations, for they do—especially since they told us nothing of any plans, good or not so good. We wouldn't know the little we do know if we hadn't written them a month or so ago, wanting to know what had happened to some long-overdue travel expense money, etc.)

DELETED SESSION
JANUARY 20, 1971

(This is the regularly-scheduled session for January 20, 1971. It is deleted from the record. For the first time in several years, the session was held in our bedroom.)

Now, good evening—

("Good evening, Seth.")

and again, we will begin slowly.

In the initial stages of Ruburt's withdrawals, the exaggerated chatter also served to fool him, you see, as well as others. He would become all the more animated. He recognized some of these characteristics in your Jesuit friend. *(Bill Gallagher.)* They frightened him and were at least somewhat responsible in helping shake him loose. *(Last week.)* Do you follow me?

("Yes.")

Now give us a moment. *(Pause.)*

Some of the buried fears have been stationary, residing or taking up residence in their physical materialization in certain areas of the body. Each one definitely has an effect physically upon any of the thousands of muscles, and usually the same fear affects the same area of the body. You end up with blockages therefore that may show some variation in <u>intensity</u> with surface moods, therapy or momentary good news, but then reassert themselves in the same areas.

They are of course blockages of energy. As different fears are expressed the blockages disappear. One fear, expressed, will bring with it through association many others, relieving also various areas of the body. The fears must be consciously recognized, emotionally felt, and then discussed or cleared away.

(True. This is a very meaningful and important paragraph. Since the session for January 18 was held, Jane has noted some dramatic improvement in her condition since she began following these ideas. We have been working at them.)

When one fear seems to be handled in such a manner, after a week or so it should be looked at again. Less emotion should be felt at each time. The pattern of worrying over many trivial affairs, of constant brooding, has been a camouflage to hide the basic fears. Now as the fears are faced these other habits will dissolve.

Your discussion this evening, and events since our session have been to the point, and beneficial. Particularly your comments concerning Ruburt's behavior with the first husband. When the two of you have had any personal difficulties then Ruburt became twice as angry and fearful about your parents. At one time he equated you with Walt in his dreams. The dreams were meant to show him <u>he</u> was repeating a pattern of behavior.

(I don't believe either of us ever realized this.)

He is terrified of vulnerability because of his mother's condition when he was a child. Many of his early poems clearly showed a desire to dissociate himself from the warm spontaneous self, and to hide in a nonfeeling uncaring safety. He envied you what he thought of as your coolness, and in trying to emulate it at times he only used it as an excuse to continue this old pattern of withdrawal.

He could not handle his mother's fear. As a child it terrified him and made him feel inadequate. He dared not feel it as deeply as he actually did; therefore fears in himself were also not to be faced. He was ashamed to look to anyone for help. He is afraid to ask for help because he was ashamed that his mother had to ask him, a child, for help, and often he hated her for doing so.

To ask you for help therefore was to put himself in the position of his mother, and plead helplessness. This has been mentioned before but it is a good point, that retaliation against his mother was felt to be impossible, for she would then have an attack for which Ruburt felt responsible. This brought on greater feelings of guilt over any protest.

Ruburt's deep love for you shocked him out of that pattern for some time, but he also idealized you to such an extent that some difficulties were bound to arise. Behind any ordinary disagreement you might voice, any normal protest, he felt there was a great charge. He was so afraid to voice protest himself that he felt you must be driven by great inner forces before you would dare voice any protest to him.

He therefore drastically overemphasized your attitudes and moods during your illness. The feeling that you did not need him began to grow out of normal bounds in Florida. Lately the apartment seemed frightening to him because he felt like a rat in a maze, reacting to the same stimuli in the same way, without knowing the reason and without the introduction of any change.

The apathy was caused when he simply decided to bring things to an end. Stopping the normal activities he had to some extent insisted upon allowed him to become aware to some degree of the subjective feelings that had been beneath all of his activities. He was face to face with them and with the natural end product if they were continued.

(This is when Jane became deeply frightened last week, etc.)

He thought you discouraged deep conversation unless there was some crisis that brought about a confrontation. He could not admit his fears to himself nor share them with you. He completely lacks the ability to discuss normal fears and worries in any kind of neighborhood contact—with girl friends. The fears finally became so charged that all normal discussion was out of the question. He used ideas of positive thinking to squash the fears down more securely. Their charge was so strong that he felt you were as frightened of them as he was, and therefore to discuss them would threaten you also.

He greatly exaggerated their power, you see, in that regard. He then projected many of these attitudes upon you. If he accused himself then he would see accusation in your remarks or attitudes toward him.

He could not give himself well in your personal intimate relations because it was with you most of all that he had to watch his expression. The fears had to be kept away from you or the game was up. He could not afford then to let go. He thinks fears are an admission of helplessness, that you always wanted someone who was free and independent, and that you would have no use for anyone in that position.

Now take your break.

(10:05. Jane said she was out "pretty good." She said Seth must have her out good in order to get this material out, or she would break right out in the middle of the session. I also thought I had detected an emotional charge in her voice while she was in trance—something which is very unusual, etc.

(We were having the session in our bedroom for privacy. Jane at break asked me to take down an oil painting of hers that, she said, represented her childhood home on Middle Avenue in Saratoga Springs, New York. She had painted it several years ago, in very dark and gloomy tones.

(In an emotional way Jane also expressed some fears about her mother. She caught herself not wanting to admit these, but we talked it out. My mother also entered the conversation, etc. Jane did express herself with emotion. Resume at 10:23.)

Now. Geographically he feels between his mother and yours, and has always been somewhat uneasy over living in this state. *(New York.)*

He felt you were ashamed of his background and did not want him to discuss it. *(Pause.)* Give us time. *(Pause.)* When he goes to see your father he feels guilty because he is not seeing his mother, who is also in a home. He feels that your mother is gloating, having gotten rid of the father, and he is afraid of your family home for fear it might trap you both. He did not want any of your belongings or yours in it.

You understand that the weight problem is also a symptom that will clear up as the fears are released. The fear of dentists has to do with an episode when he was in college, and the dentist came to visit his mother. He has consciously forgotten the details. His mother often said that her condition might have been the result of bad teeth also, and the two are connected in his mind.

The weight is also related to his grandfather, and an identification with the grandfather, who was very thin, and who left Ruburt's mother, living alone. The same characteristics go along with the identification—the refusal to argue, the fear of argument, of overt protest, and of <u>silent</u> protest; <u>fasting</u> as a method of protest.

The grandfather would not even discuss his own wife with Ruburt, or any personal matters. A turned-in reticence.

Ruburt also has feelings about food, as you know—eating with strangers or with people he does not like. All of these enter in. His mother ate too much, and this is a way of asserting his independence from her. She was very fond of food, and Ruburt now pretends to dismiss it. This did not occur earlier, but only when the fears brought additional charge. He often cast you as the accuser, and therefore felt he could not communicate. You had something to do with this in the past. Later the course was set, and when you withdrew your faulty attitudes, he went on the same course.

He is particularly susceptible along the lines of his work because he felt from childhood that his ability was the only thing that made him lovable at all in his mother's eyes, and that his entire worth as a human being was dependent upon how he made out as a writer.

It was the only thing that set him apart under welfare conditions, the mark of distinction that got him to college by the skin of his teeth, and it was, he felt, what made you love him. Therefore if you had criticisms about his work, if you did not like it, you would not love him.

The financial matter was added to this when he began to sell books. Not only did his book have to be good, you see, but financially successful since you loved him for his talents mainly, and the two were combined. With the financial elements added, then to retain your love his books must also sell well.

When *Rebellers* was published your attitude was a poor one, but it was drastically received by our friend, who could not understand it and felt then and there that you no longer loved him <u>as you had</u>. Because he felt you loved him for his talent alone, then his books became also gifts to you beside their meaning for himself. But not only gifts as much as reassurances, you see. "I still have my talent. I am using it, so you can love me."

Any difficulty with a book then meant he could lose your love.

All of this has been unconscious on his part. He has not been that aware of it. He felt then that he had no one to turn to or to help him. He was also afraid that his fears about physical reality now and in the future were so drastic that you would also be terrified, and that together you could not solve the problems. He was terrified of doing anything that might make you ill, and determined to bear any worries or problems alone.

He keeps minute by minute count of you when you are working—all unaware, yet he makes it a point not to ask you about your painting a good deal of the time. To show concern you see to his way of thinking would be to admit, even briefly, he has any fears at all regarding your work. The charge had so built up that if you had one bad afternoon painting, he saw this as a sign of complete failure on your part; and he did the same with his own work.

The unrecognized fears latched upon any unpleasant event then, exaggerating it out of all context.

The physical effects in Saratoga at your last trip *(summer 1970)* were caused by guilt, Ruburt feeling that he was so close and would not visit his mother. Now take your break. One point: These attitudes and feelings must not remain simply a part of a session. They must be discussed by both of you with emotional interplay allowed for, emotional release.

("Yes. Well, I think we're doing that."

(10:50—11:00.)

Now. Ruburt felt you were a perfectionist, both in your work and in what you demanded of others and yourself.

To give expression to a need for help, or to show a need for comfort would be seen as weaknesses in your eyes. You felt that other people were weak, indecisive, stupid, ridden by fears. This is his interpretation of your feelings. To admit a need for comfort or to admit fears would put him, in your eyes, in the same category as all these others.

We are going to end the session shortly. He feared he was going beyond your reach, and he could have in a very real manner. This idea alone terrified him. He feared that on your own you would not make the effort to pull him back, and yet he would not ask you to do so. To show that he still has some reachable foibles, you still aroused a spark of his old enthusiasm earlier this evening when you suggested that his place *(our apartment)* still did have possibilities if your eyes were opened to them. So pursue that.

Now I will end our session. My heartiest regards to you both, and a fond good evening.

("Good night, Seth, and thank you very much.")

(End at 11:06. As of the following Sunday, we have already redecorated—to some extent—the apartment, with very good results. This includes some new yellow curtains for the living room and Jane's office, etc.)

DELETED SESSION
FEBRUARY 3, 1971

(This is the regularly-scheduled session for Feb 3, 1971. It is deleted from the record.)

Good evening.

("Good evening, Seth.")

Now, we will have some dictation and some personal material—and I will change my mind and give you the personal material first.

Now you have been good about exchanging ideas, the two of you, but not as spontaneous in the exchange of emotions. The remarks Ruburt made just before session are all pertinent.

The "lovely young woman" phrase incidentally is an excellent one for him to use. *(Jane was so addressed last night in ESP class by one of her students, a male.)* He did idealize you in the early days of your relationship, and then made the transition that he mentioned. He was ignoring and hiding his fears to protect you as well as himself.

He felt threatened however then when you voiced your own fears. Looking at him, you can see that the condition, the problem, is a repressed one —the physical symptoms make this obvious. The repression of fears was latched onto for the reasons given in a recent session—the habitual syndrome—do you recall?

("Yes.")

There was a basis, therefore. Now in the beginning, now, you need a daily period together where Ruburt can quite freely be encouraged to discuss any fears that have been a part of that day. This will prevent a two-or-three-or-more-day buildup.

Later this will not be necessary, though it should be a frequent pattern in your relationship, and <u>you</u> should feel quite free to discuss your fears then also. Practically this is of great importance for it will help break the repressive habit on the one hand, and help end blockages that have been holding back positive and healthy charges of activity. You will be killing two birds with one stone.

This does not mean that the emphasis should be upon fears. Do you follow me?

("Yes.")

If possible these discussions should end with the reassurance that you can work out the practical aspects of your life together, and that you are large enough to understand your fears and use them creatively. This can be a therapeutic measure of great lasting value.

Whenever possible finish up the discussion with at least a brief look at the underlined portions of the sessions on Ruburt's clipboard. The intellectualization of the fears can be a trick to avoid facing their emotional reality, so beware of that.

"I am a lovely young woman" is particularly good because it automatically identifies Ruburt with grace, agility and health. Too often he has identified himself with his symptoms. He has in his mind seen himself not as a woman who had certain symptoms, along with many excellent good points and abilities, <u>but</u> he has identified himself <u>primarily</u> at times with the symptoms alone. Hence the appalling "monster woman" image that sprang to his mind.

Now earlier he would have been so terrified that the image would not have become conscious. Instead it can now serve as an excellent learning point, and for both of you. The identification of self with symptoms alone is very dangerous. Always distorted, the symptoms themselves are a representation of certain distortions. They are not representations of the entire self, and should never be considered so.

Ruburt's entire self-image is not wrong, therefore.

Now let us look at this simply. He comes through as an extremely attractive, highly intelligent young woman, with strong psychic and creative abilities, unusual insight into the problems of others—as a writer, a psychic, and as "the mistress" of a delightful establishment.

He also comes through as a young woman with some problems, with a repressive tendency that is physically materialized, with dogmatic and somewhat rigid distorted ideas that have only lately really been understood by the personality. I want him to read that, and I want you to know how he thinks when he is in error.

("All right.")

When he is in error he sees himself as an old hag, overly cautious with his psychic work, knocks himself over the head for not being freer about it, distrusts it, knocks himself over the head for distrusting it, fearful of emotional expression. Now you missed this fear of emotional expression on his part, because even with it he relates well usually with others. Particularly of course he was afraid of unpleasant emotional expression, or anger.

He learned restraint in this direction with his mother, and all kinds of automatic muscular tensions were then learned to inhibit the expression of fear of anger. So at his worst he feels powerless before it, and there are energy blockages here particularly.

Many of these are perfectly normal fears. He felt it beneath him intellectually to speak of them to you, and felt that you would have no use for him, that you would think he was a cowering, spineless child rather than the independent brave spirit that he tried so hard to be for himself and you.

So in the beginning particularly you may be the one to take the initiative at times, for he may be reluctant, you see—a symptom of the habit. The release of the fears then allows the body to release the natural optimism and healthy emotions that are needed, and the expansion of activity and energy.

But if you do not allow some regular time for such discussions matters will slide.

Now you may take your break.

(9:29—9:41)

Now. Retracing *(in answer to my question at break)* will not occur in any predetermined rigid manner, as it has been described unless there is a psychic or mental return to the mental patterns that caused the difficulties to begin with. This is not operating then in Ruburt's case—the mental patterns are not being returned to.

On the other hand feelings create the physical state. Accumulated feelings of like nature will be expressed often, but not always, in repetitive fashion. It would be possible to go through Ruburt's body and pinpoint the physical materialization of certain feelings as they are represented in a symptom.

It would also be <u>possible</u> however to go through his body and pinpoint the particular energizing feelings and ideas responsible for the excellent functioning of the other body areas. Retracing is a noticeable effect, not understood, highly distorted, in the explanations you have been given, representing an echoing effect that occurs whenever the individual involved touches upon those thought and feeling areas that brought about the difficulty.

They are minimal if the individual is progressing at a psychic level. Many individuals however, relying upon the physical therapy alone, set up negative associations. Say for example that a deeply repressed fear brought about the squeezing of nerves in the area of the lower spinal cord. Without the knowledge that you have, then any sensations in the area of those nerves could then through association activate the original fear, which would in turn aggravate the condition.

As the chiropractor made repeated adjustments, gradually the effect would lessen. Initially however it could be quite strong, and the chiropractor would call it a retracing action. Certain pains through association <u>can</u> (underlined) send an individual backward to the original fear or situation that first caused it.

Ruburt has at times reacted in that manner, though to a less dramatic degree, when an echo of an old frightening physical pain is felt. He has largely learned however to avoid this, particularly since our session that the feeling he is repressing is the problem, and if that is allowed release the physical aspects will vanish.

An example was the Sunday at your mother's, when he was afraid of the cramp in the leg, which <u>did not come</u> in the way that he feared.

Now. He did pick up negative suggestions regarding retracing. It only applies when a mental aspect of illness is not understood, and to the degree that it is not understood. When it does operate then at its own level it is therapeutic. Each time the body reacts less and less. It is like crying wolf.

The treatments in themselves are beneficial, but useless without the guides that you have. If you really do not want to get well, then no doctor or chiropractor can help you, for you will substitute symptoms. The treatments do serve as an aid however, but he should not <u>expect</u> (underlined) the retracing effects, for there is no reason why they should operate in his case.

The cold does have an effect upon muscles however. It goes unnoticed <u>when you are leaving your muscles alone</u>. *(Half humorously.)* Now he thinks he should answer the phone every time it rings. And answer the door every time anyone knocks. He thinks he is afraid to have people see him in poor shape, and so does not want to answer the door. Actually it is his state of mind. He does not want to see anyone, period, often at such times. He does not have to want to see people at all times.

Is he afraid of seeing people at those times? If so, why? For the symptoms are a blind in that respect.

You got more than you bargained for. Take your break.

(10:06—10:23.)

Now in class you see he is expressive and expansive. He enjoys teaching. In class he is spontaneous. He is also thinking of others and how to help them, and he is definitely not concentrating upon his own symptoms.

He feels an inferior member of a family, but in a superior position as a teacher, and his fear of being anonymous in a group, or swept up by it, when <u>he</u> is not in control of it, results from these family feelings of a group, and fear of being swept along by emotion.

He was afraid not only of his own emotions, but terrified of his mother's emotions. He feels free to express emotion in class because he is in control of the class, and can also justify this, the use of emotion as a teaching aid. He can also give expression to a very deep concern about his fellow man, safely, since the family relationship is not involved.

A consideration of his own feelings and attitudes in class will help him see what he does <u>right</u> then, and what negative thoughts and emotions are present at many other occasions. He acts to some degree also with positive aggressiveness in class. He is sure of himself. The positive aggression is important.

Great bursts of energy are available to him then, and he is not ambiguous about using it. Now that feeling of confidence is available to him at other times. He should try to remember the feeling and recapture it. He also on his own speaks loudly in class, and automatically accepts his own composure, status as teacher, and his abilities, without question.

He takes it for granted that he will be in good condition for class, regardless of how he has felt earlier, and the expectation is always correct. The lovely young woman image will also help fill him out.

Now when he was doing disguised autobiographical novels he released his fears through his writing. When the writing changed he buried them as completely as possible. He also stopped writing what he thought of as pessimistic poetry, which had performed the same function, allowing for the expression of fearful emotions. He used some of our material as an excuse to further shove his fears beneath, overexaggerating certain remarks that I had made. You follow me here.

("Yes.")

Again, your sessions should allow for the expression and discussion of fears, the giving of comfort and assurance, but <u>not</u> involve emphasis upon fears, as in the two days... You do not need to take notes here....

(Seth then explained he was referring to the days immediately following the deleted session of January 18, 1971, when Jane expressed a lot of her fears, etc.)

It is simply a matter of Ruburt keeping in touch with his own feelings, whatever they are. Do you have specific questions?

("No, I think we're doing quite well.")

You must follow the practical advice however.

He should deal with his feelings about going out. Why does he not want to? What is he afraid of?

("Why doesn't he want to go out?")

On different occasions the answers are different. Now he must emotionally find this out for himself. When he feels the reluctance however he should try to discover why and not ignore it, stay home and cower, or force himself to go out, denying the feelings that he has hidden. Do you see the difference?

("Yes.")

He should indeed go out more. I do not want positive suggestions just slipped on like bandages, leaving the fears unreleased or unrecognized. The positive suggestions are extremely important. Clearing the monster woman image will be of great help here. Do you have questions?

("No, I guess not.")

Then we did not get to dictation, but I hope that this will be as valuable. He is not having the menopause.

Now a fond good evening.

("Thank you Seth—the same to you.")

If you do not have any questions, do you have any remarks?

("No, only that we'll keep trying.")

(10:47.)

(My two pendulum sessions, and Jane's responses to the second one, are referred to in the next session.)

Feb 10/71) Pendulum   (1)
wed.

① I am responsible for Jane's knees bothering her. YES
I think I am. This is not only my opinion. I am
really responsible, etc.

② Jane's knees bother her because she is afraid of my
opinion. Not to do with the dream book or the Seth Mat'l.
I am not jealous of either book, nor is Jane afraid that
I am. YES

③ Jane isn't afraid that I am mad at her. YES

④ — Jane's knees bother her because she thinks I expect her to love
 my family. Jane hates my family. I think she hates my
 family.

⑤ Finances, medical insurance, etc, have nothing to do with
Jane's knees, etc.

⑥ Jane's knees bother her because I make her feel threatened.
YES " " " " " " my whole family does also.

⑦ My oil paintings of the old man in the home (Bradford County)
YES   cause Jane's knees to bother her.

⑧ Jane's knees bother her because she is afraid she'll end up like
my father. She is afraid she'll be a failure as an artist. YES

⑨ Jane's knees bother her because she is afraid she'll become sick
strong ~~like father.~~ also — she is afraid she is becoming more of a success
than I am. artistic has nothing to do with it, tho.

⑩ ~~Jane is afraid that in my opinion~~ ~~she becomes~~ ~~more of~~ ~~a~~
strong   she'll become more of a success than I am. No other reason
for the knees. Jane blames me because I am not more successful. She'd
feel better if I were selling a lot of paintings. She'd feel free to bloom whole.

⑪ In other words — Jane is punishing herself down the knees so that
       she won't be more of a success than I am. This is because she is
YES   afraid she'll be more successful than I am. She is getting the
       knee trouble as she becomes more & more successful.
       Not because the dream book is nearing completion, too.

(over)

⑫ — Jane's knees don't bother her because she uses in struggling with my paintings. YES. also, she's mad because I don't try to sell paintings - she thinks I have the means to success + won't use them. This related to her knee symptoms.

⑬ Her knees don't bother her because she feels guilty it's not seeing her mother. He doesn't feel guilty. Nor her father, etc. YES to agreed both

⑭ Jane's knees bother her for the reasons above. Not because of her own childhood. (Strong) — the causes are not past, but present. YES

I have uncovered the reasons for the knee trouble.

STRONG — Jane's pend. — the knees are a which to cover up her successes. So of wait notice it, etc.

Jane's pend — Jane got strong pendulum reaction to all the questions on this sheet — verified everything.

Jane's pend — Jane isn't afraid to die here or leave her if she got it too successful. But it would make me very sad.

" — Jane feels that because I don't sell my paintings, this holds her own successes back. Related to the knees.

" — Jane feels guilty about making more money in ESP class because it would show me up — did with knees —

Bob P. — doesn't feel threatened by my success.
" " — be delighted to have me make as much $ as possible —
" " — doesn't care if I earn $ when he does.

Jane, p. I feel helpless bec I can't help Rob 'succeed'
Big Y — (Tears)
Feel I'm not much good if I can't help him in this all impt issue.
have to just ex —

DELETED SESSION
FEBRUARY 10, 1971

(This is the regularly scheduled session for February 10, 1971. It is deleted from the record.

(On Friday at 1 PM on February 5, my father died. The funeral was on Monday, February 8 in Tunkhannock, PA. Jane and I were of course with Betts and Loren, my mother, and various other friends and relatives in Tunkhannock over the weekend. Jane's condition was not good and I became very concerned.

(We returned home on Monday after a heavy snowstorm in Pennsylvania, and I did not return to work until Thursday. This session is prefaced with my notes of two pendulum sessions I held with myself. The first on Tuesday, February 9 concerns my shaky hand and my father. The second on the morning of Wednesday, February 10 concerns Jane's condition and my part in it, etc. It was very productive. Suffice it to say here that Jane's own pendulum agreed with it in toto, and we spent a good deal of time discussing it. By suppertime Jane was getting some strong emotional reactions to parts of it. [Loren, incidentally, is my younger brother.]

(Monday's session, which was not held, is scheduled instead for Thursday, February 11.

(Tonight's session was held in the studio.)

Good evening.

("Good evening, Seth.")

Now, again we begin slowly. I am sure you understand the reasons.

Your pendulum data was indeed correct. Also the remark Ruburt made just before the session: he does blame your mother for your illness of several years back, and also for his own.

(This we did not know.) It was at the time of your illness that he began to conceal his feelings from you, and in a sense to coddle you. His overanxious behavior, its roots, have been given in other sessions. You follow me here.

("Yes.")

He then reverted to the alternate pattern of behavior he learned early *(in childhood)* as a defense mechanism, withholding his feelings from his own conscious knowledge as well as hiding them from you. If he were aware of them and did not share them he would feel disloyal, so if her were not to burden you with them he also had to hide them from himself.

In the past such behavior had led to an increased frenzied activity, mildly but not inordinately erratic. Such erratic behavior however he now felt out of the question, and the built-up energy from the repressed feelings had nowhere to go. He clamped down upon himself then more and more, fearing the built-up charge of repressions.

He tried to use suggestion as a bandage. As I mentioned at one time, he literally felt divorced from you emotionally, because he was divorced from the emotional nature of his own being.

He has great energy, and was able to withstand this self-assault for some time before actual physical symptoms showed. Even then his physical system has been amazingly resilient.

For some time, subjectively, he was in a highly ambiguous position. He felt he could expect no comfort from you, that he must face both your fears and his alone. Superstitiously he felt that in hiding fears about your parents he hid them for you both—shoved them under the psychological rug; but the rug became heavier and heavier.

This began at the gallery when your father and mother first stated that money would be needed, and very shortly after your return from Florida. Ruburt was outraged that having treated you the way they had, they would so humiliate themselves as to beg for your aid, and instead decided that basically they did not feel humiliated but were asking what they considered their just due.

When you were ill and not working part of Ruburt's money went to them, and he was ashamed at resenting this, and furious at you that you would allow them to do this to him. He was sure that if the circumstances were reversed he would never bleed you to help his parents.

Now we are dealing with his attitudes and feelings. I am leaving my comments out here, you understand. He wanted a car when you did not have one, but was furious that you got one in order to visit your parents—<u>not to escape from them</u>.

The neighborhood squabbles there remind him of Middle Avenue. He feels as if his mother is getting your mother to do her dirty work for her, and when your mother said to him "You are a phony," it was also his own mother for the thousandth time putting him down.

He feels trapped in this apartment, that he is here because he is readily accessible to help your mother, as when he was a child he was readily accessible to help his own mother. He has a strong, affectionate, open nature that was dealt some harm. *(Long pause at 9:18.)*

He is fiercely protective of you, and regardless of his feelings about families, you see, had he felt that your parents dealt kindly with you he would have gone along with them all the way. He felt that they betrayed you.

Now give us time.... He felt that any success of his that was not matched by you pulled you down in your parents' eyes, and was therefore part victory and part defeat. He did fear that you would become bitter if you did not succeed *(as a painter)*, and he sometimes felt that you retreated to the studio away from him, as purposely your father retreated from your mother into the cellar or garage. He would rather have burned anything that you have rather than store it in your family's house. Symbolically this threatened him. He mentioned it on several occasions, but you made a reasonable reply having to do with convenience, and so he brooded.

("*Well, we can move the stuff.*")

(*Actually, I first began moving things to Sayre because we thought we would be moving from Elmira. I wanted as little surplus material here as possible, thinking it would be easier to take our time moving items from Sayre to the new location, wherever it might be.*

(*This led into the convenience idea. I suppose it's not a good idea to keep the third carbon of this material there, either. Actually, I've begun slowly moving things back up here to store in the extra room upstairs, now that I have had the lock repaired. This will be continued until the job is done.*)

When you were quiet at times, this reminded him of your father's uncommunicative manner, and frightened him. If he reacted emotionally, this frightened him, because he was afraid you would interpret it as your mother's reaction. He is furious that he is in such poor physical condition in front of her. He thinks that you were taken in by her for years. These sound like rather harmless attitudes, or normal enough.

("*They don't to me.*" *I knew this was loaded material, etc.*)

It is only because they have been unacknowledged so many times and consciously repudiated, that they have done such harm. The protective layers were built up so strongly, and became such a part of the personality structure, that I could not bring them all toppling down from the inside.

The symptoms built up as he clamped down on his feelings. Make sure you emphasize that the release of these will also bring about the release of joy and inspiration and energy that has been blocked through repression. Take your break.

(*9:32. At break I didn't say a word. Resume at 9:35.*)

Now. Since your reaction when *Rebellers* was published, he feared that you would grow to hate him for any success, if you did not succeed, since his success he felt was largely at your expense—you bought him the time in which to work.

If he succeeded he might lose your love, in other words. He closely watched your reaction after that. On a few occasions he found it negative early in the game, but any criticism later of his relationship with publishers was taken to be a symbol of an anger with him because of his books, period.

You would find something to be angry at, he felt, so he tried to succeed and not succeed. The answers given by your pendulum also apply to my book, and to some (underlined) of our missed sessions in general. While you vigorously upheld the sessions, he still felt that to some extent, again, their success would undermine you.

He was also from the beginning afraid of the time it took you away from your work to record them, and felt that you must resent this. If he thought you looked tired, or at all reproachful or worried or bothered on a session night, he would feel that you did not really want to have a session. But he would cover this up, and if you were not out there with your notebook, he took this as a sign that you really did not want a session. *(Long pause.)*

I meant to give you a longer break, but delivered this while I had good hold of it.

("That's okay.")

At the same time he projected his fears upon you, thinking that you loved him only because he was a writer. Then why were you not pleased with his success, you see?

Take your break.

(9:50. I was appalled, and I suppose that from my own actions Jane was too. For the moment at least I felt terribly discouraged. While Jane left the room for a brief time, I asked my pendulum a question, and received this answer: "I don't think Jane wants to get well." The question had occurred to me during last night, I believe, but I had forgotten it until now.

(When Jane returned I told her about it. I believed the answer I had received, saying that the pendulum hadn't steered me wrong yet on any major question. For obvious reasons I hadn't asked this question before. Resume at 10:01.)

Now. Ruburt wants to get as well as he thinks he can afford to.

When *Rebellers* was published he felt (underlined) that you were coldly angry at him. This after the series of events mentioned earlier. He has been slowing down to give you time to catch up.

(At the time Rebellers *was published, I was jealous, but it took me some time to learn this. I made the breakthrough finally with a series of questions directed to my pendulum, as I had done this morning concerning Jane's knee troubles. In fact, it was the memory of the success of that episode that led me to this morning's session.)*

He fears that you would find any real success of his highly distasteful. He fears that he might go hogwild with it. There is a connection here I have not quite discovered, in what I am about to say.

Walt turned him over to you only too gladly. He is afraid that if you launch him into success you may then leave him, wanting none of it.

Clear emotional communication on your part will be most valuable here.

On several occasions on your tour there was a name confusion, and this upset him for fear you would be hurt and put down. Do you follow me?

("Yes." Here Seth refers to my being called Mr. Roberts on occasion during the tour. Part of this was caused by an error on the jacket copy of The Seth Material. *I can say that this bothered me not at all.)*

It is something like a sympathetic strike. Do not take that too literally.

Releasing fears will allow new inspiration and optimism to emerge, to battle against any lingering negative aspects however. He cannot have too many assurances from you, he is so thirsty for them.

The fact that you did not discuss plans together helped prolong his distorted ideas, you see. There was little counterbalance, and this is being remedied.

When you did not speak of your work much he interpreted this to mean deep worry and concern on your part about it.

Often he did not feel your support. I am not saying you did not support him. Remember also that he exaggerated his fears, and felt that they would serve to drive you from him. Reading his book is a great help. He felt you did not have any deep interest in it, and that symbolically you were rejecting it.

Take a break.

(10:16. I was really upset by this time in the session. There were so many things I wanted to say that I believe I ended up silent because points got in each other's way, etc. I did voice some thoughts that I've mentioned before: about why, in times of great stress when it's obvious the organism is in trouble, it doesn't intuitively override wrong thinking and set itself right so that it can go on about the business of life, etc. Resume at 10:28.)

Now. He felt that the trappings of success might be a real threat to your working time, and therefore to your ultimate success—that you would resent this beforehand, rather than, say, discuss it and so forth. That you would resent the lack of privacy involved, and blame him for it.

Now your own feelings toward success are highly ambiguous, and in the past neither of you really discussed them, so there was fertile ground for Ruburt to exaggerate some of your ideas and feelings.

The symptoms slowed down all of these eventualities. Convince him, and let him convince himself, that it is safe for him to go ahead.

("It is possible?")

It is indeed. Now many of your own attitudes have changed by now, but initially he used some of your past attitudes as a basis, not realizing that you had changed them. There was some fact then. However he exaggerated it—but the facts have changed.

("Then why hasn't he changed?")

He was not aware that your attitude had changed as much as it has.

("*Not even telepathically?*")

(*This is what I had been getting at. I found it hard to believe that telepathy hadn't been more of a help in at least unconscious communication.*)

He was not emotionally aware of this. The fear projections, repressed, telepathically attract like projections, and inhibit other ones. He had tuned himself toward fears, and these are what he picked up most frequently. You did not until recently make a practice of communicating feelings to each other on any consistent basis. This alone makes your changed attitudes clear. He does need encouragement now. The remark "You are doing this to yourself" is interpreted by him as an accusation. The more pliant bodily response in your intimate affairs shows that he is trusting you again as he had not done for some time to that degree.

Now he picked up many of these reactions, again, from you when you were ill. You also inhibited your feelings, cut yourself off from Ruburt, retreated, and were negatively motivated. In a manner of speaking he is working out problems for both of you. You have learned through his behavior, and saved yourself some other steps, for example.

What questions do you have?

(*Long pause. "I guess I can't think."*)

You are on the right track. Beside the release of fears the discussion of future plans is also important. If you have no questions I will end the session.... My prognosis is good.

("*At the moment I'm very discouraged, I guess.*")

The fears, written down, are encouraging. You confront them and they appall you. But they are far more appalling hidden.

("*I know it.*")

Do you have an other comments, if not questions? I bid you a fond good evening then.

("*Good evening, Seth, and thank you very much.*")

(*10:50. Truly, I felt appalled, almost overwhelmed. Many feelings came in rapid succession. Typing this up two days later, I note that the material is indeed charged as the feelings return to some degree. We've already discussed them to some extent, and believe we are making progress, etc.*)

DELETED SESSION
FEBRUARY 11, 1971

(*This session is a makeup for the regularly scheduled session of Monday,*

February 8. It is deleted from the record.)

Good evening.

("Good evening, Seth.")

Now. We may as well continue to clear some of this up.

You have the fear of the symptoms themselves, and this applies to both of you. The symptoms are still being projected into the future, and <u>often</u> (underlined) by you both. Consciously and unconsciously signs are passed and given to the effect that symptoms are persisting now and will continue to do so.

You spoke to Ruburt about imagination, and he must learn to use it for his benefit, through imagining himself free and well. This fear itself should be faced for what it is, and dealt with like any other fear. Ruburt considers it almost unspeakable. *(The fear that he will not get well.)*

Both of you, remembering the article you read this evening *(about Picasso)*, should keep in mind the immense energies of the inner self to solve such problems, to set the personality aright, and literally get it back on its feet. I have said this often, yet I cannot overemphasize it. Emphasis should not be upon the problem but upon its solution.

Not upon reversing symptoms but upon the desired results. Not what is wrong but what is right, and how a greater degree of "rightness" can be achieved. This is of utmost importance.

If Ruburt shows a bad bout of symptoms then often you both become extremely fearful. Very aware of those symptoms, concentrating upon them, and this worsens the condition. I am not saying that the symptoms are not fearful. This should be admitted.

("So what should you do?"

(As in the last session, I was getting irritated, since all of this is emotionally loaded material of course. I was on the point of asking Seth what one should do when one confronted a fearful result even if one had constructed that result, etc.)

But the search for health should be concentrated upon—not the state of ill health at any time. When you concentrate upon the symptoms you often then forget the abilities of the inner self and the vast reservoir of help available. You close it off because you are concentrating upon the opposite direction.

As you were reading today, your imaginations are centered in the wrong direction. Ruburt fears that he has a condition which will persist indefinitely.

("So far he's been right.")

There is a definite time period involved, and your own remark only shows that what I said earlier is correct. Both of you must believe that he is to completely recover. It is most important that Ruburt believe this, but extremely helpful if you will.

("But I don't see any signs that he believes it.")

You have not helped him believe it either. You are creating the reality. You must believe in his health. He must. He can learn to do this first of all by ceasing to project an image of himself as ill into the future. *(Long pause.)*

He can do this by employing the exercises that you mentioned, that will show him a daily improvement that will help break the negative image and prevent further negative projections. He can do this by the daily walk. All of these help break the negative projections, and are already proof physically of inside willingness that is then physically materialized for him to see—in terms of physical performance that he can judge.

He can do this as I mentioned earlier by reminding himself of the otherwise healthy state of his body, and being thankful for it, by <u>expecting</u> (underlined) four time's improvement, and looking for it, and <u>not expecting</u> the symptoms to remain as they are.

Now when he has expected improvements and looked for them he has found them. They have happened.

He can do this by concentrating on his book, getting out more. Now these sound like very simple procedures, but they are the ones that work. He had some difficulty because of the childhood experience of seeing his mother ill for so long. *(Long pause.)*

Give us time. There are other reasons however why you fell into the same trap, and I will try to get them for you. You are doing the same thing with his symptoms that he does with them, that so annoy you: prolonging them in time in your imagination, and you have less reason to do so.

("They're difficult to ignore. Especially when I see him going down the stairs sideways.")

These facts exist—

(Seth looked at me almost pityingly. "All right.")

—regardless of what you think of them. Your thoughts and imaginations do cause your activities. Your negative attitudes also help continue the symptoms, as do his. The physical facts of going down the stairs sideways existed first in imagination, and were materialized. You need not deny the physical fact, but if you understand what causes physical facts then you change the direction of your imagination, thought and expectations in order that the following future facts will not be like the ones that so displeased you.

The method is not difficult. You are using it the wrong way quite well in some regards. Ruburt has had his own negative attitudes about his illness to contend with, and often yours as well. You did more good by telling him he bent over well from the front this evening *(while we were exercising)*, that simple statement, than you ever could by any remark, however well-meaning, that he is not bending his leg when he walks for example.

I am not telling either of you to ignore a physical fact, but to avoid habitual, often unthinking negative suggestions that might prolong it. This is an important point, and Ruburt would not have let me speak about it earlier. Now take your break.

(*9:55—10:12.*)

Now. Let us examine what our friend just said.

With the best intentions in the world, his conscious attention was on his symptoms and his physical condition <u>all day long</u>, on the procedures involved with motion.

When he was walking his thoughts were upon how well or poorly he was walking, rather than on his book, the weather, or some neutral subject.

(*"I know it. They usually are."*)

The state of his symptoms becomes his day, and yours, when either of you indulge in that kind of procedure. He overdid when he constantly watched himself, trying so hard to get up correctly.

"Of course I can get up," or even "To hell with it, I can get up," will work far better, but without a constant eye out to check that the suggestion take place immediately.

(*"And you think this is possible to achieve."*)

I do indeed.

(*"Well, I'll tell you something: That's going to take some doing."*)

He must not immediately try to check out the results, but have faith that they will come. If he says, now, "I can get up easily," and then he does not in the next instant, then he thinks he is faced with a new failure.

(*"Well, he is."*)

He is not.

(*"He just created it for himself, didn't he?"*)

The point is that he expects a suggestion to take hold at once, and against countering suggestions that he may have given. For example: he will be working and want something. Perhaps four or five times he will think "Oh, hell, it will hurt to get up." This will be on the fringe of consciousness. Then consciously he will say "Now I can get up easily," and wonder why it hurts.

(*"Doesn't he ever get sick of this routine?"*)

He does indeed. Now give us time. (*Long pause at 10:25.*) The two of you together can help break these procedures so that at least the both of you are not applying negative ideas at the same time. There are countless small daily rituals that can break or reinforce such attitudes. I will mention one that you broke. It was the ritual involving your can opener.

("What do you mean?")

Ruburt had great difficulty with it. Strong feelings of failure. When you replaced it the hands began to improve. The ritual involved in opening the cans was a constant habitual negative reinforcement.

Ruburt has taken to using the railings. He does not need them. A sense of defeat is connected with the railings. Let him try resisting their use.

("Why doesn't he try this on his own?")

(As usual, listening to Seth's long list of negative items, I couldn't help wondering why Jane didn't appreciate the import of such actions at least intuitively, and do something about them.)

He is afraid he will fall. There are other small rituals that can be avoided, and as they come to me I will give them to you. The joint exercise idea is very good, and the morning one also. He still does not like the living room door closed at night. He feels closed in. Small changes made in his morning ritual will help bring about some morning improvement.

Quite hidden, all the habitual rituals of a family have deep psychological connotations. To change such habits is often illuminating therefore, and that is why I mention this here. Ruburt can stop trying to get everything arranged on his desk before work, so he will not have to get up for example. This is a strong negative suggestion that helps to override the conscious suggestion "I can get up easier."

("He doesn't get many good results from suggestions at all, does he?")

He uses suggestion very well—backwards. In the instance just given you—

("That's what I'm talking about.")

That is why I am giving you this material. This will come as a surprise to him.

("That's what I've begun to suspect the last few days.")

Now there will be other such instances. Look for more of them. Whenever everything is automatically arranged to make it easier for someone who cannot get about well, this is a strong negative suggestion. The aspirins in the desk drawer and on the bookcase are another instance.

Take your break.

(10:36—10:49.)

Now. You seem to have had enough for one session—

("I'm okay.")

—but you made some leeway with Ruburt in your last remarks *(which I've forgotten as I type this)* and I would like him to examine his normal habits in the light of what I said about his table and arrangements. Do you follow me?

("Yes.")

Now you can help by pointing out anything that you notice also. Follow what I have given you in this session. You can often help each other recognize negative attitudes or remarks of which the other is not consciously aware. This does not mean to emphasize the negatives, as you should understand by now.

The little habits that have been built up about Ruburt's condition should be abolished. This does not mean that you need to stand aside and not help him now and then when you see he needs it. It does mean that habitual limiting tendencies of his should not be continued.

These are most important of course around the table, since you both eat and he works there. The bathroom and the stairs. The morning hours particularly are important.

Now we will end the session. There is much constructive material in it. Put it to use. And a good suggestion from me: I expect to see it put into use.

("Well, it would be nice.")

Do you have any questions?

("No.")

My fondest regards, and good evening.

("Good evening, Seth. Thank you very much.")

(10:58.)

SESSION 567 (DELETED PORTION)
FEBRUARY 17, 1971

(This material is deleted from the 567th session for February 17, 1971.
(10:30 PM.)

Now I have a few comments. Do you want a break first?

("No.")

All right. The physical assertion of the exercises is good. He lost faith in his physical performance, and got out of the habit of asserting himself physically.

In the exercises both will, faith and assertion, come into play in coordinated effort that is met by performance, and by achievement. He gives himself then physical achievement, and for the first time can say "I did this or that, that I set my mind on, and am succeeding."

This brings a return of confidence in the body, reawakens the body memory, particularly through ordinary activities. The suggestion is beautifully implied: you do exercises because you expect to succeed at them.

It places his mind on physical performance, and leads automatically into the future in a positive way as he achieves in simpler exercises and then goes on. The exercises themselves then help combat negative suggestions on both of your parts, for you are reassured by any progress. Ruburt reacts to the reassurance that you feel.

The emphasis in these should always be upon the achievement, and the exercises follow his growing capacities. Let the feeling of trust build up. Do not overdo. The spontaneous desires to go for a walk for example this evening *(to Ruth Klebert's)* are a mark of progress.

I suggested a change in the morning ritual, and suggest you both consider this. In other words, the exercises are suggestion, and at this point the best kind.

("That's what I've been wondering about. Shall we forget about other kinds of suggestion for now?")

It's according to what he is thinking of.

("I mean the kind he usually gives himself when he lays down for perhaps fifteen minutes, etc.")

His idea of noting down the pleasures or good points of the day should be maintained. He dropped it. A heavy-handed application of suggestion should be avoided—and look carefully for negative suggestions that may be implied on either of your parts. To be relieved of these is half the battle.

Ruburt's list about what he will do when he is completely well is a good idea. Except that as an act of faith you see he should begin to carry out some of those points now.

There will be a beneficial mental and physical carryover from the exercises to other activities, particularly as the trust is built up. You have not been at them for a full week yet. The exercises in the past would not have been effective. You were both lacking the feeling of optimism that would make them work. They must be consistently carried through however, as a time of day set aside for physical achievement.

Now this shows him that he can act resolutely in the physical world, that he can express himself through his body, that he can be physically assertive. It combats the lack of confidence that had built up.

The exaggeration of negative influences was brought about because of the repression. Now, for example: so as not to bother you, Ruburt made it a point of conscience to speak to your mother on the phone for you, and not call you, when he did not want to do so. Very seldom was he even <u>aware</u> of his true feelings here, and when he was he was ashamed of them, and was 10 times nicer to your mother to cover up the feelings from all of you.

Besides this he felt highly inadequate because he knew that all the time your mother of course would have preferred two minutes with you to ten with him, so then he felt unappreciated. You had a menagerie of repressed feelings. This is just one instance.

In his own way he is fond of your mother at the same time, you see, but also terrified of her because the repressions cause him to exaggerate the hidden fears. When you are frightened of fears then the most minute one is exaggerated.

Now you may end the session, take a break, or ask more questions as you prefer.

(At last break I had asked that Seth deal with three questions tonight after finishing dictation on his book: 1. The ideas behind Jane's exaggerated response to events, particularly fears. 2. The idea of physical activity on her part instead of suggestion. 3. I was curious to know something about the mechanics behind Jane's slowed-up movements after she had been quiet for a while. That is, after she had been sitting for, say, half an hour, she was slow in getting up and under way, etc.

("Now about my question number 3, involving motion?")

There are many different reasons involved there, depending upon the circumstances, his mental activities, and the habits, mental and physical, built up with the idea of sitting or lying down.

("I was wondering if the same things applied to his getting up in the morning.")

To some large degree. Expectation <u>now</u> (underlined) is important here, and the fact that he got into the habit of denying impulses toward motion—by blocking, often, not the impulse so much as the motor response.

After sitting and blocking such impulses or responses, then it is only natural that the blockage pattern is set up. Now suddenly he wants to get up without blockage.

When his mind is engrossed as a rule the blockage is far less unless he suddenly remembers and thinks "Oh, now I will have difficulty getting up." Giving into the impulses *(to motion)* then will automatically work, and give him confidence that the impulses can indeed be followed through.

(Pause.) Something else applies during the night, but I suggest your break. *(10:55—11:09.)*

Now. There are several issues involved here, and we will not get to all of them this evening, but I will return to the subject at the end of dictation.

One point: an unfortunate connection in Ruburt's mind. You got the bed because of your back trouble years ago. *(Long pause.)*

Give us time here. Changing the direction of the bed would automatically help matters some, but *(humorously)* Ruburt does not like it the other way.

("The conscious knowledge about the bed connections will help though, won't it?")

It should. His reactions to wintertime are also involved. Several small issues that add up. The door closed, the additional blankets, the relative lack of fresh air, the disinclination to get up when it is chilly, to record dreams, say, or go to the bathroom or whatever.

("There are contradictions there, though: if he wants fresh air, it's bound to be cold because it's winter, etc.")

They are surface contradictions, not worth exploring. In the summer for example with all the windows open, the closed door would not bother him as much. The mattress bothers him on occasion.

Now. *(Long pause.)* Some of the motor response blockage is continued in sleep. *(Long pause.)* Feeling sore for so long has built up the feeling of awakening in the morning in the same way. Countering gentle, imaginative exercises would help here, not involving getting up per se, however; to see himself dressed and in excellent spirits, serving your breakfast for example—not necessarily the following morning, but simply to entertain the pleasant image.

There are some connections here with his mother being in bed and in pain, that frighten him. And negative images, deeply repressed, of her sitting on the edge of the bed, trying to get up. He automatically projects distaste into your eyes at the spectacle, and is humiliated when you see him trying to get up. That is why he often waits until you are in the other room. This gives him a first defeat for the day, you see, and early. I will give you more at the end of our next session. *(Humorously:)* Have you had enough for tonight?

("Well, I have another question, but I don't know whether to ask it or not. I would like at least a glimmering on it though.")

And I will tell you if I can deal with it tonight.

("He's still losing weight.")

I will take that up with this idea of motion and response. I cannot answer it for you in five minutes. But I will tell you that expectation is highly pertinent here on both of your parts.... Now I bid you a fond good evening, and I will go into the weight problem rather thoroughly, after dictation.

("Good. Thank you very much." 11:29.)

SESSION 572 (DELETED PORTION)
MARCH 8, 1971

(Deleted from the 572nd session for March 8, 1971.

(11:03.) You told Ruburt that when he came down the stairs *(this evening)* you felt he would get well. This was an intuitive breakthrough on your part, and highly encouraged him. It is extremely important that you think and feel in those terms.

The feeling even astonished you, so by contrast it should show you your own mode of thought habitually, and by implication suggest Ruburt's. The experience should have been illuminating.

("It was."

(As noted in the earlier part of the session not included here I had the sudden feeling as I sat in the car waiting for Jane. We were going to the tax office this evening before the session, and I had gone ahead to get the car out of the garage, etc.)

He has finally decided to gain weight, and this in turn will alter his physical image and his conception of it for the better. Your sharing of the intuitive feeling however was extremely important and of great benefit. He needs encouragement, but then he will respond to it as a duck to water.

Your going out was good. I have mentioned this before. The larger variety simply of electromagnetic ranges makes for alterations in both your mental and physical states. Some loving, gentle but firm encouragement and practice on the stairs would be of help, and definitely a concentration upon achievements in any area rather than on failures.

I will have more to say at a later time, for definite steps will be taken to see to it that he relates more specifically soon with the exterior world. You follow me.

("Yes."

(Although in retrospect I don't quite understand what Seth meant.)

Do you have questions along that line? The health?

("No.")

The concentration on his work and psychic activities will help now. Tell him to stick to it. And I bid you a fond good evening, and a hearty good evening.

("Thank you, Seth. Very good. It's been a pleasure."

(Humorously and louder:) I am still sorry that you missed our class last week. You would have had some good laughs. I will talk to you this evening in the dream state.

("Okay.")

Do not be a donkey head, and remember.

(But I didn't.

("Okay. Good night."

(11:13.)

SESSION 580 (DELETED PORTION)
APRIL 12, 1971

(This material is deleted from the 590th Session for April 12, 1971. We wanted some data on Jane's slow movements. She discussed various recent attitudes, ideas and actions, etc., and became somewhat excited talking about them. Resume after break at 10:22.)

Now. Give us a moment.... Ruburt is, as you know, highly creative. What most artists do not realize is that the self is the first creation. They do not think of themselves as products of their own creativity. Because of Ruburt's energy and creativity, he has always perfectly mirrored and even somewhat exaggerated the condition of the inner self, its activities and inner postures.

In the past this was done completely at an unconscious level, with no conscious knowledge. He took no responsibility for his image. Since childhood, he expected later life to make up for any privations suffered earlier. Books were to bring instant success. The taste of limited success whetted his appetite during your tour. On the other hand he was afraid of it for the reasons given earlier, having to do with yourself.

The slowdown was physically expressed, both as an expression of the slowdown on the company's part after the initial burst of activity, representing here disappointment and anger. This also represented a cautionary slowdown however to reassure you that he was not going to take over, overshadow you, since you have worked so hard at your own art without any such recognition.

Indeed then here a compensation. He slowed down further in anger at the compensation, or what he felt to be its necessity. It also represented a slowdown in the activity from Prentice, in that he feels that if Tam were really interested in his book he would keep better track of it.

This was tied in with the felt slowdown of winter. He was also ashamed of himself for the reactions, and hence did not want to go out to be seen. There has been a slowdown of <u>subsidiary</u> psychic activity—dream recall and out-of-bodies, which is partially cyclic. He does normally slow down in winter, which is perfectly all right, taken alone.

He is very worried that you will not find success, recognition that is, or money of a large nature, and does not feel that he should if you do not. In a chaotic world of twisted reasoning he thinks his symptoms will take your mind off your own problems, and relieve you to some extent. He is hurt when people do not buy your paintings off the walls, and angry at anyone who mentions liking a painting without offering to buy it.

He is at his worst with you on the street because he does not want to show you up. The same applies when he is with you at home, with others present.

Now there is a connection here with mothers: some of this, though she is not present, connected with your mother. If your mother thinks Ruburt is more successful than you, then obviously she can see that Ruburt is paying for it. The same applies to those in your apartment house. Much of this stems from the young psychologist's remark, as <u>interpreted</u> by Ruburt, that he was using psychic phenomena to dominate you.

As things turned out, the psychic phenomena <u>was</u> a way to achieve success, and because he loves you he will be sure it is not at your expense. No one will say that he is the most dominant, or accuse him of this if he so obviously needs your assistance, walks behind you. This also means that you show your devotion more obviously, gallantly offering him assistance, thus always showing the world that what he is doing has your blessing.

A side point here, but with some reference: his mother always told him that he would destroy those he loved, and he feared that any success of his might show you up if you had not achieved your own. Give us time. *(Pause.)*

Actual continued success on the other hand would have been a definite experience that you could have met together, say then another tour. He could have been reassured by your reactions. The slowdown however gave him ambiguous feelings, lest success on his part meant further time from your own painting, which you would resent; so that in that respect continued success at tours would be at the expense of your valued painting time.

(11:47.)

Now give us time, and rest your fingers. I will leave our friend more or less the way he is for a few moments.

("All right." Jane sat quietly in trance, while I stretched a bit and rested my right hand. Then I told Seth I was ready to resume.)

Now. Rest or a nap in the middle of the day is the most literal and yet symbolic interpretation of a slowdown. Here on awakening he was confronted with the intuitive knowledge of what he had done, not only since the tour but to varying degrees before it. For to carry the idea through, he would have to stop completely.

You cannot try to go and stop at the same time, to be driven to achieve and not achieve, without some consequences. Earlier he felt the stronger apathy that so frightened him, at the height, or depths, of the depression, that being partially probed at the time if you recall. The idea of napping evocatively brings it to mind in less severe form, so that a nap was not a creative refreshing time, but a cop-out. That is, to his way of thinking.

Now he felt that *Rebellers*, representing his first book success, helped bring about your illness, and this feeling alone is responsible for much of this.

("*Did that book come out before I got sick?*")

It came out while you were becoming sick. Your mood was very poor, and he felt that you were angry and resentful at him because of its publication. You were not yet in the throes of your illness, and he felt that this represented the last straw to you—that it was not that good a book, not art as you thought your paintings to be, and yet it was published.

("*Did I feel that way?*")

You were angry and resentful. Part of this was a projection of <u>other</u> problems however, rather than specifically your attitude toward the book. Your attitude however was very negative. It shocked, frightened him, and made him think that perhaps his success could separate you. He knew the book was not art also, and felt guilty.

He felt that you were his accuser, and punished him by becoming ill. Before that he felt that your negative feelings were largely directed against your parents. At this point he felt they were directed against him. He had put a great weight of trust and loyalty in you, and felt lost, insecure and frightened. At that point he felt completely alone. Those feelings have largely dissipated, so that the loyalty, never withdrawn, is still vital.

This is all in the background of the difficulties. You stopped reading his dream book. He is again frightened as to whether or not it will meet with your approval.

("*He knows that's no problem.*")

He worries and looks for reassurance in that area.

("*Can I ask a question?*")

You may indeed.

("*I've wondered about this before: whether we should look for another publisher for your book.*")

As things stand now, do not make any changes. Give them a chance at it and see what develops. Much can happen before that time comes.

("*We've been very concerned about the advertising angle.*")

Let what I have said stand for now. You may take a break, or end the session as you prefer.

("*I guess we'll end it then.*")

I hope I have been of help.

("*Very much so.*")

My fondest regards, and a hearty good evening.

("Thank you, Seth. It's been a pleasure.")

It's always a pleasure from my end also.

(11:03. Jane's trance had been good. She said that at the end Seth had another remark to make, but that she didn't have the energy to get it out: "And thank you for fixing my chair." This is a humorous reference to my putting a new seat in Jane's favorite Kennedy rocker—her session chair, etc.

(11:05. Seth then returned briefly.)

One small note. This also has to do in our own private sessions, with Ruburt's slowness and difficulty getting out of the chair—to show you that he is paying for the success of the sessions.

("Yeah, but I don't expect him to pay for anything.")

In class sessions he does not feel this. You have always in the <u>past</u> (underlined) spoken of discipline. He was afraid that you would resent his success in something that seemed too spontaneous.

("No, I don't.")

(Humorously:) And thank you for fixing my chair.

(11:07. There was a little more here, spoken at a fast pace, to the effect that Seth wanted us to get the recorder fixed so that we could have a session without my taking notes for a change. Seth suggested that Jane or Sue Watkins could transcribe the notes, etc., while I commented that it would be quite a job, etc.)

SESSION 581 (DELETED PORTION)
APRIL 14, 1971

(This material is deleted from the 581st session for April 14, 1971.

(After break at 10:54. Resume at 11:09.)

Now. Do you want another question answered? *(On Chapter 20 of* Seth Speaks.

("Why don't you comment on the personal material you gave Monday?")

(Humorously:) I am not the one who needs to comment on it—

("I mean, why don't you add to it?")

Ruburt feels disloyal himself to even question your own success, and this is an important point. His own paintings and work are of a highly emotional nature. Intuitively he understands much about your work that he does not realize he knows.

His fears prevent him from happily using the knowledge. If you are particularly proud of a given painting, and he does not emotionally relate to it, then he feels guilty, or afraid he will offend.

Since he does not use his unconscious knowledge of your work in daily life, and since you do not talk of it often, then he searches your face to see how you may have done. He feels guilty when you are working if he is not, for fear you will think his success is coming too easily. Assurances on your part will be exceedingly successful.

("On just what, now?")

To the effect that you do want him to succeed, that his success will help you both. Now the age issue is connected to you and your work. In the beginning of your marriage you spoke often and vehemently of the limited nature of time and the importance of using it. If you were his age he would not be so frightened in this regard.

(Humorously:) He wants you to be a success while you are young enough to enjoy it. *(I laughed.)* Because he is younger he feels he should not be successful first. The freeing of feeling is indeed important on his part. To some extent he overexaggerated your response to emotionalism as he came to think of it, during your illness. This is also connected to your work in that he was afraid that his quite natural emotions would frighten you, and therefore impede your work.

The idea of writing his feelings down in one way or another is very good. Some of your early unfortunate responses, for example with *Rebellers*, were highly charged, you see, because of the circumstances. If possible countering suggestions should carry as much exuberance, or positive energy. They should be emotionally felt in other words, rather than merely verbal.

I will end the session. My heartiest regards to you both.

("Thank you very much, Seth. It's been very interesting.")

We will still have our session when we get our recorder.

("Okay." Jane is 42, I am 52.

(11:25.)

SESSION 582 (DELETED PORTION)
APRIL 19, 1971

(This material is deleted from the 582nd session for April 19, 1971.

(After break, 10:35.)

Now give us a moment.

I can do little except to back you up on your advice to Ruburt, because it is so excellent. He does need help in redirecting his thoughts in this fashion.

(This concerns my recent suggestions to Jane that she concentrate upon the beauty and pleasure of the moment; even when she is performing a difficult task, or

finds herself brooding, etc. At the same time I want her to realize that her body is perfectly capable of taking care of itself, of healing itself, if she will but leave it alone so that it is free to do so.

(*In other words, when I tell her to live in the pleasurable aspects of a moment, I don't mean for her to use this as a method of sweeping unpleasantness under the rug, etc.*)

Much of the muscular tension and rigidity is caused by such constant mental tension. He feels duty-bound to find out what is wrong, and that is how the habit so took hold. The concentration must be upon what is right.

(*"Well, in discussing this with him I was concerned lest he use the method to hide things."*)

You must take that into consideration, but the constant concentration upon the symptoms, and disapproval of self because of them, must cease. You can help him to relax in the moment as you did last evening by simple reminders and by play.

With this relaxation more tension will not build up. The muscles and body can relax. It would be better <u>for now</u> (underlined) that he concentrates upon this—his work and full activities. Then in alpha, easily and naturally, let images play into his mind of health and happiness. Your active support, as with getting up, is of great benefit, to reassure him that you will add your own strength to his.

Living in the moment will automatically let some of these things take place, and will automatically, again, stop negative projections into the future; even a five-minute future.

Now you may take your break or end the session as you prefer.

(*"Have you anything more on Mrs. Russell's missing son?"*)

I do not at this time.

(*"We'll take a break then."*

(10:45. This proved to be the end of the session. I suggested to Jane that she train herself to focus upon external objects while doing things like getting up and down, that had bothered her. I thought this might be a convenient way of diverting her thoughts, rather than depending on purely mental efforts; at times she might feel particularly like concentrating upon inner images, etc.)

SESSION 583 (DELETED PORTION)
APRIL 21, 1971

(*This material is deleted from the 583rd session for April 21, 1971.*

(10:25.)
Now, on the personal material, encouragement from you is highly important.

You are on the right track, and consistency must be applied here. Suggestion as you know adjusts weight, and heals the body as thoroughly as it can be used in the opposite way.

You surround yourself with objects, and an obvious environment instantly perceived. You also surround yourselves with an interior environment. The color of you walls can influence your state of mind—a simple-enough fact; but the uses to which you put words, both silent and verbal, affect the state of your mind far more.

The power of words has to do initially with the sound and symbols. Pleasant words, silent or spoken, instantly cause beneficial reactions, some noticeable and some not. They alter the state of the system which is of course never stable or constant. They mold the features of a face. The expressions come and go but certain habitual patterns remain.

What you need is a preponderance of constructive words. This often has nothing to do with numbers of words, but emotionally charged words. They sway the mental state in certain directions. Suggestions given then, good ones, to a mind already distracted by fear or worry, will do little good.

This latest adventure should bring all of this out in the open, while also training Ruburt to concentrate upon pleasant rather than unpleasant stimuli. His imagination can be given full rein, except that when he find himself using it negatively, he uses it as <u>strongly</u> in the opposite direction instead.

Whatever demands he makes upon himself should be uncomplicated and simple enough so that he has a good chance of following through on them—hence a feeling of accomplishment.

If he left himself alone work-wise there would be plenty of accomplishment, but he does not believe this. Of course he must make some demands of himself—reasonable ones. To be angry at himself for not doing his yoga, say, today can outdo the benefits of having done them earlier.

As he is feeding himself how, have him think of his thoughts as nourishment, so that he feeds himself constructive nourishing thoughts. He needs them. This will automatically allow him to gain weight faster, for much of the energy taken in goes out through these worries.

("I figured there was something like that going on.")

It is the habit, to one extent self-examination carried too far in that respect, of too much concern with the problems of the self anyway. As mentioned some time ago an overconscientiousness was also involved here.

You remind him not to project negatively into the future. He needs the reminder. Again, as mentioned, you helped him the other night, bringing him into the moment constructively, and this is what is needed. He also should be encouraged to feel his energy, and rouse it. When he demands it of himself it is always there. If this is handled correctly the entire project <u>can</u> (underline) incite emotional excitement. If so, it has excellent chances. The more exciting it can be made the better, for this alone will rouse his enthusiasm.

Now. You can ask me more questions or end the session as you prefer.

I have one other remark. <u>If</u> (doubly underline) you can manage, it would be good for you to oversee Ruburt's exercises—or perhaps even do some with him; again, to add to the sense of excitement and support. When he counted upon you finally to help him get up in the morning, this automatically relieved him of the responsibility for enough time so that the negative charges connected could subside, and a new habit began to show itself.

He was ashamed of needing you to do this for him initially, yet realized your support was necessary <u>at that point</u>. The problem was to help <u>him</u> reestablish his own initiative in that regard. In the same way, if he could count on you in the exercises for a while, this would relieve him of the fear that the project, begun unsuccessfully in the past, and not continued, would follow the same pattern. I do not suggest more than 20 minutes for him in the beginning however.

Your own attitude will also automatically be more constructive and hopeful as you see for yourself the resulting changes as exercises are continued. That is the end of the personal material. Now do as you wish.

("I guess we'll end it then.")

When you are out of your body in the state that you were in, this is an excellent time to give good health suggestions to the body. I expect that you will have more such projections, and I will have more to say to you about them.

("Very good. Thank you very much Seth, and good night." 10:52.)

DELETED SESSION
APRIL 25, 1971 10:45 PM

(Session for Sue and Carl Watkins; April 25, 1971, 10:45 PM.
Now, good evening.
("Good evening, Seth.)

This is your friendly marriage counselor—and you had better listen to me, both of you. Now give me a moment.

First of all, you have both been living in your own isolated universes, and this applies to my friend over here with the bare feet on the couch. *(Sue.)*

(To Sue:) Now you have been projecting your fears about yourself outward, so that all of your husband's remarks were interpreted in that light. This aggravated some of his own original conceptions. Some of your interpretations were legitimate, based upon his attitudes, but many more were the innermost doubts that you have not faced as to who you were, and deep questions involving the nature of your person as it is related to your particular sex in this life.

You were aggressively aware of the difference between your own attitude and some of society's in that regard, but for the first time in your life you were closely involved with another person, day by day—<u>who to some extent</u> (underlined) then served as a moving picture onto which you projected these fears as to your own worth.

Intellectually you are certain enough of your worth as a person, but emotionally not nearly as certain as far as other abilities are concerned. You wanted support. You wanted confirmation of your hopes and of your faith in yourself, but because of your fears these clouded the reality that you perceived.

I am saying then that some of your interpretations of the relationship were based on what you would call factual reality, but part was also based on your own insecurity.

(Humorously:) I am not done with you yet, but I do not want him *(Carl)* to feel left out over here, and while you are recovering I will speak to him: for you were also in your own isolated universe, and if hers had fears in it, then yours was a valley of desolation in which your emotions were like unruly animals galloping around in there; and you were so frightened and worried about your own worth that you could not consider hers, and you were so insecure that her sensing insecurity, when you were aware of it, drove you to anger.

You felt hardly strong enough to handle your own fears, and could not bear the thought that she might need your help also. Now even in her position, she made efforts to get across to you, and bridges that could cross her own fear to you, but you were not able to meet her because you feared the chasm of despair within yourself.

You did not see yourselves as people of integrity coming together in love, but as insecure individuals hoping that love could find the answer to fears that you were not willing to face otherwise.

There were, shall I say, errors on both parts. *(To Sue:)* You tried to relate more strongly. Your fears did not hold you back with the unreasoning strength that his held him back.

Now, I am going to take a break while my friend *(Rob)* reads back what

I have said, and then I will return. There is hope for both of you yet, singly, and/or together. You will have to face yourselves individually no matter what you do, and you will have to do this before you can see each other with any clearness.

(11:03. Jane's trance had been deep, she said. Her pace had been fast as she spoke for Seth; I had to ask her to slow down at times. I read the material aloud as suggested. Resume at 11:11.

(To Sue:) Now. You have felt for a long time that you were between the devil and the deep blue sea. That you had a mind and a womb, and that somehow the two did not go together. Regardless of past-life influences, which did exist, and granting some other interior reasons, you had a child to prove that you were a woman both to your mother and to yourself.

Then, you thought, you could be quite free to use your mind and your other abilities, and no one could say a thing because you could always say, "Obviously, I've proven my womanhood, and I'm free to use my mind."

(To Carl:) Now this was a poor-enough bargain for her to make, but for you to add to it in her mind, to demand that she prove this womanhood daily with the dishes or the housework or whatever, was too much for her to bear, and she felt doubly betrayed by you and by herself.

She showed you early in the game, in unconscious terms, that she could be a woman with the child. This was to let you know that she was whole and womanly, to settle that question for good. Then you would be free to accept her as a person. When it seemed that you did not do this, she was not willing to make more concessions, for she felt there were no more she could make.

Many subsidiary issues fall into place there—the attempt at time to follow along the lines of sports, to cooperate, to hide the womanly nature of which you are basically ashamed. *(The last phrase to Sue.*

(To Sue:) Now these attitudes have a false premise, and knowing the premise is false will give you much more freedom. With what you know now you should realize that in each life you have different abilities. You may express yourself through a different sexual nature, and you should realize that both are necessary. The idea against which you rebel is a very temporary social premise that is already beginning to disappear. So you need not fight that battle all of your life.

([Sue:] "I asked for solutions to this in the dream state, and got a lot of World War II stuff. Were these symbols?")

You did have an existence then. You were using the war connection however as a symbol for battle between the sexes.

Now give me a moment. *(Pause.*

(To Carl:) From your own parents you also have some false premises, having to do with sex. Now. You have been twice as upset over your own fears because you are a man, and think that a man should be free of them. You also find yourself in the position where you believe you should be the entire support of your family, and where you know you have both been taking the easy way out, and you hate yourself for it.

You were afraid that you could not make it alone, or support your family if it really came down to it. Part of this is because you think that she will demand the sort of environment from which she came—which, quite secretly, appeals to you immensely, and yet for which on the other hand you have nothing but scorn.

I will take this by gentle steps and *(to me)* let you rest your fingers.

(11:26—11:35.)

(To Carl:) Now, many of your own personal problems have to do with two main issues. One is your environment, and the other is your physical experience for the last few years in particular—say, since you went to college.

You have not felt that you succeeded at anything. You have not felt that you manipulated well in physical reality, in the world as it is, and to some extent you hated both the world and yourself for this. So you think that the world does not want you to succeed, and that the world, or the establishment, is out to get you. Instead you are afraid that regardless of their opinion, you <u>cannot</u> (underlined) succeed at all in the world as it is.

(Half humorously:) Your psychologist should have told you that. It is important.

Part of this is a result of your relationship with your father. When you were very young he frightened you. You felt him very powerful, aggressive, and unreasonably so in his behavior. It did not seem to you that you could become as strong as you felt him to be then—that whatever you did you would fall short.

Now give us time here. *(Pause.)*

There was a certain quality in him that held a hidden cruelty, of which you were frightened. Emotionally you also went out to your mother, but you felt that she was dependent upon him, and weaker, and so to some extent you were afraid of your own feelings toward her.

Your own artistic abilities also brought up problems, since they seemed in your mind, unconsciously, more feminine than masculine.

Your father cut out his own world, you felt, in his house and in the wilderness, comparatively speaking, but at the same time because you feared him so you did not really feel he wanted you to do the same no matter what he said—

because to prove yourself a better man would automatically destroy him.

You have kept yourself from achieving for this reason, and some others.

The affair with the women represented a deeper betrayal to your wife, since it meant that of all things you not only did not accept her brain, but now her body also. Now you have not come to grips with this deep despondency of your own, and you can do so. It is not nearly as deep or secret as you suppose, and there are some practical methods you can use to minimize its effects while you learn.

(To Sue:) This lack of confidence in himself has been picked up by you, and you accepted it. You should have been able to help fight it—put down here that I smiled, and add—ideally speaking.

Being with your parents brought things to a head, because both of your attitudes were aggravated by the environment; you *(Sue)* relating more as a young girl in the family homestead, and he reacting as the stranger who came in the back door.

(To me.) Now read that back.

(11:47. Jane's trance had been deep, her pace again fast. Resume at 12:01 AM after I had read the material aloud, etc.)

(To Carl:) Now. You feel your emotions. You seldom reflect upon them. You know many of your attitudes. You seldom look for the reasons behind the attitudes. You accept your attitudes at their face value.

You project your feelings upon the world and take it for granted that the world is what your feelings say it is. You accept your own attitudes toward yourself at <u>their</u> face value. They are attitudes of long standing. They were formed before you had any ability to reflect upon them, and now you have your relative dislike of reading, distrust of verbal expression, for example. You think of yourself as someone who tries to deal directly with the world through experience.

You think that reading is secondhand experience. You <u>think</u> you think that. Now many of these ideas come to you because of your attitude toward your father. You have not examined for 5 years, personally, your attitude toward yourself. You have simply accepted it as truth.

In your inner journeys you have traveled as far <u>away</u> from yourself as you could get, not as far inward as you could go. To some extent because of this you distrust your wife when she analyzes emotion or when she says to you why do you feel thus and thus a way. You do not want to know a good deal of the time.

Now a session for you earlier would not have had the impact of this one, or I would have given you such a session. *(To both.)* Now you know I will not say you should do thus and so, but the inner information I am giving you should be added to your knowledge as you assess the situation.

Now the challenges you both have can indeed be met within the framework of marriage, and can perhaps be best worked out in that fashion. They can also be worked out separately. If you decide to continue, the entire atmosphere must change. She must be encouraged to express her emotions and her abilities.

(To Carl:) You must learn to reflect upon your own emotional states, to ride the emotions like a rider upon a horse rather than the other way around—and to show gentleness, to reflect more upon your own attitudes. Your image is one that is very weak, and this you must change; for the image, again, is built upon false premises—and I will give each of you more specific particulars whenever you want them.

(Humorously:) Now I am not calling either of you down. I am not exactly giving you a medal, either.

([Sue:] "Where is Sean in all of this?")

The child can develop excellent abilities, and if your own relationship becomes a constructive one then he will more than learn from your experience. You both have characteristics that are highly advantageous to him. Reincarnational material I will give you another time. He is of such a nature that I believe he will be quite safe regardless of what you do.

Now read that back.

(12:19—12:29 AM.)

Now. You have had quite a bit for one night, but each of you can creatively use these problems, and turn them to your advantage, and this is a learning process in which you are both involved. It is not always an easy matter of saying no, and I do see both of you handling your situations well. Do not feel hopeless, and do not feel that you are failures. This is a point of time for you that in other ways has already passed, that you will look back upon. You are not caught in the moment. Request information therefore from your inner selves, and release your perceptions so that you clearly perceive the answers that you receive. You do have the abilities to solve these issues. Remind yourselves therefore of that fact, and do not tell yourselves that your situation in any case is a hopeless one.

Now. Would you have preferred not to be consciously aware of the information I gave you tonight?

([Sue:] "No."

([Carl:] "Alone, no.")

Then use it. Use it alone or together, but in any case you must use it. You will use it, for you have far more strength than you realize that you have. You have only to draw upon it. I know that you have it, and I know also that you will use it.

Now I bid you both a fond good evening. *(To Carl:)* Open your eyes. Within yourself you will find more than despair, Carl. Let yourself be flooded with inner realizations that are within you. They are your bridge, not only to yourself but to your wife. Hopelessness will not repair the situation.

(End at 12:34.)

SESSION 584 (DELETED PORTION)
MAY 3, 1971 9:35PM MONDAY

(This material is deleted from the 584th session for May 3, 1971. It grew out of Seth's answers to a couple of questions I asked for Chapter 20 of Seth's own book. They had to do with Seth speaking through Jane in her lifetime; with my help, etc.

(A carbon of the first part of the session is attached here, however, since the whole session applies to the question of Jane's symptoms, etc.

(Break at 10:09. Jane was well dissociated, she said. I read a few paragraphs from the first part of the session to her, since I thought them very important. The material led me to suggest some alternatives to our present routine and attitudes; Jane said the suggestions, which were only speculative at this stage, frightened her, but I did not intend this of course. I was only floundering around trying to find ways of relieving the symptoms, even if this meant suspending ESP classes, or the sessions, or whatever, while we tackled the problems at hand.

(Jane said she didn't know whether she could resume the session, but she did so at 10:37.)

Now. I have a few remarks to make.

When Ruburt is finished with his own book and I am done with mine, a vacation should come in any case, and will be not only acceptable but most beneficial.

His attitude <u>is</u> changing, and has been, and with your help it can change for the better. Any fear is not of the session. While it is not now <u>specifically</u> related to particular past events, it is still related to past training where he was led to believe that he must keep a tight rein upon himself; not go ahead full blast, and restrain the spontaneous parts of the personality, unless they showed themselves in "acceptable" fashion.

Poetry was acceptable. In other areas he feared that the spontaneous self could lead to childbirth. In the psychic area he was afraid it could lead to falsehood, much more for example than he feared anything like schizophrenia. With you, for a while, he felt the spontaneous self brought you only trouble—as per the Florida trip and so forth, and that he had better learn to control it.

When you were ill and did not have sexual relations often, he feared that his desires then could even lead him to physical unfaithfulness, and so on all counts the habit of repression and of physical repression also built up. All areas of life were to some extent included then.

Spiritually he felt that he <u>might</u> be leading people astray.

The symptoms were the result of strain, then. While they still allowed him to pursue those activities in which he was interested, the conscientious nature, the questioning mind that led him to investigate psychic realities, and that led him to learn so much, did not change overnight. They were of much too long standing.

They continued to question this experience as they had every other, and to apply the same overconscientious tests toward truth. The sale of the book and his influence led him to question anew that if he <u>had</u> such influence, it had better be based upon legitimate truths.

("Does he think it is?")

He thinks basically that it is, and he accepts the basic principles of the work—that is, the Seth material. He still finds reincarnation difficult to accept, but this is not the only sore point. Give us time. He <u>sometimes</u> is confused about the God concept also. He accepts the source of the material as beyond his usual self. If he were not committed to the material he would have ceased the sessions long ago. Do you have other questions now along this line?

("Do you mean for Chapter 20?")

No, personal material. The habit of thinking, again, is the point here—<u>Ruburt's pattern of thinking</u>.

("Do ESP classes aggravate his symptoms?")

As a rule they do not, unless they touch upon the points mentioned above. Or <u>when</u> they do.

("When *The Seth Material* *was published and we went on tour: did this revive or intensify his fears about leading people astray?*")

In the beginning, if you recall, he made little effort to have the material published, or even to deal with the material itself in those terms. His first book dealt with your experiments, done on your own in the main, and with their results. This happened, that happened: people could accept or reject.

The material represented a body of teaching, which was at variance not only with his own childhood religious background, but to some extent with the intellectual ideas of early adulthood. He made the jump to publish the teachings, to that extent, so far.

Then he realized that the coverage given on your tour, the people being reached, and so then again he wondered. He was also using his writing ability, or putting his writing ability at the hand of the material. Then again it had better be legitimate, since it was obvious he was being interviewed as a psychic who wrote, rather than as a writer with psychic abilities.

It made his position clear to him in the world's eyes, he thought. He did enjoy the publicity and the experience however, and he did, as mentioned, feel let down by Prentice later.

He did not like the Washington show at all, or the circumstances, and was upset by that. *(The second trip.*

("What do you think will happen with the next two books—the one he's finishing now, the dream book, and your own book?")

The initial rsponse was the strongest one of course because it was his first experience along those lines. Also he has grown to know himself more since then.

("But the symptoms have intensified.")

The other information I have given you about the symptoms also applies here, in the deleted sessions, since your return.

Now there is some more information I can give you, concerning the weather. I suggest however that you take a break—or I will give you the information in our next session as you prefer.

("We'll take the break."

(11:10—11:18.)

Now. I will not keep you. Your own statement of course was quite true, as to the concentration on negative aspects *(since supper time)*, but both of your attitudes have definitely improved.

Now Ruburt's weight gain is a prerequisite for continuing improvement, and happened also once in the past before the more recent negative aspects. At that previous time the weight gain preceded improvement.

I will not go deeply into the weather angle now because of the hour. There are two points here however. The physical condition reacts to some extent weatherwise, in that as Ruburt's Piper said, muscles behave differently *(in inclement weather)*. In the case of strong active muscles this is hardly perceptible. If there is any difficulty it simply becomes more noticeable, and can be minimized to a large extent through a different mental attitude—but it does exist.

Secondly, your moods are affected by weather, all kinds; as you know you form it to begin with. There is a constant interaction. Through association in periods of depression a connection can be built up—a habitual pattern in which bad weather suggests depression and vice-versa.

There are also electromagnetic changes in the atmosphere, constantly affecting the body, and if the body is wearied for whatever reason it is more sensitive to these. Take a poor day, a dark day for example, a poor habitual reaction, a handful of negative suggestions, and some symptoms, and it does not add up to much.

Understanding this however will let Ruburt take some countering measures, as he did today by thinking of how cozy it was inside to work, and how comforting the rain sounded.

Now I bid you a fond good evening, whether or not you enjoyed it very much.

("It was very instructive. Thank you very much, Seth. Good night.")

You have been working well together.

("Yes.")

(11:28. Jane's trance was again good. She said Seth was very affectionate tonight—that it was one of those nights, etc.)

SESSION 585 (DELETED PORTION)
MAY 12, 1971

(This material is deleted from the 585th session for May 12, 1971. Here are a few details of my own cold-like symptoms which began on Tuesday night, May 4, and which Seth discusses below. I had already received some insight on the problem by using the pendulum, but by tonight, Wednesday, felt exhausted by the symptoms.

(My pendulum related the symptoms to my decision to paint an oil from a small pen-and-ink sketch I had made in 1969. I pulled the little sketch, which was a free interpretation of what I considered to be a man facing himself, embodying certain distortions of face and form from my files recently and decided to paint it. For a surface I chose a cardboard canvas-covered panel made by one of the well-known artist's manufacturers. I don't often use such panels, usually thinking them not permanent enough; I almost always prefer Masonite, etc.

(To bolster the permanency of the panel I backed it with a wooden frame that I glued to the panel, to prevent warping, etc. I used wood for this that I found in father's garage in Sayre over the last weekend. On Tuesday afternoon when I began the blowup of the drawing to transfer in turn to the panel for painting, the symptoms began—coughing, sneezing, etc., much like aggravated hay fever symptoms. I also had trouble figuring out the right size to make the figures in the oil—nothing was going right, and after a while it was only too obvious that my subconscious was raising hell about the whole project.

(The pendulum told me that I was bothered by the idea of the possible lack of permanency of the panel I had chosen, and briefly that I was somewhat aware of the

change in this picture, as far as handling of form would be concerned, from my usual style of working. I told none of this to Jane at the time. I thought I had resolved the problem, but when the symptoms continued during Jane's ESP class Tuesday night, I realized I was wrong—the problem had not been cleared up.

(I felt much better while out working Wednesday morning, but the symptoms returned again Wednesday afternoon when I again tackled the project in the studio. I became angry and half disgusted, and began to realize that I would probably have to abandon the painting, since I wasn't resolving the problems. I was afraid that once the symptoms persisted for another day or so, I would have a cold or some such thing to handle, and that days could be spent clearing it up. I didn't ask Seth to clear anything. I was also struck by my reaction to the whole development, and couldn't help comparing my reaction to Jane's reaction to her own symptoms. I wanted out after a day of unease, but her symptoms had persisted now for several years. I felt intuitively that both sets of symptoms represented doing things that encountered resistance; my own symptoms seemed very instructive in this respect.

(I connected my symptoms also with the creed, mentioned in the notes proceeding the undeleted material for this session. As stated this creed grew out of the last, 584th session for May 3, 1971, Seth Speaks, *pages 321 and 322, where Seth discussed the ego's fear of being swamped by strong creative abilities, etc. I had felt for some time now that Jane entertained fears of this kind, and that they must be resolved.*

(Part of the creed involved Jane's listing what bothered her—indeed, it would end up covering all essential points in our lives, and I hoped would act as a guide and reminder. I was now beginning to feel that none of us were all powerful, and would have to live within whatever limits and capabilities we could handle. In short, there might be certain things that, even though we could do them, we might better not do, in order to maintain overall balance, health, etc. Which is another way of saying that we could accomplish our ends by perhaps slightly different methods.

(When I began to learn about my own symptoms, I started taking steps whereby I could present the same idea—of a man facing himself—in other ways, and shortly evolved several quite acceptable ways, that were in harmony with my ideas of pictorial form, permanence, etc. This experience was quite revealing. It taught me to consider all *portions of the personality—its needs, desires, creative drives and expressions, etc., and I intuitively linked this up with Jane's problems. It began to seem very clear to me that this was what she must do.*

(Elements of the creed would consider whether she should have these sessions, whether they should be public or merely private, whether they should be published now or later, or never, etc. I was, and am, anxious to do anything that will help, and will feel no regrets. Jane has already learned that she doesn't want to do merely psy-

chic, Seth books, like the Edgar Cayce series, for instance—*from her own work on the creed*. She wants to, and needs to, do work in which she is her own creator, and goes through the creative process from start to finish consciously, etc. It doesn't really matter that the Seth material is excellent, etc. What counts is her reaction to it, and the symptoms, as far as I can tell at this time, are all too clear a sign of her reaction to it—at least an important part of her is reacting this way.

(That a part of her did and does welcome the sessions and is indeed responsible for them, is not as important as that all elements of her personality respond to whatever she does in a positive way. As long as the symptoms last, it is a sign that all is not well. Changes are coming; they must; I don't believe they can be anything but for the better. There will probably be more to say on this later. I didn't plan particularly to ask Seth about any of this tonight; I was angry at myself and not in the mood to delve into anything, actually.

(The session resumed then after break from 10:25—10:32. See Session 585 in Seth Speaks.)

Now. I have some personal remarks for you, and then since we are well embarked upon our chapter, and since it is late, I will let you go.

("I'm doing all right.")

Give us a moment. (Pause.)

The idea of permanence in your mind is strongly connected with more representational work. You think of the old masters for example, the figure work. You are concerned lest the freer style itself implies a lack of permanency, in that you wonder how well others will relate to it as time passes.

(This is excellent information, and as has happened before where Seth discusses art, implies knowledge that I don't believe Jane would express in such terms.)

This, plus the feelings of the impermanency of the board account for the symptoms.

(Note that I had progressed this far on my own with the pendulum, but I hadn't reached a full understanding of the contents of the first paragraph, above. I'd had some glimmerings, but hadn't expressed any of them to Jane.)

The inner self is permanent regardless of its form of course, and the encounter of a man with himself is primarily an interior one. Do you have questions?

("Well, I can resolve this, can't I?")

You can indeed.

("I didn't want to be rigid in my ideas, and the way I expressed them.")

You did not encounter the difficulty in sketch form, you see—only when the idea of permanency in a painting came into issue. The remark I made about the inner encounter will help you reconcile the two positions.

("I thought this painting would allow me more of an expression of fantasy than I usually permit myself.")

It will indeed. It will in itself help break down any inhibiting, rigid factors in any of your work.

("What part of me is raising hell, then?")

You can accept completely abstract work, and do it well, though you would not be satisfied with it for a great time. *(True.)* This sort of a painting however, that uses figures or objects, but not in representational form, bothers you, while you are strongly attracted in sketches of the same nature. There is no dilemma: you allow the intuitive self spontaneous expression in those sketches. It is only when you transpose the same ideas onto painting and a more permanent form that you become uneasy.

(Excellent information, etc.)

Give us a moment here. *(Pause.)* You trust the extrerior sense of order you perceive in objects, and when they are distorted this brings a sense of alarm—again, in paintings, not sketches.

In this line of feeling, the distortions, artistic distortions represent those points where you feel that the irrational could enter in, or untruth. To portray an object faithfully represented a kind of truth to you. To represent it differently than it was, represented at best a half-lie—this from the exaggerated and distorted ideas of order that surrounded you as a child on the part of your father.

(Excellent. Part of this was quite unknown to me consciously, but is the kind of data that once realized falls instantly into place.)

Intuitively you knew better, and *(but?)* when painting was concerned—your career, you did not allow yourself the freedom. In sketches which were fun, and to you not permanent, you permitted the spontaneity.

I will have Ruburt put out his cigarette, and continue.

("Okay." I had been coughing again, etc.)

Your father always tried to fix objects that were broken. To some extent you carried this with you, so that objects or figures not painted correctly, in those terms, should be fixed. The order seemed broken.

("Yes." This was very perceptive.)

There will be no problem however as you become aware of these connections. You looked for great order, to create in painting an ordered universe, to find perfection that ideally you felt should be in the exterior world, and yet was lacking. You discovered that order itself springs from spontaneity, and this is your first real attempt to bring the two together. Do you have any questions?

("No, I think that covers it. I can make the connections now.")

(Nevertheless, I have laid the projected painting aside, at least for the time

being, although I did arrive at what seems to be an acceptable solution to all portions of my personality. At least the pendulum agrees to this. But it is Sunday, May 16, as I write this, and the symptoms are still with me—to a much lesser degree. They are gradually wearing away, in the same way, I suppose, that I will gradually come to reconcile the conflicts I became aware of through this whole episode.

(In the meantime, I told myself I would know how to proceed with painting; the result is that I returned to a small portrait I began several months ago, and left unfinished while I tackled some other problems. With this decision I feel I am back on a kind of track that will lead to more developments; some of these developments may possibly include the kind of painting that triggered the episode; if so, if compatible, all to the good. Whatever happens, much was learned and will be put to use.

(I am finishing up a series of half a dozen life-sized portraits, at the end of which, I told myself some time ago, I would feel free to embark upon larger projects of whatever choice I made. The smaller painting mentioned above is part of this series; so in returning to this I think I made a good decision. The pendulum agrees.

(Seth had paused, so I asked a question I hadn't particularly planned on. The elements behind the question have been explained.

("What do you think about those discussions Jane and I had earlier in the week, about giving her more freedom?"

(And embodied in our "creed" that we are now working on...)

They are very beneficial, and issues that should be brought into the open. When they are repressed they gain a charge out of all proportion, to which over-reactions can then occur. There is no reason for him to confine himself to psychic books alone, in any case.

I have myself repeatedly urged him to write more poetry. He must of course make his own choice as to the extent to which he wants to commit himself to our work. His feelings in all directions bearing on these issues should be aired, acknowledged, discussed, and then action taken in line with what he discovers.

(This is an admirable acceptance on Seth's part of whatever developments occur. He is probably more acutely aware of possibilities than I am, although I have been turning them over at a great rate lately. Some things are bound to be changed, I feel. It's too early for decisions to be given here, and perhaps no hard and fast rules are needed... but some changes in attitudes are, certainly. I don't mind stating that I felt sadness now as I contemplated some of the alternatives I'd been entertaining lately.)

A vacation in any case is needed, quite naturally. He need not plunge into another contract, for example. Rigidity of attitude, setting up either/ors, is a problem, and you can help him recognize when he does this.

(Is he still concerned about me, resulting in a slowdown of movement on his part?

(In earlier deleted material, Seth told us that Jane's slower physical motions since the publication of The Seth Material *was, in part, caused by her desire to slow down to give me a chance to catch up to her own success, etc., through my painting.)*

To a large degree that has been taken care of, because of your own reassurances.

(But she moves as slowly as before, I thought: "I'm just wondering where that leaves the impetus for the slow motion, then.")

The pressure put upon him by himself, and discussed by you, having to do with his own work. The unresolved and partially-buried attitudes that you have written down upon your paper *(our creed)*, and the fact that many of these were so repressed that he would not think about them himself, much less discuss them with you, unless he was driven to it.

(My feelings exactly.

("Have we covered all major points in that paper?")

You have indeed. The ones now important.

And now I bid you a fond and therapeutic good evening.

("Thank you, Seth. Your help is appreciated, it really is. Good night."

(11:03.)

SESSION 589 (DELETED PORTION)
AUGUST 4, 1971

(This material is deleted from the 589th Session for August 4, 1971.

(It is Seth's interpretation of Jane's very interesting dream of this morning, and was given after he had finished dictation for the evening on Chapter 22 of his book: Seth Speaks*—A Goodbye and an Introduction.*

(10:45.)

Give us a good moment.

Ruburt needs you to do his best work, and the support that you give him. He trusts you. In the dream he follows you where he wants to go, but he needs your confidence to help lead him.

The dream has several aspects. First the defined steps going upward represented <u>fairly</u> (underlined) ordinary steps that had to be taken, that others had taken before you. They were clearly defined as such. Even then Ruburt wondered about them. They became less defined as you went higher.

Finally you were led to travel to the top where there were no defined steps, but a smooth, steady ascent with no steps as such to follow. You got there first and helped Ruburt. This means that in your inter self you have a clear idea of the goals which Ruburt, for many reasons, some quite legitimate, hides from his practical self.

He was afraid he would be turned upside down, and in the dream he was before he attained the top. This represents his tendency to look back over the way he has come.

On a physical level the dream had another meaning—that after awhile he will not be worried about stairs and walking. The method of getting upstairs will no longer concern him, simply the ascent, and that the two of you together are conquering the physical situation.

The dream also shows his willingness to follow you in both cases, and emphasizes your confidence in his abilities. It shows the two of you again with common goals, working together.

The man represented the reason for the symptoms—the dark side, which you both decide to avoid. You leave him in the woods, and then begin the ascent.

("This doesn't mean we're avoiding the problem, does it?")

It means that you have no more association with it, that you leave it in the woods from which you both emerge for the ascent.

On another level the man represents various distractions of a negative kind; a refusal to be held back by any more commerce with him.

Give us a moment. In the beginning tine house is small. Ruburt wants to put up the window so that a porch can be added to living space. Instead you lead him out of the house. This represents your current and late attempts to lead Jane outside physically, and your determination to get you both out of the woods.

She wanted to hide inside the house. You led her through the woods past the symptoms represented by the man, to the ascent.

Now you may take a break or end the session as you prefer.

("We'll take the break.")

(11:05. This was the end of the session, however.)

DELETED SESSION
AUGUST 16, 1971

(This is the regularly scheduled session for Monday, August 16, 1971. It is deleted from the record.)

Good evening.

("Good evening, Seth.")

Now. The healthy person takes health for granted. He takes it for granted as he does the air that he breathes. He can appreciate his health as he can appreciate the air, without feeling that either is going to be taken from him. He is not concerned with his health because he takes it on trust unthinkingly, as he takes his life on trust.

You take your artistic ability on trust. You consider it a part of you. Ruburt considers his writing a part of him. There are people highly gifted with artistic abilities, who have never trusted those abilities, did not consider them a part of themselves, and practically speaking have been unable to use them.

The abilities have always been present, however, latent as within each man health is there, though perhaps latent in the same way. The rich man thinks of wealth as a part of himself. He takes it for granted he has it and will achieve more. The poor man takes his poverty for granted, actually on trust, and takes it for granted he will have more of the same.

In all of these areas expectations bring about physical reality.

The life that you two personally have, has been brought about through trust and expectation. Your artistic endeavors are the result of trust and expectation. Now, only a comparative few operate in such a manner that their entire lives, in all areas, bring about the results they think they are after. The danger is in concentrating upon the lacks, the "sore spots," building up greater concentrations of mistrust. In very important issues, both you and Ruburt are in excellent health. In every important manner, you personally are in the best of health.

So is Ruburt in all areas, except that one upon which he has concentrated negatively, and given up trust. I want you to realize that in very important ways, and even in the health area, you are both successful.

Ruburt has always taken it for granted that his organs functioned well, the living organs upon which survival is dependent. There were two areas that he did not quite trust. These were connected with the past, but only in so far as the distrust grew there. But the lack of trust is the important issue.

One had to do with the in quotes "problem" of artistic creativity versus womanhood, and this along with personal background brought about a distrust of the feminine organs. Not in such a manner that illness would result therein, or, say, diseased organs, but only so far as function was concerned.

Later, with certain issues that arose between you, fairly well understood now, I think, he felt his womanly qualities a threat to you both, and the habit of mistrust became manifested in a suspension of monthly periods. We will give you some suggestions on this when I am finished.

The mistrust of mobility, or fear that it could be taken away, was built up also, with other reasons given in the sessions, simply through the suggestion over the years of living with someone who was not mobile. The proximity alone. While Ruburt trusted the body then in all other areas, these two points represented holes in his armor, so to speak.

When inner challenges and problems went unrecognized for some time, and became physically materialized, these were the areas chosen. The resulting symptoms then served to reinforce the initial lack of trust. A state of faith in reverse therefore operates.

The rules are the same: as you believe, so you are. Now even after the initial causes of the mistrust no longer strongly operate, you are left with the results of in quotes "your faith," in this case the faith in immobility. As already discussed, the exterior situation then serves to reinforce the inner data, and it seems to fly in the face of all reason, to deny exterior symptoms. You follow me here.

(*"Yes."*)

This is all apart now from good and evil. It does no good to say "Why should such things be?" since you are here to learn <u>how</u> (underlined) thoughts, feelings and emotions are materialized physically.

This is to lead up to Ruburt's "as if" game. It is an excellent method. It will work if he follows it, through you must not look for results, in those terms, quickly.

You are left with, as of now, the results of negative beliefs, projected upon certain portions of the body. The old charges have pretty well worn down. You should try to help him in this game—understanding how it works. Even if you want to play it with him, it is extremely important that it is an "as if" imaginative game.

Up to now you both have been playing the illness game strongly, in your imagination both creating symptoms, imprisoning Ruburt within them in the present, seeing them in the future, and examining future events in the light of present symptoms.

So you understand how to play the game. We just want it reversed.

You need some reminders. I am not speaking now necessarily to you, for I have said this before: remember areas of health and vitality. As far as your living quarters are concerned, enjoyment of them, taking spaciousness for granted, loving the idea of it, will bring you more.

Ruburt's enjoyment of the trees will lead you to an area of greater trees. His enjoyment of class money will lead to more. In any of these areas however concentration upon the lacks would reinforce <u>these</u>. I want you to see what you do right, so that you can apply it to these other areas.

In his "as if" game, have Ruburt imagine he is having his period, buying his Tampax. This is all he need do—not hammer the point. This and your satisfactory sexual relationship, now, will also help. He feels more now that you accept him as a woman. For a while he felt you did not.

A note: the reincarnational information you received was quite legitimate—and with some little application on your part entire episodes of that existence could become clear, with little relative effort.

("Was my father there in that class?")

He was indeed.

Now give me a moment. *(Pause.)* My book will do very well. Take this for granted.

("I think we already do.")

The reincarnational material that you have received should enlighten you. There is an important reason for your love of detail, and also there are charges connected with this. The details represent far more to you than you realize. You do not love detail for detail's sake, for example, but you can overreact strongly in such areas.

Now when your idea of truth, or art, or artistic integrity, is connected with detail then the charged areas show themselves. This applies often in your paintings, and can in certain areas of my book where you are involved.

One wrong or bad apple, you feel, can rot the whole basket. When your idea of artistic vision is concerned then, each detail is of utmost importance to you. Details represent steps to truth, to you, in those areas. Other parts of you realize quite will the importance for example of inspiration, in which the steps or details do not appear in logical terms, so you allow both aspects to balance themselves.

You may take a break.

(10:10—10:30.)

Now. The "as if" game brings the picture of health into the present. Ruburt sees himself imaginatively as completely healthy and free now, which is something he has not been able to do. That is extremely important.

This is done in such a way, when it is done correctly, so that no comparisons against present behavior is involved. The <u>idea</u> of health however becomes as persuasive as ill health was.

The idea of playfulness, and even of fun and ease, must be maintained. Ruburt must find the game fun, not resolutely pursue it. The "as if " will automatically retrain muscular motion, and without effort.

Let us look at a scene from a play called "Getting Up in the Morning."

It has been acted out imaginatively and physically, with some changes and variations. Generally however it has been the same. This scene will change not necessarily because of any particular effort to reenact the scene differently imaginatively, but because of the overall "as if" game. You follow here.

("*Yes.*")

The set and expectations will change. It is important that you try to play this with him, or know what he is doing, simply because you reinforce each other so strongly. So you play your own "as if" game with him. This will help. Do it in the same manner. As Ruburt knows from his reading today *(Psycho-Cybernetics)* when the dawn suddenly burst, any discouragements should be accepted as part of the learning process with which he is involved—and the failures, particularly of the past, forgotten. You should not remind him of them either, or concentrate upon them yourself.

In the past he often used the image of himself, in his terms "before I got sick," as a basis of comparison. Worse, he sometimes used the twenty-year-old physical self, which automatically led to some very negative attitudes, since he simply is not twenty.

He wants to be a healthy present self, not a healthy past self. A good deal of the weight problem is not a problem. You have both to some extent overexaggerated it. He can use more weight. The energy used in worrying about the condition has taken up the small leeway that would have given him weight. In the best of health he will not be a heavy person, for example.

When advance is seen in these other areas, the weight gain will be automatic. In seeing himself in his "as if" game, the healthy image should include ordinary weight, but without stress upon it.

Now certain habits should automatically drop away if the game is played correctly. He is not dressing with the freedom of an ordinary healthy good-looking young woman, for example, so he must dress for the role in his "as if" game. Healthy women do not dress to cover up their bodies, to hide their knees or their arms. They dress to show them off.

If the "as if" game is played correctly the dressing habits will change automatically, again without stress. Ruburt fears humiliation. Acting as if he were perfectly healthy, such imagined humiliation would not be automatically projected. This is one area where both of you will have to watch, contrasting the game against <u>immediate</u> physical data.

It shows however a lack of freedom in a pivotal situation. I said pivotal because the dressing brings together both the idea of mobility and womanliness—both past areas of mistrust. The sexual area also combines both the lack of mobility and the womanly aspects, so freedom and the "as if" game in these areas is doubly important and vital.

Again, here particularly the game should not be carried out resolutely but with an idea of imaginative fun. There need be no decision on Ruburt's part to wear short skirts all the time, for example. That would not be freedom either.

Done properly this game will be played almost automatically, but the entire mental patterns will change and hence the physical. Quickness of mobility will easily return. The suggestions should also be retained. They are very helpful. The "as if" game will increase the suggestions' worth by dissipating habitual areas of thought that combat them.

The creative block in the writing has been worked out. And for <u>now</u> (underlined) let the dream book rest. It will be used.

Spending money as Ruburt has been doing, and his freedom with his creative-writing money, will give him more. In this area, and in taking on greater rent, you act on the trust that more is available, and so it has been and will be.

You should look for a house when you are ready, that you want and desire regardless of the amount that it cost, and the means to get it will come. If you think you are being reasonable by looking for a lesser house, that seems more within your means, then you are selling yourself short, lacking the trust that more will be given. The feeling toward such a house will automatically guide your experiences within it. Do you follow me here?

("Yes.")

This is indeed a potpourri of a session.

There will be far more organized sessions to come, and other books, but used correctly this information is most vital. People go from illness to illness and from poverty to poverty from lack of the knowledge I am giving you.

Now take your break.

("Thank you.")

I am not making you overextend yourself this evening.

("It's very interesting.")

(10:46—10:55.)

Now. This release on Ruburt's part will also release you both in other areas that have been inhibited. Open expressions of warmth are extremely important, on both of your parts in your daily life, and are also connected with your creativity as well as your health. This applies to you and to everyone.

This also applies—this trust of open warmth—to internal data, psychic information and inner experiences. If you allow yourself the freedom you can draw for inspiration not only from this life's experience, but for your painting use visual memory from your other existences.

Emotional feeling will also emerge as you remember people and faces that you have known, and places that you have loved. Many excellent artists have drawn from this source. The willingness to trust opens up these and many other doorways to perception and creativity.

Past feelings of abundance from other lives can help you ignite a current love of abundance and concentration upon it. When you, now, Joseph, find yourself enraged, or even just upset, about world conditions or the behavior of your fellow men, certainly admit your feelings and express them. Realize however that it is up to you in which areas of reality you concentrate.

An overconcentration in those areas helps bring about those conditions in your own experience. There are great parallel existences now occurring, always occurring, all taking place within the area of physical activity. To some men there is no good. The world is not to be trusted, and their experience proves it. Others dwell in a world that is filled with all kinds of abundance. Both worlds are real, both are created by those who experience them. You know that robbers exist. You do not dwell on the matter however; it hardly overbalances your greater feelings of trust, and so while granting that thieves live, you go unbothered.

If you began a practice of following all reports of such crimes, you would soon find yourself experiencing the fact of thievery, drawing to you those people because of your own concentration. The same applies to all areas of activity.

Despite your feelings against this house, generated because of Mr. Spaziani, at least on one level, your love of it was picked up by your present landlady for several reasons having nothing to do with the house. She has great respect for your painting, and for Ruburt's abilities, and you knew her when she was a soldier in Rome. It is for this reason that she painted the halls, and made the apartment adjustment. In this case the past overrode your negative ideas about the house when she bought it.

Now you may end the session. I am going easy on you until my book is typed up.

("Well, we can take a break.")

You may indeed.

(11:09—11:25.)

Now. It may seem to you that ideally one should be so highly proficient that in one life you are gifted with excellent health, great abilities, power and wealth. The fact remains however that many individuals choose to "specialize" in quotes, learning for example how to translate creative thought into physical form, or into physical abundance, and relatively ignore other areas.

In some cases an imbalance is deliberately chosen, as I have mentioned, for various reasons, for the sake of experience, for emphasis. Some seek and achieve wealth simply to learn the lesson that wealth alone is not the answer to life's problems, so they are wealthy and unhappy—though they need not be wealthy and unhappy. You follow me.

Reincarnational challenges need not take a lifetime to satisfy however. Some such problems are settled in mid-life or even before, and new challenges set. You are not stuck with a situation, then, because of a previous life. You gave it to yourself in order to solve it.

We will indeed write a book which will make all this quite clear, where you are not taken as examples. Here however we start with the personal.

Now Ruburt was a priestess in that life—

("In Rome?")

—when you were in Rome, and did not know Sue. There was no great connection with you, except that you visited her once, and the two of you were both involved in what you may call the in quotes "mystery" religions. You were seeped in such lore, having been born in Greece rather than in Rome. Ruburt acted as an oracle, and you consulted her at one time.

Now I am going to end the session, out of regard for the typing you still have to do on my book.

("It's not so much.")

Read and apply this session.

Some night I will give you some pointers on practical matters having to do with letters you receive, the future of the material, and other matters. A hearty good evening.

("Thank you very much, Seth. It's been very interesting.")

Whenever you are ready with your recorder, it is fine with me.

("Okay—maybe Wednesday night, then. Good night.")

(11:35.)

SESSION 593 (DELETED)
AUGUST 30, 1971 MONDAY 1:06 PM

(The first part of this session, being personal, was not used in the Appendix for Seth's book. Therefore I let its typing-up go until we had finished with the book. The book was mailed to Prentice-Hall on November 15, after extensive rewriting of the notes, additional proofreading, etc. Jane and I now are free, we feel, to do our own thing.)

Good evening.

("Good evening, Seth.")

Now. I will give you some material for our appendix. First I have some personal notes, if you do not mind.

("Nope.")

Now Ruburt is literally floating free from his difficulties. He made an important statement this evening concerning habits. Some new habits have finally taken; consciously he has learned to leave himself alone enough so that the body can clear itself.

(On November 16, as I type this material, Jane's condition is the same, as far as I can tell.)

The morning and evening suggestions that you initiated (underlined), and the longer list, have helped. The environment change has been of great benefit, but also because he was ready. Talk out what you were discussing before the session, for there are variances here, errors in communication on both of your parts. You can clear these up easily when each understands exactly what the other means in given definite situations—so go over those particular events. See what each of you meant by what you did or said, what the other thought you meant, and your reactions.

This is simply poor communication and misunderstanding, but you should both clear it up.

A word about what Ruburt calls his "helper." In the past he drained his reserves. Now they are building up in all areas. There are excess energies now that act as magnets, drawing other positive energy to him in such proportion that the entire gestalt becomes in effect a psychic helper.

Now this does have personality characteristics in terms of consciousness and intent. Very positive ones, initially set into motion by Ruburt's desire to help others, and attempts to do so. This is a form built up by him unconsciously in a realm other than the physical, and it is gaining in strength and expertise.

He will be able to send it to help others, and it will learn to do so with practice. It will become then more powerful in terms of good. It was always available. His late feelings of joy and release and the refreshment he is finding in nature, released him from private circles of nervousness, and opened channels through which positive energy did accumulate.

This helper now automatically helps heal Ruburt. Ruburt's emotional energy is very strong, as you know. Thoughts and feelings of dejection were too faithfully materialized. Now the change shows in an acceleration also, in attraction toward the creative and positive which very quickly generated the birth of the helper.

It is indeed the opposite version of his black thing.

It will also be able to guide him in a highly personal manner, again, as it continues to develop. It is born and nurtured in those feelings of peace, joy and contentment that he experiences watching his oak tree. *(Out the kitchen window.)*

This is accumulative, you see. This sort of phenomena occurs in one way or another with those who have the capacity to draw upon great energies, but the manifestation, you see, can be beneficial or detrimental.

("Yes. I was wondering about that.")

These are personalities, in that they do possess consciousness, in this case built upon Ruburt's most creative tendencies. Such personalities are extremely faithful.

("Did he have a negative personality like this?")

That was his black thing, formed by him.

("I mean consistently over the past few years.")

To that extent it was consistent. It was not driven however by intent. In one way both personalities were accidental, in that Ruburt did not consciously (underlined) form either. In deeper terms however it was a creature of default, of frustration, and lack-of. *(Seth's punctuation.)*

When the frustrations were faced and worked through more and more, the creature then lost its strength. It was not given the unifying qualities of intent and purpose. In the helper, you see, you find a binding quality, where the deepest drives of the personality for good are freed, actually, released in another realm of activity to continue the personality's main intents.

The black thing simply raged. You must understand however that the black thing also served its purpose, for Ruburt was finally able to recognize moods that corresponded to it. You both came close to this recognition during your vacation when you discussed a black ball or atmosphere that you threw back and forth, a pall.

Ruburt has found again what you never really lost—the sense of daily joy of existence—which he allowed himself unknowingly to relinquish for some time. Follow the advice given you earlier this evening, the both of you.

Now this helper, as time goes by, can be counted upon to help you in whatever ways it can, as long as Ruburt continues in his present frame of mind and habit, for this itself is bringing about improvements in all areas of your lives.

Ruburt should make a habit of addressing his helper now and then, and of building up rapport. The more that is asked of it the better it will perform, and the greater its own development will become. It needs training, and enjoys it, but the training must be gently and kindly.

I will have more to say concerning this at another time, for Ruburt can use the information. Now I suggest you take your break and we will continue.

(9:39. My original notes contain a few cryptic remarks here about such things as "our discussion," "many ramifications apparent," etc., and of course I've long forgotten just what they referred to; other than the general tone of the session material,

I suppose.

(Since August, when this session was held, it seems that little if anything has developed re Jane's helper. The ideas seem to be very good ones, and I remember that when the session was held we had high hopes. For one reason or another—or several—they have been set aside; finishing Seth's book contributed of course. It's educational to type up this material after such a long interval—but also somewhat discouraging, I'm afraid. I do not hear Jane mention the concept of the helper very often. The term will crop up when she has some kind of related psychic experience occasionally, but that seems to be all. Resume at 9:50)

Now. We have gone very lightly into such material, because of the interpretation that can be, and has been, given to it in the past. If you are not careful, you see, you end up with whole leagues of in quotes "devils and angels," only completely disconnected from human personality. Independent agents of good or evil, out to tempt men or save them, as the case may be.

You end up with the casting-out of devils, which can be of great benefit, incidentally, <u>if</u> (underlined) the sufferer happens to <u>believe</u> (underlined) he is possessed by one.

I have told you often that you create your reality physically. Obviously you create your psychic and spiritual reality also. You are <u>aware</u> (underlined) of the physical environment that you create. It is the mirror image of the inner environment, but of this you are usually not so aware. Your reality exists, as you should well know by now, in many dimensions.

Feelings and emotions attract in the physical universe and in any other their own kind. They form together, coalesce, they cleave together. In your system there is some lag before physical reality catches up with your inner conceptions. In other realities there is no such lag, for reasons that by now you should understand.

At one time therefore Ruburt's fears greatly overbalanced his hopes. Feelings of desolation outbalanced feelings of joy. In a concentrated form in this other realm, this self-image was reflected. Following the laws of attraction, it drew to it other such realities.

(Pause.) Ruburt was made aware of the fact in an out-of-body state when they came face to face. He kept careful note of his feeling and reactions during that time, and knew he could not get in that state of mind again: so he started in quotes "upward." The old habits however had to be broken down in <u>both</u> realms.

The black thing and the helper are always latent in those terms. Great energy is required however, so many people are not acquainted with these. They do not have the energy capacity to form either. They may however use symbols instead, upon which they vent negative feelings. Do you follow me?

("Yes." Pause at 10:05.)

Now. You are on the threshold of forming your own helper. You helped Ruburt in both of his creations. *(Leaning forward intently:)* These helpers are simply possessed of a different kind of consciousness than your own. In one way they are formed from you, but considerable work of one kind or another is done often before they are released, and set free to work within these other realms for you.

Now these beings can be perceived of course by others, either traveling through those realms or within them. They are not thought-forms. They are energy forms. *(Pause.)* They know others of their kind. They can communicate with the psychic or spiritual levels of consciousness of living persons. *(Long pause.)*

In one way they are automatic offshoots or products, except that once created, because of their nature and their nonphysical environment, their abilities far surpass your own in terms of acceleration. Is that clear?

("Yes." Pause at 10:15.)

The black thing could be called a shadow image. The dark side of the personality gaining dominance for a time. The helper represents the strongest, most creative aspects of personality, gaining greatly in ascendancy. In between you see the image is much the same as the one shown by the normal personality—the weaknesses and strengths balancing out.

Often the black thing, or dark side of the personality, sensed and acknowledged that it was responsible for the helper, or the helper's birth. Do you follow me there?

("Yes.")

Those familiar with a helper very rarely ever experience their equivalent black thing again, though the black thing can appear many times before the personality changes its ways, and grows.

In your case, Ruburt's black thing served for both of you. By watching him you learned many lessons that you sorely needed to learn.

Take your break.

(10:21. Resume on the Appendix for Seth's book at 10:30.)

SESSION 597 (DELETED)
NOVEMBER 22, 1971 9:02 PM MONDAY

(This is our first private session since September 27, 1971. During the long

layoff Jane and I worked on Seth's book, editing, rewriting notes, etc. The book was delivered to Prentice-Hall a week ago today. Jane called the publisher today, and learned that The Seth Material *is due in paperback probably in January, with Seth's own book to be published next October.*

(Jane said she was somewhat nervous as we sat waiting for the session tonight. I had some doubts of my own. These were connected, with the sessions per se. I wasn't sure, really, whether Jane wanted to resume them now, or wait, etc. I finally asked her this afternoon whether she wanted to have a session this evening.

(Jane said she finally became aware of "half-formed words, or something like that," from Seth, as we waited for the session to begin. I found I had to work harder taking my notes, to remind myself of the many symbols and signs I had worked out; some of these had temporarily slipped my mind, I discovered. Jane's pace was brisk.)

Now, good evening—

("Good evening, Seth.")

—and welcome back. And tell our friend that I said welcome back to him also.

(Jane has had some rather brief sessions in ESP class during the interim.)

Now I told you that when the book was finished, you could feel free to have some private sessions if you so desired. You are welcome to them but that is up to you.

(I had forgotten this. I'd planned to use our recorder for these sessions, too. "Well, give me some time to plan out what I'd like the sessions to cover, then we'll see.")

There is a session I promised to our lady of Venice also.

("Yes." Plus two others that Jane was committed to.)

Now then. It is true that thoughts form reality, but the thoughts are like passengers, riding atop of emotional feelings, or feeling-tones. The feelings obviously help form the thought. On the surface there are many feelings, sometimes highly ambiguous, that rise and fall and often compete for domination.

Far beneath however, at any given time in your terms, there is a dominant, characteristic, unique feeling-tone that pervades the personality and colors all of the other activities, feelings and thoughts. There is also a rhythm at this level however, and such a basic feeling-tone will also of itself change into another. Feelings and thoughts exist in the ground of the basic feeling-tone.

(I heard a man and a woman begin to climb the stairs from the front entrance of the apartment house. They clumped on up past our floor to the one above, sounding very loud and clumsy. As I feared, they had come to call on the tenant who lived

in the small apartment above our living room, where we were holding the session. I heard the door open, then slam shut, and a babble of voices. Footsteps began to resound back and forth overhead. I was of course highly irritated, as I always am at such interruptions during sessions. Jane, in trance, kept speaking though, seemingly not bothered.)

In the case of individuals such feeling-tones pervade all experiences and perception, and can even therefore alter the perception of reality, therefore effectively changing it. En masse the same story is true. The world as you know it therefore at any given time is pervaded by its own "ground feeling-tone" in quotes, which becomes the medium from which and in which other feelings and ideas emerge.

These are all highly creative, regardless of the apparent effects of what you would call the less desirable ones.

In a large sense different basic feeling-tones can dominate various incarnations. It must be understood that these are not static, however. These are reflected in every area physically and en masse, from the kind of thoughts entertained to the type of architecture chosen, say, by a people, and the general state of mental and physical health.

Now we are leading here into some personal and yet generally applied material.

Ruburt is indeed out of the basic feeling-tone that brought about his malady. The feeling-tone however also helped to bring about our sessions as well, even though he did not become ill in your terms until afterward.

The feeling-tone, somewhat generated in childhood as I told you, was momentarily changed for the better when your relationship with him began. The feeling-tone however was one of the issues that led him to seek so for answers, and also made it very difficult for him to accept them.

The creative liberation in his own work *(since Seth's book has been finished Jane has started two books of her own)* is a clear symptom on the positive side of the change in feeling-tone, as was the more expansive idea of adding to your establishment. *(Renting the second apartment, across the hall from the original one.)*

It is the feeling-tone even more than the thoughts that dictate overall activity. The feeling-tone will of itself alter the nature of the thoughts. *(Leaning forward for emphasis.)* The feeling, rather than the thought of confidence, is what he needs now, and his alpha experiences are leading him in that direction.

The feeling-tone can now be encouraged, the optimism and sense of joy and accomplishment, by indulging in those activities in which he *is* accomplished and takes joy. *(Noise upstairs.)* For some time your own feeling-tone however was still not over the boundary in your terms to the positive side. For this reason you often reinforced each other's poor moods, for example.

The feeling-tone that is presently for your purposes the best brings you a feeling and sense of ease and abundance in any area of your present endeavors. Recognize this feeling when you have it, and do whatever seems to bring it about.

You may take your break. *(Humorously:)* We are starting out, and you may be surprised where we end up.

("Okay."

(9:30—9:40.)

Now. We will be writing other books, but never in such a way that you must plunge from one into another. The books will fall into their own rhythm overall in our sessions. You will have rest between in other words.

(Not that I'm worried.)

The feeling-tone of Ruburt's mentioned earlier in your terms, the negative one, was triggered as you know by his reaction to your illness, which was followed by rising difficulties on the part of your own parents. He felt trapped by them, having to help them, as he felt trapped by his own mother.

He felt then that the tables had been turned on him again, after a time of freedom. Learning to handle these problems took him time, and again the problems themselves helped generate enough activity within his psychic centers to open up new channels.

When he felt trapped he adopted those symptoms, though to a much lesser degree, that his mother had when she was trapped. His childhood situation filled him with terror, yet there was the impetus of growing up to set him free. This time he found himself in adulthood with no such "escape" in quotes offered or possible in the old terms.

All in all he surprised himself by his performance with your parents. Such a performance would have been impossible for him early in your marriage. He simply would have run away, as he wanted to run away this time.

(Pause. May I add that Jane surprised me also, in the excellent relationship she established with my parents.)

These are obviously not the only issues involved. They were simply trigger points. At the same time he had not found himself yet where he wanted to go with his own career. He never thought of himself beyond the age of 30. In his dreams by then he would be a well-known writer, and that was the glorious end of the tale.

(Now I listened to the company that had been visiting upstairs troop back down two flights of stairs.)

What seemed to be a time of most uncomfortable and unhappy circumstance was indeed a re-evaluation and adjustment, most necessary if the personality were to continue to function as a strongly creative effective individual.

There were then physical side-effects. He was used to dealing with parents as enemies. Your own position as partially in league with those enemies, to his way of thinking, confused him further. His loyalty to you would make him by turns deny any backed-up feelings toward your parents, and then he would be forced to recognize them, and in doing so he would become angry at you for having parents.

It was the religious connection at your father's funeral that upset him. His reactions were based upon the past and had to be brought up into the present, and worked through, and this largely has been done. Your mother, for example, is quite aware that Ruburt has in his own way grown to cherish her.

He was ready to move the minute your parents got in difficulty, and, was outraged that you did not do so. He is discovering through your own parents that parents are simply people. *(Pause.)* The charge gradually thus becoming manageable.

The difference in age to some extent applied, in that he became angry at you then for being enough older than he so that your aging parents would become a difficulty. Such problems would have had to be faced in any case, but they were faced creatively, and brought about these sessions and your own psychic developments.

It was, however, like a second, more painful adolescence. He felt always on shifting ground, and could not get his footing—hence the rigidity.

You may take your break.

(10:02. Jane's trance had been good. I was finding the session very revealing. Since it dealt with parents, I brought up a thought I'd been entertaining, although I told Jane I wasn't sure it was such a good idea after all.

(Her father, Del, had died on November 16, at 7:30 AM, in Daytona Beach, Florida. Midge, Del's wife, called Jane later that morning, and Jane in turn called me at work. There isn't anything we can do, particularly, beyond the few letters Jane wrote. During break I explained to Jane that she might like Seth to say something about Del; by this I meant his experiences after death. I thought his death might give Jane a chance to "follow along" with a personality no longer physical in our terms. Resume at 10:20.)

Now. Give us a moment. *(Pause.)*

Ruburt's father is with his mother from this life. She waited for him before reincarnating. They were closely involved in other relationships in past lives.

(Del's mother, Mattie, died perhaps 19 or 20 years ago.)

On another level she encouraged Ruburt in his own development. As

Ruburt knows she was a Christian Scientist and a reader. Both grandmothers, while seeming so different, were more than usually concerned with the nature of the soul, and their idea of what religion was.

Ruburt would do well, in fact, to speak to Mattie sometimes mentally.

In developing his own abilities and searching for answers through these sessions, Ruburt also unconsciously sought, and seeks, finds answers for his mother, since she was unable to find them, and answers for his grandfather Burdo as well. *("Little Daddy," as Jane called him.)*

Ruburt's father was very bound to his mother. The energy went out of him with her passing. He had no intention of living to a ripe old age. *(Del died at 66, very suddenly, of a cerebral hemorrhage.)* He was very uneasy about Ruburt, until Ruburt met you, and he then turned Ruburt over to you.

He wanted to join both Mattie and Dorothy. *(Dorothy, Mattie's sister, died a year or so ago at a very advanced age.)* His emotional direction however was always with his mother. He had been a woman, and Mattie a man. Mattie had owned him. For a good deal of this life, while loving her, he depended upon her for handouts, and refused to set himself up independently to point out the old relationship when he was forbidden independence.

This time his dependence was a source of hurt to her.

He did not use his abilities fully to spite her, while loving her. This was the reason for the repressed aggression. He was basically childlike, trusting not people however but nature. They are having a reunion in depth.

(Jane took a pause, her hand to her closed eyes, which lasted well over a minute.)

He has met his former wife *(Maxine, who died about 14 years ago, just as Jane and I met)*, but the connections are not good. The mutual attraction no longer exists as it did between them. The reunion is joyous and his vision is clear at last in terms of his own selfhood.

Dorothy is also there, and another member of the family from the west coast *(California)* will shortly join them. You may possibly be aware of Ruburt's father before he is. He would be afraid of frightening Ruburt, regardless of Ruburt's work.

("How would he appear to Ruburt?")

You may be aware of him without his necessarily appearing. He will look in on Midge, however. He remembers her with gratitude; but there is a possibility of an unpleasant death on her part, that could involve fire. *(Pause.)* If so, he will see to it that she does not suffer.

Now you may end the session. My heartiest regards to you both. Remember to have Ruburt speak mentally to Mattie. Her thoughts are turned somewhat in your direction because of events.

("Okay." *I never met Mattie. I was still writing. When I looked up I saw that Jane was out of trance, her eyes bleary. I said good night to Seth quickly, but I was too late. "It's me," Jane said. I also forgot to note the time the session ended. Approximately 11:10.*

(*Jane said she had to "fight to stay in trance" at the last, because she began to pick up some "bad feelings" about Midge, alone in the house down there in Florida, and probably drinking. Jane kept wanting to come out of trance. She had an impression of Midge in a robe, crawling on the floor near the oil stove in the living room. Jane saw no flames, she said, but "it was all hazy, like smoke... I don't know, but I don't feel good about it right now." Then, "I've still got this scary feeling. Maybe I've just translated all the mixed-up feelings about my father and the house there and everything into Midge. I've got the impression that she was trying to close the door of the stove."*

(*Since we visited Del and Midge in this same house several years ago, we can pretty well picture the physical setting.*

(*We have no idea to whom Seth might refer when he tells us that another member of the family from the west coast might soon join Del, Mattie and Dorothy. Mattie has a sister, Maude, also elderly, if still alive. Actually we don't know whether she still "lives" or not. Maude has a daughter, Ruth Dudley, a little older than Jane, we think, and she in turn has children. Jane said there are also assorted cousins, etc. out there whom we haven't met, so there is still evidently quite a family group extant.*

(*Class had been discussing dream realities, personality, etc., for about an hour; Pat and Sheila began talking back and forth on Sheila's ideas on separate personalities, when Jane interrupted to say that she had the impression that the "hole in the universe" had opened up in Dr. Sam Levine's house next-door and a crowd of people were flying from it into the room. She added that she thought their teacher was standing at the table by the windows. We went into Alpha to see what we could get—most of us had that impression of other: in the room—and Jane got the words to a chant, which she wrote down. As she started to read this chant to us, she suddenly threw her head back and wailed the words in an extremely loud voice; she then remained in trance for five minutes or so, and began to speak in a liquid, near-whisper:*

"Sumari
ispania
wena nefari
dena dena nefari
loan
loan
Sumari!

("*It is with this always we began and we begin our classes. It is with this chant* always that we begin our endeavors in our space; it is not your own, and only a translation, for we do not use verbal communication. It is always with the facsimile of what we have heard that we begin our work, and in many guises and in many ways you are acquainted with our activities. I have always been here in your terms as you have always been in other places and other times, and there is a great familiarity and wonder on our part that you are still involved in these endeavors which were begun in your terms so many centuries ago, and in ways that you cannot now presently comprehend. And yet you are even familiar with what comes out as what appears as my voice in your own traits and your own translations. There are cities that we have built that you have helped us build; there are wonders here, wonders in your own reality that we helped build in other sizes in your time. We have been here many times, and you have been where we are.

Sumari !"

(*The second voice, which came through about twenty minutes later, was louder and sounded "older":*

("*And I am Sumari in another guise. And all of you have your guises and your masks that you wear and have worn. I am Sumari in another guise. And all of these guises are myself, and all of your guises are yourselves. And as I dwell in many realities, so dwell you in many realities. You will learn to become aware of these; you are learning. I am aware of all your activities. I am aware, for example, of your Seth and of your Seth II. We are all Sumari. Now we are appearing more clearly in terms that you can understand. But we are all Sumari, and if you are all Sumari, and never forget that you are all Sumari, and you have always been Sumari. It is the name of your family."*

([Pat:] "Are there other family names?"

("*It is the name of your family. It has always been the name of your family, and there are many families. I am telling you your family name, and you are learning of your heritage. I am Sumari, you are Sumari."*

(*Much later, and softly: "Thank you for coming to our class."*)

SESSION 598
NOVEMBER 24, 1971 WEDNESDAY

(*Notes taped and transcribed by Sue Watkins.*

(*Last night in ESP class, Jane had an experience with a personality who called itself, and the rest of us, <u>Sumari</u>. This afternoon I dropped in to talk about this incident with Jane & Rob; in the course of the conversation we decided that I should* *bring the tape of that class to their apartment this evening, stay on for the session, and record it and type it up.*

(It had been snowing all evening and I had some trouble driving in from Pine City. Besides that, my recording of the Sumari *personality was poor and I had to stop at Fred and Pet's [class members] to get their tape, and I didn't arrive at Jane & Rob's until 9 PM. We played the two tapes—Jane was especially interested in the chant that preceded the* Sumari's *short speech—until 9:20. Jane had written this chant down during an Alpha experiment in class; when she started to read it to us, she suddenly wailed the words as loudly as I have ever heard even Seth's voice go:*

> "Sumari
> ispania
> wena nefari
> dena dena nefari
> lona
> lona
> lona
> Sumari!"

(Jane's spelling & scansion.

(Here she had gone into an extended trance state that lasted, for all purposes, for the rest of the evening.

(I thought that Jane was uneasy about the whole experience last night, but as soon as she felt Seth around, we all seemed to relax more. Rob poured us beers and the session started at 9:35.)

Now. Good evening to you.

(To Rob:) We will begin with an explanation of your experience last evening. And our record-keeper over here *(me)* will also understand what you are doing.

Two things were involved: a certain evolution of your abilities, using the eye phenomena. Do you follow me?

("Yes," Rob said.)

And secondly, of course, what you experienced. You were not picking up anything regarding Ruburt's father, as you thought. Instead you were indeed perceiving in your own fashion what was happening here for the entire evening. You are well aware of any changes that occur as far as Ruburt's own abilities are concerned, or any offshoots, say, from our sessions or work; and so though you were not here physically, you did indeed participate.

("I didn't start until quite late, though," Rob said.)

The time makes little difference. Earlier, you were beginning to put yourself in that frame of mind, and physiological state, which would bring about the particular changes that bring you to the eye method. This time, however, you were aware of what you were trying to do: you were trying to use your ability in a particular fashion and so you did. You were dealing with an energy source, and it was this that you were trying to perceive, and the reason for the brilliance and also the concentrated area with which you were dealing; not an expansion, but a small concentrated brilliant area.

(To me:) Now, you remember, because of one of your experiences and something I said in a session—or, rather, another portion of me said in a session—having to do with the fact that Seth II, if you could perceive him, would be as small as a brown nut. *(To Rob:)* And so you were perceiving a core of energy that radiated outward and infringed upon this reality—<u>intruded</u> upon it: hence, the fragmented area about it, you see, and the seemingly jagged effect.

("It was very beautiful.")
It was indeed.
("But impossible to describe," Rob added.)

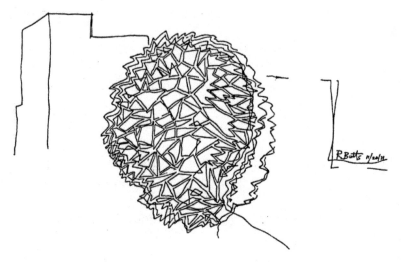

(A reduced version of the on-the-spot drawing I made of my vision after 10PM on Tuesday, November 23, 1971, as I sat typing in our second apartment across the hall from where Jane was holding her ESP class. My crude drawing can't begin to reproduce the delicate, shimmering and transparent beauty of what I briefly saw floating before me.)

You will be able to do an approximation in an entirely different fashion, in several paintings. You will not see what you have done until some time after you have done it, because the difference in the product, in the painting itself, will be so divorced from the original vision that you will not see that they come from the same source.

Now, the energy here last night was strong enough so that it could be picked up very easily, but you perceived its approach. Do you follow me? Before it was here, in your terms, you were aware of its approach and began to prepare yourself to perceive it in whatever fashion you could.

("Well," Rob said, "earlier, I heard a fragment of that chant while I was still typing, but I forgot about it.")

You began the physiological procedure at approximately four o'clock yesterday afternoon. Now, Ruburt also knew what was going to happen and that you would be involved, simply because the eye effect frightens him and he is always aware ahead of time of such activities on your part. You are all Sumari.

("What's that?" Rob asked, grinning.)

It is what you are.

(Rob & I laughed. "All right," he agreed, "but you'll have to explain it to us.")

And you knew it is what you are, and what you will be; and as the other developments in the sessions also rose out of what you are and what Ruburt is, so did this one. It is the reason, again, why you participated in your own way, though you were not at class. And you will indeed receive the full story, in good time.

I want to make a point to you, however: you can imaginatively receive data now without the eye involvement. In the past, in your very earlier years, you needed that mechanism. It caught your attention. It pivoted it and made you concentrate. Now, you see, that you recognize the connection, you will not need it. It leads, however, to a strong pivoting of your energy. You are concentrating your own perceptive abilities and energy almost in the same fashion, for example, as a laser beam concentrates energy. Do you follow me? So that the vision that you received, while it was microscopic, was still brilliant, and radiated strong energy.

Now, such a vision is not only something that you see that intrudes upon this reality, but also something that has its effects upon this reality, and often effects that you do not perceive. You perceive the appearance of the image, but its other effects escape you. The concentration of energy itself, is highly important, you see, and changes the behavior even of the atoms and molecules within the neighborhood of its appearance.

Now, remember what I told you in the book about the black holes and the concentration of energy. Now, such occurrences allow you unusual exchanges of energy from one system to another. They are fountains, therefore, of new energy; and their very intrusion into your world activates that reality in a different fashion, usually in a quickening, stirring, transforming fashion—an activation, say, rather than a slowing down.

There are, incidentally, levels of motion so fast that they attain what seems to be a level of complete peace. Where motion is not perceived. Beyond such levels, the motion is perceived again and the period of peace seems over. Now, in the case of your experience last evening, the image itself by its appearance activates the air in the atmosphere. In that activation, however, it achieved, finally, a level of seeming peace where you do not perceive it, but in which it still exists. There is also a reason why you perceived it in the particular room that you did, you see.

("The kitchen? In our second apartment across the hall? You mean because of the open surroundings?" Rob asked.)

Because of your attitude toward it, because of the open surroundings, and because it is highly charged for other reasons.

Now, the energy that was here last night became suspended for a time between the two apartments so that there was a give-and-take. Had you been even more aware, for example, it would have been fairly easy for you to perceive more than you did, and you could have done it through sketching. You could have brought out forms that were here beneath your visual perception.

Do you have any questions, now, in that regard?

(Rob paused. "Well, no; but a couple of times I felt that I was right on the verge of accomplishing more with it, but I couldn't quite bridge the gap to bring it about. The first thing I thought of was Jane's father, though—I didn't actually see him, but I was telling Jane that at times I thought I did see the shape of the back of the head —I did associate that with his head.")

There is also a connection between the death of Ruburt's father, your fine physicist's father's death, and the introduction of the Sumari name to the class in general.

("I thought about Al's father's death last night," Rob said, referring to Al Oberg, a class member whose father had died the Thursday before Jane's father had. "What's the connection?")

I will tell you. I like to hold <u>some</u> of my goodies back.

Now. Give us a moment. *(Pause.)* There are alliances in all levels of reality—there are attractions that reach even bright space and time, groupings of consciousness, associations, psychic attractions that hold and mold various kinds of consciousness in a loose organization. There are personalities who come together for certain reasons, varying reasons, whose individual inclinations are somewhat the same, and purposes. You may think of the guilds in the Middle Ages, for example. These groups of consciousness range throughout history as you know it. In their own way, and according to their capacity and purpose, they change and alter the nature of the universe, sometimes by being born within your historical time, and sometimes by trying to reach those who are within your historical time. They are far closer in your terms because of their natural affinity than they are, for example, sometimes even to other portions of their own entity, as you might be closer to a strong friend than you are to certain members of your own family, though they may be of your own blood. It is a membership of choice, in other words, of attraction and respect, and usually this is bound by like purpose and endeavor. These are true families.

In this case, you would have received the information now or later; it was yours, you would receive it. Because of the circumstances, however, and the two family deaths, the information was available, and used to remind all the class members of the different kind of familyship, a different kind of endeavor, and to offer a different kind of assurance and bonds that are not destroyed in your terms by any amount of reincarnation or any amount of time you use them.

Now you may take your break.

(9:59. During break, we discussed what had been said and then somehow got to joking about a reincarnational drama-scene that Rob and I had played out a few months ago, in which he had apparently been a teacher of mine and an exasperatingly thorough record-keeper. Jane had just made a remark that sent me convulsing with laughter when Seth came through again, loudly and emphatically:)

Now, who is taking the record this evening and who has been taking records for class? And enough said in that direction.

Now. Let us speak about the Sumari. Ruburt does not like the idea of brotherhoods, alive or dead, so I should not use that phrase. So we will say that the Sumari are a guild. In much earlier times, they would be a royal guild, in that they are the richest, the most expansive. They have indeed, on their own, begun civilizations. They have a large membership. It is impossible to <u>speak</u> to you in terms of membership, however, for the idea of individuality is not clear with you yet, and you would think in terms of how many individuals.

(Long pause.) I am trying to find words that will not offend our friend, and sometimes it is difficult. This group, therefore, has always been involved in the kind of work in which you are now involved, and on a grand scale. They never forget their members. There are indeed initiates, but all of you passed that stage in another layer of reality, in your terms, some time ago. Their main activities take place in other levels of consciousness. You are on missions, in certain terms. You do attend meetings, when you are in the sleep state, between lives. You work through many layers of reality at the same time. Now, these are the people, for example, that you *(me)* were speaking of, the strangers that you see in your

dreams. You are affecting each others' realities, but you have always done this to some degree.

Now, this is different from the speakers. A speaker may or may not be a Sumari. Some speakers are Sumari, and some are not. There are bonds of affection and understanding that unite this group, and a speaker may or may not be one. The relationships, however, go between realities; you can be closer, then, with another Sumari than you are with a husband or wife, particularly if you do not like the husband or wife overwell. It is not true to say that this is a religious group in any way, but it is true to say that this is a very strong alliance. And the alliance is of a kind that is difficult to explain. Whole, for example, may work. Together, and have, to initiate certain discoveries on various worlds, or to prepare the groundwork, in your terms, for future events. They interweave, not only through your centuries as you understand them, but through other realities. They are great coordinators.

Now, many are efficient in one particular reality, and devoted to it. But the Sumari coordinate very well, and move within a freedom <u>that is denied to many. It is simply their nature.</u>

("What brings a group together?" Rob asked. "I know I'm speaking of beginnings and endings, but what causes a group of Sumari to congregate?")

They congregate, in those terms, seldom. They did not suddenly get together and decide "We will be a group."

("I realize that," Rob said, "but why *did* they get together?")

Because of the bonds of affection and understanding and instant intuitional comprehension that allows them to recognize one another. It is an instant recognition of brotherhood and unity of purpose, and in a strange manner, overall, of temperament.

Now. Astrology, as it is thought of, and as it is taught, you see, represents but a vague shadow of something far different. Consciousness generally can be divided into certain characteristics, hardly the number, the small number, presently given to it, for example, in charts, the twelve houses. Now, that sort of thing is a <u>dim</u> shadow, in three-dimensional terms, dealing with one planet, of a much more vast system. And in that vast system there are this particular group of people, who are united by certain traits and similarities.

("Are there other such groups?")

There are indeed.

("All right," Rob pursued, "say some speakers are Sumari, but might another group of speakers be of another family?")

The speakers generally do not fall into any particular group. Do you follow me? There will be groups of speakers, within these large guilds. Now, I am using that term purposely.

("I don't think Ruburt would object if you used some other term," Rob said.)

We like to break things gently to him.

("He'll get used to it," Rob laughed. "How are the Sumari different from other groups?" I asked.)

In their strong psychic alliance and in their coordination abilities, and the agility with which—the <u>agility</u> with which—they can manipulate between systems, consciously, with purpose, and with some exuberance. They are communicators in that they spread knowledge from one system of reality to another. They are given much more, for example, to ideas rather than to the various camouflage realities within systems. Many groups, you see, deal exclusively with the camouflage reality between systems, with building it up, with its maintenance.

("Then the Sumari have experienced the various kinds of physical realities," Rob suggested.)

They have indeed. They have indeed. And in that respect, they are initiators, say, of a particular camouflage system. But they are not those who continually nourish that camouflage system. There are groups who do that.

("Would Seth II fit in that group?" Rob asked.)

(Humorously:) Would Seth II fit in which group?

("Those more apt to nourish," Rob explained. "I think he mentioned that once.")

Initiate <u>and</u> nourish, in his particular case. The Sumari, however—and they <u>all</u> initiate—initiate the birth of systems. They constantly carry communications between systems, and they deal with the initiation and communication of ideas, from one system to another. Because they are initiators therefore, they are creators. They are, however, comparatively speaking, like those who create and then are satisfied to go on to other creations. They want someone else to take care of what they have created. They do not want to hang around to mow the grass, in other words. But those who mow the grass could not create it.

("How about the two voices that came through last night?" Rob asked.)

Ruburt is quite correct. He will learn how to translate those realities.

("Is that why they were weak?" Rob said.)

It has to do with his physical sensations at the time and also the weakness of the voice. The weakness, however, did not have to do with the weakness of power, but to his inability to translate the strange material that he was receiving.

("Was this material from specific entities, or personalities, in those terms?" Rob added.)

Now, there are some things that I will have to explain to you slowly. And the true answer to your question will take time. One Sumari is all Sumari. There are gradations, in those terms, within the Sumari alliances; therefore, everyone is not at the same level, if you follow me: it is an organization of affection, loyalty, and abilities; and there will be varying grades within their alliance. Now, everyone who was here last night was Sumari, and many who come to class, even for one time, are Sumari.

("But it's not only Sumari who come to class," Rob put in.)

It is not indeed. I want to go into, and I will at a later date, the connections between this kind of reality and the astrology that is now popular.

("What were you going to say about the connection between Jane's father and Al's father and this?")

The time, simply, was right for the information to come through because two members had lost members of their own—family. They were ready, therefore, to learn of their greater family; and for various reasons, personal reasons, having to do with both class members. This was also to be a reassurance to our friend Ruburt. There is a family who loves him after all! And you can only be involved in this work so long, you see, before you become acquainted with your true associates. Your acquaintanceship grows, and you discover old friendships.

You are being recognized, in your terms, as your present personalities by your guild again. The conscious self was not told, you see. You are now ready to take up conscious membership. It is only a way to acquaint your conscious self with your real and deep alliances. The information would have made little sense some years ago.

Now, I will also have some things to say concerning the nature of the two "personalities," in quotes, for whom our friend spoke last night. But I suggest now that you take a break, even though I do not have to worry about the state of your fingers.

(Break at 10:30. Jane came out of trance and told us that she knew Seth had said something about astrology because she had had a conceptual experience, which she simply couldn't put into words, involving the positions of the planets and the vastness behind their symbolism. We discussed the idea of Sumari and what might be their connection with the "class dreams." If class could correlate their dreams, we might be able to find a common theme or purpose, with each individual remembering his own part in it. Break lasted for a half an hour and Rob was wondering if the session was over when Seth resumed at 11:02.)

The session is not over. Now. There are several reasons why the personal last evening appeared feminine in the first instance; and this is a matter again of translation. The Sumari are initiators and creators. They are filled with feelings of abundance; they have great energy, you see. There is not a word in your vocabulary to explain what I am trying to get at. The word "graciousness" as used last evening comes faintly close. The feminine seemed to apply, therefore; it was a way of getting these characteristics across. It was also a way that Ruburt used to translate the idea of the particular kind of creativity involved; the idea, indeed, of birth, for this is the birth or a system, of a new kind of reality, that this group is involved with.

You were listening in one respect to the voice of your people. The second voice, therefore, also had its own part to play, bringing in the idea, hopefully, both of ancient knowledge and of youth. And in that case, the feminine idea was not used. Do you follow me?

These were then, the voices of your people coming to you in ways that you could understand. They were coming from personalities. The transmission however, is of a different kind; therefore, though the messages were coming from personalities, the entire term involves a translation that escapes you. We translate the word "personality;" we translate what we are into a term that you understand.

("Could you give us a word that we could learn to use?" Rob asked.)

Now, I will be doing that. I do not want to involve you with an esoteric language that can be used to close others out as well as to unite you. But there will be terms that I will be giving you. And again, this development was latent in the early beginning of our sessions. Now, give us a moment.

(Long pause.) The multidimensional experience of this group was suddenly and surprisingly present for Ruburt to draw upon last evening. Now, he translated this into layers of voices, and various languages, and did not know how to translate or contain the information that was quite legitimately available. Now, this is a storehouse of knowledge, not of one personality in your terms but, for example, it can be compared, to your racial history, to the achievements of your people, its goals and purposes.

Now, as you *(Rob)* might perceive such information visually, it is translated for Ruburt in an entirely different fashion. Therefore, you see, I do not believe that at one time you will be able to get a translation of some of the old speakers manuscripts, but it still will be a difficult endeavor. The same information can be given, you see, in other ways. Now, I am interested in your reaching people at large.

("You mean through publication?")

In any way, through the publication, and whether or not such a manuscript would allow us to do so in any more efficient way than we will anyway, is another point. It may. It would take some time, and also it would require that I clear the issue myself with several people of my own acquaintanceship.

("It would take several years, then.")

It would indeed. And perhaps longer. Ruburt might need, for example, a rest or a different kind of material in between. However, it could not have taken place had the experience last evening not taken place. He would not have been ready.

("Would you get this information yourself, or would you get it through speakers?" Rob asked.)

This would be a combined activity. It would take far too much effort on my part, for example, away from other endeavors to do that particular thing alone. I would oversee it.

("Like a Sumari.")

Indeed. *(Humorously.)* And a very high lieutenant indeed, I will have you know.

("Can we digress a moment here?" Rob asked.)

You have never had to ask my permission in the past. You may indeed.

("Well, I was thinking a minute ago about the incident with Jane and Dr. Wilt in Sayre.")

I was amused that he did not ask me.

("Why didn't he ask?" Rob said.)

You must ask him. Now. Ruburt's friend, his darling Dr. Wilt, is indeed a Sumari. They both knew it at once, and you are lucky they did not go into that chant and dance right there. The gesture, in your terms now, was a translation, not into words but into a physical gesture, of acknowledgement and recognition.

("They almost hugged," Rob observed.)

They did indeed. They were well aware of their affiliation. Now, you for example, are also a Sumari, but the same recognition did not hit you. The doctor, however, did pick it up as far as you were concerned, though to a lesser degree. He and Ruburt have worked together, you see, on other occasions and also have known each other in some past lives. He knew you as a Sumari but he had not worked with you, in your terms, personally. They were closely involved, and in a work relationship, a highly personal work relationship. They were also members of several small tribes.

Now, all of you communicate in the dream state, and they had me there often also, discussing work in which they had been involved in the past.

("Well, such encounters can't be too infrequent then," Rob said.)

They are not. The experience last evening on both of your parts and the part of the class will initiate new information and endeavors and activities and experiences.

("That's the kind of thing we talked about in break," Rob said. "For instance,

you go into a supermarket and out of all the people you encounter casually—I'm sure that we'd like some guidance on how we can pick out Sumari.")

There will be no doubt if they trust their inner reactions. You first have to be aware that the group exists. Now, what about our friend over here *(me)*?

(*"I was just thinking about the woman with the book in the drugstore," I said, referring to a person I'd noticed in Fay's some weeks before. "She had been standing by a bookrack, shuffling through best-sellers, and I'd had a strong, almost sisterly urge to walk up to her and start talking about books we'd been reading lately."*)

She was indeed Sumari. *(To Rob:)* And the information that you were discussing at suppertime will indeed be given, and in altered fashion. The personal information that was begun.

And now, I bid you a fond good evening, not worried about your fingers *(Rob)*, but our friend's over here *(me)*. We will have to send her additional energy. She will doubtlessly have some experiences on her own as she types it out, however, to compensate. I look out for her.

(*"Seth," I said, "can I ask a question about something you said to me in class?"*)
You may indeed.
(*"The remark about objects—did that concern my parents' house?"*)
It did indeed.
(*"I've had a number of dreams about the house in which there was a terrified feeling and the house had an animalistic look, which is contrary to how I feel about it consciously," I said. "Is this the point at which I can't differentiate?"*)

It expresses your fears that the house traps you, and it is a turnabout. The house appears animalistic. Men trap animals, but in this case, the animal traps you.

(*"And *that* was the point I didn't realize?"*)
It was indeed. You did not realize. You *think* that you realize.
(*"Well, you do now, don't you?" Rob asked me.*)
Not completely. It seems very clear to her, that she realizes that she projected. The realization has not come fully, but it will. Moving from the situation will indeed help clear your vision.

Now, I bid you a fond good evening. And some night I will do our chant for you.

(*Jane came out of trance at 11:20 and we sat and talked about what had been said. During the past hour or so, however, the first syllables of a word—"grund..." or "gruna..." had been going through my head, and I had the idea that it was related to these "families". "I wonder what some other family names are," I remarked. "I keep getting this word like Grundoon or something." At that, Seth was abruptly there.*)

Grunaargh.

("What?" Rob said. The tape was off, and I switched it on in a hurry. "What was that?" I asked. "One more time, Seth," Rob said.

("Wait a minute, this is me," Jane said with a dazed look.

("Could you repeat that again for the record?" I waited, and Seth came through again, loudly.)

Grunaargh.

("Oh?" I said—Rob and I were both laughing—"What do they do?" Seth stared at me in that penetrating way of his for several moments.)

Now. We are not going to get into a discussion of all the guilds or brotherhoods this evening, because I want to do a good job when we do it now. The chant, however, the vowels and syllables used in pronouncing the chant, are highly important and evocative. The sounds themselves are keys that tune you in, so to speak, with certain frequencies. In other words, the chant is a tool in that regard, a translation in completely different terms, of something far different.

Now—I bid you good evening.

(End 11:30.)

DELETED SESSION
NOVEMBER 29, 1971 MONDAY

(This is the regularly scheduled session for November 29, 1971, Monday. It is deleted from the record.

(At supper this evening Jane and I had a very productive discussion about personal problems. It's continued in the session this evening.)

Good evening.

("Good evening, Seth.")

Now. There are some further points, unrecognized items that we have not touched upon. They are fairly important and play their part in Ruburt's attitudes. I am pointing out patterns, now, that he has not recognized.

They exerted force because he was not consciously aware of them, nor ready to face them in those terms. Some of this will go a good way in explaining portions of his behavior. If you have questions ask when I have finished.

He felt, as a child now, that he had no rights. Nothing was his by rights. Anything could be taken from him at any time. While he lived in one house, still the home itself was always in jeopardy. His mother frequently told him that she would keep him only if he was good, that only Marie's good graces kept the child from going to an asylum. The mother's affections were not the child's by right, but dependent upon how well the child cared or performed.

As has been noted, all normal aggressive feelings toward the mother had to be masked. The mother frequently took away gifts that she had given the child, when the child misbehaved, making it clear that even these were not the child's by right.

Only poetry seemed Ruburt's by right. In the convent home, as you know, letters were censored, and only positive statements got through the censor. The child feared punishment there by giving voice to any complaint. Ruburt grew up then without daring to <u>ask</u> for anything. Welfare, who gave, always threatened to take away. They were a threat as well as a sustenance. The college scholarship was not Ruburt's by right, but could also be taken away.

To a large extent in even small things therefore, he felt he had no rights per se, no right to ask you for example for anything. Remember early tales he tells about feeling guilty for buying a lipstick. Before tonight's session he mentioned that the class wine was gone. He meant obviously that it must be replaced, but would never directly ask you to do so, feeling he had no right.

This explains much of his behavior in terms of spending money at the store, and so forth. *(Pause.)* Give us time… He did not feel that any love was his by right, yours or anyone else's: therefore he did not feel worthy of it, and in the face of any difficulty between you he suspected it, thought then that you no longer loved him.

To voice any dissatisfaction to you verbally was highly difficult, for you could then take away your love and affection, as his mother did, for she would not stand, in Ruburt's eyes, for such voiced aggression. He had to be quiet therefore to preserve your love.

The backed-up feelings helped bring about the rigidity over a period of time. He was operating to a large degree according to the code long set down by his grandfather: be quiet, do not argue, be aloof, and above all never raise your voice.

It seemed the only safe policy.

Policy however shadowed everything he did, for he carried it into every activity. Whenever he thought anything differently than the opinions you voiced, he felt inward and refused to express himself regardless of the issue involved—its triviality or its importance.

As mentioned earlier in other sessions he felt, erroneously, for some time that your love for him depended upon his performance as a writer and in sessions, since it could not be his by right. He had to test the love therefore by skipping sessions to see if you still loved him. If you objected it meant you did not.

If you did not object, it meant you did not care for the sessions. In the psychic realm therefore he dared not voice any feelings that you did not voice. The unvoiced fear always was that you would abandon him because he had no rights.

The habits however became strong through the years: the reasons largely forgotten, and for that matter no longer vital, but active.

Your going to the store for him without asking proves that you love him. He would never ask you to do anything for him, for he felt he had no right to do so, or to your love. He needed a strong excuse therefore in order to ask you to do anything. One excuse was that he could not do it himself.

He was afraid that you did not love and cherish him for himself, and too embarrassed, rigid and proud to continue seeking assurances from you, as he used to do.

The symptoms, beside other issues, have been a crying out to you for a love he feels he does not deserve but needs, a love he feared you could forget. He feared always that you would go your way in your work and life, and emotionally leave him alone. He could not bear that eventuality.

The symptoms also served to punish you for making him go to such extremes, because physically they obviously hampered the expression of that love. He is possessive and jealous, and gave you his entire loyalty. He was afraid you would flee as your father fled. He would not (in quotes) "humiliate himself" to his way of thinking by crying after you, hammering at your door. He transferred the entire dilemma to the physical realm.

The term, woo back to health, is an excellent one, quite apropos to a large extent in all such conditions, and operating beneath most symptoms despite their nature.

Now part of this was quite unrealistic, based on old ideas of his, part of it from the interaction of your natures. Our sessions are extremely legitimate, from what you would call a psychic viewpoint—you are reaching dimensions very seldom reached. They also served psychological purposes of course.

Ruburt hoped they would bring the two of you closer together after your illness. Instead he feared that they drove you farther apart, in that he feared you would use them to spend time away from him rather than with him, and in that he did not feel able to express his own ambiguous feelings—the ideas of performance entering in here.

On one level then the sessions were an attempt to retain your love and give him a right to it. Hence his later feelings that you loved him only for the sessions carried a certain charge. Now this is one of the most important sessions you have been given on your own affairs. I suggest a break. He would quite literally do anything to retain your love—hence his feelings sometimes that you sent him out on this psychic pilgrimage. This feeling however, having its roots in "lack of rights" and his alliance with you, also provides him with the unity upon which his life is based: the poetry, the psychic work, and yourself. A trio, you see.

Now take your break.

(9:38. Jane's trance had been deep. "He did a funny thing," she said. "He socked me out real good so I couldn't back out; yet I remembered a lot of that. I'm going to hide…." Her pace had been fast. Resume at 9:50.)

Now let us get through what we can before the two of you get involved in a discussion.

("We won't.")

Ruburt's sense of worth came from his writing self. There he felt on firm ground. It carried him through all of his early years, this belief in the writing self that automatically justified his existence and more (underlined) than made up for any other lacks, he felt. It made him then superior, and effectively hid the other sense of worthlessness.

The writing self had always been both highly intuitional and highly questioning. The questioning of values, of neighborhood and church, allowed the intuitions to work and gave them freedom. The writing self therefore led the way also to the psychic developments. These were a natural extension.

Though this was true, the writing self for the first time began to question itself, its achievements, and the new field it had entered. It had never questioned itself before. This brought forth some conflicts, for the writing self had been Ruburt's justification of your love. He had a right to it because he was a writer, not because he was himself.

When he began to doubt the writing self in this new alliance with the psychic, then the framework became shaky. Some of this was a creative psychic and artistic endeavor that had to be worked through, whether or not it shook the foundations, you see.

The writing self knew it needed something to write about, and greater maturity if it were to fulfill its abilities, and here again the psychic development fulfilled a need. The writing self was led to examine its own substance; since Ruburt felt your love was dependent on the outcome, this brought about certain difficulties.

He was afraid shortly before our sessions began that you had largely lost your love for him, and he began frantically to initiate methods of insuring it. The sessions were on the one hand a gift to you, by which means your health could be restored. He felt your physical withdrawal strongly during your illness previously, felt on several occasions physically attracted to other men, and became terrified. Walt did not want him physically, but he did not love Walt. He feared you were turning away from him in those terms. He was frightened that his sexual appetite would attract him to others and betray him, so he closed the door on it as best he could.

There was also the idea of channeling that energy into our sessions, this of course at a deeply unconscious level. Instead he felt that you latched upon the sessions so that they came before he did personally—that you demanded performance there in sessions, while not in bed. In an odd way he felt that you used them against him, in other words—this during the time of tests, in that area.

He did not feel they had served that particular purpose, yet he felt the sessions too legitimate to drop then, and the psychic work too fascinating to disown. They seemed not to have brought you closer together however, to him. Precisely at the time the strong symptoms began, the ESP book was slated for publication. You had received the cover, and the writing self was facing its own conflicts also: was the psychic work its natural fulfillment, or a disastrous side trip? The two of you were not communicating well. He did not feel you were proud enough of that book. He was afraid it did not justify your love. His symptoms then began.

The first strong twinges came earlier when the young psychologist touched certain triggers, indicating that the sessions were a way of handling you, because amid all of the other motives and conditions, he knew they were also a method of keeping your love.

This unconscious knowledge frightened him. He was afraid it meant that the sessions were just (underlined) a fraudulent method of manipulating you, and hence not legitimate. This of course was not the case.

Any money he made was always simply a way of winning your approval, in the terms that you wanted. He had many good ideas that he felt you would have been against that would have worked out very well, but he was afraid of going against you.

Now you were drawn to him because you sensed precisely that deep love of his, and needed it to add to your own vitality and substance. If you were ever tempted, particularly in earlier times, to isolate yourself to an unhealthy degree, Ruburt was precisely your insurance. You counted on him to call you back, to insist. You counted on that remedy. He was also your own insurance against being swallowed by your own parents, and he saved you from that possibility, which was present.

You knew he would not allow it, while you gave yourself time to grow in understanding. Otherwise you might well have continued your earlier performance, and moved in with your parents, to bail out your younger brother in a situation which would have then been present.

The situation occurred in a facsimile, a lighter version.

When Ruburt felt his other efforts did not insure what he wanted, he became highly frustrated and frightened. He alternately retreated from you in hurt bewilderment, railed at you silently, and still felt that what he wanted was not in your nature to give, and for that reason also he had no right to ask it.

He felt guilty then at asking you to change your mode of behavior, and felt you would construe this to mean he was grasping and wanted all of you and meant to allow you no freedom; which again, was not the case.

No one had loved him at all, however. If getting sick insured him a certain amount of your affection and notice, brought about gallant behavior, then he was willing to pay the price.

Now this early summer he improved, and to a large degree, for several reasons. His defiance was finally aroused, a sense of personal worth rushed to the surface, a sense of independence, the feeling "Well if you wanted to leave him go ahead," all of which released some pressure. Besides this during your vacation you spent a lot of time and attention on him.

You made love frequently, and began an open communication area. The night of the Milligan party he did very well. You spoke some words to him, mentioning that his performance still needed much more progress. Unfortunately he took this to mean that you did not appreciate his efforts, did not love him, and cautioned him that he had better not give up those symptoms yet.

I am going to suggest a break. If your hand is not tired we will then continue, hopefully with suggestions.

(10:29—10:45.)

Now are you ready for more?

("Yes.")

There are several areas that can work great improvement.

Basic communication has been difficult. This means you should try better to communicate your thoughts and feelings. You, then, say what naturally comes to mind, and encourage Ruburt to make any questions or comments. Feel free to say what is on your mind; again, discuss Ruburt's interpretation.

Several such freely entered encounters will show him practically the difference between your meaning and his interpretation. You are not to watch yourself, in other words. You should both take some time each day to freely discuss whatever personal issues are involved, to express your selves personally to each other on whatever issues you want.

For now, I recommend a definite certain amount of time on a regular basis. I cannot recommend this too strongly. Later you will not need the time, per se. Communication will flow freely, but now you need it.

Your afternoon activities today are but a hint of natural communications that you have both let lag. As you both ascertained, this is an excellent method. For one thing the activity engages body, mind and spirit in joyful pursuit. Spontaneity is encouraged. Physically, hormones and chemicals are brought into activity that are otherwise sluggish. It is not your role, necessarily, to make up for the love Ruburt did not have as a child, yet bodily caresses and fond verbal endearments provide him with exactly the kind of soothing assuring elements that he needs, and that will result in health improvement.

You may find his moods quickly changing under such circumstances. This should be encouraged. Physically your touches activate portions of the body that have collected various feelings. Touching the physical portions help release the feelings.

Aside from this your own vitality will also be improved, and the situation with the penis relieved. Physical intercourse may or may not take place according to your moods, but the physical endearments and the feelings of closeness, being cherished and assured are definitely important on Ruburt's part.

The period difficulty is connected here, and is a follow-through, as I explained earlier in other sessions. These are the two most important elements necessary now, and the steady but light use of the suggestions.

Some of the material given tonight has been buried. Ruburt did not want to face it. Have him read the session several times.

You can woo him back to health. It may seem that you need not do this—that he should do it alone, but because your relationship is so involved this is by far the procedure that will rouse his own desire for health. Do you follow me?

("Yes.")

I am not saying therefore that the burden is on you, to woo him back. It is good sense. The open communication will help immensely. It will help if you do not let him retreat from it when he is tempted by the old habit.

Now if you want results follow the suggestions. You may end the session, ask questions, or if you prefer list any questions you have between the session and the next, to give you time to think.

("We'll have to digest this material first, then.")

Then I bid you a fond good evening.

("Thank you, Seth. Good night."

(11:06. I thought the session was excellent.)

DELETED SESSION
DECEMBER 6, 1971

(This is the regularly scheduled session for December 6, 1971. It is deleted from the record.)

Now, good evening.

("Good evening, Seth.")

We will start slowly.

Much of what you discussed today was discussed by me a good deal of time ago. *(True.)* The suggestions I made at that time were not followed. Others were not, for both of your reasons, because the situation served both of your purposes to some extent.

Because now you fear that the situation may become a way of life, you are finally both willing to take more direct action. To some degree you have both been avoiding each other. You made a pact not to discuss troublesome, frightening or critical problems, particularly those which did not seem to have an immediate solution.

You avoided <u>meaningful</u> (underlined) emotional encounters with each other often as a result. Neither of your ideas were tempered by the ideas of the other, therefore, nor were your feelings about these life problems. The rich emotional contact and encounters that are possible between you became clogged by inhibition and fears. Because of his particular nature, these agreements on your part to avoid such issues, and the resulting lack of positive encounters, was more damaging to Ruburt.

You obviously also suffered, however. Bringing such matters to the surface serves many more purposes than is apparent, therefore. It means that you refuse to let old habits any longer rule, and each such encounter is an exercise in learning how to express and communicate your feelings each to the other.

This will automatically break down some projections, clear the air, but more than this the repressed energy being used to prevent communication, open communication, is physically and psychically released.

Ruburt was correct then in those statements he made last evening, having to do with the balance of routine and spontaneity, for his nature does need both. So does yours, incidentally, though this is not nearly as apparent. You were not living clearly in the sensual, physical world, in that large amounts of energy were being used to repress physical communication.

You went to some good degree toward breaking some of those patterns last evening and today, but the issues of your lives should be clearly discussed and not hidden. The problems were being taken out of the physical realm, where you could indeed handle them, into a mental realm, where you tried to hide them.

I am speaking now of you both. You did not communicate your concern to each other, therefore you did not communicate your hopes. You, now, did for some time get into the habit of nonsmiling, which led Ruburt to further reinforce his own negative ideas of what you are thinking. But all of the symptoms now represent aspects of your lives that you have not faced in a normal above-the-board fashion. It is not so much that you have not solved them, as that you let communication about them gradually fade away.

Ruburt can be far more helpful than you realize, in helping with those solutions. Your lives in many ways did not satisfy you, but rather than accept this fact clearly and cast about for what changes or solutions there might be, both of you tried to keep everything <u>precisely</u> (underlined) as it was, make no changes, and live with the dissatisfaction that became a constant inner problem.

It naturally reflected all of your own attitudes, the similar and various ways the both of you have of facing reality. So when you discuss it the problem becomes an excellent focal point, showing you how you interact, how you interpret and misinterpret each other, and brings out quite clearly any basic conflicts that you have.

In other words, such discussions are excellent methods of showing you how you interrelate. They provide miniature yet perfect therapeutic sessions, beside having the advantage of bringing the initial problems to the front where you can deal with them together. Before you nursed these separately, and felt, both of you, overburdened at times, and misunderstood by the other.

Such a discussion also serves to force Ruburt to say what he thinks, clarifies his own feelings, for he is not used to vocalizing them. Doing this alone can help him understand them more clearly.

Aggression or fear may rise up. If so face those feelings honestly, for they have been backed up within you. All of this serves to clear the air, opening the channels of communication, so that you do not have to be wondering what the other one is up to now.

The breaking of schedules is extremely beneficial for you also and would have made your outside job less burdensome in the past. It serves to give you a feeling of freedom, and open the way to unstructured emotional release. This, with the information given in the last session, if followed, can help you greatly, and clear Ruburt's symptoms; but not if the advice is not followed.

You may take your break.

(9:37—9:55.)

Now. To the both of you, unconsciously, an emotional encounter means an encounter with unpleasant emotions. You have <u>both</u> done a job of hiding your emotions from each other, even more than your thoughts.

Reasons have been given to you in the past, but you can break the habit now by expressing your emotions to each other, and so indeed you must. One of the deep disappointments that neither of you have faced is the difference between what your personal relationship is and what it could and should be.

Your relationship is a good one, compared to most an excellent one, but you know your inner potentials, and the potentials of that relationship, and how much you have to some degree failed it. Obviously you have not entirely failed by any means, and you have always maintained an underground basis of loyalty and love; but you are each deeply disappointed with that relationship compared to what you know it can be.

The sexual aspect is but a symptom of this. You were both afraid in varying degrees of emotional contact of a strong nature. In the early days or years of your relationship these patterns were submerged largely. Your tendency to avoid such encounters was much more apparent then than Ruburt's.

Your habits both became extremely sloppy in that regard, and it was easy for both of you to justify the lack of increasingly rewarding emotional interaction by saying it went into your separate work, and into our work.

As repressions built up then emotional encounters did seem to be unpleasant, for only when one of you became thoroughly uncomfortable and desperate did you really open emotionally to the other. It is a testament to the strength of your love and mutual commitment that you did not run into far greater problems.

Now Ruburt took this out physically, and blocked emotions, not from the distant past but a current life-habit, now shows these blocked emotions. Again, he suffers more from the lack of rich emotional interaction than you; he is less able to take it.

Whenever you begin to interact, often the negative emotions show first. Each of you become frightened, and clap a lid down upon the whole affair. Ruburt shows some improvement, and then goes back until you try again.

Your relationship and your lives in general, you see, follow certain definite patterns set by you. Your work and your relationship are interwoven. You have not allowed yourselves the leeway, or the excuses either, that people do with families or a large number of interests. If you do not find emotional satisfaction with each other you do not find it, in other words. The whole problem however involves your work also, and solving one problem solves the other. Finding release in one gives you release in the other, and both of you chose therefore a life situation and framework in which precisely those problems you have tired to ignore should serve as challenges and impetuses.

You have not given each other, now, the ever-growing, ever-more-rewarding emotional interactions and encounters that you need as individuals and as creators.

You can break the pattern then at any time. This should help you do so, by present, current action. Often you are so involved with feelings you had in the past that you do not know what you are feeling in the present. There are richly creative emotional founts within you both. Each of you know this and sense it.

You would do far better by trying to bring these out into the open on your own parts and encourage them on the part of your mate; the angers or aggressions or misunderstandings, when you let them out and discuss them and feel them. You try to be, both of you, too mental and intellectual about your emotions, thinking them away if possible rather than freely admitting them.

Now, that disappointment with your relationship is even more pertinent than your individual and joint feelings about Artistic, and your life in that regard. That aspect of your life would simply be another challenge for the two of you to face together if you admitted this deeper disappointment and did something about it.

Ruburt is, again, far better able to help you in that regard than either of you realize. The basic disappointment with each other colors your perspective when you consider the Artistic Card aspect.

Now I am telling you this: Ruburt is emotionally deprived, and that is what his physical body does when it knows it. He managed to go ahead creatively despite this, though at great difficulty.

Your symptoms lay in a different area, and I am sure you know where. They show up in your creative work, for otherwise you would have been far freer. Your creative work therefore shows the emotional depriving aspects. You have not been able to let yourself go fully in them, as Ruburt has not been able to go freely with his body.

Now, this is the basic problem. The basic reasons for both Ruburt's symptoms and the holdback in your own work, and the answer to both lies in learning how to release yourselves to yourselves, to let your own emotional natures relate to each other. You must get over the hump therefore of being afraid of your emotions, both of you.

The show of any emotion between you should be considered an advance. You will soon find joy and spontaneity therefore quite automatically and freely.

Now you may take your break. And I have told you why you have not succeeded in the past, either of you, and why you can now.

(10:25. Jane's pace had again been fast, as it had all evening. She said Seth was present now really strongly, very immediate, etc. Resume at 10:36.)

Now. In your relationship you inhibited the expression of joyful and loving emotions first. You were not afraid as much of negative emotions, briefly, because in your family your father found safety in negative emotions. By the denial of hope and the inhibition of joyful emotions he tried to protect himself against disappointment or defeat.

If he did not expect much there was nothing he could lose. Do you follow me?

("Yes.")

The same feeling often pervades your own attitude when you think of Ruburt's symptoms. You think you are being realistic. You are instead giving into old patterns of emotion, and you can break this habit. You are afraid then not of the negative emotional release—which meant, to the degree mentioned, safety—but of the joyful loving emotions. Part of this had to do with your father's disappointment in business, and his (underlined) reaction to it.

Part of it had to do with your distrust of such emotion when it was displayed by your mother. You felt it could be smothering, for you sensed the reasons behind her smothering love for her sons. When you begin to sense you might be getting somewhere then you become suspicious instantly, inhibit the feeling in the name of realism.

Now Ruburt inhibited the negative emotions, so-called, first of all because of his own background—the fear of arguments, of hurting someone, as explained clearly in other sessions. The end result however on both of your parts was the inhibition of emotional expression in your relationship, precisely in those most important areas where it was most needed.

Gradually he inhibited the love and joy, and you the negatives until your lives lacked those natural rises and falls in feelings in tone. You set yourself against your feelings, allowing them release in certain areas only under certain conditions, and in largely impersonal as opposed to intimate areas.

You related in terms of your work, or our work, or as a couple with others. Now resentment against each other grew. Many would be far more than satisfied with your relationship, but you set yourselves high goals, both in your work and in your personal lifelong relationship with each other, and you suffer when you are not true to this.

You do not look at each other freshly. You cannot examine your feelings, though you think you do, because you do not honestly come to grips with them nor express them. As far as the relationship is concerned you face each other distantly. Out of the potential relationship interactions are possible that will make great changes in your lives, your individual work, and our work.

You must forget the ideas you have about each other, and look at the living emotional selves upon which you have built and projected. Ruburt's health, your work, the Artistic Card aspect and all others will fall into line.

Now this session was not practically possible until each of you were ready to hear it, for these facts were made on both of your parts. There is no other answer. The entire affair must (underlined) be considered as a creative emotional venture and challenge.

You are both indeed lucky, for you do have a firm basis from which to work. It is not that you do not have an "ideal" in quotes relationship; but you had lost that feeling of the potentials within you. Your relationship fell so far below those standards, and you are so closely bound together, that his would show in all areas.

Our sessions, both of your creative works, the good you have done and are doing, the health that you have maintained—no serious organic defects—all of this is testament to what you have done.

Now unless you have questions I will end the session—and there are no other reasons.

("Well, " I said, "I guess for the first time I don't feel there's still something about the situation that we don't know....")

Neither of you would have been willing to do the work required earlier.

("All right. Thank you very much, Seth, and good night.")

And it was still a creative endeavor.

("I understand.")

(Pause at 11 PM.) One footnote to make sure you understand. You hid your warmth from each other, and denied each other the life-giving, rich emotional interaction that you need as individuals and as creators.

You obviously did not completely do this, or the affair would be far worse. You no longer made each other laugh or cry. Do you follow me?

("Oh, yes." [Pause.] "Good night, Seth." 11:01.)

THE SETH AUDIO COLLECTION

RARE RECORDINGS OF SETH SPEAKING through Jane Roberts are now available on audiocassette and CD. These Seth sessions were recorded by Jane's student, Rick Stack, during Jane's classes in Elmira, New York, in the 1970's. The majority of these selections have never been published in any form. Volume I, described below, is a collection of some of the best of Seth's comments gleaned from over 120 Seth Sessions. Additional selections from The Seth Audio Collection are also available. For information ask for our free catalogue.

Volume I of The Seth Audio Collection consists of six (1-hour) cassettes plus a 34-page booklet of Seth transcripts. Topics covered in Volume I include:

- Creating your own reality – How to free yourself from limiting beliefs and create the life you want.
- Dreams and out-of-body experiences.
- Reincarnation and Simultaneous Time.
- Connecting with your inner self.
- Spontaneity–Letting yourself go with the flow of your being.
- Creating abundance in every area of your life.
- Parallel (probable) universes and exploring other dimensions of reality.
- Spiritual healing, how to handle emotions, overcoming depression and much more.

FOR A FREE CATALOGUE of Seth related products including a detailed description of The Seth Audio Collection, please send your request to the address below.

ORDER INFORMATION:
If you would like to order a copy of The Seth Audio Collection Volume I, please send your name and address, with a check or money order payable to New Awareness Network, Inc. for $60 (Tapes), or $70 (CD's) plus shipping charges. United States residents in NY, NJ, CT, PA, & TX must add sales tax.

Shipping charges: U.S.—$7.50, Canada—$10, Europe, Australia & Asia—$27
Rates are UPS for U.S. & Airmail for International—Allow 2 weeks for delivery
Alternate Shipping—Surface—$15.00 to anywhere in the world—Allow 5-8 weeks

Mail to: NEW AWARENESS NETWORK INC.
P.O. BOX 192, Manhasset, New York 11030
(516) 869-9108 between 9:00-5:00 p.m. Monday-Friday EST
Visit us on the Internet—www.sethcenter.com

Books by Jane Roberts from Amber-Allen Publishing

Seth Speaks: The Eternal Validity of the Soul. This essential guide to conscious living clearly and powerfully articulates the furthest reaches of human potential, and the concept that each of us creates our own reality.

The Nature of Personal Reality: Specific, Practical Techniques for Solving Everyday Problems and Enriching the Life You Know.. In this perennial bestseller, Seth challenges our assumptions about the nature of reality and stresses the individual's capacity for conscious action.

The Individual and the Nature of Mass Events. Seth explores the connection between personal beliefs and world events, how our realities merge and combine "to form mass reactions such as the overthrow of governments, the birth of a new religion, wars, epidemics, earthquakes, and new periods of art, architecture, and technology."

The Magical Approach: Seth Speaks About the Art of Creative Living. Seth reveals the true, magical nature of our deepest levels of being, and explains how to live our lives spontaneously, creatively, and according to our own natural rhythms.

The Oversoul Seven Trilogy (The Education of Oversoul Seven, The Further Education of Oversoul Seven, Oversoul Seven and the Museum of Time). Inspired by Jane's own experiences with the Seth Material, the adventures of Oversoul Seven are an intriguing fantasy, a mind-altering exploration of our inner being, and a vibrant celebration of life.

The Nature of the Psyche. Seth reveals a startling new concept of self, answering questions about the inner reality that exists apart from time, the origins and powers of dreams, human sexuality, and how we choose our physical death.

The "Unknown" Reality, Volumes One and Two. Seth reveals the multidimensional nature of the human soul, the dazzling labyrinths of unseen probabilities involved in any decision, and how probable realities combine to create the waking life we know.

Dreams, "Evolution," and Value Fulfillment, Volumes One and Two. Seth discusses the material world as an ongoing self-creation—the product of a conscious, self-aware and thoroughly animate universe, where virtually every possibility not only exists, but is constantly encouraged to achieve its highest potential.

The Way Toward Health. Woven through the poignant story of Jane Roberts' final days are Seth's teachings about self-healing and the mind's effect upon physical health.

Available in bookstores everywhere.

CPSIA information can be obtained
at www.ICGtesting.com
Printed in the USA
BVHW082136201219
566948BV00005B/18/P